Mick Brown was born in London in 1950. He wrote for the *Sunday Times* for ten years as well as for national and international magazines. He is now a freelance writer and broadcaster. He lives with his wife Patricia and their three children in London.

Richard Branson

The Authorised Biography

Mick Brown

HEADLINE

First published in Great Britain in 1988
by Michael Joseph Ltd

First published in paperback in 1989
by HEADLINE BOOK PUBLISHING
Second revised edition August 1992
Third revised edition September 1994
Fourth revised edition April 1998

4 5 6 7 8 9 10

ISBN 0 7472 3216 4

Typeset by
Letterpart Limited, Reigate, Surrey

Printed and bound in Great Britain by
Mackays of Chatham PLC, Chatham, Kent

HEADLINE BOOK PUBLISHING
A division of Hodder Headline PLC
338 Euston Road
London NW1 3BH

To Patricia

ACKNOWLEDGEMENTS

I would like to thank all those who have given so generously of their time, advice and confidences in the preparation of this book.

Contents

List of Illustrations

Prologue

On a late summer's evening in August 1997, four days after the death of Diana, Princess of Wales in a car crash, Richard Branson took a walk in London's Kensington Gardens.

Something extraordinary had happened in London that week. A mood had settled on the city compounded of grief and disbelief. The gardens around Kensington Palace, Diana's home, had been transformed into a sea of cellophane-wrapped flowers, votive candles and heartfelt tributes to the dead Princess. An atmosphere of tangible sadness permeated the air. Like the hundreds of thousands of people who made the pilgrimage to Kensington Gardens that week, Branson had come to pay his respects, to bear witness to the extraordinary outpouring of public grief. 'It's so terribly sad', said Branson, as he walked slowly among the piles of flowers, pausing to examine the hand-written notes and tributes. 'Such a terrible waste.'

Branson and Princess Diana had been friends. They had played tennis together, lunched together, exchanged the occasional telephone call. At a time when she was anxious to escape the hounding of the media, Branson had lent her his Caribbean island, Neckar, as a hideaway. She reciprocated the favour in 1993, after declaring that she was 'retiring' from public life, by choosing to make her last appearance unveiling a new Virgin aircraft, guaranteeing Branson unparalleled press coverage for the event.

When Branson won his fight against British Airways over their 'dirty tricks' campaign, she had been among the first to send him a congratulatory note. And when Branson and his family were involved in a near-fatal car crash on the way to their home in Oxford, she had been the first to send flowers and a note expressing her concern and relief that nobody had been killed.

Now as he made his way slowly through the drifts of flowers, people came forward to shake his hand or simply touch him on the shoulder. Several congratulated him on the news in that morning's papers that he would be helping to establish a charity in Diana's name, and organising an album by sundry pop stars of 'songs for Diana'. A family asked if he would pose for a photograph with their children. As he obliged, a small crowd gathered round, brandishing cameras, pens, scraps of paper, the power of celebrity momentarily eclipsing the mood of mourning. Patiently, with an air that seemed to commingle embarrassment and obligation, Branson did as he was asked. It was as if in some peculiar way, in the absence of any members of the Royal family, or ministers of government, Branson had found himself cast as her representative among the people.

In the wake of Diana's death, there was some almost tangible change in the public mood of Britain, as if the near-canonisation of Diana as an icon of compassion gave shape and meaning to the mood of change coursing through the country in the wake of Labour's victory in

2

the general election three months earlier. There was talk of a new Britain: caring, tolerant, optimistic; as if the greed, materialism and sleaze which had become synonymous with eighteen years of Conservative rule had been banished at a stroke. Three figures, it was said, characterised this mood of renewal: Diana, 'the People's Princess'; Tony Blair, 'the People's Prime Minister'; and Richard Branson, 'the People's Businessman'.

The People's Businessman? Businessmen do not usually attain the status of public heroes. But then Richard Branson is an unusual sort of businessman – the 'adventure capitalist' who has come to embody the idea that capitalism does not necessarily mean greed; that it can carry with it a sense of moral responsibility, and furthermore, that it can be fun.

The rise of Richard Branson is a paradigm of the changing face of Britain over the past thirty years: the public school drop-out turned student magazine editor who sowed the seeds of his fortune in an era of cultural rebellion and reaped the fruits of an age of pragmatic commerce to build a global business empire which, in 1996, was estimated to be worth £1.6bn.

The Virgin name, first attached to a hippie mail-order record business, now extends to almost every facet of the entertainment and leisure industry. There are few people in Britain whose lives have not, at some point, been touched by a Virgin product. People can buy their records in a Virgin megastore. Listen to Virgin radio. Take a Virgin holiday in Florida or the Caribbean, flying there on a Virgin plane. They can watch films in a Virgin cinema, while glugging on a Virgin cola or 'energy drink'; arrange their personal investments or a mortgage through Virgin finance, ride a Virgin train, stay in a Virgin hotel in the highlands of Scotland or on the

Ballearic island of Majorca. They can even have their wedding arranged by Virgin Brides, the bride no doubt walking up the aisle wearing Vie cosmetics – another Virgin product.

The strongest selling point in all these services and commodities has been Richard Branson himself. He is a man whose inexorable rise, his personable nature, and his daredevil exploits in power-boats and hot-air balloons, appears to have equipped him – at least in the popular imagination – to fulfil virtually every role public life has to offer.

In every opinion poll, speculating on who should be President in the event of Britain becoming a republic, or who should be London's first mayor, Branson's name is at the top of the list. Asked who would be the best person to re-write the Ten Commandments, a poll of young people decided that after Mother Teresa, the Pope and the Archbishop of Canterbury, it would be Richard Branson. He is, as the television commentator David Frost remarked, 'the most popular bearded man in Britain after Santa Claus'.

To the casual observer, Branson appears as a walking series of paradoxes: an entrepreneur who has built a business empire by breaking almost every rule in the businessman's book; an extremely wealthy man who has never lost the common touch. He is one of the most recognisable, most frequently photographed and quoted figures in public life, and yet he remains at the same time curiously elusive, and enigmatic. Clearly, behind the ready smile, the tousled hair and the apparently hesitant, somewhat awkward public manner, lies a shrewd and astute business brain. But who exactly *is* Richard Branson?

In the mid-1980s, when Branson launched Virgin

Atlantic airways, and his public image as 'the hippie entrepreneur' was first in the ascendant, a quite specific picture solidified in the public imagination. You could draw a caricature with four or five easy brushstrokes: the big, boyish grin, the piratical beard, the endless selection of brightly coloured jumpers, the houseboat where he lived and worked – a thirty-something Peter Pan at play in the world of big business. At forty-something going on fifty, the tousled hair is now cut shorter, and the piratical beard is flecked with grey. The figure is stockier, but kept in shape by regular tennis and early-morning swims in the pool of his London home. The famous jumpers have been put in the drawer; nowadays he more often favours sports-jackets by Armani and Cerutti – not that Branson himself would necessarily notice the label. His clothes are bought for him by his wife Joan, and he wears them all with the careless indifference of a schoolboy who has been dressed by his parents. His wristwatch is a £35 Swatch. He has still never been photographed in a tie.

He left the houseboat long ago. Nowadays he lives in a large, rambling house in the Holland Park district of West London, adjacent to an identical property which functions as his office. But his professional style remains relentlessly informal. Far from being a model of the clean, efficient work-space, his office more closely resembles the study of a particularly untidy student, cluttered with Virgin memorabilia, model airplanes and trains, awards and posters which no one has yet got round to putting up on the wall, and probably never will. His desk is virtually invisible under a sea of papers. He sits in a reclining chair, telephone cradled in his neck, a 10 × 8-inch notebook on his lap, in which he scribbles details of conversations, deals, lists, ideas, random thoughts, newspaper headlines, his son's or daughter's parting shots on the way to school. A computer stands on a rickety desk, but he seldom uses it.

He takes his holidays on his own island in the Virgin Islands, Neckar. It is the last word in homely luxury: a large house atop a hill, built and furnished in the Balinese style. There are blissfully empty beaches, a selection of wind surfers, dinghies and speed-boats for recreation. Typically, Branson turns the hideaway to practical use. He is a generous host, regularly flying out family and friends for holidays. But when he is not using it himself, the island is run as a holiday retreat, much favoured by high-rolling Hollywood stars and businessmen.

When in London (although nowadays he is frequently in the air, commuting between Britain and America, South Africa and Japan) he works civilised hours, arriving at his office at 8.30 am, usually leaving by 6 pm – but continuing to play the telephones long into the evening, sitting on the sofa at home. At weekends he escapes to his home in Oxford. This is modest and comfortable rather than opulent – certainly no country mansion – but bordered by 300 acres of land which he has turned into a wild-bird sanctuary, creating a huge lake, stocked with rare geese and swans.

Each year he hosts a series of parties at his home for all the Virgin employees – flight attendants, shop assistants, aero-engineers, secretaries. There is a fun-fair, barbecues, bouncy castles, punting on the river which runs alongside the land. It is a fair bet that Branson will end up in the water more than once over the course of the weekend. One is hard put to think of any other businessman or captain of industry, in any field – Lord Hanson or Donald Trump, Alan Sugar or Bill Gates – who would entertain his staff like this. Equally hard to think of another chairman of an airline who would greet his passengers at the door of the aircraft, or dress up in full drag as a stewardess to serve them in-flight drinks, as Branson once did.

This informality is at the heart of the Branson style. It was always his claim that he ran Virgin as a family. In the early years of the company, every employee was given his home telephone number, and encouraged to call if they had a suggestion or a complaint. Virgin is now a multi-national company, employing some 15,000 people in Britain alone – a large 'family' by any standards – yet it retains a distinctly familial feel. All and sundry in the company continue to know and address him as 'Richard'. Branson likes to be liked, and most people who meet him do like him. But the amiable and apparently casual manner can be deceptive. Those who fail to take him seriously – like Lord King in Virgin's famous battle with British Airways over the 'dirty tricks' – do so at their peril.

The question remains: what does Richard Branson want? He is one of Britain's wealthiest men, yet a man to whom wealth in itself means very little. His fame is as much a cause of awkward embarrassment as it is of pleasure. Power for its own sake does not interest him. Not a man given to existential angst or deep self-analysis, Branson prefers to articulate his ambitions in more nebulous terms. What he relishes, he says, is 'a challenge'; what he likes from life is 'fun'. On such apparently simple principles he has built a business empire which straddles the globe. Challenges and fun. Clearly, you think, there is more to Richard Branson than that.

Chapter 1

Childhood

'This will do,' said the blonde-haired woman sitting in the front seat. The car came winding down the narrow Devon lane between high hedgerows, and rolled to a halt. It was an antiquated saloon, modified by a previous owner to accommodate a curious wooden and glass structure at its rear which looked like a greenhouse. Known to all and sundry as the 'Bumpety-Bump' car, it had carried the family to Devon, as it did each year, for the summer holidays. Today, it had carried them to the beach and back, to within half a mile of the farmhouse where they stayed. 'It's not too far,' said the woman. She turned to the four-year-old boy, sitting in the back seat. 'Come along,' she said, soft yet insistent. 'It's time you became a man. You see if you can walk back to Grandpa's on your own from here.'

'Are you sure this is the right thing, darling?' Her husband drew on his pipe, concern in his voice.

'He'll be perfectly all right, won't you, darling? It's only a short distance.'

The little boy climbed out and stood and watched as the Bumpety-Bump car vanished round the corner. He crossed the road, climbed over a farm gate and set off across the fields. The afternoon sun was dying slowly in the sky. He had never been alone like this before, and he felt a little frightened. He stopped to sit down and suck on a piece of corn; followed a butterfly on its trail across the hedgerow, and walked on. He was silly to be frightened. This wasn't frightening at all. It was fun. He began running around the field, his arms outstretched to make airplane wings; then fell on his stomach and crawled through the grass, looking out for snakes and tigers. It was almost dark now. He had no idea of how long his parents had been gone, nor of where he was going, but down in the valley he could see lights. He made his way down the hill and walked up to the front door. It wasn't his grandfather's farm, but he rang on the doorbell just the same.

At another farm, a mile away, apprehension had given way to sharp words and now to tears. Coats were being pulled back on, flashlights turned out from drawers, the worst of all possible fates pushed to the back of everyone's minds, when the telephone rang. 'Have you lost Richard Branson . . . ?' asked the voice.

The birth of Richard Charles Nicholas Branson, on 18 July 1950, was unusually traumatic. Doctors Pink and White, proprietors of the Stonefield Maternity Home, Blackheath, in South London, believed in natural childbirth methods; no drips, no forceps, no painkillers. The boy was three weeks overdue and, as his grandmother later recalled, his head was 'simply enormous', occasioning Eve Branson considerable pain and a postnatal operation for a prolapse. Her son came into the world 'an absolute handful. And he has been a handful ever since.'

From his father, Richard Branson inherited his physique, and an air which at times could be diffident, almost apologetic. From his mother he took the blue eyes set wide apart, a broad forehead – a physiognomy which suggested her Nordic ancestry; an indefatigable energy and a determination which could border on the obsessive.

Richard Branson was born into the class of propriety and comfort. The class of the clergy, the City and the Bench; administrators of the spirit, the law and the share portfolio. The class which both defines the parameters of social convention, and disregards them with the greatest impunity.

The law had belonged to his father's side of the family for three generations. Richard's great-grandfather, James, was a lawyer with the colonial service who had risen to become the senior barrister at the Calcutta Bar in India. James's eldest son, George Arthur Harwin Branson, followed illustriously in his father's footsteps. An exhibitioner at Trinity College, Cambridge, he studied Classics and won a rowing Blue against Oxford in the boat-race of 1893 (they lost). He went on to rise through the legislature – writing the definitive book on Stock Exchange law on the way – to become a High Court judge. Richard Branson grew up in awe of his grandfather. As a young boy he was taken to the Chamber of Horrors in Madame Tussaud's waxworks. 'Do you see that man?' his father Ted said, pointing to one or another particularly grisly murderer. 'Your grandfather hanged him . . .'

An executioner, if only by word, was something that Ted himself could never be – nor would he have wished it. For Edward Branson followed his father into the law and became a barrister, against his own better judgement, bowing to the indomitable weight of family tradition. At an early age it had been clear to Edward, if not to his father, that he had no vocation for the law. He had been keener on carpentry and collecting fossils than English or arithmetic. His Common Entrance pass had fallen far short of the rigorous requirements of Eton – his father's choice of school. Instead, he had been sent to Bootham School, in Yorkshire, a Quaker establishment where the inter-house rivalry and élitism of traditional public schools was frowned upon and artistic pursuits and a sense of fraternity and egalitarianism encouraged. Edward had grown up a thoughtful and kindly young man, with a self-awareness of his privileged social position tempered strongly by an abiding sense of *noblesse oblige*.

Breeding ensured that Edward respected the family tradition, but it was the one member of the family who had most spectacularly departed from it that he secretly admired. His father's younger brother James – Uncle Jim – had been a successful solicitor in India, until he fell from his horse during a polo match. He was in a coma for two weeks, returning to consciousness with a profoundly different view of the world. Abandoning his law practice, he returned to England and bought a farm on the Surrey-Hampshire borders, planning to breed polo ponies.

But, alas, Uncle Jim was not a success at business. Potential buyers were fully appraised of the ponies' weaknesses, but not their strengths. Because of his philosophical belief that it was morally wrong to sell eggs at more than a penny each, the farm produce side also incurred frightful losses. Eventually, he was obliged to sell the farm and move to a flat in the lugubrious London suburb of Balham. Curiously, this did not hinder his pursuit of a life close to nature. He bicycled everywhere, collecting interesting shrubs and blossoms from the hedgerows and grass from the fields. Arriving at his brother George's home, Uncle Jim would delight young Edward by emptying the contents of his 'nose-bag' into a porridge bowl, adding a sprinkling of raisins and milk, and eating it. This eccentricity eventually brought him minor celebrity, when the magazine *Picture Post* published a photograph of him making hay in his bathroom in Balham, for his own consumption.

Edward had no desire to eat hay, but Uncle Jim was, in his own curious way, an example. If he could carry his dinner around in a nosebag, perhaps Edward would be allowed to be, say, an Egyptologist. But while tradition had been overruled by Uncle Jim, and in Edward's own education at Bootham, it would not be overruled when it came to his career. Like his father before him, Edward arrived at Trinity College, Cambridge, to study law. It was a step that was forced upon him; that Edward accepted with good grace, but which he would always, privately, regret.

When war intervened, he volunteered for a cavalry regiment organised around the Inns of Court. In Palestine, he took part in one of the last horse charges in British military history. Later, he served in tanks in the Western desert, Italy and, at the war's end, as a staff-major in Germany administrating the dispersal of refugees and displaced persons. In 1946 he returned to England and, reluctantly, his law studies; he was a dashing and refined young man with good prospects and a practised eye for the opposite sex. In short, Edward Branson was a rather desirable catch.

Evette Huntley-Flindt materialised at a cocktail party in London. A trim, strikingly beautiful young girl with blonde hair and piercing blue eyes, she approached him with a plate of cocktail sausages and the suggestion that 'the best way to a man's heart is through his stomach'. At twenty-seven, Eve Huntley-Flindt was a strong-willed, purposeful young woman who had overcome more intimidating forces than Edward Branson's reputation as a ladies' man.

Spirit – and longevity – ran in her family. Her grandfather had been a clergyman. His wife had worked as a secretary of the Bishop of Edinburgh until she was eighty-three and had died at ninety-four. Eve's mother, Dorothy, displayed similar vigour. At the age of eighty-nine she became the oldest person in Britain ever to pass the advanced Latin-American ballroom dancing examination – an award achieved in between energetic afternoons on the golf course.

Dorothy had married Rupert Huntley-Flindt, a London stockbroker who retired at the age of thirty-eight, with two children and a guaranteed income of £500 a year, to run a fruit and chicken farm in Devon. It was not a success. The Devon climate was unsuitable for fruit-farming; Rupert worked himself to the bone, and his wife to near-breakdown with boredom and isolation. Dorothy Huntley-Flindt did not approve of Devon, or 'Devony children', and had no wish for her own children to be brought up there. One by one, Michael, Eve and the youngest daughter, Clare, were despatched to boarding school by their mother. As a family friend, Douglas Bader, the Second World War fighter pilot, later remarked, in the Huntley-Flindt family it was always the women who made the decisions.

Meanwhile, Eve showed great promise as a classically trained dancer. By the age of twelve she was on stage in the West End, as one of 'Bucky's Bears', in a dance revue written by Marie Stopes (who later founded the Marie Stopes family-planning clinics) and her son. Eve went on to become the youngest member of Cochrane's Young Ladies dance revue, and then an actress on the West End stage. The aftermath of war brought a new career, as an air stewardess, flying the first scheduled services between Europe and South America for British South American Airways. To the 'Star Girls', as the airline's stewardesses were known, the 'glamour' of transatlantic travel was tempered by acute discomfort. The journey to South America took a week, via Europe and West Africa. The aeroplanes, decommissioned Lancaster bombers, were noisy and precarious; crossing the Andes passengers were obliged to wear oxygen masks, arriving at their destinations with frozen fingers.

Now, at military historian Cyril Falls's cocktail party, Edward Branson was transfixed by the pale, gamin-like – and, by now, utterly nerveless – beauty. A whirlwind courtship climaxed in his proposing marriage as they sped along on his motorbike. They married on 14 October 1949. Richard, they thereafter insisted, had been conceived either on the first night of the honeymoon, in the Savoy Hotel, or on the third, in Majorca. Bride and groom returned to England, and found a new home, a cottage in the Surrey village of Shamley Green, five miles from Guildford.

Shamley Green was one of those pretend villages the character of which is determined by its commuting distance to London; a picture postcard, resolute in its orderliness and respectability. There was a church, a post office and general store, a scattering of artisan cottages, later gentrified, around the green; its picturesque beauty ensured by the outlying protection of Tudor and gabled Edwardian family houses, each set comfortably at the apex of a gravel drive and expansive lawns. It was a community lubricated by good manners, discretion and generous measures of gin and tonic; an agreeable enough place in which to bring up a young family. But the

Bransons' happiness was somewhat tempered by the surprising fact that they were poor – at least by the standards of the Surrey stockbroker belt. The couple had returned from their honeymoon to bad news: Ted had failed his final examinations to qualify as a barrister. Worse, as a punishment for his son marrying before he was qualified, Sir George Branson had reduced Ted's allowance to a pittance. Even their cottage, Easteds, had to be acquired at a knock-down price from a friend.

The hasty, and not altogether planned, arrival of Richard added an extra urgency to Ted's need to qualify. Egged on by Eve, he applied himself to his studies in earnest. A sidecar was attached to Ted's motorbike, in which the baby Richard was placed; while Ted drove, Eve rode pillion behind him, chanting law cases into his ear. But even when Ted eventually qualified, circumstances did not improve much. As a junior barrister he had little choice in which cases he handled and was obliged to take insurance work for motor-accident claims. This often meant being asked by solicitors to persuade clients to offer a plea against their own best interests, but in the long-term interests of the insurance companies. Many barristers accept such work without a murmur, but Ted's conscience was troubled by it. The briefs became fewer and further between. Everybody acknowledged that Ted Branson had a kind and sensitive disposition, but nobody would have ever described him as ambitious. Ambition was Eve's forte.

To help make ends meet, Eve converted a small shed at the bottom of the garden into a workshop, where she made embroidered cushions, matchboxes covered with velvet and other fancy trinkets, to be sold in Harrods. After the birth of her second child, Lynette (Lindi), in 1953, she even trained briefly as a gliding instructor.

When it came to money-raising schemes, Eve applied herself with a gusto and enterprise which was identifiably a family trait. Money was not there to be squandered; the imperative of saving pennies was impressed on Richard from an early age, fostering a cautiousness with money that has never left him. However, the shortage of money as he grew up was an irritation to the Bransons rather than a permanent handicap. Sir George's fit of pique on Ted's marriage did not extend to his grandchildren: a family bequest would pay for their education – the notion of state schools was, of course, unthinkable.

Despite the family's financial worries, Richard's childhood was happy and secure. If ever the Branson parents were invited out for an evening, Richard and Lindi would travel with them and sleep in the car. They provided their children with constant love and attention: Richard's earliest memory is of being carried back to his own bed late at night, his father's voice reassuring in his ear, 'It's only me . . .'

On the other hand, Eve was determined that her children should be just as independent and single-minded as she was herself. Independence, motivation, 'being a self-starter', 'standing on your own two feet' – all were strongly encouraged and cultivated in the Branson family. To a woman accustomed to flying over the Andes in an oxygen mask, sending a four-year-old off to walk home across the fields of Devon was nothing. She regarded shyness as a weakness; hiding behind skirts was not tolerated. Richard, Lindi, and – much later – the youngest child Vanessa were regularly pulled from their rooms to sing or offer some performance for dinner-party guests, their squirming protestations of bashfulness firmly overruled by Eve's admonition that 'shyness is selfishness. Come on, you're only thinking of yourself when you should be thinking of other people. Make them feel at home.' It was a dictum that eventually became enshrined into a kind of family code: have faith in yourself; nothing is impossible, but the only person likely to make anything happen is you. To Eve, anything was possible for Richard and his sisters, but only the very best would ever be acceptable. One day, she told friends, her son would be Prime Minister.

Richard himself wanted to be an explorer. Scott of the Antarctic had been a cousin of his grandfather, Sir George Branson, and twice a year the Bransons would visit an elderly and distant relative who had known Scott well enough to regale Richard with stories of his blighted expedition to the South Pole.

On an excursion to London, Ted took him over Scott's boat, the *Discovery*. That same afternoon, he was sketched by a pavement artist on the Embankment – a cherubic seven-year-old with a blond kiss curl, rosy cheeks and eyes shining with excitement, a picture torn from the pages of a book by Mabel Lucy Atwell. The kiss curl was deceptive. For Richard was one of those boys whose angelic demeanour was directly proportionate to the amount of trouble they cause their parents, and whose childhood was measured out in scarred and blood-ied limbs and broken windows. He showed little interest in the more docile pursuits of boyhood – train sets, Meccano – and no interest at all in books. Television was forbidden at home; Eve believed it was a waste of time. Watching what other people had achieved or done was not constructive; one should always be doing things oneself. One should always be constructive.

Richard Branson spent his childhood stalking through fields and woods, shinning up trees and down embank-ments. What he liked above all else was to go hunting with his father, 'spotting' for rabbit and woodpigeon. Under Ted's expert tuition, he could skin a rabbit by the time he was ten.

Holidays were spent at his grandparents' farm in Devon, or with Eve's sister, Clare, who lived in Norfolk. Clare lived in a real millhouse, with water coursing past the back door; she smoked cigars, parachuted from aeroplanes for fun, and later bred her own flock of black sheep. Richard adored her.

In Devon, any number of relatives slept in a large barn adjacent to the Huntley-Flindts' farmhouse and set out each day on expeditions: rock-climbing, fishing and hunting for sand-eels along the beach. During one of these stays, when Richard was seven, an aunt promised him a pound if he could learn to swim before the holiday was over. Rain kept the beaches deserted for two days. On the last day of the holiday, a small convoy of cars set off to a nearby river. Like Richard's walk across the fields to the farmhouse three years before, the swim had assumed the dimensions of a rite of passage.

Mother, father and sister Lindi, aunts and uncles, lined the bank in a steady drizzle, shouting encouragement as the seven-year-old waded into the water and struck out for the other side. The waters closed over his head, he broke to the surface, gasping for breath, and thrashed and struggled his way to the other side, dragging himself out triumphantly and claiming his one pound. The Branson family believed in sharing tribulations and accomplishments.

Richard's closest and most constant childhood friend was a boy named Nikolas Powell. They had met at Longacre, the private junior school to which Richard had been sent at the age of four. Powell's father was a senior civil servant; he lived a short sprint from the Bransons in a house with a larger garden and better access to the adjacent fields and copses where Nik, his elder brothers and Richard and Lindi played. Nik was a gangling boy with dark, tousled hair and intense eyes. He suffered from epilepsy, which threw a shadow of caution over his activities, and made him prone to saturnine moods. Nik was cleverer than Richard, more cerebral, but circumstances decreed he could never be as carefree, nor as daring.

There is no sentiment in children's friendships, and little equality. Nik regarded Richard with a curious mixture of admiration, envy and disdain. Richard's ability to climb trees higher than him, to court disaster with greater indifference than him, marked the friendship for years to come – with Nik metaphorically tugging at Richard's shirt-tails, both enjoying and fearful of his friend's daring, simultaneously urging him on and telling him to be careful. Where Richard led, Nik invariably followed. And yet, as is so often the case, it was the leader who frequently needed the follower more. Their friendship assumed a recurring pattern: of Richard getting himself into scrapes and Nik attempting to get him out of them. One afternoon, it was decided to 'christen' Nik's new bicycle by taking it in turns to race downhill towards a fast-running river, seeing who dared to stay on the longest. Nik skidded to a halt a few feet short of the river bank. With a whoop, Richard hurtled down the hill – and straight into the river. It was Nik who fished him out with a piece of wood. However, careful dragging of the river failed to retrieve the bike, and the Bransons were obliged to cover the cost of a replacement – money which they could ill-afford.

Ted and Eve grew to regard Richard's behaviour with a weary resignation. He was a high-spirited, headstrong, not to say wayward – sometimes impossible – child; but high spirits – and high jinks – were, after all, the mark of the independence of mind, the self-reliance which his parents sought to cultivate. However, while his disposition was frequently mischievous and disobedient, Richard was seldom malicious. He had an innate sense of fun; he was quick to tease others, but, unlike his sister Lindi, he could see the joke when teased himself. Brother and sister squabbled frequently, usually as Lindi fell victim to yet another of Richard's torments. Ted and Eve's punishment was to send both of them to their rooms, irrespective of who was to blame. That way, as Lindi remembered, the children then united against their parents – and the anger was soon forgotten. 'We became a family that would kill for each other.'

Whenever Richard was naughty Eve would threaten him with, 'I'll tell your father when he gets home.' Ted would come in and tell his son to hold out his hand. But Richard was never hit. The threat was enough. However, on one occasion, a family friend, similar in age to Richard, came to stay for a weekend. The Bransons were not a churchgoing family as a rule, but Eve insisted that on this Sunday the children should be taken. In bad humour, Richard was dressed in his school blazer and dragged to the service. Worse, he had no time for his guest; a dull and complaisant boy. In mid-sermon, Richard stood up, and moved across the church to another pew, to sit with a friend. Eve looked daggers at him for the rest of the service, then furiously dragged him home and, for the only time in her son's life, told Ted the boy should be beaten. With a grave face, Ted took Richard into another room, bent him over his knee and administered six gentle and painless taps, while Richard howled theatrical squeals of pain.

When Richard was eight, Eve decided that he should be sent away to boarding school. Ted was against the idea; he knew from personal experience the unhappiness that could result from being sent away to school, and he wanted Richard to remain at Shamley Green. Richard protested, too; life at Shamley Green, with the Powells nearby, was always fun. But Eve was adamant. None of the local schools was 'suitable', and with her cottage industry thriving at the bottom of the garden she could not give Richard the attention he required at home.

Scaitcliffe preparatory school took its place as a rung on the ladder of privilege with due gravitas. A large pre-war house, set on the borders of Windsor Great Park, its close proximity to royalty seemed only to reinforce its delusions of upholding some grand, pre-ordained social order. Its seventy-odd boys – sons of the military, diplomats, families which deemed themselves 'good' – were marched through the park each Sunday in a neat crocodile of pressed blue serge, cringing at the taunts of passing oiks.

Richard arrived at Scaitcliffe, homesick and miserable. On his very first night, he awoke to find he had vomited all over his bed. He was soundly scolded by the matron and forced to clean up the mess himself. It was a bad omen.

The homesickness was short-lived, but another problem reared: Richard was a slow learner – at eight he could barely read – and at Scaitcliffe he fell increasingly behind with schoolwork. To the further exasperation of his parents and teachers, he did not appear to *care* that he fell behind. He had discovered competitive sport instead. He quickly became captain of the school rugby, cricket and football teams. Each sports day reaped a new harvest of cups and certificates for the family sideboard, Eve's satisfaction as Richard stepped forward to receive them clouded only by the certainty that the school report would bring further news of abject failure in the classroom.

The encyclopaedias and improving books pressed on Richard at Christmas and birthdays by his anxious parents and relatives all went unread. He had made friends with a boy named Johnny Best. The son of Lord Wynford, Best was the second fastest runner in the school, and almost equal to Branson in his blithe indifference to schoolwork. With monotonous regularity, they took the walk together to the study of the headmaster, Mr Vickers, for caning – punishment for 'ragging' in the dormitory, or some infringement of school etiquette.

Branson was big for his age, untidy, and with a personality that Best remembers as 'very assertive and pushy. He had this attitude that anything was possible, and if it's not possible, why not?' If there was any conspiracy afoot, it was likely that Richard was at the heart of it. The constraints and academic disciplines of school bored him and the only absorbing activities were sporting ones – he was now dreaming of a career as a cricketer, or perhaps an Olympic athlete. When not on the sports field, life for Richard became a constant challenge to create opportunities to make it interesting. This often involved telling other boys what to do and he was not particularly liked for it. But even at that age, as Best remembers, 'the energy level was phenomenal, which, if you were close to him, rubbed off'.

At the age of eleven, whilst playing in a football match, Richard suddenly heard a deafening scream. It took some seconds for him to realise that it had come from him, and that he was being carried off the pitch with a searing pain in his leg. He was taken to hospital, where a torn ligament was diagnosed and rest prescribed. It was not until some weeks later, the pain still acute, that he was taken back into hospital to have the cartilage in his knee removed. He returned to Scaitcliffe on crutches, his sporting activities – and ambitions – effectively over.

The accident accelerated Richard's parents' concern for his future from acute worry to near panic. It had also been discovered that Richard needed to wear glasses; an optician expressed surprise that he could even read from a blackboard. Too late, this partly explained why he had fallen so far behind in his schoolwork; for the prospect of his passing his Common Entrance examination and winning a place at one of the better public schools, as Ted and Eve had always hoped, looked increasingly remote. In desperation, they decided to remove Richard from Scaitcliffe and send him to a 'crammer', for a year's intensive tuition.

Cliff View House, on the Sussex coast at Seaford, resembled an academic prisoner-of-war camp, peopled by disconsolate middle-class boys, paying the price for a lifetime's indolence or lack of ability, constantly being reminded that their last chance for a privileged and fruitful existence now stared them in the face.

In this joyless climate, deprived of his beloved sports and urged on by his parents' dire warnings about the bleakness of a future without qualifications, even Richard began to work. To make matters worse for Richard, Cliff View was a Catholic school, and he was the only Protestant there. In these monastic surroundings, a variety of conflicting emotions began to fight for supremacy in his mind: guilt on the one hand, pubescent desire on the other. The object of his desire was the headmaster's daughter, a comely eighteen-year-old girl named Marianne.

Word spread among the boys that Marianne – who worked in the school dispensing aspirins and sympathy – had a habit of 'adopting' a boy each year to whom she would give special encouragement and comfort. To his delight, her glance fell on Richard, and a ritual was quickly established. Each night after lights-out he stuffed his pillows under his sheets, climbed down the drainpipe outside his dormitory window and stole across the lawn to the neighbouring building. A fire escape gave access into a corridor, and thence into Marianne's room for a pleasant hour or two engaged in what was euphemistically known as 'feelies'.

One night, however, the entrance from the fire escape was barred. Richard swore under his breath and shinned back down. Sneaking around the building, he found a ground-floor window unlocked, pushed it open and clambered through into a bathroom. A teacher stood there watching incredulously as the boy in his pyjamas dropped to the floor. The next morning, he was summoned to the headmaster's study and put on his word of honour to explain what he was doing clambering through a toilet window, in the wrong house, after lights-out. Branson was astonished to hear himself telling the truth. 'I was on my way to your daughter's room, sir . . .'

'And what were you planning to do there?'

Richard thought it prudent to avoid any mention of 'feelies', but the damage was already done. The headmaster's rage was incandescent. Branson was told he was expelled and that he should prepare to leave immediately. His parents were contacted by telephone and asked to collect their son the following day.

That evening, Richard decided there was only one way out of his predicament. In the hour after tea reserved for prep, he drafted a suicide note, describing how he could not live with the shame of expulsion and the wrath it would incur with his parents. Marking the note with the strict instruction that it should not be opened until the following day, he gave it to a boy who could be relied upon to open it immediately, and set off out of the school grounds and towards the cliffs, fittingly named Lovers' Leap. Slowly.

Walking up the hill, he looked back with relief as a knot of boys and grown-ups appeared below him, swarming up the slope in hot pursuit. Having slowed down to enable them to catch up, he was pulled back from the precipice before the dramatic sacrifice could be made. The next day, he was reinstated in school and caned soundly.

Edward Branson took his son's disgrace in his stride. He was mildly shocked, of course, but slightly envious, too; Marianne, he thought, was 'a very pretty girl'. But what the Bransons felt above all was a sense of relief. To Ted's mind, sexual indiscretions with the headmaster's daughter, even a bogus suicide attempt, were a small price to pay for Richard making some academic progress.

The problem of where to send him now took on added urgency. Richard, as Eve had long realised, was 'a very difficult, very unusual child' who would not easily fit into any school system. Applications had been filed for Eton, Winchester and Charterhouse: all deemed him unsuitable. The headmaster of Cliff View advised that because of Richard's weakness in maths it 'might prove disastrous' to persevere with another choice, Radley. Branson, it seemed, just could not add up.

One school, however, detected a glimmer of something that might have been promise. Stowe School agreed to take him on the strength of his interview alone, whatever his examination results.

The headmaster of Cliff View filed a note to the headmaster of Stowe. 'Branson,' he wrote, 'is an intelligent boy who has certainly worked hard and willingly. He enjoys art and thinks he can play the banjo.'

Thus commended, in September 1964, thirteen-year-old Richard Branson set off for public school, having passed his Common Entrance with above average marks.

Chapter 2

Stowe

The car carrying Richard Branson travelled along leafy roads from the town of Buckingham, past tranquil pastures and turned down a narrow lane, leaving behind the twentieth century, to approach Stowe School through the Oxford Gate. It came over a narrow stone bridge, between two pavilions standing like pepperpots on the crest of the hill, and then proceeded along a driveway, a mile in length, flanked by lime trees, with rolling pasture and woodland beyond.

Through the trees, Richard could glimpse the school itself, an imposing grey stone Georgian house, three storeys high, flanked on either side by palladian arches, the walls embroidered with stucco. The car pulled to a halt and Richard clambered out, stiff in the new jacket and trousers and shining black shoes for which, as Eve reminded him, 'sacrifices' had been made – although of what order he could not be exactly sure. He gazed at the flight of majestic steps, flanked by doric columns tapering upwards to an imposing portico.

To the successive generations of barons, viscounts, earls and dukes who had built and modified Stowe through the eighteenth and nineteenth centuries, the effect of humbling the visitor with the wealth and magnitude of the surroundings and thereby elevating their own importance yet further, was both intentional and desirable. Thirteen-year-old Richard felt awe and trepidation – quickly followed by resentment at being so intimidated. Richard Branson approached Stowe as a challenge.

Stowe House had been the ancestral home of the Temple family. Like so many families of the English aristocracy, the Temples owed their power not to innate nobility of birth but to business *nous*. The land on which Stowe School now stands was acquired for the family in the sixteenth century by one Peter Temple, a sheep and property speculator who had profited from an era of rampant inflation. His son bought the estate outright, and for the next two hundred years the family climbed the ladder of social rank by a mixture of guile, money and marriage. By the early nineteenth century, the family acquired the title of Dukes of Buckingham and Chandos; by the early twentieth they teetered on the verge of bankruptcy.

In 1921 the great house and its accumulated treasures were sold by public auction. In 1923, Stowe School was founded. Stowe was conceived as a new kind of public school. The Great War of 1914–18 had swept away many of the shibboleths and conventions of the Edwardian era and a spirit of liberalism was abroad in England. At Stowe, it was claimed, boys would enjoy a 'purposive freedom', from which the individual would mould the school, not the school the individual.

Gone were the Victorian sartorial traditions of sewn-up trouser pockets and wing collars. The young gentlemen of Stowe could disport themselves comfortably, but with dignity, in sports jacket and flannels as they laboured over irregular Latin verbs beneath the majestic ceilings of the house, or wandered the magnificent estate shaped by a succession of landscape gardeners through the eighteenth century and scattered with temples and statuary to inspire thoughts of the nobility of man and the dominance of reason over nature.

Yet, despite its comparative liberalism, Stowe had not abandoned all the public-school traditions. Richard Branson arrived at a school where the 'house' system remained fundamental; the hierarchy of boys and the practice of 'fagging', with all the clandestine rites of bullying and buggery it implies.

Branson was shown to his new quarters in Cobham House, sited in what had once been the stables. A new régime quickly imposed itself on his life. Each morning, the boys rose at eight for 'call-over' and passed along a stone-flagged corridor – what had once been the servants' passage – to the State Dining-Room. There they sat on forms, twelve boys to a table, and ate breakfast under a portrait of Caroline, wife of the 3rd Duke of Buckingham and Chandos. The day's lessons were followed by evening 'prep' in the houseroom, ninety minutes of silence under the supervision of a senior boy. Then it was upstairs to the dormitory, with linoleum on the floor, curtainless windows and iron bedsteads with sagging mattresses.

Cobham House had a good reputation for sports – an unkind irony for Branson, given the continuing hindrance of his knee injury. Sports periods he spent either in the art room or in the library, lined from wooden floor to ornate ceiling with text books, its enormous windows providing expansive views across lawns and a lake to the triumphal arch a mile beyond. There was hardly a room in the school that did not evoke reflections about the social order and a boy's own place in the scheme of things.

Branson did not bridle immediately against the régime of Stowe. But neither did he show any particular interest in subordinating himself to it. He knew that qualifications would be useful, not to say necessary, for his future life. But at the same time schoolwork, and the Byzantine rituals of life at Stowe generally, seemed intrinsically *pointless*, seldom interesting enough in themselves to repay the effort of persevering. Nor did his teachers harbour any illusions. To Brian Stephan, his tutor in English and Classics, Branson's lack of interest academically stood out a mile. 'It was apparent that his one aim was to get on and out into the world.'

Stowe's headmaster, Robert Drayson, also noticed the desire to get on, and if necessary to cut corners. Although nobody could be quite sure, yet, where or what Branson wanted to get on to. He was a disconcerting presence: a tall boy with an unruly shock of blond hair, prominent teeth, horn-rimmed spectacles, raging acne and table manners that haunted his teachers for years to come.

His classmates thought him the complete maverick; the boy who didn't give a toss what anybody else thought of him. 'If he got in trouble it wasn't because he was making a radical statement against the system,' said one of them, Tim Albery, 'but because he simply wasn't interested in doing what was demanded of him. He was only interested in doing what he wanted to do, and if he could inveigle other people into doing it, so much the better; if he couldn't, too bad.'

As at Scaitcliffe, Richard had few close friends: it was as if his single-mindedness kept others at bay, and he felt no empathy with the clubbishness, bonhomie and male-bonding of public school. A secret literary ambition encouraged him to seek out the boy who became his closest friend. In school holidays, and at odd moments after evening prep, Branson had been working on what he fancied to be an erotic masterpiece, distilled from his own strictly limited sexual experience and a feverish adolescent imagination. Jonathan Holland-Gems was eighteen months younger than Branson, a clever boy who was always talking about poetry and literature. Branson sought his opinion on the masterpiece. It was not encouraging. Holland-Gems pored over the notebooks which Branson produced from his locker, and pronounced it 'like Daphne du Maurier' and of limited literary merit. A firm friendship began, although the two boys could hardly have been more different.

Although younger than Branson, Holland-Gems was in many ways more worldly, certainly more cultured. His father was a painter and sculptor who had diversified into the manufacture of wax models and mannequins. Holland-Gems lived in London, and affected a suitably metropolitan air; he knew about literature and painting, admired Baudelaire, Rimbaud and the poets *maudites*. He was quick-witted, sardonic, troublesome. To Holland-Gems, Branson was a startling visitation, peculiar-looking, yet 'as if he was on fire the whole time', a dynamo who did everything with the most tremendous outpouring of energy and whose disruptive presence was impossible to ignore. 'He was incredibly incoherent – impossibly so, as if he had hundreds of things to say, but he didn't know how to say them. It was like a tornado of frustration.'

Branson did not affect the languorous air so assiduously cultivated at public school. It often seemed he did not know how to, and had no interest in learning. He had a terrier's enthusiasm for life; a bounding, wild-eyed excitement and energy and an insatiable appetite for practical jokes which resulted in either fun or spillages and broken bones – which could be either tremendously stimulating or enormously irritating.

'He wasn't a popular boy,' says Gems. 'One of the most insulting adjectives you could apply to somebody was the word "keen", and Richard was keen.' While other boys pushed the boundaries of sartorial acceptability to their furthest limits – taxing convention with a provocative check, a pointed shoe, a glimpse of cacophonous, Day-Glo sock – Richard showed no interest or awareness of fashion at all. He had no sense of whether he was conforming to convention or bucking against it. He never noticed what other people wore, or what they looked like – or at least, he did not judge them by it. He was not a swot, but nor was he an insurrectionary. Nobody knew quite where to place him. Branson identified with neither the cricketers nor the Bohemians, the rugby-players or the putative intellectuals. The athletics people were right-wing, philistine and élitist. Branson liked athletics – although his injuries mostly consigned him to the sidelines – but demonstrated none of the boorishness or self-interest to belong there. The artistic people were aesthetes and would-be socialists. Branson enjoyed art, but nobody could have accused him of having a poetic soul. In Holland-Gems's phrase, he had 'no prejudices', and no consistent set of morals either. 'He would happily go and do something really quite criminal one day, and then the next do something to help out the headmaster. He was a totally independent-minded personality, a free agent. He'd just go wherever he could use up this energy.'

Branson did not fit in anywhere. But energy, like power, abhors a vacuum. And the single-minded drive which at Scaitcliffe had been turned towards sport, and for a year at Cliff View towards schoolwork, now sought some other outlet and purpose.

Broach any housemaster at Stowe in 1964 with the term 'student power' and as likely as not he would have thought it applied to the muscle which drove the rugby First XV.

It was not until 1967 that a student protest over the appointment of a new director at the London School of Economics led to a mass sit-in, in turn triggering a chain reaction of student protest in universities and colleges throughout Britain. Not until 1968 that the relationship of 'student power' to public schools was addressed by the director Lindsay Anderson in the film *If* – a savage allegory about the 'nurseries' of the British Establishment in which a group of public-school boys arm themselves and assassinate the visiting dignitaries on school speech day in a bloody and cathartic orgy of revenge against the three symbols of Establishment power – Church, school and Army.

Throughout the 1950s, the advances of the Welfare State had left public schools feeling beleaguered and uneasy – if not yet vulnerable. With the turn of the decade came further evidence that the old social order was breaking down. The new Labour government of Harold Wilson, which came to power in October 1964, seemed to presage a bolder order of social egalitarianism after thirteen years of Conservative rule. The triumph of Wilson's bluff, avuncular provincialism over the remote, aristocratic diffidence of his predecessor, Douglas-Home – his promise of 'a hundred days of dynamic action' – sent a shiver of nervousness through the public-school system and perhaps a frisson of excitement among those toiling under its anachronisms.

In universities and polytechnics, dangerous talk could already be heard about 'democratising' the education system, making places of learning 'answerable' to their students. Stowe, with its liberal traditions, perhaps had less far to travel than other public schools, which had remained in a state of ossification for, literally, centuries. But a modest spirit of dissent was already abroad in the Cobham houseroom.

The usual response of any schoolboy to the system he labours under is either to quietly bend to it, to exploit it to his own advantage as best he can, or to rebel against it. Few think of attempting to reform it.

As the friendship between Holland-Gems and Branson deepened, they found much common ground in their distaste, not to say loathing, of Stowe's more arcane and immutable practices. Holland-Gems, who was physically slight, had suffered particularly badly from fagging. It was a practice that Branson abhorred; he did not like bullies, and a sense of justice, or at least fair play, was one strong legacy from his barrister father. Many things at Stowe seemed unfair; others impractical; some simply ridiculous.

There was the anachronism of the Combined Cadet Forces, for example – in which boys dressed up as soldiers and paraded with antiquated rifles. There was also compulsory church attendance. Neither of these particularly affected Branson personally; typically, he had somehow managed to duck CCF altogether, and avoided church by the simple expedient of never having attended from the outset and therefore never being missed. He loathed doing anything that he regarded as a waste of time.

Holland-Gems hated school. Branson hated it less. However, as Holland-Gems put it, 'We felt, like all kids do, that the education we were having stuffed down our throats was quite inappropriate to a) what we were interested in; and b) what was useful to know as far as the outside world was concerned.' Together, the two boys talked long into the night about reforming the education system – or that part of it that pertained to their own lives.

Branson decided to get things moving and wrote a detailed memorandum to Mr Drayson, the headmaster, helpfully spelling out ways in which school might be improved. 'There are many boys now who are thirsting for knowledge through interesting conversations,' he began, setting the tone. 'One of the best times to talk is at meals – but at Stowe this is practically impossible.' He went on to spell out the social advantages, and economic savings, of a canteen-style service ('We can cut down on the Italian and Spanish waiters by at least half'); argue for the establishment of a sixth-form recreation room, serving alcohol ('3 times a week sixth-formers should be allowed to drink two pints a night'), in order, he wrote, 'to encourage social life throughout Stowe – leading on to discussing religeon [sic] etc.

'I am bitterly opposed to "fagging", for reasons I will give you if you can spare the time. I am also against the utter waste of time that is spent in compulsory watching of matches. If one is unable to play for the First XV one should be able to spend one's time in better ways than that. I know this sounds a frightful break against tradition etc. – but I feel very strongly about this. If 450-odd people watching matches spent that time in Buckingham cleaning windows, for instance, they would gain at least something more than "*watching others achieving something*".' The years of parental injunctions against time-wasting and encouragement to 'do something yourself' had left their mark. Drayson studied the memo carefully, decided he could live without Branson's thoughts on fagging, commended him for his enthusiasm and filed the letter quietly away.

Together, Richard and Johnny plotted a magazine for Cobham House where these and other ideas could be floated. But permission to do that was refused on the grounds that anything that needed to be said about the house could be said in the existing school magazine, *The Stoic*. What about an alternative school magazine then? Permission for that was refused, too.

Then what about an inter-school magazine, to be circulated among all schools? A forum for what Holland-Gems had grandly taken to calling 'radical and reformist ideas'? In the houseroom of Cobham, along the servants' passages; in the State Dining-Room, under the inscrutable gaze of dukes and duchesses – the icons of a nation's greatness – the two friends drew up their new agenda: the abolition of fagging, corporal punishment and compulsory attendance at church and games. No more Latin, and the introduction of new, more useful subjects on the syllabus: plumbing, car maintenance, electrical wiring. In the flag-stoned and parquet-floored corridors of Stowe the ghosts of the ancestral Dukes of Buckingham and Chandos groaned.

It had never occurred to Jonathan Holland-Gems that Branson was not wealthy until Holland-Gems started coming to Shamley Green for holidays. At dinner one evening, with all the family gathered around the table, he was struck by Eve's sigh of frustration as she eyed a jar of brown pickle and remarked, 'I wish we were Branstons, not Bransons.' It was the sort of remark that would usually pass as a joke, unremarked and unremembered, but for a reason he could not quite explain, Gems sensed it was invested with something like longing.

For years, the Bransons had been hard-up in the way that only the English upper middle classes can be – which is to say, at no apparent detriment to their standard of living or interference with their pleasures, and certainly at no cost to their gentility; held aloft by the invisible wire of family inheritance, Ted's modest income from the law and Eve's enterprising and dextrous financial management. The family drove a car and took holidays every year. Ted continued to shoot for a hobby, with the hand-barrelled William Laing and Holland & Holland twelve-bore shotguns, worth several thousand pounds apiece, which had once belonged to his father.

But recently the family fortunes had taken a turn for the better. After his unhappy start in insurance law, Ted had changed to criminal practice and was frequently in court as both a defence and prosecuting counsel. The family had moved. Easteds, the cottage on the village green where Ted and Eve had lived since their marriage, had greatly appreciated in value over the years and they were able to sell it and buy a much larger, albeit somewhat dilapidated house on the other side of the common, and still have some money to spare for improvements.

Tanyard Farm was a sixteenth-century farmhouse on to which had been grafted a succession of extensions and outbuildings, presenting a child's delight of low-beamed rooms, twisting corridors, bolt-holes and hiding-places. At the rear, the lawn sloped up towards a vegetable garden and an orchard. There was a barn where, in time, Ted installed billiards and table-tennis tables; and, beside it, a dovecote in which the birds multiplied over the years until the roofs of the house and barn seemed alive with them. There was even an outdoor swimming-pool. It became in time the idyllic family home.

Richard loved Tanyards. His parents could now indulge their natural gregariousness and sense of fun, and the house was often the scene of parties full of Eve's friends from theatre, Ted's from the law; and, always, family, with no distinction made between young and old. The only certainty was that, at night's end, somebody would end up fully-clothed in the Tanyards swimming-pool. It was usually Richard.

He was no less accident-prone as an adolescent than as a small boy. At the age of fourteen, while riding with his sisters and showing off to a girl friend of Lindi's, he tumbled from the horse. As the girls ran over to him, Richard lay on the ground, alternately laughing and complaining that he was in agony. 'Don't be so stupid,' said Lindi, kicking him in the side. The laughter turned to screams of pain. It transpired he had fractured his pelvis. The girls had to make a stretcher out of the chicken coop to drag him up to the house, and an ambulance carried him to hospital.

Nik Powell was a frequent visitor to Tanyards. He too had been sent away to school, to Ampleforth, the Roman Catholic school in Yorkshire, but the friendship between him and Branson survived separation, and the occasional fiery argument, and was renewed each school holiday.

At Eve's instigation to 'do something useful with your-selves', the two friends embarked on a series of money-making schemes during the school holidays. Branson thought of Christmas trees. Enquiries at a local nursery revealed that one hundred conifer saplings could be bought for five pounds. Christmas trees sold for a pound a foot. Branson worked it out: in four years' time, when he and Powell left school, they would be some £600 in profit. An area of wilderness at the top of the Tanyards garden was reclaimed and the saplings planted. But the Christmas profits were slowly eaten away by wild rabbits as the boys' enthusiasm for horticulture waned.

Another scheme to breed and sell budgerigars, hatched in high enthusiasm when Richard brought home a pair of the birds from Guildford market, also came to nothing. True to expectation, the budgerigars multiplied at a prodigious rate, but by that time Richard had returned to school and it was left to Ted to spend his weekends constructing ever more cages for the flourishing bird population until at last he tired of it and the birds were given away.

The relationship between the two boys had hardly changed since they were small. Sometimes they cycled the few miles to the cinema in Guildford or Cranleigh. Branson was invariably the one to suggest a game of 'chicken' – sitting on the white line in the middle of the darkened road with the last one to dash for the curb as a car approached the winner. 'He liked playing that,' Powell remembers. 'I pretended to play. But really I was more intelligent than that. I wasn't going to kill myself for two shillings.'

The boys occupied themselves mainly with country pursuits. From an early age, Ted had instructed Richard in the proper handling and use of a gun, and he and Nik would frequently hunt in the surrounding woodlands for pigeon. On one occasion, returning from a weekend away, Ted opened the refrigerator and was astonished to find large pieces of raw, bloodied flesh tumbling out on to the kitchen floor. It was a young deer which the two boys had shot, on land where they had been given permission to shoot for pigeon. Contemplating the legality of shooting the deer, Ted took the pragmatic view. In the circumstances, the most prudent thing was to keep quiet about it. And the venison was, in any case, delicious.

★ ★ ★

In the semi-rural fastness of Shamley Green, the vagaries of what was coming to be recognised as 'youth culture' made little or no impact at all. To be mods or rockers was the calling of working-class teenagers in towns, not middle-class boys, such as Branson or Powell, home from public school. Across the world, from San Francisco to London, rock music was imparting a new sense of earnestness, a call to arms, defining not only a generational divide but a whole ethos. But in Guildford, its messages fell on blithely indifferent ears. Branson could not get on with Bob Dylan. The argument about whether the Beatles were better than the Rolling Stones interested him not one jot. Neither he nor Nik collected records, and rock music sounded no atavistic chord of communion, rebellion or yearning in their lives. To Richard, the idea of simply listening to records, immersing yourself in their rhythms, messages and dreams, fell into that category, along with television and the compulsory watching of games, of something which was not *useful*. His favourite record then, and for some years to come, was 'Bachelor Boy' by Cliff Richard, although much later he also developed a liking for the theme from *Borsalino* – a film with which he fancifully identified. Cliff Richard's simplistic and irritating confection had a particular resonance for Branson. He had discovered girls – one girl in particular, named Rudi, whom he had met when she was on an exchange visit from Holland, adolescent passion blossoming in fevered letters and reunions during the school holidays.

Nik Powell was perhaps in the best position to observe his friend's early dalliances. 'Richard never had any problems meeting girls. His devil-daring always put him in a very good position to make relationships, and it was

certainly turned to that use a fair amount of time. Other
boys would hold back at parties and look at girls wistfully; Richard would always just barge straight up to
them. He was certainly very keen to be the first person on
the block to have sex.'

In fact, it was to Jonathan Holland-Gems that Richard
first broke his news, as the train pulled out from Euston
bearing them back to Stowe for the beginning of the
autumn term. Branson was just sixteen and beside himself with excitement.

'You'll never guess what I've done ... I've had a
fuck ...'

Gems was agog. 'No ... Was it good?'

'It was fantastic ... like a religious experience. But the
only thing is, I'm worried about the tide-mark.'

'Tide-mark?' Gems was doing his best to disguise his
ignorance of such matters. 'What tide-mark?'

'Don't you know?' Branson mustered as much authority as the situation allowed. 'Every time you go with a
woman you get a tide-mark, you know, where you can't
go in any further. The mark fades after a few days. But
I'm dead worried about being found out at the school
medical.'

Holland-Gems too had been busy during the holidays.
His father had provided a ream of headed notepaper,
stamped with the symbol of a sun with the legend
'*Student* – an inter-school magazine'. With the notepaper
the project now took on an added momentum. The
prospectus had broadened. More than just a magazine
about parochial school issues, *Student* would be a magazine about all manner of issues of interest to students
and sixth formers. Fired with enthusiasm, Branson borrowed *Who's Who* from the school library and began

writing to as many people as possible, asking for an interview, an article, money, whatever. Mr Drayson, the headmaster, noted in an internal memorandum at the time that Branson was 'employing any and almost every boy in the houseroom', copying letters and licking stamps. His skill for inveigling others into his projects by sheer enthusiasm alone was already being recognised.

Partly as an acknowledgement of Branson's initiative; partly to make his own life easier, Drayson made a room available in school where Richard could sit during games periods to plan the magazine. 'It was clear that *Student* was his consuming interest,' Drayson remembers. 'We had a school prize, donated by an old boy, which I offered to any boy with a good idea for a summer adventure holiday. Richard put his name down for it, but since he was rather busy with *Student* he asked if his girlfriend could go in for it on his behalf. She couldn't, of course, because she wasn't a member of school, but I thought it was very typical of him to think of a very good idea of how he might get the prize and win a holiday with his girlfriend, because he couldn't spare the time to go in for it himself.'

What neither Drayson nor anybody else realised was that for three days Richard had installed the same girlfriend in a tent, pitched on the furthest perimeters of the Stowe grounds, close by the armoury, where he would join her each night after lights-out.

Branson and Holland-Gems could hardly have chosen a more fortuitous moment in history to embark on the idea of a student magazine. Or at least, a moment when they could have been assured of a more sympathetic, not to say eager, reception. The notion that youth was a blessed state of existence and that the young had 'something to offer' – even if nobody could be altogether sure what – was already broadly established. Youth was a fashion, if not yet a tyranny. It was not only the young who were seized by a sense of their own possibilities; everybody else was too. Everybody wanted to be young, or, failing that, to be liked by the young. If nothing else, there was always the possibility of selling them something. The increase in disposable income among the young had turned the attention of advertisers towards them in an unprecedented way: the 'youth market' had become the Holy Grail, pursued by clothing manufacturers and pop-music moguls, shamans and political ideologues of all shades.

This curious state of grace enjoyed by the young would prove greatly advantageous to *Student* in the short term – and aid Richard Branson and his endeavours considerably over the coming years.

The replies from *Who's Who* started flowing in. In his enthusiasm, Branson had made the mistake of writing to every Member of Parliament, soliciting their thoughts on 'youth', for inclusion in the magazine. To his initial delight, and ultimate tedium, many of them replied at length. The celebrated violinist Yehudi Menuhin, whose name Richard had also found in *Who's Who*, wrote to apologise for not having had time to compose anything specifically for *Student* 'before leaving for Gstaad'; he enclosed instead some notes made for German students at a graduation ceremony he had attended. They were never used.

Robert Graves, one of the greatest English living poets, contributed an erudite thesis on his ancestors, each page initialled in his florid signature. That would never be used either. It was, thought Richard, 'too boring'. Reputations did not mean a lot on *Student*. Edward Heath, Bryan Forbes, Peter Sellers, William Rees-Mogg and scores of others sent letters of support.

For Branson *Student* provided an indispensable education. If you want to contact somebody, no matter how famous, all you need do is put aside any nervousness; don't contemplate failure. Just write to them and they will write back! Had he been five or six years older, the ludicrousness of the idea would have prevented him doing it at all. As it was, he was young, naif and brash enough to knock on almost any door – and find that by knocking it invariably opened.

Student gave Richard the sense of purpose, of vocation, which had been utterly absent since his arrival at Stowe. In the back of his mind, he even began to dream of editing the magazine full-time, as a job. He would be a journalist! His plans grew more heady by the minute. He and Holland-Gems had not, of course, actually produced an issue of the magazine yet, but in July 1966 he wrote a short article for the official school magazine, *The Stoic*, in which he announced that *Student* would be sent to 3,500 schools and universities throughout Britain, with plans to expand to America, Australia and New Zealand. '*Student*,' he wrote, 'is a non-profit-making project, and all proceeds will be devoted to students who have ideas for unusual and interesting trips abroad to follow these up.' His grandmother, Mrs Huntley-Flindt, pressed into occasional secretarial service on his behalf, had already typed and despatched the letters of introduction to the Archbishop of Canterbury and to President Lyndon B. Johnson, asking whether the President would be so kind as to launch the magazine with 'a short message to the young of today'.

Branson's plans gained an enormous fillip that same summer term when he won a school essay competition, The Gavin Maxwell prize. Maxwell was an Old Stoic, who in 1960 had won international acclaim for his book *Ring of Bright Water*, which had done for otters what *Watership Down* was later to do for rabbits. Maxwell came to Stowe to present the prize, with his friend, the *Observer* war correspondent Gavin Young. Over lunch, Branson poured out his dilemma to the author. Should he please his parents, and the school, by staying on at Stowe, studying hard for university and a safe career; or should he follow his own instincts, leave as soon as he could and try to make something of *Student*?

Maxwell was unequivocal. It was Richard's life. He should do what would make himself, and not other people, happy. That evening, Maxwell and Young drove Richard back to Shamley Green. On the way down they stopped at a friend of Maxwell's, Douglas Botting, who lived not far from the Bransons, in the village of Compton. Over dinner, Richard announced that he had made up his mind: he was leaving Stowe as soon as possible.

Branson now began the long and difficult process of softening up his parents to the idea, countering their protests with promises about polytechnic college courses and further qualifications – the options of a career in journalism, the Law, politics. Ted and Eve Branson would not be the last to experience the full weight of their son's powers of persuasion, negotiation and tenacity when he had an objective in mind.

Richard's letters home became increasingly didactic in instructing them how they might aid his plans for the future and extricate him from Stowe. 'Have you had an interview with the commerce man at the Technical College yet?' he wrote in one. 'It is absolutely essential that you get ahead with it *quam celeriter*. If possible within the next day or two.' To the letter he attached a separate note, with the instruction that Ted should copy it in his own handwriting and send it to Richard's housemaster, 'and at the same time you should write a letter to the HM on the same lines':

We have decided after much consultation to move Richard from Stowe to the Technical College in Guildford. Our reasons for doing this are as follows. Since Richard's knee has handicapped him since going to Stowe he has wanted to forget about games and get on with writing and other academic subjects. He wishes to go to the Guildford Technical College so he can do A-levels in one year instead of two . . . His aim at doing a one-year A-level course is so that he can get on to his degree for Law straight away or go on into a University.

I have also discovered from speaking to him that he wishes to go into politics and feels that by going to a technical college he will have the chance to mix with a class of person he has never had the chance to mix with before.

Richard has had a very happy time in Cobham and we cannot possibly express our thanks to you for all you have done for him – not only as a housemaster, but in religion.

Yours, Edward Branson.

Ted Branson never wrote the letter.

It was Branson's directness about his objectives alongside his almost Machiavellian cunning which made him so disarming. Following Gavin Maxwell's advice, he began writing to, and telephoning, commercial companies and institutions in an attempt to sell advertising space in the forthcoming magazine. Drayson was astonished when

Branson approached him one day and suggested he would stay on at Stowe for a two-year A-level course if Drayson would put a telephone in his study. 'He wanted it to run the magazine, and he couldn't do that from the public telephone box. I said that wouldn't be easy, so he said, in that case he was afraid he would have to leave.'

Branson's school reports measured his declining interest in academic subjects. 'Too ready to make facile generalisations' in history; in maths, 'his background knowledge is very weak indeed'; physics: 'his only interest in the course has been to criticise it'. Summing up, the long-suffering Drayson wrote, 'I have all the time in the world for his enthusiasm and interest in what is going on around him. But he lacks a sense of judgement in making his choices and demands, and I hope he has not bitten off more than he can chew.'

Branson's O-level passes in Scripture, English Language, English Literature, History, Ancient History and French were only average. He tried for, and failed, Elementary Maths three times. None the less, both Drayson and his parents continued to hammer into Richard the need to apply himself to A-levels.

At the beginning of 1967, he wrote to his grandmother, requesting more help with typing. 'To tell you the truth I'm finding everything seems to be closing in on me. I have got to get up at four o'clock every day and do *Student*, prepare letters, get the dummy ready, prepare interviews etc., etc. Apart from that I have schoolwork. Life is altogether full up.'

He had already written to Drayson in the autumn, outlining his reasons for wanting to leave Stowe that summer – a letter which typified that curious mixture of the unctuous and the arrogant which his schoolmasters always found so trying. What Branson said was usually self-important, often impertinent, sometimes outrageous, yet it could, when he chose, be couched in terms of such fulsome politeness, given of a degree of reasonableness so infuriating, that they sometimes wished he would just be rude and leave it at that. 'The fact that I am asking to leave may well sound gutless and inexcusable, after all you and Stowe have given me. I fully appreciate and am extremely grateful to you for *everything* you have done. I sincerely wish that I could remain at Stowe for my full-time, and through my qualities I might possess, do all I can help in the school, and in the new house. But I also feel that it is impossible to stay.' By leaving that summer, he wrote, he could 'give more to Stowe and Britain'. *Student* could well mean 'a great deal in the lives of a great many . . . By giving a platform to students and others, we aim to spark off enthusiasm and a new drive in Britain, beginning with its young. I realise now that this could not be achieved by remaining at Stowe.'

Drayson, however, continued to believe that the regeneration of Britain could wait until Richard Branson had secured a proper education. He wrote again to Ted and Eve, saying that for Richard to leave at the end of the summer term 'would be against all common sense academically. He is an impetuous young man with a lot of ideas, some good and some not so good. I think it would be a great pity if he got things wrong at this point.'

That Easter, when Branson returned to Tanyards for the holidays, Ted walked him on the lawn for a fatherly chat. He implored Richard to stay on at school, attempting to convince him that *Student* was too perilous an enterprise to offer any proper future prospects, that a career in the Law offered more security. If Richard applied himself to work now he could get the required qualifications for Cambridge; Ted had set sufficient money aside to see him through university. Richard listened patiently, then launched into his argument. They had been working on the first issue of *Student*. It would be ready in the summer; he and Johnny had put everything into it, and he knew it was going to be a success. He repeated what he had said to Drayson, that *Student* could mean 'a great deal in the lives of a great many'. But, on the other hand – and here he adopted the voice of the responsible and obedient son – if going into the Law was what his father wanted, then how could he, Richard, act against his wishes . . . ? The conversation unsettled Ted. On the one hand, he had got his way. But the more he thought about what he had said to Richard, the more he was reminded of how unhappy he had been following his own father's wishes. He told Richard, before his son's return to Stowe, that he would write the letter he wanted.

In April 1967, Drayson wrote again to the Bransons. 'Thank you for your letter in which you say that Richard will be leaving Stowe at the end of the present term. I feel sure that this is the right step, as it would be pointless for us to try to persuade Richard to stay against his wishes.'

That year, Branson collected his single A-level, in Ancient History – a reflection, his housemaster noted 'more of his natural, native wit than academic study'. He had, by this time, moved houses, from Cobham to a newly inaugurated house, Lyttleton, where he spent his last two terms.

Some twenty years later, revisiting Stowe for the first time, Branson was approached on the lawn by an enthusiastic master. 'I'm in charge of Lyttleton now,' the master said. 'Your old house.' Branson confessed he had no memory of it whatsoever.

He walked out of Stowe in the summer of 1967. But it was clear that he had left the school in his mind some considerable time before. 'Branson,' said his headmaster on the day he left, 'I predict you will either go to prison, or become a millionaire.'

Chapter 3

Student

The first issue of *Student* magazine appeared in January 1968. Its cover showed a drawing of a symbolic student figure – kipper-tied, his jacket lapels covered with badges. The drawing was an original by Peter Blake, whose cover art for the Beatles' *Sgt Pepper* album the year before had made him the most famous painter of the day. Inside, Vanessa Redgrave, an actress then in her first flush of political radicalism, held forth in an interview conducted by Branson.

There were further interviews with an impressive selection of the most esteemed artists of the day – Henry Moore, David Hockney, Michael Ayrton, Gerald Scarfe, Kenneth Armitage and Peter Blake, all conducted by Jonathan Holland-Gems. The Dean of Liverpool and Paul Ferris debated sexual freedom; John Le Carré donated a short story; and Gavin Maxwell, Richard's old mentor, a thoughtful piece on education. There was also the first 'inside story' ever to appear in a British magazine about the Provos, the Dutch anarchist group which advocated the abolition of the motor car in towns and filled the streets of Amsterdam with white bicycles. Richard's Dutch girlfriend, Rudi, had effected an introduction.

Between Holland-Gems's precocious knowledge of the arts and London cultural life and Branson's precocious powers of persuasion – his willingness to knock on anybody's, and everybody's, door – *Student* boasted a list of contents and contributors which would have been the envy of any colour supplement or established publication. For a first issue of a new magazine, it was a work of remarkable professionalism and maturity – all the more astonishing given that the average age of the staff was sixteen. The first editorial sounded a clarion call:

> At a time when the student population of the world is growing rapidly, when topical and controversial issues fall more and more into the court of the young and recently qualified, many feel it is essential that the exploding student population should have the hearing it deserves. We want *Student* to develop as a platform for all shades of opinion, all beliefs and ideas . . . a vehicle for intelligent comment and protest.

Establishing a useful precedent, in the spirit of the times, not one of the prestigious contributors was paid.

The first issue of *Student* had been conceived in enthusiasm, gestated in persistence, and born in conditions of extreme squalor. There had been no question, on leaving Stowe, of Richard moving back home to Tanyards. Ted and Eve had made it clear that they could not, and would not, support him. He made it clear that he did not expect them to. Utterly miserable, and unable to tolerate public-school life any longer, Jonathan Holland-Gems had also left Stowe, with a view to going on to another school in London. He would continue working on *Student* in the meantime. The basement of his parents' house in Connaught Square, a few minutes' walk from Hyde Park, was in a condition of disrepair, but vacant: *Student* could operate from there.

In the autumn of 1967, Branson and Holland-Gems moved in and quickly set about reconstructing their new office and home into a scene that one early visitor described as 'like the aftermath of Hiroshima'. The room was small, dark and dank; its sole furnishings a rickety wooden table and a selection of old mattresses leaking springs and stuffing on to a linoleum-covered floor. Piles of papers and scraps of artwork were scattered at random around the room. Unwashed coffee cups grew mould and dust settled on the dinner plates, congealing colourfully with the remnants of food which had been pilfered in nocturnal raids from Mrs Holland-Gems's kitchen upstairs.

The campaign to sell advertising, begun in the public telephone-box at Stowe, gained fresh impetus. Branson was a telephone actor; one of those people for whom the telephone is an instrument of transformation. Awkward in person, on the telephone he could lower his voice and invoke an air of purposeful confidence and responsibility, if not exactly gravitas. Those on the other end of the line hardly realised they were talking to a spotty seventeen-year-old and he quickly sold some £6,000-worth of space, to customers as varied as the Metal Box Company, the *Sunday Times* and J. Walter Thompson recruitment.

In search of a designer for the magazine, Branson, with characteristic directness, broached the offices of *Town* magazine – then the epitome of stylish publishing – and asked the art editor, Ian Howes, if he wanted another job. Howes put him on to a colleague, Bob Morley, who became *Student*'s honorary art editor. Howes himself would contribute photographs. 'Richard was basically a spotty little yob who'd gone through all the magazines and decided who he wanted to design his,' Howes remembers. 'He just wouldn't go away. He was one of those people who it was just easier to do what he asked and get rid of him; otherwise he'd be on your doorstep every five minutes, driving you mad.'

For printing, Branson approached the old-established firm of Waterlows. Taken by his persuasiveness and the by now dying remnants of a good public-school accent, they agreed surprisingly to give *Student* three months' credit. Not until the first edition was about to go to press did they discover Branson was only seventeen, under the legal age for signing contracts and therefore not responsible for his debts. Waterlows demanded that he provide a guarantor, or the magazine would not be printed. Branson turned to his father, Ted, who advised him that as he had a contract in writing he should go back to Waterlows – 'Don't crow about it' – and say that if they did not print then their good name would be damaged, and he, Richard Branson, would expect some compensation. 'So he went to see them and obviously they had taken legal advice, because they said, it looks as if we shall have to sink or swim together, and they went ahead and printed.'

Sixty thousand copies of the first *Student* were printed, distributed through a network of contacts in colleges and universities throughout the country. Branson persuaded W.H. Smith to handle a small amount. The rest were sold on the streets by him, Holland-Gems and the small band of people who began to turn up at the door in Connaught Square establishing a ritual which greeted the publication of each new edition of *Student*. Lured by the promise of easy money, what passed for London's 'alternative' society would arrive on the doorstep of the *Student* offices, long-haired, bejeaned, and bleary-eyed, to be given a bundle of magazines by whomever happened to be 'distribution manager' that morning. The magazines were then peddled up and down Oxford Street and Piccadilly Circus to any likely-looking target, particularly credulous back-packing foreigners. Sometimes, the street-sellers would return with the agreed 50 per cent of the proceeds. Often, they would never be seen again.

Nik Powell, Branson's old friend from Shamley Green, had arrived, in a hiatus between school and university, to lend a hand looking after the magazine's accounts. Other friends from Stowe and Ampleforth drifted in, and some from nobody quite knew where, materialising with some journalistic or design skill to offer, or simply in search of the ready cash from selling the magazine. The offices of *Student* became half creative hothouse, half a resting place for public-school drop-outs. The Connaught Square basement grew ever more cramped, fetid and dirty; Mrs Holland-Gems's cupboards ever more bare; her patience thinner and thinner . . .

The London of January 1968 on to which *Student* magazine was launched was on the cusp between the politics of ecstasy and the politics of confrontation, shivering between the memory of 'the summer of love' and anticipation for the forthcoming spring of discontent.

The 'summer of love' had appeared, in Britain at least, largely as a phenomenon of the media. But the bells, beads and silly newspaper headlines were to provide a last, heady moment of euphoria on which to bid adieu to a fast-evaporating mood of idealism and optimism. London already had a press which served what was loosely defined as 'the underground'. *International Times* (or *IT*) had been launched in October 1966, with a party that typified the heady and hallucinatory mood of the times. Two thousand five hundred people had gathered in a disused railway engine shed in Camden Town called the Roundhouse to listen to music by The Soft Machine and Pink Floyd. The invitation urged guests to 'bring your own poison', but each person entering was handed a sugar cube, one in twenty of which – according to legend – was dosed with LSD.

IT concerned itself with studiously fermenting revolution and chronicling the harassment and persecution of the counter-culture by the Establishment – some of it imagined, much of it not. *Oz*, founded by an Australian named Richard Neville, argued the politics of hedonism and ecstasy. Its graphic style, resembling an explosion in a paint shop, with purple printed on green, orange on yellow, was a graphic metaphor for the psychedelic experience, conveying a theology which was dazzling at first glance, migrainous on closer examination. Both *IT* and *Oz*, to a greater or lesser extent, addressed the interests of 'students' – at least, the more insurrectionary ones: revolutionary politics, drugs, sexual freedoms, rock and roll music. In fact, students were a positive growth industry by 1968. The population of universities doubled in the 1960s. The expansion of the red-brick universities, and the increasing emphasis in the curriculum on the humanities – sociology, politics, economics – had fostered a large, and highly critical, student population, with a growing sense of their own potential and power. At Sussex, Essex, the LSE, as well as in Paris and Bonn, Lenin's 'stormy petrels of the revolution' were stretching their wings.

Student magazine, it was clear, was neither neo-psychedelic nor radical. The list of those to whom polite thanks were given in its first issue – Richard's and Johnny's parents, Marjorie Proops, Peter Scott, Edward Heath, William Rees-Mogg – hardly constituted a *Who's Who* of the London underground. And the magazine's policy of adopting a scrupulously neutral, even-handed approach became holy writ. As one editorial put it: 'We feel that we cannot fulfil our responsibilities by simply printing what X thinks of Y. We must also print why Z disagrees.' So it was that one issue of *Student* contained a fiery espousal of black radicalism by James Baldwin alongside the full text of Enoch Powell's infamous 'rivers of blood' speech; and a dialogue between Kenneth Allsop and Malcolm Muggeridge, embodying the forces of liberalism and reaction. Nor was Richard Branson himself anybody's idea of either a hippie or a stormy petrel. The outsize jumper and untidy haircut, the black, horn-rimmed spectacles, fractured at the bridge and held together with Sellotape, gave him the air of a perpetually genial schoolboy – an air which he has never quite shaken off.

For Branson, the privations of life at Connaught Square were somewhat alleviated by his being taken up by new and influential friends, not least Vanessa Redgrave. Branson had written to the actress requesting an interview for *Student*. The very first issue of the magazine announced that Redgrave would be 'sponsoring' a forum for new ideas on education. That never materialised, but she was taken by Branson's enthusiasm and by the potential platform that *Student* might provide; a friendship developed. There were soirées at her home in Hammersmith where the actress would air her views – 'anti everything American except her cheques', as one visitor from *Student* put it – and where Branson was introduced to the likes of actor David Hemmings, Tariq Ali and other doyens of radical chic. For his part, Branson was flattered by her interest in, and support for, *Student*. More than fifteen years later, Redgrave approached Richard Branson again, seeking support for a project involving the Workers Revolutionary Party – and was politely declined. But to the seventeen-year-old Branson, her moral and political certainties were exemplary, particularly on the issue which, more than any other, catalysed youthful protest: the war in Vietnam. In March 1968 Redgrave rang Richard from California inviting him to join her on the march against the American Embassy in Grosvenor Square, on the seventeenth of the month.

A contingent from *Student* duly presented themselves on the allotted day at Trafalgar Square, where Tariq Ali addressed the multitudes. From there, they set off through the West End, pausing to harangue the offices of Dow Chemicals, the manufacturers of the napalm being dropped on Vietnam, and then on towards Grosvenor Square. Branson marched at the head of the procession, at Vanessa Redgrave's right shoulder, his feelings churning in the excitement of the moment. The magic of the mob worked its spell. To be leading a procession, tens of thousands strong, and in the company of the foremost political activists of the day, gave him a feeling of power that was undeniable – if somewhat unhealthy. But to be marching for something you believed in, to stop the war; that was a good feeling. As the crowd's chants swelled to a crescendo: 'Hey, hey, LBJ, how many kids you killed today?' Branson silently reflected that it was perhaps just as well that *Student* had not published good luck greetings from the same 'LBJ' after all.

In Grosvenor Square, Branson found himself directly in front of the American Embassy, the tide of humanity beating around him, a huge, frightened heart. Redgrave and Ali were nowhere to be seen. There was only the shouting and the sound of horses' hooves and the sight of batons raised against the sky and people being dragged, screaming, from the crowd. Branson himself was chased across the square, pursued by a policeman with his truncheon raised, but he outsprinted him and melted into the safety of the crowd, from which darts arced out towards the police horses and marbles were rolled under hooves. The newspapers next day lamented the demonstration as a nadir in 'civil disobedience'. Two hundred and eighty people were arrested, including Jonathan Gems, who was soundly thumped and dragged kicking and screaming to a police van by three policemen. Richard paid his fine the next day at Marlborough Street Magistrates Court.

Branson joined another march on the American Embassy later that year, but protesting against the war in Vietnam was the limit of his political radicalism. 'I suppose I am left-wing – well, only to the extent that I think left-wing views are sane and rational,' he told a reporter from the *Guardian*, one of the increasing number that began to thread their way over the mattresses and recumbent bodies to where Branson was playing the telephones. Rather, he had absorbed the idealism of the era and assimilated it into a hazy benevolence, 'to do something for young people' – particularly if that something provided fun, excitement and a challenge for himself.

Richard's friends working on *Student* reflected the broad swath of liberal opinions on subjects such as South Africa and apartheid, the reform of the drug laws and Vietnam. The magazine treated all these issues seriously, but without revolutionary zeal. For Branson, however, the passion lay much more with the act of publishing the magazine itself than with its potential as a polemical platform.

Student's reputation began to grow, and Branson's with it. He was featured in *Vogue*, in a spread on 'British Talent in its Stride', which also included Lord Snowdon, the painter Allen Jones and Terry Hands, who later became director of the Royal Shakespeare Company. Branson was described as 'very much a student – a great woolly jersey, a cheerful, rumbling energy and a slight surprise that the world should be thought difficult'. Branson spoke of his wish for the magazine to galvanise the British student into an awareness of things other than his grant and his digs, to 'give expression to the feeling of internationalism, the wish to know about other students' problems, and also to get him involved'. There were even a handful of television appearances, in which Branson was usually characterised as 'The Voice of Youth'. This was something of a misnomer; for, while persuasively fluent when cajoling advertising or 'selling' the importance of *Student* to newspaper reporters, as a public speaker the 'Voice of Youth' ummed and aahed in a manner of agonising incoherence.

At a rally on the students' role in revolutionary struggle, he was invited to appear on a platform with German agitator Daniel Cohn-Bendit and Tariq Ali, outside University College, London, in front of an excitable crowd of students and activists and the beady glare of German television cameras. The two revolutionaries fulminated against American imperialism and the need for international solidarity for forty-five minutes each, without notes, while Branson waited his turn anxiously. He had tried to memorise his speech, but after two minutes of perspiring under the television lights he dried up and the speech fell into an incomprehensible garble. Stuttering and stammering, he fled from the platform red-faced.

The patronage of political firebrands did not last long as they realised that they stood to gain nothing from *Student*. Max Handley, who arrived at Connaught Square one day with a friend and stayed on to become *Student*'s features editor, observed the way in which Branson would quickly discern anyone approaching *Student* with ulterior motives. 'A lot of people saw Richard as someone they could turn to their advantage, whether it was young slickers wanting to take the magazine from under him, or established political figures who wanted to use it for their own platform. They saw this young kid with broken glasses, boasting about this huge circulation, and thought he was ripe for the plucking. They all underestimated him, and all of them came out with nothing.'

Jonathan Holland-Gems's parents had grown increasingly distressed by the activities in their basement, the nocturnal comings and goings, the general air of squalor and disrepute. *Student* magazine was given notice to quit.

For Ted and Eve, the thought of Richard being without somewhere to live, as well as being without a proper job and prospects, was too much to bear. In need of an occasional London base, the Bransons had taken a short lease on a four-storey, end-of-terrace Georgian house in Albion Street, across the Bayswater Road from Hyde Park, and coincidentally around the corner from Connaught Square. It was a street of shuttered windows and locked doors, inhabited by professional couples, comfortably off widows, Ukrainian exiles and the like. Number Forty-four Albion Street was owned by the Church Commissioners, and had previously been used as the vicarage for the local church. Within a fortnight of its being taken over by *Student*, a letter had arrived for the Bransons from a neighbour, complaining about the noise and appealing 'to either ask the kids to wear slippers or make some other arrangements. Incidentally, its no concern of mine, but your front door is ever open, day and night.'

The fond hope of Ted and Eve that their son might still take the path to further education and respectability was fast evaporating. Allowing him to use Albion Street was both bowing to the inevitable and giving support, even for a project with which they were still far from happy. Only the drawing-room on the first floor, filled with Eve's furniture, was officially out of bounds – a restriction observed on pain of expulsion. Relations between parents and son had been strained, not least because of Ted's and Eve's fears that in leaving Stowe to pursue *Student* Richard had 'led astray' his younger friend Jonathan Holland-Gems. The accusation upset Richard.

Sitting at his desk in Albion Street, he wrote a long and detailed letter home, denying that he had persuaded Gems to leave Stowe or that he had led him into smoking and drinking. It was a letter of portentous gravity for a seventeen-year-old, written in the manner Branson sometimes adopted of a boy old before his time, who had progressed from childhood to adulthood, with all the burdens and responsibilities it implied, but with no adolescence in between.

Dear Mum and Dad,
I know only too well that all your advice is always, of course, sound and sense. I accept it, increase it to my vocabulary and silently thank you both for it.
    It is, I think, in my nature to question everything. You will have to forgive me for the many occasions I

have stubbornly and openly rejected your sound suggestions – but have inwardly, I think and hope, benefited enormously.

Johnnie has learnt a lot with *Student*. I have not seen him for some time. He has, I hoped, been getting on with exams. He has rejected school after school – system after system, and now he may, for all I know, be rejecting society. And perhaps society will reject him. I will try to see him soon and see what I can do. But if I were to blame myself I think I would be unjustified.

Replying to his parents' suggestion that he may be 'scornful of others staying on at school to learn – or others who go to university', Richard wrote,

Please – don't put words in my mouth. Why should I be scornful? Of course I'm not. Only perhaps slightly filled with the hope that I soon might experience the atmosphere of a really first-class university. I hope you'll excuse me answering your questions in this way. I hope too I'm making the time to think of others. I have ten people – almost a large family – here who are depending on me all the time. Four of them have put their future careers in my hands. It is an enormous responsibility and my only way to think of others right now is to work *very* hard. To prove this I write this letter at 3 a.m. . . .

Gems had, indeed, left *Student*, partly to continue his education at a comprehensive school, but also to improve his sex life. 'I was very shy with girls; I'd go through absolute hell to make a girl notice me and then Richard would suddenly sweep in and carry her off. This kept on happening, and at last I thought "I've got to leave" . . .'

More arrived to take his place. In some curious confirmation of Parkinson's Law, the numbers of people involved in *Student* had increased to fill the space afforded by the move to bigger premises. By Issue Three, the masthead was listing more names than could be comfortably accommodated in the offices of a national daily newspaper, as well as 'correspondents' in Czechoslovakia, East Africa, France (seven people), Greece, Nigeria, Spain, America and Vietnam. Many of these were people who had happened to pass through the office en route to foreign parts and who would despatch nothing more than the occasional postcard. But the Vietnam correspondent was real enough – and a testament to Branson's growing facility for deal-making. In this case an arrangement with the *Daily Mirror*.

In order to get seventeen-year-old Julian Manyon out to Vietnam, Branson contacted the *Daily Mirror* and offered them a diverting human interest story about a young correspondent for a student magazine covering the war from the front line: all they had to do was pay Manyon's fare and expenses. They agreed and from this promising beginning Manyon went on to make a career in television journalism.

A similar deal was struck in order to cover the war in Biafra. The Nigerian government had clamped down on journalists entering the country, but Branson was able to persuade the London consulate to grant visitors' permits for 'students'. He then approached ITN news, offering entry to Nigeria for a camera crew on his student visas, if they paid all fares and costs for the *Student* writer.

It became increasingly apparent that Branson's real skills lay less in journalism than in the less tangible art of

fixing. While he enjoyed editing and conducting interviews, the reluctance of anybody else on the magazine to
handle the more prosaic business of selling advertising,
and therefore actually keeping *Student* afloat, meant it
fell to him alone. To persuade a company to part with
£300 for a page of advertising was an achievement – and
usually a crucial one. Without revenue, the magazine
could not be printed, and there was never enough revenue
to bring it out regularly. Branson's journalistic endeavours had, anyway, always relied greatly on bluff, reflecting his impatience with the time-consuming and often
tedious business of reading, researching and writing. He
once presented himself at the Hilton Hotel to interview
the visiting American author James Baldwin. Insinuating
his way to the door of the Baldwin suite, he made his
explanations, and was ushered in by a gracious, accommodating and exceedingly dapper black man whom he
dutifully began to interview. After a long and interesting
exchange, his subject rose from the sofa and said that
actually he was Mr Baldwin's aide and that Mr Baldwin
was next door.

As creative publisher Branson could play the telephone
– always his great skill – and allow his imagination full
rein. The list of distinguished people persuaded to give
freely of their talents continued to grow – Jean-Paul
Sartre, Alice Walker and Stephen Spender all contributed
to Issue Three – as did Branson's plans to project *Student*
as the biggest, best, most important, most exciting project
imaginable. 'Richard's interest in the magazine was more
about image than content,' says Max Handley. 'He'd say,
let's get Sartre to write something, but what Sartre wrote
would be incidental. Richard was always the guy with the
next idea and even if they weren't very good ones he'd
pour energy into them and make them work.'

His telephone litany – 'I'm Richard Branson, I'm eighteen and I run a magazine that's doing something really useful for young people' – burst forth in a single gush of enthusiasm, guilefully inflating the circulation of *Student* from its actual 50,000 to a wildly fanciful 100,000 in a matter of seconds, and yielding promises of advertising from the unlikeliest quarters. Branson was the inspired salesman, or, in the words of one Albion Street resident, 'the supreme bullshitter'. Whenever a newspaper reporter arrived to prepare another profile on the coming 'whiz-kid', somebody was despatched to the nearest telephone-box to ring Branson constantly, thereby creating an impression of frenetic activity.

For Nik Powell all this came as a revelation. 'It really surprised me how easy it was to con people into thinking you had something successful when you quite patently didn't – journalists, in particular; if something made good copy they'd write it, and it made much better copy for *Student* to be an enormous publishing success rather than the modest failure it actually was.' However many, or few, copies were printed, the piles accumulating in the corners of Albion Street never seemed to diminish. No audited circulation figures were ever produced, because the magazine was distributed through universities and sold on the streets; there were thousands of copies all over the country gathering dust in bedsits and junior common rooms, unsold; and any receipts were seldom collected by *Student*. The honest salespeople who did bring money back did not know how few in number they really were. 'Advertising was sold on the basis of an estimated figure,' says Powell. 'Whenever anybody questioned the figures more closely – which very few people did – Richard would quickly change from talking circulation to talking readership – the old sleight of hand. He was quite brilliant at it.'

★ ★ ★

Branson's enthusiasm was at its most contagious, and most necessary, in the offices of *Student*.

When Christopher Strangeways first arrived at Albion Street with his cousin Harriet, who worked on *Student*, he was somewhat taken aback to be greeted by Branson with a big kiss. 'I thought, Christ, this is odd, but also what an interesting and exciting place to be – because it was a friendly kiss.' It needed to be. Nobody on *Student* was being paid a salary. Many remarked on Branson's capacity to get people working for no money or apparent reward to themselves, inspired by some indefinable, yet strangely palpable notion that to do so was for the greater good, in the cause of some noble idea that nobody could ever quite put their finger on. Somehow, to endure financial hardship – or at least forgo financial reward – was 'fun'.

'Fun' was an essential Richard Branson word – a simple reason for doing things; the rationale for the practical jokes and schoolboy pranks to which anyone in the office could be subject at any time; the currency which sufficed in the absence of money. Branson was neither witty nor sophisticated, but he had an intuitive grasp of what was going on in other people's minds, and was quick to analyse a situation correctly and take advantage of it. 'His ability to pull someone's leg in any circumstances was remarkable,' says Strangeways. 'He could fool you at any time he chose – phoning up and pretending to be somebody else, playing some kind of trick.'

'Fun' was the component which kept the peace in Albion Street when tempers flared and dampened any potentially mutinous sentiments. 'Richard was very good at releasing tension,' Jonathan Holland-Gems remembers. 'He'd say, "Come on everybody, let's go to Hyde Park." Everybody would say "Fuck off, Richard." "No, no, I've got something to show you." "Not another practical joke, Richard." But eventually he'd force everybody out and we'd traipse to Hyde Park and he'd just push people in the fountains and behave like a crazy man. People loved that. The girls thought it was fun because they felt like being part of some happy family; the boys thought it fun because they could rub against the girls. It all helped.

'He was a good captain of the ship, because he knew what people were thinking; he could anticipate and create scenarios so that people would not sink the boat through frustration or hostility.'

And yet, for all the appearance of tribal communality, there was no doubting who was chieftain. While the others slept in a constantly fluctuating arrangement of numbers and people, Richard maintained his own room at the top of the house. An indefatigable captain by day, he seemed less at ease in the 'unwinding sessions' that occurred each evening over a bottle of cheap wine or a few marijuana 'joints' which at first were consumed in the manner of holy sacrament but soon assumed a habitual mundanity. Branson drank sparingly, and had a low tolerance of alcohol. He would puff at a joint tentatively, and then, it seemed, only to be polite. Cerebral contemplation, communal giggling at nothing in particular, and getting lost in the latest Pink Floyd record was not the sort of relaxation he relished. In fact, relaxation did not appear to be a word in his vocabulary. He was forever preoccupied, plotting schemes to promote the magazine, support the household or extend in some way the empire.

'He was always extraordinarily single-minded,' remembers Max Handley. 'You couldn't have a conversation that wasn't about the magazine. If you talked about anything else he would just lose interest and start making phone calls.'

Projects associated with the magazine flourished almost overnight – and were invariably dead by next morning – conceived in a flurry of enthusiasm, but never properly developed: the Student Fashion Agency, the Student Literary Agency, the Student Art Exhibition. Most of these ideas were addressed to one purpose: how to keep *Student* solvent. For the piles of magazines accumulating in the corners and cupboards of Albion Street suggested that while intellectual credibility was served by the presence of Jean-Paul Sartre and James Baldwin on the cover, a more popular name was required to actually promote sales of the magazine. As the autumn of 1968 turned to winter Branson set off for a brisk stroll across a Hyde Park brown and orange in the hazy sunshine, on his way to No. 3 Savile Row, to seek audience with the most popular names of all.

The Beatles' announcement, earlier that year, of the inauguration of the Apple Foundation for the Arts, had brought an immediate throng of supplicants to the Apple door. Each day found a new batch of artists, performers, pilgrims, mendicants and simple confidence-tricksters, in search of benefaction and support for plots, wheezes and schemes for the betterment of mankind in general, and themselves in particular.

The four Beatles had little to do with the administration of largesse. The bulk of this creative outpouring accumulated, unopened and unread, in the office of the Beatles' press officer and majordomo, Derek Taylor. A slim, moustachioed man, with the deceptively clipped speech of the officers' mess, Taylor played his role as the principal link between the Beatles and the outside world with an abiding graciousness and sense of responsibility. The Beatles promised to make people's dreams come true; the very least Derek Taylor felt obliged to do was to let them down gently, with a drink, a smoke and a few minutes' civilised conversation.

Richard Branson arrived at Apple with a more modest request than most. The forthcoming issue of *Student* would include an interview with John Lennon; could John and Yoko be prevailed upon to provide an original recording which could be distributed in the magazine on flexidisc – singing, or talking perhaps, preferably customised for *Student*. Taylor listened sympathetically. The idea was feasible, and he thought that Branson had 'good manners'. Taylor believed good manners were very important.

He introduced Branson to Ron Kass, the managing director of Apple, and to a manufacturer of flexidiscs. The agreement made, Branson persisted. Hardly a day passed without the phone ringing in Taylor's office: 'Sorry to bother you, Derek, any news?' As Christmas neared, Branson became a frequent visitor to Apple, sitting on the floor of Taylor's office, addressing envelopes while Taylor bashed out signatures on Christmas cards. 'One day,' says Taylor, 'he looked up and said, "The record will be OK, won't it, Derek?" and I just scribbled on a card, "Trust me, Derek" and threw it down, and he looked very relieved.'

1969 arrived, but without John and Yoko's recording. Life had weighed heavily on them both in the preceding months. In November, Yoko had lost the baby she was expecting. The following week, John had been convicted for possession of cannabis. Now they had become mysteriously unavailable, secluded in their Weybridge mansion, rumoured to be 'not well', inaccessible even to the entreaties of Derek Taylor. Taylor began to fret about the assurances he had given to *Student* magazine. He was a man of his word, and he would hate to see Branson let down. Then, in late January, on his way out of the Apple office to see a performance of *Peter Pan*, Derek Taylor was handed a writ: *Connaught Publications* vs. *John and Yoko Lennon and Derek Taylor*, for breach of promise. Among the promised exhibits was a copy of the Christmas message Taylor had scribbled – Trust me.

Branson was getting desperate. In anticipation of *Student*'s celebrity exclusive, he had already prepared the cover of the spring issue. The print run had been doubled to 100,000 copies, and the famous, and expensive, illustrator Alan Aldridge had been commissioned to provide cover art, leaving a white space in the middle for the Lennon flexidisc to be stuck on to. All that was missing was the disc itself. Without it, the cover would have to be scrapped, and *Student*'s perilous financial situation rendered nigh on terminal. Branson was not a barrister's son for nothing. His father had told him often enough that if you want satisfaction in a case, you go to litigation – or at least threaten to go. It just might force the Lennons into providing the record. The fact that he was an eighteen-year-old threatening the best-loved pop institution in the world did not occur to him, let alone deter him. He was within his rights . . .

Derek Taylor received the writ with a heavy heart. He immediately sent a memo to John Lennon. Being sued for breach of promise by a student magazine was hardly the kind of publicity the Lennons were seeking in their drive for world peace. As Taylor had made the promise himself he was prepared to personally pay the damages claimed, £10,000, to avoid the matter going to court, but it had also become a matter of honour for Branson that he should have *something* to put on a record.

In April, Branson, Derek Taylor and their respective lawyers gathered in the basement of 3 Savile Row to unveil the tape which Lennon had delivered. The hiss of the speakers quietened conversation, then the room filled with a curious sound: ba-boom, ba-boom, ba-boom, ba-boom.

'What's that?' Branson asked.

'It's the heartbeat of Yoko's baby,' replied Taylor.

The sound stopped.

'Is that all there is?'

'That's when it died . . .' There was an awkward hush. 'It's reality,' said Taylor at last, with the expediency if not the conviction of one who had grown accustomed to explaining John Lennon climbing into bags and gathering acorns. 'It's conceptual art. It's something that belonged to John and Yoko. And anyway, it's all we've got.' The record was never used.

Branson returned to Albion Street, worrying over printers' bills. Taylor went back to Savile Row, expecting to have to pay £10,000. He heard nothing more. Four years later, Taylor received a letter from Richard Branson explaining that he had been in dire straits with the magazine; the threat of legal action was an act of desperation. But it had been withdrawn; would Derek accept his apologies?

Taylor wrote back, 'Don't worry, Richard. All you need is love. Yours ever . . .'

In 1968, whilst still living among the detritus of the Holland-Gems' basement in Connaught Square, Richard Branson made his girlfriend pregnant . . .

She was not a particularly close girlfriend (in later

years Branson had difficulty even remembering her name); simply one of the number who had drifted into the *Student* offices and ended up in his bed. Branson was alarmed at the news, for both their sakes. And when she said she would have an abortion, he arranged it at a clinic in Birmingham and travelled up with her on the train to support her.

The difficulty in arranging the abortion was an alarming revelation for Branson. What happened to people who failed to make the connections he and his girlfriend had done, and were unable to extricate themselves from the situation? Release had been founded in July 1967, to advise those 'busted' on drugs charges; and there were other existing agencies to give advice on birth control – and termination. But what about those people who wanted help or advice on unwanted pregnancies, sexual matters, financial or housing problems and who were unwilling or unable to turn to the 'adult world' to find it? Here was a way for Branson's hazy ideas of benevolence and idealism – of 'doing something for young people' – to assume tangible form. The Student Advisory Centre was one of the few schemes to grow out of the chaotic machinations of *Student* magazine which actually bore fruit, all the more sweet because they were purely altruistic.

The Student Advisory Centre was born with an announcement in the magazine and a circular distributed by hand around London. 'Give Us Your Headaches,' it urged. Legal advice, abortion, adoption, contraception, drugs, pregnancy testing, psychiatric help, venereal disease . . . The response was immediate. A queue began to form at Albion Street of distraught mothers-to-be, alcoholics, lesbians with severe personality disorders and people afflicted with anti-social diseases. Urine samples began dropping through the letterbox. The telephone rang constantly with pleas for help. The *Student* editorial team quickly became expert at referring people to a body of sympathetic doctors, psychiatrists, hospitals and specialists for qualified advice, while offering immediate applications of sympathy and reassurance themselves.

The new venture put an extra strain on the accommodation at Albion Street; additional premises would need to be found. Branson approached the Revd Cuthbert Scott, vicar of the local church of St John, to see if he would help. Scott offered him the use of the church crypt – in return for Richard preaching a sermon in St John's about the work of the Student Advisory Centre. It was, remembers Scott, a quietly moving sermon, 'which conveyed the fact that these young people weren't being looked after. And that he loved 'em.'

The crypt had not been opened since being used as an air-raid shelter some twenty-five years before. It was cold and dark, but spacious. The paraphernalia of the magazine began to spill through the catacombs. Branson placed his desk across two marble tombs.

The crypt stayed open day and night, and there was sometimes confusion between the distressed young persons queuing for the Advisory Centre and the nannies and well-to-do young mothers wheeling their children to the nursery run by the church, but the Revd Scott took it in his stride. 'There were rude words written all over the church at times, but it was all right, they were cleaned off again. There were periods when it seemed as if the place was on fire – there would be billows of smoke coming out. But they always put it out. Richard always contained it, and apologised in the right quarters.'

While averting potential suicides, stamping out sexually

transmitted diseases and generally easing the burdens of the young, the good offices of the Student Advisory Centre had a further therapeutic effect. Among the perpetually destitute residents of Albion Street it provided some definable, worthwhile rationale for why they should be working for next to nothing. Money – or the lack of it – was an enduring source of consternation, not least to Branson himself.

Ducking creditors was a new addition to his skills. Bills for the telephone took priority – the telephone was a lifeline from which more money might yet be conjured. Bills for printing went unpaid for as long as possible. Branson treated money with a curious ambivalence: trusting to the better nature of those who distributed *Student*, he allowed hundreds of pounds to slip away; yet those honest souls who undertook to distribute Advisory Centre leaflets were usually obliged to return to Albion Street more than once for payment. 'One of Richard's major tricks was not to be around at six o'clock when people started trundling in for their two pounds,' says one former resident.

Life at Albion Street was becoming ever more beleaguered, its freedoms and pleasures not without hazards. Indulging himself in the luxury of a visit to an expensive barber, Christopher Strangeways was mortified to be loudly informed that he was the carrier of head lice. The stench of medicinal preparations filled Albion Street for weeks afterwards as every inhabitant was ritually doused.

Tom Newman, a musician with plans to develop his own recording studio, occasionally came to Albion Street with his girlfriend, who worked on *Student*, bringing with him bags of frozen chips stolen from the backdoor of a nearby Wimpy Bar. 'It was like something out of Dickens. There were half a dozen undernourished people sitting in the basement, like waifs and strays. One imagined some kind of Fagin upstairs controlling them.' When at last Newman was ushered upstairs to meet Branson, he was bemused to find not the 'greasy, middle-aged businessman' of his expectations but 'this unbelievably scruffy room, clothes and papers everywhere, and Richard sitting in a big brass bed with a girl and a telephone, flashing that enormous grin'.

The appearance, even the mood, of Albion Street may have been in the communal spirit of the day, but it was a co-operative, as someone put it, 'only in that all the people who worked there co-operated with each other from time to time'. There was little that was ideologically co-operative about it.

As Branson himself emphasises, 'Because it was the Sixties we had long hair, but we were always running a business.' The most important thing about *Student* was the advertising, 'because without the advertising there would have been no editorial at all.'

A few of the staff were, by now, on a wage but the dispensation of it was ever erratic; extracting money from Richard held the air of a challenge. Wendy Mandy had answered an advertisement in *The Times* which read 'international magazine needs assistant editor', arrived for the interview and been appointed Branson's personal assistant. She quickly found out that one way to guarantee being paid was to take his chequebook out of his drawer, forge his signature and pay herself. 'I would tell him this and he'd think it was funny. The cheekier you were, the more he liked it. All he really wanted from anyone was loyalty.'

In fact, to Branson it was a cause of irritation that the people in Albion Street never seemed to fully appreciate the realities of the situation. The house, the magazine – them, to a certain extent – all were his responsibility.

While they sat around getting stoned, he was the one who worried about the bills, to such an extent that it began to exact a toll on his health. He began to look tired and wan. Unless they found money soon, *Student* would collapse – and Branson with it. The late-night conversations turned, with mounting urgency, to ways of making money. Almost every avenue that could be related to students, or be of interest to them, had been considered. It was Branson who at last thought of selling cut-price records by mail-order.

The abolition of retail price maintenance had been one of the last acts of the Conservative Government in 1964, yet its effect on the record retail business had been negligible. Fearful of a repetition of what had occurred in America, where discounting had driven many businesses to the wall, record retailers in Britain operated an informal and unspoken cartel to keep prices stable. In fact, to the occupants of Albion Street, record prices were quite obviously 'a rip-off'. There were thousands of young people, readers of *Student*, who would jump at the chance of buying rock music cheaply. Branson knew nothing about music himself, but there were enough people in Albion Street who did, and the magazine provided the perfect medium for advertising.

The name for the new enterprise also came out of an evening of communal joking and suggestions – Student Records? Slipped Disc? Then, Virgin – because, as Branson and myth would for ever have it, 'We were novices in business.' But also, as somebody pointed out, and the night dissolved in laughter, because virgins were the one thing, apart from money, in short supply at Albion Street.

Chapter 4

Sex and Drugs and Rock and Roll

The very first advertisement for Virgin mail-order appeared in what turned out to be the very last issue of *Student*. It offered a 10–15 per cent discount on any rock record of the purchaser's choice. The response was immediate. Along with the regular morning delivery of urine samples and final demands came a deluge of postal orders, and with them the promise of an end to Richard Branson's heavy financial burden.

As expected, the orders came, in the main, from people who took their music seriously. They did not want records by popular artists, familiar from the Top Twenty, but 'progressive' rock, some so progressive that even the musical scholars in Albion Street had not yet caught up with them. Volunteers were despatched to HMV Records in Oxford Street to find out which companies particular groups recorded for, so that Branson could start haggling over orders. This proved more problematic than anyone had anticipated. Suspicious of discounting, and of a company that called itself Virgin – *Virgin??* – the established companies refused to give credit. Instead, Branson negotiated to buy in bulk from a retailer named Raymond Laren, who owned a chain of shops in the East End of London.

The *Student* staff were put to the new task of opening envelopes, processing orders, building shelves and tucking records into brown envelopes. Seeking a job between O- and A-levels, Steve Lewis arrived in the school holidays to answer telephones. 'One call would be, "How much is the Principal Edwards Magic Theatre record?" The next would be "I'm pregnant, what do I do?" ' The fact that Lewis knew what Principal Edwards Magic Theatre was made him invaluable in compiling a catalogue of 'hip' records, to be made available to the cognoscenti. Virgin's reputation for musical élitism and discernment was taking root, in an atmosphere Lewis describes as being 'like the best moments at school. It wasn't a hierarchical structure at all. It was like being in a gang, with Richard as leader. It wasn't a job; it was a lark.'

The inauguration of the new business brought with it another change of premises. At Albion Street, the Church Commissioners' agents had struck a final, and fatal, blow. Branson's ploy of temporarily removing any trace of office equipment and paraphernalia whenever notice of an inspection was given by the estate agents had been uncovered during one visit by the persistent ringing of a telephone from inside a cupboard. It was opened to reveal a switchboard of the kind not normally found in private homes.

The magazine, the Student Advisory Centre and the mail-order company were now consolidated under one roof, in a warehouse in South Wharf Road, in Paddington – the first premises on which the fledgling Virgin organisation was obliged to pay rent.

Student magazine was proving a constant worry to

Branson. Attempts to bring the magazine into profitability by bringing it out every month and selling more advertising had failed. Somehow, the magazine resisted any attempts at punctuality. Branson found it exhausting and time-consuming. The idealistic impulse from which the magazine had been born had been worn thin by the sheer grind and effort of producing it. Mail-order was already providing the steady flow of cash which had never been forthcoming with *Student*. The future, Branson decided, did not belong in publishing – at least not for the moment. The plans for expansion in the publishing world, with which he had regaled a reporter for the *Guardian* a few short months before – an American edition of *Student*, an 'arts' magazine, a scheme to revive the photo-news magazine *Picture Post* in partnership with a television company – were now quietly abandoned.

While Branson concentrated on running the mail-order business, he handed over the editorship of *Student* to the magazine's features editor, John Varnom, who worked on resuscitating *Student* for a few months, until Branson lost interest altogether.

IPC, the magazine publishing company which specialised in publications for the youth market, had long expressed an interest in investing in *Student*. Negotiations now started again in earnest for IPC to make a £75,000 injection into the magazine, with Branson to continue as publishing director. Branson went to lunch at IPC's Farringdon Street offices with the publishing director Patricia Lamburn and spent the entire meeting trying to sell another idea for young people's hotels. The IPC executives decided his enthusiasm for magazine publishing was less than total; the investment plans were quietly dropped, and *Student* magazine was finally laid to rest.

However, the Student Advisory Centre lived on, changing its name to Help. Branson continues to finance it, right up until the present day, making it his most long-established project.

For Branson, the move to South Wharf Road also brought with it a change of home, a new love affair and the discovery of a relative he did not even know he had.

It had long been a fancy of his to live on a houseboat. Walking alongside the Regents Canal one day in search of a suitable vessel, he stopped by one boat to make enquiries. Mundy Ellis was entertaining some friends on deck. 'Richard simply barged through the gate and shouted over that he wanted to buy a boat, and how did he go about it? I launched into a great explanation about how hard it was to get them. He stayed for lunch, and then tea, and then I just couldn't get rid of him.'

Mundy was two years older than Branson; stylishly dressed, with long, fair hair, blue eyes and quintessentially English features. She was intelligent and quick-witted and had a practical, purposeful disposition which warmed to the air of boyish helplessness which Branson could contrive over matters of eating, dressing and daily routine. Within a matter of weeks she had given up her job as a press officer at the Greenwich Theatre and was running the Student Advisory Centre, and living with Branson on his new houseboat, the *Alberta*.

The new relative appeared in similarly unexpected fashion. Simon Draper was Branson's second cousin. He had grown up in Cape Town, South Africa, passionately interested in rock music and yearning for the day when he could make the pilgrimage to its source. After finishing a degree course in English and Political Science, and with the added incentive of avoiding National Service in the South African Army, he set off for London, with his younger brother, a friend and £110 in his pocket. Draper had seen *Student* magazine in South Africa and immediately sought out Richard at South Wharf Road, where he explained who he was. Branson took to Draper at once: they shared the same family; they were almost exactly the same age – Draper a day older. It was like meeting the brother he had never had. Over bacon and eggs at the nearby Riviera Café, Branson excitedly sketched out a picture of the empire he was planning to build. It was obvious, he said, that there was money to be made in records. With mail-order up and running, his next plan was to start a record label. 'We're going to attack the record industry on every level,' Branson enthused. Tony Mellor, who worked in mail-order, knew about music; he was probably going to run the label. 'But you can run it with him,' Branson told Draper. In the meantime, if he wanted a job, he would work in mail-order as a record-buyer – £12 a week, and £15 if he worked on Saturdays.

The ritual of being a 'record-buyer' had already been established, as Draper quickly discovered. At eleven each morning, Tony Mellor would take out his tobacco pouch and ceremoniously roll a succession of joints – a pleasant adjunct to a day spent packing records, writing down catalogue numbers and listening to music. Draper spent his first few months in London in a marijuana haze, until Virgin's increasing turnover, and the mounting difficulty of conducting a coherent conversation with the EMI sales people while under the influence obliged him to desist. The world of business, as it was fast becoming clear, had a way of imposing itself on the world of pleasure.

By 1971, the counter-culture, such as it was, was fast going into liquidation; its most obvious legacy, a lost army of young people with long hair, a shared interest in soft drugs, some ill-defined consensus about 'rock culture' and the nagging sense that the party was over.

The turn of the decade brought with it a series of squalid deaths – of Janis Joplin, Brian Jones of the Rolling Stones, Jim Morrison and Jimi Hendrix. Their symbolic value as abrupt punctuation marks to an era's aspirations and its most empty conceits about the 'romance' of self-destruction only became apparent in time.

The power of rock music as an evangelical force, a lever for social change, had been found wanting. And no event symbolised the transformation of rock's possibilities into betrayals more graphically, or more swiftly, than the pop festival. The gathering at Woodstock, in upstate New York in August 1969, had seemed to offer more than just proof that 400,000 people could sit in mud for three days in relative harmony – notwithstanding overflowing lavatories, three deaths, two births and four miscarriages. It seemed to presage the triumph of a new spirit of humanity. The festival at the Altamont racetrack in California, in December, in which a young man was beaten to death by 'official' Hells Angels bodyguards as the Rolling Stones performed, seemed to indicate its peremptory defeat.

Utopia had lasted precisely four months.

By the time of the Isle of Wight festival in 1970, it was penned behind corrugated-iron fences and buried under a sea of detritus and drinks cans – a spectacle which moved one member of the audience to leap onstage during the performance by Joni Mitchell and declare the event 'just a hippie concentration camp'. Mitchell was singing her tribute to Woodstock at the time.

And yet, the opportunistic, or prescient, eye might also

have seen another vision. It was the spectacle of hundreds upon thousands of young people wanting to buy things. In its transactions, as well as its seething humanity, and its air of squalor and licence, the pop festival resembled nothing so much as a Middle-Eastern *souk*.

Being a 'hippie', particularly of the weekend variety, did not, it seemed, constitute a complete rejection of materialism and acquisitiveness. People did not stop buying things. It simply changed the things there were to buy, and meant they had to be sold in a different way. Commerce, in its most naked and unadulterated form – an unseemly interest in 'bread' – was certainly a little uncool, but commerce it was none the less, in loon pants, cheese-cloth shirts, peace patches, patchouli oil and records. Particularly records.

Record sales, which had fallen in the mid-Sixties, had begun to climb again as the decade moved to a close. In 1970, albums outsold singles for the first time ever. The pop music explosion of the Sixties had created a new, neo-aristocratic class of 'superstars', and with it a new set of musical values. Following the precedent set by the Beatles and Bob Dylan, all performers now wrote their own songs, often creaking self-consciously under the burden of 'art'. The 'important' artists – Pink Floyd, Led Zeppelin, the Rolling Stones, the Who – conceived their work as long-players, often as 'concept' albums, sometimes as 'suites', just like 'serious' musicians did.

Soon rock music and the great, passive congregations in its honour were all that was left of the 'counter-culture'; a way to show some allegiance to revolutionary gestures, without actually being a revolutionary oneself. For student protest too had largely died of inertia. The loudest dissenting voices now raised among the young were those in the correspondence columns of *Melody*

Maker, disputing whether or not Alvin Lee could indeed play Eric Clapton 'under the table', or vice versa.

Virgin was perfectly positioned to tap the new mother-lode. Without even trying – in fact, precisely because they *were* the people they were selling to – Virgin's founders connected immediately with the sensibilities of their customers. To be selling records more cheaply than anybody else was, after all, a beneficent act of sorts – if not exactly revolutionary. To be long-haired – seemingly not of the world of men in suits – was a distinct advantage. Virgin, it seemed, was not one of 'them', but one of 'us'.

It was ironic that the person at South Wharf Road whose instincts steered him more assuredly towards the requirements of the market-place was also the person least in tune with its tenets. It had not been necessary for Branson to know the difference between Van Der Graaf Generator and Blodwyn Pig in order to spot the business potential of discounting records. But nor was it calculation as to how best to exploit the burgeoning 'youth market' which accounted for Virgin's initial direction. It was much more random than that, dictated not by grand design but by the imperatives of survival; the mail-order business had grown out of the requirement to raise money for *Student* and subsequently eclipsed it. Just as record shops would shortly grow out of mail-order, again by chance, and eclipse that. Branson did not need necessarily share the tastes of his peers to cater to them. One of his skills was to know how to use the knowledge of those around him. He was the enabler, the catalyst who made things happen, even if he did not always understand what their happening meant in a wider cultural sense. Even Simon Draper had noticed, within days of arriving in London, how his second cousin differed so markedly from almost everyone else working at Virgin.

He quickly pigeon-holed Richard as 'a true blue capital-ist'. Branson carried with him an aura of privilege, and the 'other' world to which privilege belonged, which the shapeless jumpers and threadbare corduroy trousers could never quite disguise, and which could reveal itself in most unexpected ways.

One summer's weekend in 1971, Richard and Mundy, Richard's secretary Caroline Gold and her husband Rob, set off for a weekend in Suffolk, staying at a cottage belonging to Caroline's mother. Richard had brought with him two of his father's shotguns. Out shooting for pheasant on private land, however, they were caught by gamekeepers and brought before the landowner. The police were called and things looked grim until it was discovered that Richard was indeed the grandson of Sir George Branson who had lived in neighbouring Bradfield Hall. The police insisted on the charges being pressed, although the landowner tried to stop the prosecution, and Branson was fined a nominal amount. But more importantly, given their value, his father's guns were not confiscated and destroyed, as might have been the case, but returned to him. John Varnom, for one, was struck by the delight with which Richard recounted the story the following week over a convivial lunch in the Riviera Café. Varnom says he formed the impression then and there that Branson 'ultimately wanted to be one of the great and good'. It was not an ambition that many of Virgin's customers would have shared, or even thought to dream of.

By 1971 it had become apparent to all of Britain that the optimism of the Wilson years had proved utterly ground-less. His vision of a New Britain, forged in the white heat of technology, now seemed as distant as England's World

Cup victory, as chimerical as 'Swinging London', replaced by the reality of rising inflation and rising unemployment. In 1970, Edward Heath had returned the Conservatives to office, but the downward spiral had only accelerated in intensity. By 1975, unemployment would reach one million for the first time. Caught between panic over the visible shrinking of the value of the pay packet through inflation and the expectations of an improving qualify of life, peddled so tantalisingly throughout the Sixties, British industry moved into a cycle of higher and higher wage demands and lower and lower productivity. 1971 was to produce the worst record for strikes and stoppages since 1926.

In January 1971, Tom Jackson, the general secretary of the Union of Post Office workers, a man whose twinkling eyes and handlebar moustache lent him the deceptively jocular air of an Edwardian publican, called an all-out strike by his members in support of a 15–20 per cent pay claim. The strike was to last five weeks, but its impact in South Wharf Road was immediate and catastrophic. Overnight the flow of cheques and money orders dried up. Faced with shelves of records, Richard Branson made an instant decision: Virgin would open a shop.

Within a matter of days premises had been found, up a flight of stairs above a hi-fi and electrical goods shop at the end of Oxford Street where the wide pavements and spacious department stores give way to a jostling mass of cut-price boutiques, jewellers and the atmosphere of an Arab bazaar. Within a fortnight, the doors of Virgin's first shop were flung open to accommodate a queue stretching all the way from beneath its rainbow-patterned awning to the steps of Tottenham Court Road underground station.

As record shops go, the Virgin shop was unique, with

an ambience that owed everything to financial destitution. Scant attention had been paid to decor or fittings, but its hastily improvised, makeshift air only enhanced the mood of cliquish intimacy. Virgin carried only the most 'correct' stock: the best of British rock, imports of American West Coast bands and the latest bootlegs – illegal *samizdat* recordings, usually of live performances, by the most cultish performers of the day. It was a point of principle that there were no 'middle-of-the-road' records to be found in Virgin racks; no crooners' mush or pre-pubescent twaddle.

No shop assistant clicked their tongue impatiently and insisted you vacate the listening booth because others were waiting. In the Virgin shop you could wear headphones, sink into cushions and deliberate at your ease over whether or not to buy a particular record – rather as you would an expensive painting. It was a microcosm of how self-serious rock music had become. To shop at Virgin was an experience rich with the ambience, and often the aroma, of an evening relaxing over Red Lebanese or Afghan Black in one's 'pad'. Not surprisingly, some people stayed all day and never got round to buying a thing.

This atmosphere was to prove so contagious that among the staff there grew up what Nik Powell recognised as 'an ethos problem', in which the basic requirements of stock and till checks were widely disregarded as too much of a 'hassle'. To Powell fell the role of sorting it out, by dismissal where necessary. So brisk was business in the Oxford Street shop that it was decided to open another as soon as possible. Powell travelled north on an exploratory mission and secured some run-down premises in Liverpool, at a knock-down rent. That opened to a completely different set of problems: drug-users nodding out in the corners and rival street gangs disputing their territorial 'right' to spend all day in the shop almost closed it before it had properly opened. To Nik Powell fell the role of sorting that out too.

In fact, 'sorting it out', in the most general sense, had become Nik Powell's forte. Powell's initial involvement with *Student* had proved to be only temporary, yet, in its own way, crucial. His role at Albion Street had been the nebulous one of 'office manager' – a job which entailed bolting together Richard's wilder schemes, attempting to pacify distraught creditors, keeping a beady eye on the accounts. Powell was methodical, punctilious, with a keen, active intelligence . . . but somewhat dour. Everybody agreed on that. While Branson governed by enthusiasm, encouragement and the perpetual dispensation of 'fun', Powell reinforced his rule by a nagging, nit-picking attention to detail. 'Nik played an important role in establishing Richard's position,' says Christopher Strangeways. 'They were really a pair; Richard had the charm and the flair and the ideas, and Nik provided the intellectual rigour and credibility, the back-up.'

But in 1969, when *Student* was still in publication, Powell had left Albion Street. As much to pacify his parents as to satisfy himself, he had taken up a place at Sussex University to study English and American History. He enjoyed it more than he thought he would, and had made up his mind to finish the course. Then Branson telephoned. He told Powell that he had started a mail-order business: he was feeling the strain of running things on his own. Would Nik come back and join him? Powell was reluctant and said no. Branson cajoled, persuaded and promised him a generous share in Virgin. At length, Powell relented, gave up his studies, and moved back to

London. Within a year, an agreement was drawn up giving Powell 40 per cent of Virgin.

The relationship just picked up exactly where it had left off: 'Richard going out and splattering the world with ideas, and Nik coming along behind him, tidying up, budgeting them and holding them together,' as Mundy Ellis put it. But it was not without tears. Just as their childhood friendship in Shamley Green had been marked by spats of temper and fisticuffs, so the business partnership thrived as much on tension as friendship. 'Nik always used to say that partnerships are like marriages, but this one struck me as more like a marriage than most,' John Varnom says. 'Richard would go out and hunt, and Nik look after the housekeeping, as it were. It was like feckless husband and nagging wife constantly arguing with each other.'

On one occasion, on Branson's houseboat, Varnom, Powell, Branson and Simon Draper were playing a game of Diplomacy. During the game, Branson reneged on a treaty with Powell. Powell was furious, leapt to his feet screaming 'You bastard', kicked Branson hard and stormed off the boat. To John Varnom, it seemed a more extreme reaction than a simple default in Diplomacy warranted. 'The kick obviously hurt Richard, but he just lay back, laughing his head off.'

But whatever the tensions between them, it was clear to both that they needed each other, even loved each other as only old friends can. Nobody but Branson knew the difficulties Nik had experienced because of his epilepsy. Later, when Powell moved on to the boat, Branson nursed him through awkward attacks. While Nik was unfalteringly loyal to Branson's vision of Virgin. Through stoicism, methodical attention to detail and the occasional display of belligerence, Nik dealt with recalcitrant shop managers, local authority planning regulations and the chores of stock-taking, grumbling the while but bearing the brunt of the jobs Branson had no time for.

The mundane requirements of stock-taking and accountancy which characterise the world of record retailing held little attraction for Branson. There was also the irritating business of bootleg recordings. More than once, Virgin had been taken to court for stocking bootlegs; on one occasion, Branson and another Virgin employee were obliged to fabricate a fictitious letterheading and invoice from a non-existent American company, to make it look as if they had bought bootleg recordings in good faith, believing they were genuine imports. The case was kept out of court. The record shops proved yet another example of Branson gestating an idea in high enthusiasm, executing it in a rush of energy and activity, and then growing bored with it, restless for some other challenge or distraction. He found both in the Manor.

The idea of a recording studio had first taken root in Albion Street. Tom Newman, in delivering the frozen chips, had taken up more or less permanent residence in the basement. Newman had played the guitar for a 'psychedelic' band called July, which enjoyed a modest recognition on the London club circuit, but nowhere else. With the band in liquidation, Newman struggled on as a songwriter, recording his own makeshift demos by the simple, and cheap, expedient of 'bouncing' tracks back and forth between two mono tape-recorders. Tinkering with his rudimentary technology, Newman decided that what would really be fun would be to have his own recording studio.

Newman was similar to Branson in some ways; charming and guileful, he had an open face fixed in a perpetual grin – only partially attributable to his regular intake of marijuana. His total lack of experience in recording was no barrier to his plausibility. 'Tom,' as a friend had it, 'could make something out of a piece of string and sealing wax and make you believe it was going to go.'

Richard greeted the idea of a studio excitedly. The mail-order business had begun to unveil a myriad possibilities in his mind. Selling records, producing them on your own label, actually making the recordings in your own studio – it was all of a piece.

The idea of establishing the studio in a country property had a certain commercial logic. Not only were properties cheaper, but the notion of the pastoral life as a boon to creativity was abroad in rock music. More and more groups nowadays spoke dreamily of retreating to the countryside to 'get our heads together' and plan their next masterpiece. Referring to a copy of *Country Life*, Branson and Newman set off to find an affordable mansion.

Branson had earmarked a 'fairy-tale' castle in Wales, but when they arrived it turned out to be in the middle of a less than romantic industrial trading estate. Driving back to London, Branson saw an advertisement for another property, the old manor house at Shipton-on-Cherwell, twenty miles from Oxford. They arrived in the early evening, without an appointment, climbed over the wall at the back of the garden and strolled through the stone cloisters and on to the terrace. The gardens sloped gently away and vanished in the woods beyond. Behind them, in the dying sun, the house assumed the appearance of freshly baked ginger-bread. It seemed a kingdom beyond compare. 'We looked at each other,' remembers Branson, 'and both knew instantly that this was the place.'

Built in 1660, Shipton Manor had in more recent years been occupied by the Sheriff of Oxford, an American heart-surgeon and, latterly, an elderly and puritanical spinster whose final contribution to its history had been to paint a censorious black cloud over the genitals of a naked male god in the *trompe l'oeil* painted on the balcony wall. Branson was beside himself at the prospect of owning the house; the next weekend he took Mundy Ellis on a guided tour, roaming through the baronial entrance hall and up the grand staircase, expansively pointing out the six main bedrooms, the domestic quarters, the staff cottages, croquet lawn, swimming-pool and tennis court. 'He absolutely loved it,' she says. 'I think it made him feel grown up, and gave him a sense of being on his way.' It was very typical, she thought, when he picked up a sledgehammer and started knocking the bricks out of the fireplace. '. . . And we'll have that open . . .' Whack. The contract had not even been signed. In March 1971 the manor and grounds became the possession of Richard Branson, for £30,000 – secured with a loan of £7,500 from his aunt Joyce, Ted's sister, and a mortgage from Coutts.

Each weekend found Branson at the Manor, supervising the painting and refurbishment and the conversion of the old stables into a recording studio. To the staff of Virgin, to have come from the chaotic privations of Albion Street to an Oxfordshire manor house in less than twelve months seemed little short of miraculous, a further testament, as Chris Strangeways noted, of Branson's ability 'to make the most unlikely things happen . . . This sense that anything was possible, and nothing would stand in his way.'

Such appearances, however, were deceptive. For a long time, Branson had felt unwell, and the feelings of physical and nervous exhaustion persisted. At the age of twenty, he had a growing business, some forty employees, a substantial overdraft and mounting debts; to which was now added chronic pains in his stomach.

His doctor warned him that they were the preliminaries to ulcers, and that Branson was exhibiting symptoms more common to men three times his age. If Branson did not take complete rest, he warned, then he would become seriously ill.

Ted and Eve had bought a second home, in Minorca – a dilapidated and picturesque villa set on the end of a promontory into the sea and which they had christened Little Venice. Richard, they urged, must come to the island for an indefinite period, and Mundy must come too. 'Here he was,' Mundy Ellis says, 'with this terrible ultimatum hanging over him, trying to decide what to do with his life. We spent three days relaxing; by the fourth day he was making plans to buy the local newspaper and a small island out in the bay. It was impossible, and obvious he was never going to slow down.' After a fortnight, Branson was back at work, and the symptoms eventually passed.

Branson's inability to relax, however, manifested as a kind of mania which informed even as cerebral a pastime as chess. Playing against his friend Rob Gold, Branson would finish one game, then immediately want to play again, and again, determined to win. Winning was one thing he took terribly seriously. 'Richard,' as one friend put it, 'would cheat at snap.'

His abiding sense of being 'on duty', as he was wont to put it, was taking its toll on his relationship with Mundy. Their affair had never followed the usual course of excursions to the cinema or a concert, or quiet evenings together. As Mundy had discovered, Richard's immersion in business was so all-consuming and complete that anyone in his life was there solely on his terms. He was, as she found, 'constantly in motion'; either you moved contentedly in his slipstream, or you moved out of it. With the acquisition of the Manor, Mundy stopped working for the Student Advisory Centre and instead took on the role of Richard's 'emissary', supervising the renovation and decoration of the Manor during the week, spending only the weekends with Richard, either in Oxfordshire or London.

Once or twice at the Manor, on those rare summer afternoons when the warmth of the sun made work unthinkable, Mundy had 'dropped' LSD, under the beaming ministrations of Tom Newman. In the idyllic surroundings of the Oxfordshire countryside, that drug capable of igniting the most sublime fantasies, or unlocking the worst, and mostly deeply buried paranoia, had proved itself consistently benign.

Now she had brought some back to London for Richard to try. Richard's drug use had been confined to the occasional, sociable puff of a marijuana joint, to negligible effect. Perhaps he could never relax enough to appreciate its effects, but it seemed only to slow down his mental and physical processes, and Branson was not comfortable slowing down. LSD, of course, was somewhat different, but in the climate of the times – certainly in the climate of the record business – it was possible to consider taking it as almost normal – albeit strictly illegal. The Beatles had owned up to taking it; its imaginistic possibilities were still discussed seriously by artists and academics, while condemned by legislators and the medical profession. Branson gave it some thought. He was of the opinion that you should try anything once. Well, almost anything. That is what he would do; try it, once. He and Mundy were joined on his houseboat by their friends Rob and Caroline Gold. In the self-conscious manner befitting the event, candles were lit, Mundy produced the host in the form of minute blue tablets and communion began.

Rob had declined to join the 'trip'; a practical person, he understood that convention demanded one person remain 'straight' in case of emergencies. At first everything proceeded smoothly, Richard experienced the promised feelings of euphoria and well-being. Then, almost imperceptibly, things began to change. Every time Richard looked at Mundy, the attractive young woman he knew seemed to have been replaced by a five-year-old girl, offering a ghastly smile. He recoiled in confusion. Across the room, Rob and Caroline swum into vision, their reassuringly familiar selves, but now Mundy had become an old, old woman and then a young girl again. What was going on? He had never felt so frightened in his life, so . . . out of control. That was it. He was always in control of himself, of situations. Now things had assumed a perverse meaning all of their own which he didn't understand at all. It was an unpleasant feeling. At one point he became so distressed that the unfortunate Mundy had to go and sit on the steps of the boat watching the rain against a streetlamp and thinking 'I can't go inside because Richard doesn't want to see me. It's raining, I'm miserable. But I'm not scared.' Inside, Rob was pretending to be a doctor. He had heard that it was reassuring when on a 'bad trip' to believe you were in medical hands; now he earnestly assured Richard that everything was all right, as Richard asked repeatedly for his mother.

To Branson, the experience had afforded him two insights. Firstly, that he had absolutely no wish to take LSD again; secondly, that the relationship with Mundy was regrettably at an end. Many people who had experienced something so troubling might wish to unburden themselves of the feeling to friends. But Branson never again discussed the LSD trip with Mundy Ellis, or the Golds. The next day, he went back to work. Mundy caught a cold and went back to Oxfordshire.

Richard Branson had other, more pressing problems, which no amount of the self-revelation afforded by LSD could solve. While orders flowed in to South Wharf Road with pleasing constancy, the eagerly anticipated move into profit had still not come. The margins on mail-order were too small, postage too high; the overheads of the Oxford Street shop, and the new one in Liverpool, expenses on the Manor – all were accumulating at a frightening rate. Consultations with an accountant appeared to confirm the worst: Virgin were £60,000 in debt. The best thing to do, the accountant urged, would be to cash in what assets the company had and call it a day.

Branson refused to be downcast. After all, the Manor would soon be open for business. Something else was sure to turn up; why, only the other day a new avenue had opened up in retailing – an order had come through from a company in Belgium, the first from abroad, and worth a substantial amount. The company's white transit van was duly laden down with records and Branson set off for Dover. On landing at Calais, however, he was asked to produce the carnet – the permit necessary to carry goods through France to Belgium. Branson did not have a carnet; to his great annoyance he was obliged to return to England, still carrying his load.

Only as he was driving back to London did the penny drop. Under the tax laws, the purchase tax levied on goods was not payable if those goods were being exported. He now had a vanload of records, with a ship's manifest stamped by British Customs to show they had been 'exported' to Belgium, but which could now be sold at the usual price in London. Put another way, for the price of a round trip to Calais, he had just defrauded the taxman of some £8,000 in purchase tax. It was an opportunity too good to be missed, but one that needed careful refinement.

The next morning, telephone calls were made to locate a ready source of 'deletions', old records by forgotten Scottish dance bands and arterio-sclerotic crooners which could be bought for next to nothing. It was explained that they were needed for 'interior decorating'. At the same time, a further consignment of records 'for export' was ordered from the manufacturers, to be invoiced with the purchase tax deducted.

While the new records went straight on to the shelves at South Wharf Road, the deletions were loaded on to the van and driven across to Belgium. Branson had even acquired a carnet to ensure that everything looked above board. The worthless records were duly delivered to a municipal rubbish tip near Antwerp.

As a fraud it was so simple, so flawless, so deliciously fecund with immediate profit for absolutely no sweat, that it was surely possible to fly even closer to the wind without risk. British Customs never bothered to check the contents of the van on the outward journey. Why go to all the bother of buying deletions and loading the van when the records were only going to be thrown away anyway?

On the fourth journey to Dover, Branson drove a van filled only with empty boxes. There was a minor hiccup at the Customs Office, when he presented his papers to be stamped and the officer asked if he could spare a couple of records 'for my kids'. If only he knew the truth of it! But a bit of quick thinking got out of that one – not carrying anything suitable, but I'll bring a couple next time . . . have to dash. It was so easy that Branson could not even be bothered to catch the ferry. He simply drove around the docks and back to London, several thousand pounds ahead of the taxman.

He had been back at South Wharf Road for two hours when the telephone rang. The caller, an elderly man by the sound of it, did not wish to say his name, but a friend of his had once been helped by the Student Advisory Centre and one good turn deserved another. 'You're about to be raided by Customs and Excise,' he said. If Branson were to buy a sunlamp and examine all the records he had bought for export, he would find them marked in fluorescent ink with an 'E'.

In a panic, Branson rushed to a chemist and bought two sunlamps. Back at the office, the entire staff began hastily pulling records off shelves and examining them under the lamps. To their horror, the 'E' markings glared back accusingly. By the end of that evening, all the incriminating records had been sorted and loaded on to the van and were on their way to the Manor for hiding.

The Customs men arrived the next morning, simultaneously raiding South Wharf Road and the shops in Oxford Street and Liverpool. As they gathered up Branson's papers, the mood of the officers was relentlessly jokey: 'Didn't you head off for Belgium yesterday? Got back quickly, didn't you?'

That morning Branson was driven to Dover, pausing only for a congenial lunch at a restaurant on the A2. At Dover police station he was charged under Section 301 of the Customs and Excise Act 1952, that on 28 May 1971 at Eastern Docks, Dover, he caused to be delivered to an officer a ship's manifest being a document produced for the purpose of an assigned matter namely Customs, which was untrue in a material particular in that it purported to show the exportation of 10,000 gramophone records . . .

On the telephone to his mother, Branson burst into tears. It was the first time Eve had ever known him to break down. 'Pull yourself together,' she said crossly. 'Pull yourself together.'

Branson spent that night in the police cells, shivering under a blanket, unsure whether to be more fearful of the disapprobation of the law, or of his mother. The next morning he appeared in court. Eve had travelled down to Dover on the first train and now regarded him across the court with an even gaze. In a moment of temerity, Branson stood up and made an application for legal aid. If he could not afford to stand his own costs, the magistrate replied, then he would have to be remanded in custody for three weeks until the trial. Branson quickly changed his mind about applying for legal aid. When bail was set at £30,000, Eve volunteered Tanyard Farm as surety: 'I looked across the court and put up the house and thought "Can I trust him?" I had never felt so saddened, so angry. I thought then that perhaps everything we'd worked for had been lost. But one just had to put up everything.'

That evening, Branson and his mother took the train back to London. Her mood now was more resigned. Richard would have preferred unadulterated fury; that would have made him feel less wretched himself. The fact that his parents were supporting him now only exacerbated the degree to which he had let the family down and embarrassed the name of his father in the legal world.

Within Customs and Excise, there was some exultation at Branson's arrest. Several other record retailers had attempted a similar deception, but in monetary terms he was the biggest catch. Two things could happen. The charge could be pressed, and Branson go to court, with the certainty that, whatever the outcome, he would have a criminal record. But the preferred tactic in such cases is to come to a financial arrangement which at least ensures the tax is recouped.

After prolonged consultations between the Branson family and Customs and Excise, an arrangement was made to drop the charge. In return, in an agreement drawn up on 18 August 1971 – six days before the case was due to be heard in court – Branson agreed to pay £15,000 immediate compound settlement, and a further £38,000 in outstanding purchase tax, import duty and charges, to be paid in instalments over the next three years.

In years to come, Richard Branson would happily own up to his brush with the law, mindful of the fact that there was a greater potential harm in trying to conceal it. 'A night spent in the cells with just a filthy blanket and one drink,' he says, 'and you learn never to do it again.'

It was characteristic that, in time, the escapade was turned almost into an asset – evidence of youthful high spirits, with no damage done. Almost an education.

In fact, in view of what was to occur in its aftermath, over the ensuing months, the Customs and Excise 'bust' was really a stroke of luck. But then, as his friends back at South Wharf Road were coming to realise, Richard Branson was nothing if not lucky.

Chapter 5

The First Million

Richard Branson's first fortune arrived at the Manor in a rented white Ford Transit van, which crunched up the gravel drive under cold and overcast skies in November 1971.

Mike Oldfield did not look like a man about to make himself, Richard Branson or anybody else a million. Spaniel eyes peered out nervously from behind a curtain of lank, brown hair. A wispy, adolescent beard lent him the tortured appearance of a medieval penitent. Tinkering with his new recording equipment, Tom Newman took one, disinterested look at the new arrival and pronounced him 'a space cadet. A long-haired, scruffy little tyke.'

Life at the Manor had assumed an idyllic air. Newman supervised construction of the studio and Mundy Ellis the domestic arrangements. More staff had arrived to cook and carry. There was Mrs Parsley in the kitchens, and in the gardens Mr Branch tended to the roses and rhododendrons. Richard Branson would arrive in his white Mini, usually at weekends, sometimes bringing with him a prospective customer – a singer or a manager, being persuaded of the virtues of recording at the

Manor: the arcadian tranquillity; the meditative rambles along the banks of the River Cherwell; the close proximity of several agreeable public houses.

The Arthur Louis Band were the Manor's first paying customers. Louis, an extrovert, Afro-haired American, who claimed, not uniquely for the time, to be 'a cross between Hendrix and Dylan', departed after just one week, on a one-way ticket to Palookaville. The spaniel-eyed guitar-player stayed on.

Oldfield, as Mundy quickly observed, had an air of 'I can't quite cope' about him; a vulnerability which brought out the protective instincts in everybody. The girls at the Manor mothered him, pressed extra helpings on his plate and uncomplainingly patched his threadbare flared trousers. Tom Newman put a fraternal arm over his shoulder. The usually breezy Newman was in a 'soulful' period too, barely militated by his suspicion that despite a 'man-to-man' talk on the subject, Branson had never quite forgiven him for beginning an affair with Mundy. Newman and Oldfield became mutual confidants.

Oldfield's home life had been profoundly unhappy. His father was a general practitioner in Harold Wood, Essex, but his mother was an alcoholic and manic depressive. Oldfield was reticent, ill-at-ease, uncommunicative. Yet his almost chronic diffidence belied a precocious talent as a musician.

At the age of nineteen, Oldfield was already a seasoned veteran of the music business. He had made his first professional recording at the age of fourteen, with his elder sister, Sally, under the name Sallyangie. At sixteen he had become the guitarist for Kevin Ayres' group, the Whole World, recording with them on two albums. He had even had a spell deputising in the house band for the

musical *Hair*. In his free moments, Oldfield had been
working on a composition of his own, laboriously overdubbing any number of different instruments on a tape-
recorder borrowed from Ayres. Now, at the Manor, he
sought out Tom Newman and asked if he would give an
opinion. Newman thought it 'hyper-romantic, sad,
poignant . . . and brilliant'.

Ever since his first conversation with Branson in the
Riviera Café, Simon Draper had been thinking longingly
about running a record label. When Newman played him
Oldfield's tape, Draper was immediately taken with it.
Even Branson was completely captivated and played the
tape incessantly to visitors to the houseboat. Branson was
the first to acknowledge that he was no expert on music,
but even he had noticed that Oldfield's composition had
no vocals at all. It did not sound like anything anyone
had put out before. Would they be able to sell it? This, in
fact, was the unanimous verdict of every record company
in London to which Oldfield had played the tape. It was
'not commercial'. The rejections made Oldfield even
more downcast than usual. 'Don't worry, Mike,' Branson
said. 'You can be the first artist on our label.' The more
Branson came to know this solemn, introverted young
man, the more he liked him. When he heard about
Oldfield's domestic difficulties, Branson told the young
musician he could stay at the Manor for as long as there
was room. Oldfield moved in and began planning his
masterpiece, which he was now calling *Tubular Bells*.

Richard Branson had fallen in love. Truly, this time.
Branson had never wanted for the company of young
girls; rather the opposite. But he had wilfully avoided
attachment. Mundy Ellis had been his longest-standing
girlfriend, and that, in the end, went the way of all

Branson's relationships, sacrificed to his unswerving devotion to his work. As other girls had discovered to their cost, when faced with the choice of a romantic evening or a series of telephone calls in which business deals could possibly be completed, there was seldom any doubt about where Richard Branson's affections lay.

It was not inappropriate, then, that Branson should meet his new love in the place that presently constituted the biggest deficit in his bank account, the Manor. It was July 1971. Kristen Tomassi had arrived in Britain from America barely a week before and had been brought to investigate what a friend insisted was 'a quaint English country house'. Branson took one look at the slim girl with exquisite features, framed by long, honey-blond hair, and decided with a peculiar certainty he had never experienced before that he was in love. He walked up to her, lifted her off her feet in an embrace and then apologised that he thought she was someone he knew. At least it broke the ice.

At the age of nineteen, Kristen Tomassi was beautiful, clever, worldly and opinionated. The daughter of a vice-president for the Canada Dry corporation, she had been educated at the Concorde Academy, Massachusetts, a bluestocking establishment where her contemporaries included Caroline Kennedy, the daughter of the late American president. At the age of sixteen, feeling 'too much like a part of the privileged élite', she had left Concorde for a local state school, going on to study architecture and design at colleges in New York and Arizona. She had come to Britain for a month's touring holiday.

Kristen was intrigued by what she regarded as Richard's display of English eccentricity; too bemused even to be piqued when he drove her back to London the next day and refused to drop her at her house, insisting instead that she return to the houseboat with him, with the thought that, 'I'm having some friends to lunch. Perhaps you could cook it?' Any time spent with Branson, she thought, would be merely an amusing interlude; in a few days she would be in Scotland.

On the day she was supposed to leave, Kristen telephoned Branson from a call-box near where she was staying to say goodbye. Branson kept her talking. By the time she had returned to her flat, the driver from Virgin had arrived and was loading her belongings into the van. 'Richard,' he explained, 'will kill me if I don't bring you back.' Once at the houseboat, Branson took the suitcases and, with an enormous grin, turned them upside down, scattering her belongings over the floor. 'Well, nice to see you . . .' he said.

It was on the following day that Richard Branson was raided by the officers of Customs and Excise, engaged in the purchase-tax avoidance investigation. The raid was not only on Virgin's offices at South Wharf Road and its shops but also on Branson's houseboat. Kristen Tomassi's first experience of life with Richard Branson was having her suitcase upended for the second consecutive day, this time by two besuited and faintly abashed Customs officers, in search of 'evidence'. Curiously, this did not discourage Kristen. She did not leave for Scotland, but instead got swept up into the world of endless business meetings, weekends at the Manor, panic-stricken conversations about debts and overdrafts.

Money was a serious problem; one which the £53,000 fine imposed by the Customs and Excise made almost terminal. Branson and Nik Powell agreed there were two alternatives. They could sell everything, still have barely enough to repay the money, but avoid prosecution. Or they could 'expand' out of trouble, by generating as much cash as possible to pay the fine. Branson's existing arrangement with his bank, Coutts, allowed more generous overdraft facilities than most 20-year-old businessmen could expect to draw upon. That would take care of the expenses of maintaining the Manor and installing the necessary recording equipment to make it a viable commercial proposition. More enticingly, through the mail-order business and the two record shops Virgin now had 'cashflow' – a phrase with the hypnotically stabilising effect of a Hindu mantra. 'Cashflow' gave you time, breathing space, the chance to keep expanding one step ahead of your debts, in the hope that they would never catch up with you at all. With 'cashflow' you could do almost anything.

So it was that Branson and Powell embarked on a policy of opening shops – as many as possible, as fast as possible. The policy was to acquire run-down premises in city centres; decorate them as cheaply as possible, using whatever skills were to hand (Tom Newman was called back from the Manor to install the record-players in one shop). A new shop was always opened on the first day of the month, to take the maximum advantage of the two-calendar-month credit period exercised in record wholesaling, under which system records bought on any date between, say, 1 and 31 January would have to be paid for on 28 February, effectively giving the purchaser a choice of four weeks' or eight weeks' credit. Thus juggling between credit and cashflow, the Oxford Street and Liverpool shops were quickly followed by a third in Notting Hill Gate, West London; then Brighton, Newcastle, Leeds. Altogether, some fifteen shops were opened over the next two years, borne not of careful planning but of desperation.

Ted and Eve had forgiven their son's altercation with Customs and Excise, if not altogether forgotten it. Eve's sense of shock and shame had been tempered by a more immediate concern about Richard's ability to pay the fine and about whether his future prospects lay in business or in jail. Years of exposure to the consequences of life's petty temptations and conceits in court rooms the length and breadth of Britain had endowed Ted with a tolerant and forgiving view of human nature. He had dismissed his son's flirtation with the law as high spirits, but some sort of check on Richard's business practices was clearly in order. Ted had a friend in the City named Michael Davis, who was a director of the Imperial Foods group; could he keep an eye on Richard, Ted asked, 'and make sure he doesn't do anything foolish from a business point of view'. Davis was unable to help, but he did introduce a chartered accountant named Jack Claydon, who agreed to act in a supervisory role. Claydon examined Virgin's books and pronounced them 'a complete mess'. 'Richard had a turnover of £1m and quite a few people charging around,' says Claydon. 'I asked him, what about payroll and PAYE? He said, "We don't really worry about that. Everybody just gets £20 and that's it." We had to sort that out straight away.'

The quarterly meetings with Coutts manager Peter Caston became a worrying event for Claydon. Branson approached them like a schoolboy called before the headmaster, hoping that a sufficient display of the spirited enthusiasm which teachers always associated with the captain of the sports team would compensate for a lamentable performance in maths. Impatient with the mundane world of accounts, unable to read a balance sheet, and disinclined to learn, Branson seldom prepared himself properly. Forever the optimist, he preferred to talk not about the previous year's figures, which the bank were interested in, but what he expected Virgin to be doing in two or three years' time, usually adding a few noughts to the realistic projection. Hypnotised by his own patter, Branson would leave each meeting having convinced at least himself that the Promised Land lay just beyond the next mountain range; with the patient, sanguine and rational figure of Jack Claydon almost believing it too.

On one occasion, anxious to impress, Branson invited Peter Caston to lunch at the highly traditional and expensive restaurant, Simpsons in the Strand. First, Branson was refused entry because he was not wearing a tie; the restaurant then refused to accept his cheque, obliging his bank manager Caston to pay for the meal.

Nik Powell became a force of strength in imposing some semblance of order on the accounts. The methodical mind saw ways of squeezing and saving where Branson's impetuous, long-range vision could not. Powell poured cold water on Branson's and Tom Newman's scheme to develop the theme of getting-away-from-it-all recording, pioneered by the Manor, with another studio – this one to be built on a ship that would cruise the Mediterranean. He issued instructions that Richard could only draw cash from the tills of Virgin shops on production of a personal cheque; the pile of hastily scrawled IOU's were playing havoc with the books. His purges against expenditure on paper clips and toilet paper spread fear and consternation among all at Virgin. Even Branson became a little afraid of him.

Yet, for all their differences, Branson and Powell were still very much a team, unfailingly protective and supportive of each other. Powell understood Branson in a way which few others on the Virgin staff could do.

Indeed, so bemusing and maddening could Branson's character be, in its combination of enthusiasm and wilfulness, generosity and self-interest, that trying to 'figure out Richard' became a common afternoon pastime at Virgin's offices. One girl who left, tired of it all, likened it to 'being in the Moonies'.

To a large extent, this was the common pre-occupation of any group of people depending on one person for their livelihood. The bond of struggling in common adversity was not always enough to assuage the grumbles about the rising cost of living. There was even a brief agitation at South Wharf Road – 'strike' was too emotive a word to describe everyone simply not bothering to come in for a day – led by John Varnom, to acquire an extra £3 for working on Saturdays. To Branson it was a confusing experience. Didn't people understand times were extremely tight and the company was struggling to get on its feet? Above all, it was personally wounding, a sign that people felt he had let them down. If people felt like that, he asked Varnom, why didn't they come and talk to him about it themselves? They knew he was always available.

In a similar situation, Branson himself would have no fears about knocking on anybody's door and demanding his rights. He could not understand it when Varnom explained that 'not everybody feels strong enough'. To Varnom, it was a symptom of just how remote Branson could sometimes be from the real world. 'Richard felt that if he was nice to people, then that ought to be fine, regardless of what they were paid,' says Varnom. 'When people still bit the hand that fed, because they didn't think they were being fed enough, he found that hard to understand.'

On 22 July 1972 Richard Branson married Kristen Tomassi, in the small parish church of Shipton, close to the Manor. The groom wore a top hat and tails. The bride arrived at the church in a horse-drawn carriage. The groom's grandmother, the stately Dorothy Huntley-Flindt, arrived in an articulated lorry with which she had collided en route to the church, the driver having obligingly given her a lift. Some five hundred people adjourned to the candy-striped marquees which had been erected in the grounds of the Manor for the reception. Nik Powell was the best man. Another old friend and veteran of *Student*, Chris Stylianou, imbued with the spirit of the moment, made a speech in which he alluded to a common topic of conversation in the Virgin offices: the wealth of the Tomassi family. 'We all know why we're having this wedding,' he announced, 'where's the bank manager?' Stylianou was quickly ushered into the kitchen and told to sober up. The bank manager was, in fact, being fed a constant supply of champagne by attentive Virgin staff.

Business was beginning to look up at last. The Manor, in its first few months of operation, had attracted a steady stream of clients. Buddy Miles, the Fairport Convention and the Scaffold had all recorded there, drawn by its unique atmosphere and surroundings. The bucolic outlook, the dinners around a large oak table, the crackling log fire – even the second-hand curtains sent by Kristen's mother, who had found the Manor quaint but somewhat lacking in American-style refinements all struck a suitable baronial note, to make visiting performers believe they belonged to some rarefied social caste. The staff were friendly, but always deferential and efficient, as Richard insisted they should be. The girls who looked after housekeeping were instructed that anyone arriving, whatever time of day or night, must expect a drink and a welcome. One girl who declined to make a cup of tea for a friend of the maintenance man was sternly rebuked by Branson on the telephone when he heard of it.

The only shadows were cast by intermittent visits from the police – called in by a troublesome neighbour, well aware that no permission had been granted to use the recording studios at night. It became necessary to post a look-out at the end of the drive who would sound an alarm in the studio as the police approached so that the musicians could then run into the kitchen. This system was put to the test with the arrival at the Manor of Paul McCartney for two days' recording. It was deemed inappropriate to ask a former Beatle to drop his guitar and run into the kitchen when ever a bell sounded, just because a neighbour had complained about the noise; so Branson made sure the door to the studio was firmly shut. It was a warm night and Linda McCartney threw open the door for air. A few minutes later, Branson stole back and closed it. Linda McCartney opened it again. Branson closed it . . .

The McCartneys never returned, but their presence somehow affirmed that Virgin was now to be taken seriously in the rock world. In an uncharacteristic fit of extravagance, Richard Branson even bought a decrepit Bentley which had once belonged to Mary Hopkin.

Mike Oldfield had become almost a fixture at the Manor, labouring painstakingly over his masterpiece, with the patient assistance of Tom Newman, in those moments of 'downtime' when the studio was not in official use. The friendship between Oldfield and Branson had blossomed, founded on a peculiar magnetism of opposites. Oldfield was only two years younger, yet he brought out almost paternalistic feelings in Branson. Put simply, Branson made Oldfield laugh – a valued gift to one suffused in an air of almost perpetual melancholy. Oldfield envied Branson the apparent air of blithe confidence and ease with which he sailed through life. How, Oldfield wondered, could anybody remain so indefatigably cheerful? If Branson woke up each morning, as he claimed, determined that this was to be the best day of his life, Oldfield woke up rather fearing it would be the worst. Oldfield noticed that if Branson tried to do something himself he often made a mess of it, charging into things without planning or forethought; his talent was to inspire others to do their best; to make others want to please him. 'I always regarded Richard as the figurehead. He was like the house captain at public school; somebody that everybody admired, and knew was going places, and they'd follow him if they could.'

But, much as he admired Branson, Oldfield also enjoyed 'winding him up'; in a bid to get the Rolling Stones to record at the Manor, Branson had invited Keith Richards for a tour of inspection, and himself readied the master bedroom with a bottle of Jack Daniels, the bourbon favoured by the Rolling Stone. Oldfield stole into the room and drank the bottle dry.

When it came to signing the record contract that would make Oldfield the first artist on the new Virgin label, the would-be boy genius teased Branson that he had changed his mind and did not want to sign after all. Branson had never negotiated a record contract in his life before, and he was no more sure what was involved than Oldfield. Branson telephoned Sandy Denny, the singer with Fairport Convention, and asked to borrow her contract, as a model. It was said to be a 'standard' Island Records contract.

Sitting in the kitchen of the Manor, Mike Oldfield signed the piece of paper stipulating that he would make ten albums for Virgin, for which he would be paid an artist royalty of 5 per cent, less the usual discounts for packaging – a standard rate for the time. In the meantime, Oldfield was put on the standard Virgin wage, £20 a week – an advance which would be deducted from his future royalties. The signing was celebrated with a bottle of wine. It was to be some years before the recriminations began.

Mike Oldfield created *Tubular Bells* over a period of some nine months. He played a total of twenty-two different instruments, with the help of Tom Newman meticulously assembling some 2,300 overdubs into a seamless mosaic of sound. For both men the recording was a journey of self-discovery; Newman exploring for the first time the infinite possibilities offered by the complex, electronic circuitry of the Manor's new sixteen-track recording console; Oldfield inspired in the knowledge that he was creating something totally fresh, totally different. '*Tubular Bells* wasn't really engineered by any of us,' Newman remembers. 'It was organic. It just grew . . . like magic.'

On one day there was a crazy rush to collect as many cardboard boxes as possible, to be impacted in the studio for a required percussion effect. On another, Mundy Ellis – whose last performance had been in the school choir – and Sally Oldfield were enjoined to create a mass heavenly chorus, by the miracle of yet more overdubbing. In the last week of recording, Vivian Stanshall, of the Bonzo Dog Doo-Dah Band, who were using the Manor at the time, performed the role of 'Master of Ceremonies', introducing the roll-call of instruments which was to bring the first side of the piece to its climax, and become, in turn, the mainstay of many a marijuana-induced reverie. 'Bass guitar . . . double speed guitar . . . two slightly distorted guitars . . . mandolin . . . Spanish guitar, and introducing acoustic guitar . . . plus TUBU-LAR BELLS!' Stanshall knew something of the sacrifices demanded by art. In order to attain a required effect on the Bonzo Dog's own record, he had gorged himself on a particularly virulent curry, concocted in the Manor kitchens, and then locked himself in the lavatory with a microphone, awaiting the desired effect.

Tubular Bells was released on 25 May 1973: V2001, the first entry in the Virgin catalogue, and one of four records released on the new label in that week. The others were an album by a German group, Faust, with the gimmick of being sold for the price of a single; an album by a group called Gong; and *Manor Live* – a recording of a 'jam session' conducted by a number of musicians over one highly inebriated fortnight at the Manor.

But it was to *Tubular Bells* that the critics turned their full attention. Here was a work to challenge not only the perceptions of the listeners but the powers of description and comparison of the rock reviewer. Most confessed they had heard almost nothing like it before. Within its forty-nine minutes' compass, *Tubular Bells* seemed as rich and diverse as any music from the rock canon could expect to be. In its repetition of themes, it hinted at the 'steady-state' music of Terry Riley, whose albums *A Rainbow in Curved Air* and *In C* had both enjoyed modest, voguish success. *Tubular Bells* also contained fragrant snatches of melody which the elongated extemporisations of so much progressive rock lacked – even begging comparison, some said, to the pastoral romanticism of Sibelius and Vaughan Williams. Yet in its instrumentation and its rhythmic pulse it was undeniably a rock record too. It was something of everything; the reconciliation of rock's aspirations towards the depth and gravitas of classical music, with the playful coda of a version of the sailor's hornpipe, and all rendered in state-of-the-art high fidelity.

John Peel, the pontiff of progressive music, anointed the record by playing both sides all the way through on his BBC radio show. Writing in *The Listener*, he described *Tubular Bells* as a record 'of such strength, energy and real beauty that to me it represents the first breakthrough into history that any musician primarily regarded as a rock musician has ever made'. Several other newspapers also gave it enthusiastic reviews. Others pronounced it 'self-indulgent'.

Richard Branson assembled all the favourable reviews into a collage of superlatives which appeared as an advertisement in *Melody Maker*. Looking for other ways to promote the work, Branson hit upon the idea of hiring the prestigious Queen Elizabeth Hall and staging a performance of *Tubular Bells* himself. A team of sympathetic musicians was recruited to play the parts which Oldfield had overdubbed on record, Branson adding a lustre of fame by persuading Mick Taylor, the guitarist who had recently left the Rolling Stones, to join the ensemble. Rehearsals began at the Manor, and invitations to the media were despatched. A week before the concert was to take place, however, Oldfield suddenly had a change of heart. He would not perform – and this time it was not 'a wind-up'. *Tubular Bells*, he explained to an increasingly distraught Branson and Draper, could not be properly reproduced live; it was a work of the recording studio. Branson pleaded and cajoled, but to no avail. How do you force an artist to compromise his beliefs? At last, he played his trump card. 'All right, Mike – if you do the show, you can have the Bentley . . .'

'The Bentley . . . ?'

The show was a great success.

Oldfield was genuinely touched by Branson's efforts on his behalf. Oldfield had a strongly purist streak in his attitude to music which, allied with his chronic shyness, manifested as an antipathy towards any kind of publicity or self-promotion bordering on paranoia. The most memorable utterance in his first ever press interview, with the *Melody Maker*, came at the very end, when Oldfield confessed, 'I feel as if I've been raped.' Yet Branson worked relentlessly to plug *Tubular Bells*, humouring journalists and disc-jockeys, unstinting in his enthusiasm – and his advertising budget – in promoting the record. It seemed to both of them only logical that Branson should also become Oldfield's manager.

If there was any one, single model for Richard Branson in setting up Virgin Records, it was Island Records – at that time Britain's most celebrated, and certainly most adventurous, independent label.

Island had been founded by Chris Blackwell, a man with whom Richard Branson had much in common. Both came from the same upper-middle-class stock – although Blackwell's family, as part of the Crosse and Blackwell food company, were somewhat wealthier. Both had public-school educations – although Blackwell, more grandly, had been at Harrow. Both had exceptionally strong, driven mothers; separated from her husband, Blanche Blackwell ran a banana plantation in Jamaica, where Chris had been born and spent his early childhood.

Growing up in the Caribbean, Blackwell had developed a love for 'islands' music. He founded the Island label in 1962 – at a time when the British record industry was still effectively under the control of the three business 'giants': EMI, Decca and Pye. Island's speciality as an outlet for Jamaican ska music and American soul proved little threat to the majors. By the late Sixties, however, Island had become a significant force in the rock field, handling such performers as Traffic (whom Blackwell, through his long association with Steve Winwood, also managed), Cat Stevens and Free. Blackwell had also pulled together a series of production deals, through which Island released records produced by Joe Boyd (John Martyn and Fairport Convention), by artists managed by the EG Company (King Crimson, Emerson, Lake and Palmer and Roxy Music), and artists managed by Chrysalis (Jethro Tull). Chrysalis management had been founded by two ex-university social secretaries, Chris Wright and Terry Ellis, who had brought Jethro Tull to Island in 1968 on the agreement that they would revert from a 'licensed artists' to a 'licensed label' arrangement if they achieved a certain sales target. Tull quickly achieved the target, and the Chrysalis label was founded; licensed through Island.

Island's success was mirrored in the rise of the other independent labels – Track, Immediate, Charisma and then Chrysalis – all of which demonstrated how small companies with their ears to the ground could be much more responsive to the rapidly shifting trends in pop music than large ones, hidebound as they were by tradition and bureaucracy. Most of these small independents eventually fell by the wayside, but they helped to change the complexion of the British record industry for ever.

By the early Seventies the dominant companies of the Fifties and early Sixties – Decca, EMI, and Pye – had been largely usurped, their power eroded by the establishment in Britain of subsidiaries of American companies, large and small – Warners/Elektra/Asylum, CBS, A & M and Bell/Arista – or by the British independents. Of these, Island was both the largest and the most respected, its commitment to good taste and its apparently harmonious relations with its artists a role model for any aspiring young record company.

Richard Branson first approached Island in the early days of *Student*, to see if the record company would help distribute the magazine, or at the very least advertise in it. With the advent of Virgin mail-order and the record shops, the relationship had become closer. Early on, Blackwell and his managing director, David Betteridge, had taken the young Branson out for lunch. Betteridge had used the occasion to berate Branson for selling bootlegs of Island artists in Virgin shops, thereby depriving the company of possible legitimate sales. But Blackwell was intrigued by Branson's *chutzpah* and enthusiasm, and his nose for business.

So it was that as Mike Oldfield brought *Tubular Bells* to completion, it was to Island that Branson turned in search of an arrangement to get the Virgin label off the ground. David Betteridge listened to the tapes of *Tubular Bells* and offered Branson the same licensing arrangement Island had with Chrysalis. In this, Island would pay Virgin a substantial advance and then an 18 per cent licence royalty on all records sold. It was a standard arrangement, and one that made much sense to a company in Virgin's position. It gave them cash in hand, and offered considerable savings on the costs of publicity and promotion, which would be looked after by Island. It was dependable and safe, and Branson's lawyers urged him to take it. But Branson was exploring another route – the same route, in fact, which Chris Blackwell himself had taken when setting up Island as a pop label. Branson wanted a distribution deal, under which Island would act simply as handling agents – pressing and distributing the records, and taking a 10–15 per cent commission for their pains. There would be no cash advance for Virgin under this method, and it would vastly increase Virgin's office overheads. Branson was taking an enormous gamble: without immediate success, the Virgin label would be stillborn. But if Virgin had one or two immediate hits the potential profits could be enormous. On a million-selling album it could be the difference between Virgin making £500,000 and making £2,250,000. Branson was adamant. 'I'll get the money,' he told Draper. 'We're not signing away our birthright.' But Island were reluctant to set the precedent of a distribution deal with Virgin which their existing licensees, Chrysalis and Bronze, might want to follow. Only when Branson suddenly began negotiating with CBS instead did David Betteridge hastily telephone Island's agreement.

The gamble paid off. On 14 July, *Tubular Bells* entered the British album charts at number 23. And once it had started selling, it just wouldn't stop.

The profits which began to pour in from *Tubular Bells* had two immediate consequences. They reduced Virgin's perennially embarrassing overdraft, and they afforded Simon Draper the luxury of following a musical policy determined by artistic considerations, not simply commercial ones. Virgin's policy of subsidising music which other companies would have deemed a questionable investment gave them immediate cachet among musicians and the critical arbiters of the 'thinking' music press. Groups like Gong, Hatfield and the North and Henry

Cow continued to embody notions of rock music as a vehicle for statements of 'art' and zealous idealism which appeared increasingly recondite at a time when the values of the pop market-place were once again becoming dominant. As Chris Cutler of the group Henry Cow told *Melody Maker* at the time, 'Virgin have broken certain important rules in this area. They've taken people like Mike Oldfield, Gong and us, that are distinctly non-commercial in any conventional sense, and proved that by confronting people with alternative music, people are interested. It's possible for music to actually be valuable to people, and I'm not just talking about managers, agents and promoters.'

Occasionally, too, there might even be the fillip of a massive hit. The demand in Virgin's retail shops for imported albums by experimental German groups, which had led Simon Draper to Faust, also led him to another German group called Tangerine Dream. Their first record had sold some 20,000 copies, on import, through mail-order and the shops. In May 1974, having signed the group direct, Virgin released their British album, *Phaedra*. Filled with languorous synthesiser soundscapes, which defined the term 'head' music even more than *Tubular Bells* had done, *Phaedra* too went on to become a million seller.

Richard Branson was happy to let Simon Draper determine the musical policy of Virgin. He trusted Draper's musical judgement more than he trusted his own; the complexities of Hatfield and the North, Henry Cow and the orchestral composer David Bedford were, after all, light years from the anodyne simplicity of 'Bachelor Boy'. Branson was happier making deals. The arrangement he had made with Island for distribution was for England only. With the help of his lawyer,

Charles Levison, he now carefully began to assemble a series of deals to handle Virgin across the world. With only the office in London, common sense and budget dictated that these should be licensing, not distribution, arrangements, yet Branson still managed to extract the maximum advantage from the minimum of possibilities, showing little respect for the precedents set by previous English companies. The success in Britain of *Tubular Bells* gave him a powerful bargaining tool. 'Richard,' says Levison, 'would conceptualise the impossible, and get much nearer realising it than anybody else could. On a licensing deal where $.5m was a reasonable advance, Richard would ask for $1.5m, and get $1m. He could manoeuvre people into a position where they couldn't conceive of any alternative to actually doing the deal. He would push them, but not so far that they would feel unhappy about it afterwards.'

In New York, Branson called upon Ahmet Ertegun, the suave and bespectacled head of Atlantic Records. Ertegun had been forewarned of his arrival by Chris Blackwell, whose own business acumen had led Ertegun to nickname him 'The Baby-faced Killer'. In his phlegmatic way, Ertegun thought Branson 'unlike your average record company person' in his threadbare cords, tousled hair and the inevitable shapeless sweater. To the American, he became 'The Baby-faced Killer Mark 2'. Ertegun thought *Tubular Bells* 'odd', but he felt he could do something with it. Branson was paid a $750,000 advance on that and other Virgin products. What Ertegun then did was convince the film director William Friedkin that *Tubular Bells* should be used as the theme music for his film *The Exorcist*. In April, the record reached the top of the American album charts.

Whilst in America seeing Ertegun, Branson had also

been ski-ing in Vermont with Kristen and his youngest sister Vanessa. It was Vanessa's first ever visit to America, and on a sightseeing expedition to New York they rode a horse-drawn carriage through Central Park, glistening under a crisp carpet of snow, and strolled down Fifth Avenue under a yawning grey sky, midst Manhattan's symphony of car horns. Life was perfect. Branson had the girl he loved; he had just completed a deal that would make *Tubular Bells* a worldwide success. 'God,' he said to Vanessa, 'do you realise, I'm twenty-three years old and I've got everything I want . . .' How wonderful, Vanessa thought, to have everything you want. But there was a distinct note in Richard's voice, she thought, that suggested it wasn't enough.

Chapter 6
'Earl's Court Hippies'

At the beginning of 1974, Virgin moved offices to Vernon Yard, a small cobbled mews set off the Portobello Road, in Notting Hill, West London. The 'Napoli' of Colin MacInnes's novel *Absolute Beginners*, Notting Hill sits uneasily between fashionability and squalor, its crumbling Victorian terraces colonised either by Irish and West Indian immigrants, or the professional classes bent on gentrification – its contrasts mirrored in the progress of the Portobello Road marked from high-priced antiques at one end, through prosaic fruit and vegetables, to a flea market of the meanest hue at the other.

The Vernon Yard premises exuded a particular quaintness behind the yellow ochre façade and green doors and shutters. The premises had once been stabling for horses. More recently a homosexual resident had hanged himself to death from the low wooden beams following a row with his lover. From the day Virgin moved in, the offices were over-crowded. Boxes of records and ephemera piled up in the reception area, people pressed themselves against walls to let colleagues pass; partitions were shuffled hither and thither in a vain attempt to create either space or privacy. An air of perpetual confusion reigned which time would never fully resolve, manifest in jarring strains of music, overbrimming ash trays, discarded plates of health food and an abundance of long, straggly centre-parted hair. Richard Branson and Nik Powell took adjacent offices on the first floor, Branson's small but furnished with the office's one reasonable sofa, which became a sanctuary for the weary at the end of the day. Immediately below Branson, Simon Draper, in the A & R (artists and repertoire) department, entertained a steady stream of supplicants, drawn by the promise of artistic freedom. Many were the concept albums about astral travel, the pyramids and the Aquarian age which Draper was obliged to suffer.

Branson was assembling around him the nucleus of a team, many of them veterans from the time of *Student*, elevated to positions of sudden and unexpected responsibility. Draper had gone from ticking order forms to effectively shaping the musical policy of Virgin. His friend Jumbo Van Rennen, who had arrived from South Africa at the same time and packed records in South Wharf Road, was now in charge of 'international', charting the progress of Virgin acts around the world. Chris Stylianou – 'Greek Chris' – who had joined as a magazine-seller, was in charge of exports. Steve Lewis, who as a schoolboy had compiled the first ever Virgin mail-order catalogue, was responsible for a new project – Virgin management and promotions. There too was Rod Vickery, another veteran of *Student*. A young man named Ken Berry, who later rose to become managing director of the record company, and Branson's most trusted adviser, joined in what was jocularly known as the accounts department, filing invoices in cardboard boxes. Berry's qualifications included back-packing around Europe and milking cows in Denmark.

In all of this, Branson's skill lay in cultivating the flower of enthusiasm, encouraging and enabling others to do things they hardly dared to believe themselves capable of; Branson's style, as Stylianou put it, was to 'put someone in charge of something, then simply let them get on with it'. It was a practice which perhaps owed as much to necessity as to management theory – Virgin could hardly afford the wages to attract people from outside – yet it worked. People given responsibility tended to rise to it; those who could not were quietly found jobs somewhere else.

The atmosphere was one of frenetic activity, coupled with extreme informality, never more so than when the Virgin directors convened for 'board meetings'; a euphemism for a day at the Manor, playing a leisurely game of snooker, with frequent adjournments to the local pub to discuss the future.

It was a paradox that someone who could inspire self-confidence in others could so often seem so ill-at-ease and socially awkward himself. It was as if somewhere along the way, Richard had not quite learned the art of conversation, a fact of which he was aware, and even self-conscious: he had always been in too much of a hurry to read, broaden his education. At times when his contemporaries had been enjoying the luxury of self-contemplation and realisation, journeying inwards with the guidebooks of Herman Hesse or Aldous Huxley, Branson had been turning his mind to the selling of advertising space, the raising of bank loans. When he first met Branson, Simon Draper had taken it upon himself to complete his cousin's cultural education, plying Branson with books and records. He gave up when it became obvious they went unread and unheard. Branson gave the impression of someone who had never had time for the usual adolescent doubts of self-identity and purpose, who ran on instinct rather than reason. He was rooted in a pragmatic world of action and consequence. In this way, he was not a child of the Sixties at all, nor even of the Seventies; but someone awaiting the arrival of the Eighties. Business gave him a vocabulary, a framework and set of references he otherwise lacked, and which galvanised him in a way normal conversation never could. The mind bit on details like a trap. Deal-making invested him with utter certainty, and in finding the shortest distance between two points of business he acquired a fluency invariably absent in the exchange of social pleasantries, or social intimacies. He found it hard to show his feelings.

Practical jokes, creating events and happenings – *doing something* – was a way of filling the silences that might otherwise arise in conversations, and creating an equal intimacy with friends and strangers. There was not a swimming-pool that did not invite Branson to jump into it – and pull others in with him; hardly a meal that could not be enlivened by a breadroll – or meatball-throwing contest. His sense of humour could sometimes be gruesome, as he took a child's pleasure in other people's squirming discomfort. For a short while, it became the custom to hold heads of department meetings at an Indian restaurant of dubious hygiene close by the Virgin offices. When the sight of cockroaches leaping on the table became too much, there was a general plea to Alison Short, Branson's secretary, to change the venue. 'No, no, book it there,' Branson insisted. Wasn't it worth it for the expressions of revulsion on everyone's faces? Better yet . . . what could be more delicious than to be at the Manor, enjoying dinner with friends and then accidentally drop a glass in the kitchen, swiftly concoct a mixture of ketchup and iodine, smear it liberally over your face and lurch theatrically into the dining-room crying, 'Call an ambulance.' Then to watch the faces, frozen in horrified disbelief for what seems like an eternity, torn between rushing to the telephone or your aid; then to slowly transform the expression of pain on your face into one of hilarity as the chorus of groans, oaths and imprecations becomes a barrage of breadrolls and insults.

Nobody could accuse Branson of finesse, yet nor could it be denied that the Virgin offices were enlivened by an uncommon sense of fun. A birthday gift from the staff of a plastic sex doll was received with a gesture fitting the thought – Branson dropping his trousers as the girls fled screaming from the office. He was so taken with the gift that when he drove to the Manor that afternoon he insisted on taking the inflated doll with him, sticking up through the open sunroof. Sitting beside him, his secretary, Alison, blushed the entire length of the M40. Branson's favourite joke on bringing musicians to the Manor was to drive past the entrance and some four miles further on to the small town of Woodstock. There he would turn the car under a magnificent arched entranceway – pausing to point out the row of quaint cottages 'where our kitchen staff live' – and proceed up the sweeping drive to the front door of the magnificent country house. To Frank Zappa, the American leader of the Mothers of Invention, Branson explained that he was 'just off to park the car' and that Zappa should ring the doorbell and someone would let him in. Zappa duly mounted the sweeping terrace of steps to the door and tugged at the bell, to be greeted by a uniformed member of staff informing him that, actually, this was not a pop recording studio but Blenheim Palace, the ancestral seat of the Dukes of Marlborough.

Relations with musicians often assumed a surrealistic quality, for Branson's ignorance of music was so consistent and comprehensive as to be almost pathological. He had sat in front of a crackling log fire at the Manor while Keith Richards attempted to teach him how to roll a Jamaican-style spliff – an experience akin to Velasquez giving you painting lessons; he knew who Keith Richards was, but was that other man with the python-skin boots and shark's-tooth earring a Face, a Stone or something else entirely? Branson could never tell.

He became adept at bluff. By the judicious application of nods, grunts and pregnant silences, he could convey the impression that he knew far more than he actually did, whether the conversation was about who had recorded what or what exactly the copyright laws were pertaining to releases in Germany. It bought him time in striking deals with more practised negotiators, while he learnt what was valuable and what was not, what could be surrendered and what must be fought for, at almost any cost.

Record deals conform to a simple framework. In signing with a record company, an act signs a contract guaranteeing that they will provide a certain number of recordings over an agreed period. They are given an advance deductible against future royalties. These royalties are calculated on a percentage basis of the retail price of the record, and are known in the industry as 'points'. An act's 'points' will rise commensurate to their fame and selling power. Within this framework, however, there is infinite scope for variation. But to Branson one factor became paramount; think in the long term.

Owning a company fosters a different attitude to being an employee of somebody else's corporation. Corporate employees are out to make quick reputations within their companies; it is their bargaining tool for a better job somewhere else. They have little vested interest in shaping a contract to ensure that a performer will still be on the label in four or five years' time – the likelihood is they will have moved on themselves by then. An employee will sacrifice long-term advantage for short-term gain.

It became Branson's policy – an absolute rule – to sign acts for as long a term as possible, with the promise that the company would make a commensurate long-term commitment to the act's success. It is often the case that a group will return to the negotiating table long before the contract expires, either because they have been successful and are in search of more points, or to borrow more money for a tour, equipment or living expenses. Branson would not hesitate to seize the moment for a bout of horse-trading; more points in exchange for extending the period of the contract; more money in exchange for the right to sell the songs on to another company for a compilation record.

In striking such deals, Branson exercised a simple, abiding principle: the key to success in the music business lies in controlling copyright, be it on recordings or music publishing. And the longer you can control copyright, the more money you will make on it. All contracts, for example, contain an agreement on how long the record company has the right to 'exploit' an artist's work for that label, be it five, ten or fifty years – the full length of copyright. Branson became fastidious about sticking on the length of these 'exploitation rights', sometimes for the full duration of copyright.

Virgin's boast that no artist ever quit the label for another was a testament not only to how harmonious most contracts within the company were, but also how watertight. For, once signed, Branson would enforce a contract to the letter, with a single-minded precision and ruthlessness which his beaming, friendly countenance belied.

Branson's competitive instincts, and his determination to exact the best possible advantage from negotiations, could be counter-productive. He would try to make it a condition of every deal, for example, that a new group should sign their music publishing as well as their recording rights to Virgin. It was the record company that did all the work promoting the group and making hits, Branson argued, so why should another publishing company sit back and collect their 6 per cent? There was, of course, a simple inconsistency in this argument. Virgin acted as music publishers for a number of artists not signed to the label – and were perfectly happy to collect their 6 per cent. But Branson applied the principle wherever he could. In 1976, he and Simon Draper flew to Ireland to meet with the Boomtown Rats, an up-and-coming act led by a singer named Bob Geldof. Draper had high hopes of signing them. A figure for signing and royalty rates was agreed, but then Branson introduced the question of music publishing into the negotiation. Draper was angry that Branson was jeopardising a deal that Virgin badly needed to sign when a simple compromise would have the group in the bag. But Branson refused to relinquish the point. The Boomtown Rats were angry too at the tactic of introducing new conditions when they believed the deal had been agreed. They pulled out of negotiations altogether, and signed with another label, Ensign.

Even Branson's closest friends and colleagues could be disconcerted by his relish for exacting the best possible price out of an adversary. Alison Short was on the telephone, agreeing a price of £250 to have the snooker table at the Manor recovered when Branson snatched the telephone from her hand to re-open the negotiations, and beat the supplier down to £150. Negotiating a wage rise was never a simple discussion, but an opportunity for a game; the object of which was not necessarily to deprive the supplicant of what they deserved, but to delight in mental fencing. If you asked Richard to lend you a fiver, it was said, he would immediately try to beat you down to £4.50.

Branson showed no great inclination to turn the profits of his business acumen to self-aggrandisement. He drew only a modest salary from Virgin and lived on remarkably little. Like the Pope, Salvador Dali and members of the British Royal Family he seldom carried any money in his pocket. Friends grew accustomed to paying for the little things of life – taxi fares, rounds of drinks, newspapers – for it would invariably be reciprocated in time by a meal or a weekend in the country. The peculiar combination of generosity of spirit and an invariable poverty of immediate resources reached its zenith one night when Branson and his old friend Ian Howes stopped for a hitchhiker in London. Once in the car, the boy spun a hard-luck story about needing to get to Oxford to see his girlfriend. Branson was obviously touched by the story. 'We're not going that far, but we'll give you the taxi fare', he said, patting his pockets for cash; then came the inevitable coda: 'Got any money, Ian?'

The Bentley – that momentary, arriviste conceit which had been bequeathed to Mike Oldfield for the *Tubular Bells* concert – gave way to a series of nondescript saloons, all subjected to the same indifferent treatment, often skewiffed carelessly on a yellow line outside Vernon Yard, window and doors left open, the keys hanging tantalisingly in the ignition. On more than one occasion someone would be despatched to find a car which Branson had parked 'somewhere in the West End' the previous night and had been unable to locate himself.

He was as indifferent about all his personal possessions. Kristen bought his clothes; the only condition was that they were comfortable. When it was decided that the houseboat had grown too small, and a house should be found that could double as home and personal office, it became Kristen's responsibility to find and furnish it. The house she found belonged to the comedian Peter Cook. It was a three-storey Victorian property, painted pillar-box red, in Denbigh Terrace, a few minutes' walk from Vernon Yard and directly opposite a small council estate. Branson did not believe in locking his doors, and soon the house became open to children from the neighbouring estate, slouching on the antique leather Chesterfield, bought by Kristen; clustered around the small bar-billiards table in the games room.

Kristen too now worked for Virgin, in a variety of roles. At Branson's suggestion she supervised Virgin Rags, an ill-fated diversification into selling clothes in selected Virgin record shops. To Kristen's increasing chagrin, the selected shops all happened to be in Britain's least attractive provincial cities, entailing frequent train journeys to monitor the cheesecloth shirts and loon pants of various garish hues which nobody wished to buy.

Later, she worked at the Virgin offices. Then, she and Richard might at least pass each other in the corridor in Vernon Yard as well as on the way to and from the bathroom in Denbigh Terrace. Branson's passion for work continued unabated by marriage. Often, work would be brought home to Denbigh Terrace, in the shape of a lunch or dinner party for business associates which

Kristen was expected to cook. Weekends at the Manor were hardly a respite. Kristen began to wonder if she and Richard had not married too soon.

In the summer of 1974 they went on holiday, to the island of Cozumel, off the Yucatan peninsula of Mexico. It was an idyllic holiday, which gave Richard a novel excitement of deep-sea fishing, for tuna, marlin, even shark. On the day before they were due to leave, Richard wanted one more expedition. Kristen was not keen: the weather forecast was bad; and the fishermen they approached in the harbour refused to take them, until Branson at last found a small wooden vessel, crewed by a father and son who, with two more passengers on board, agreed to the journey for a few dollars more.

The boat set out into the straits between Cozumel and the peninsula and lines were cast. Before long, Branson had hooked a king-size marlin and the attention of the entire boat was drawn to the struggle as he fought to wind the fish aboard. Nobody noticed the storm until it was almost upon them. The sky suddenly darkened and it grew bitterly cold; spray dashed their faces and the boat pitched violently on the waves. The captain of the boat shouted not to worry, they would head for shore. But to their utter horror, the boat instead turned out towards the open water. The tiller had jammed. Now, instead of riding the waves, the boat was being hit broadside, threatening to capsize with each assault. Richard and Kristen clutched at each other, convinced that this was the end. The boat seemed hardly strong enough to withstand such a battering, or the weight of water washing over its side. Yet, miraculously, the storm abated. Now they bobbed helplessly, with a jammed tiller, at the mercy of the skies, darkening once more. Branson and Kristen quickly conferred between themselves: the boat, they thought, would not survive another battering like the last one. And if they stayed on it, neither would they. The shoreline was visible, some two miles beyond. They should swim for it. But no one else would agree to leave the boat; it was against the rules of the sea; besides, the shore was too far; the currents too strong – and there were the sharks to consider.

Branson found a plank of wood in the bottom of the boat and threw it overboard, to use as a float; then he and Kristen slipped over the side into the chill waters and struck out for shore. Kristen was accustomed to long-distance swimming; as a child she and her sister would cover distances up to five miles; it wasn't so bad; you take it easy, sing a few songs and you get there in the end. Richard was not such a strong swimmer, and the plank he had thrown overboard sank quickly in the water. The shoreline seemed far, far away. Slowly, they made their way towards it, shouting encouragement to each other, fearful of the other at any moment vanishing from view in a sudden, thrashing attack from below. The current seemed stronger closer to shore, tugging them further down the coastline. Richard's legs felt as heavy as iron, and his heart beat in his ears. Then suddenly there was sand underfoot and they were dragging themselves on to the shore, to collapse, exhausted and reborn. The beach was utterly deserted, save for land crabs, unused to human company, and the decomposing shell of a turtle. No boat could be seen on the horizon. The sense of having experienced something which only the other could possibly understand, and which could never be expressed, arose in them both. 'We'll be together for ever after this,' said Richard.

What they now had to do was get to a village and try to organise a rescue for the boat they had just left behind.

They walked for what seemed like miles along the beach and the fringes of jungle to reach a small village. They were on the peninsula of Yucatan, with no clothes and no money. A ferry ran from the village back to the island and Branson managed to explain that there was a boat stuck out at sea that needed to be rescued. They got on board, but no sooner had the ferry put out to sea than it too ran into the second wave of the storm and had to turn back. It was only as dusk fell that they finally arrived back at the harbour of Cozumel. A small fleet of vessels now put out to sea in search of the fishing boat, but it was never found, and the next day Richard and Kristen left Mexico for good.

The experience was a sobering one for Branson. It brought him and Kristen together in a way which only the shared experience of being near to death can. But it would not be enough to save their marriage. Back in London, Virgin and work imposed its familiar tyranny on Branson's life.

It was Mike Oldfield who introduced Kevin Ayers into their lives. Ayers' work with the Soft Machine, his group the Whole World and as a solo artist, had endeared him to aficionados of a particularly cultured strain of British art rock. To Oldfield, who had played guitar in the Whole World, Ayers had been something of a mentor – a role model to which any young musician might aspire. Some ten years older than Oldfield, he exuded an air of worldly sophistication and knowing hedonism. Tall, blond, white-suited and fluent in the languages, romantic manners and drinking habits of several Mediterranean countries, Ayers was to be found, flexing a fatal charm, at the most fashionable London pop parties. He had only one thing in common with Richard Branson, and that was Branson's wife.

Branson, however, believed that Ayers would be an asset to the Virgin label, notwithstanding his realisation that Kristen and Ayers were falling in love. Indeed, friends noticed that, in some curious way, Branson seemed almost to push Kristen and Ayers together, as if testing the resilience of his marriage. 'But that's Richard,' said one. 'He'll push things and push things, just to see how far they'll go. And he pushed Kristen too far.'

The first separation was not for long. Kristen came back to the house in Denbigh Terrace and both resolved to try and mend the marriage. Richard suggested a celebratory dinner together. Kristen cooked. It became, inevitably, a dinner party of friends and business associates. Soon afterwards, she left for good, to live with Ayers.

The separation affected Branson deeply, and in a way immediately apparent to close friends like Simon Draper. 'It's the only time I've ever seen Richard at a loss in terms of relationships, and where he was going. He wasn't distraught, but thrown, on edge, anxious – which is as close as he ever gets to being distraught.'

For a time Richard was hardly seen in Vernon Yard at all, but worked out of the house in Denbigh Terrace. Friends came to stay, in whose company Branson threw himself into a state of vengeful bachelorhood as a succession of willowy blondes, whose resemblance to Kristen was often remarked upon, passed through the house. The front door remained permanently open to the neighbourhood children, now even more at home with the leather Chesterfield, the bar-billiards table and Branson's possessions. Jewellery which Eve had bequeathed to Kristen went missing, as did the gold watch that had been given to Richard as a boy by Uncle Jim, of Balham hay bath fame.

Some months later, chance brought Branson, Kristen and Ayers together again once more, around the dinner table at the Manor, where Ayers had gone to record. The evening passed in awkward cordiality. When somebody spilt some water beside Ayers, Branson made play of manoeuvring a light flex into the water. The lights shorted. In the enveloping darkness and confusion, those present could reflect that this was one practical joke imbued with the faintest edge of revenge.

The enormous success of *Tubular Bells*, and to a lesser extent Tangerine Dream's *Phaedra*, both in Britain and abroad, turned on a tap of money which fed and nourished Virgin for almost three years. Almost immediately, Branson had begun a policy of diversification. Ostensibly, the idea was to expand into fields related to the 'core business' of the record company. The mail-order business was closed down, but in its place there sprang up a management company, a music publishing company and a booking agency. The publishing company would prove an invaluable source of income, but the management and booking agencies were closed down when it became obvious that it was in the best interests of performers, and the record company, for the performers' affairs to be handled independently.

Branson himself continued to manage Mike Oldfield, but this allowed little scope for creative development of Oldfield's career. With the money from *Tubular Bells*, Oldfield had bought himself a large house in Herefordshire where he had installed his own studio. Here he continued to produce a series of virtuoso rock suites in the manner of *Tubular Bells* and nurture his contempt for the music industry at large. Branson's pleas for Oldfield to perform in America to consolidate the success of

Tubular Bells had fallen on deaf ears. He refused to give interviews, or promote his career in any way. Branson's principal managerial role was to pay frequent visits to Herefordshire and while away the evenings with his diffident protégé in remote country pubs, in the company of farming folk.

Virgin Rags, the company's venture into clothing, was to prove short-lived, notwithstanding the efforts of Kristen and Rod Vickery, as was Duveens, a restaurant which was opened near the Vernon Yard offices. In fact, Duveens promised to be a great success. Under the management of Chris Stylianou, it soon attracted a regular, and free-spending, clientele. Its only drawback was its close proximity to the Virgin offices, and the opportunity it provided for staff to unwind in surroundings they considered as home. Customers seeking a romantic tryst by candlelight would have their reveries disturbed by a breadroll in the back of the neck, caught in the crossfire of some inebriated interdepartmental dispute. One night Rod Vickery was making his way towards the restaurant when he sighted a figure outside. It was Branson, standing in the road dressed only in his underwear, covered from head to foot in cranberry sauce. Vickery nodded a greeting and hurried on, unwilling to broach the carnage within.

The record company remained the principal source of income, but even this was in an increasingly precarious state. The money from *Tubular Bells* and *Phaedra* – and the more modest successes of Oldfield's *Hergest Ridge* and *Ommadawn* – had been used to subsidise a musical policy of commendable artistic zeal, but dubious commercial worth. For example, Virgin now had its own resident poet and wordsmith, Ivor Cutler, and a proper 'serious' composer, David Bedford. Bedford had helped Mike Oldfield in the preparation of *Tubular Bells* and scored the work for a performance by the Royal Philharmonic Orchestra. Largely on the strength of his association with Oldfield, he was given his own contract with Virgin, producing a sequence of orchestral albums of increasingly impenetrable complexity.

It became apparent to Branson and Draper that if the label were to prosper, its musical scope must be broadened to include performers with a more obvious commercial appeal. At various times over the next twelve months, Branson entered into negotiations to sign 10CC, David Bowie, the Who and Pink Floyd – a group which Draper noted laconically 'wanted to sign with a bank, not a record label' – all without success.

Finally, Branson bid for the biggest of them all – the Rolling Stones. Even Branson himself acknowledged that there was something slightly preposterous about the notion of Virgin chasing the Rolling Stones. The Stones' record sales had never quite matched their reputation, but they would certainly be asking more than the ever-diminishing returns from Gong, Supercharge or even Mike Oldfield could afford, and they would be seeking guarantees about distribution which Virgin could not give. Undaunted, however, Branson approached the Rolling Stones' financial manager, Prince Rupert Lowenstein, with a simple question: How much? Lowenstein was indulgent, but sceptical. There was, he said, next to no chance of the Stones signing to a label as small as Virgin; the price would be well beyond Branson's reach. As it was, the group had nearly reached an agreement with Phonogram for three million dollars. 'I'll give you four million dollars,' said Branson. In that case, said Lowenstein, if Branson could deliver a promissory note for four million dollars to the Rolling Stones' office by the following Monday, Lowenstein would 'seriously consider it'.

The next day, Richard Branson arrived at Heathrow Airport with a sheaf of air-tickets which would carry him from France to Italy, Germany and on to Scandinavia for appointments with all the foreign licensees of Virgin product. To each of them Branson made the same proposal: If you can guarantee us 100,000–200,000 dollars, or even more, through your territory, we can offer you the Rolling Stones. He arrived back in London after three days, utterly exhausted, yet bearing guarantees totalling 3,500,000 dollars. Lowenstein was impressed by Branson's acumen and drive. He would take the Virgin offer very seriously, he said. A week later, the Rolling Stones signed to EMI.

Branson was bitterly disappointed. The label, he was now acutely aware, was at a watershed. The need to sign a group that could restore both the label's flagging fortunes and add lustre to its increasingly outmoded image was paramount. Meanwhile, there would be a rigorous examination of the existing roster, to see which artists had become luxuries Virgin could no longer afford. On an autumn day in 1976, fifteen members of the Virgin staff met at Branson's Denbigh Terrace home, to argue the merits of all those artists signed to the label, and draw a blue line through the names of those who had become financial liabilities to the label.

Among those struck from the list was the orchestral composer David Bedford. The news of his demise distressed Bedford greatly and he sat down to compose two letters. To Richard Branson he wrote a warm note, thanking him for all his help and support over the years, commending Virgin for its contribution to the arts and expressing the earnest wish that they might work together again in the future. To his friend and mentor Mike Oldfield he wrote another note, expressing a somewhat different sentiment. Richard Branson, he wrote tartly, was a mercenary philistine and a shit, and he, Bedford, was glad to be shot of him. Bedford sealed and stamped the letters with some satisfaction, in the knowledge that he had both got his feelings off his chest and left open a useful door for the future. He popped them in the post-box. Alas, he put the letters in the wrong envelopes.

Chapter 7

Pistols at Dawn

Pondering the moment when the Sex Pistols became the most notorious pop group in the world, and the word 'punk' first entered the popular vocabulary as a synonym for delinquency and devilment, future historians will possibly set their clocks at 5.30 on the afternoon of 1 December 1976.

It was then that the four members of the Sex Pistols were taken, well-lubricated, from the hospitality suite of Thames Television to face interrogation by Bill Grundy on the popular teatime magazine programme, *Today*.

Grundy, a commentator known for his bilious disposition, had that afternoon returned from a lunch at *Punch* magazine and was himself feeling no pain. So it was that an otherwise desultory exchange, from opposite ends of the universe, was suddenly enlivened by the discovery of common ground when Grundy observed, 'You're more drunk than I am.' In the words of a newspaper account the following day, Grundy then asked 'a spiky-haired youth' to repeat a four-letter word he had used off camera. The youth obliged, adding a further string of expletives, just for good measure.

Four-letter words had been uttered on television

before, but never so fulsomely, so splenetically, and never at teatime. History was being made. Out in viewerland, an irate lorry-driver put his boot through his television set to prevent contamination of his eight-year-old son. Viewers jammed the Thames Television switchboard; Fleet Street pundits and leader writers reached for their pencils.

In his home at Denbigh Terrace, Richard Branson flicked off the television, breathed deeply on the tangible aroma of excitement in the air, and allowed a broad smile to crease his face. His judgement was, after all, perfectly sound.

Only a few hours earlier, Branson had telephoned Leslie Hill, the managing director of EMI Records, with a proposition. 'If you want to get rid of the Sex Pistols,' he said, 'I'll take them off your hands.' Hill declined to speak to Branson. Within the affluent premises of EMI, Virgin were referred to scornfully as 'The Earl's Court Hippies', and hardly worthy of a managing director's time. 'Mr Hill,' a secretary tartly informed Branson, 'is quite happy with the Sex Pistols, thank you very much.'

At seven a.m. the following morning, contemplating newspaper headlines which screamed 'The Filth and the Fury', and with the clamour of shareholders ringing in his ears, Leslie Hill personally telephoned Branson at home with a simple request, 'Can we talk?'

When Branson arrived at Hill's office at EMI later that day, he found a man desperate to rid himself of an embarrassment. After only a few minutes' discussion, Hill and Branson agreed a transfer of the Sex Pistols' contract from EMI to Virgin, conditional, of course, on the agreement of the group's manager, Malcolm McLaren.

McLaren was then ushered in from an adjoining office. Branson took him in at a glance. At thirty-two, Malcolm McLaren was seven years older than Branson, yet he looked only the same age, possibly even younger; a short and wiry figure dressed in pointed boots, black jeans and a tight-fitting suit jacket of Italianate design. The shock of red hair, the puckish, mobile face and preternaturally bright eyes set in an expression of mocking amusement all conspired to lend Malcolm McLaren a Mephistophelean air. He and Branson looked at each other with the candour of two people who know they are utterly different, but for one shared resolution. Not to be beaten.

Do a deal? McLaren was the spirit of expansive bonhomie. Of course, Richard; of course. Fine by me, and the boys will be thrilled . . . He reversed out of the office, pumping Branson's hand. 'And we'll be in your office this afternoon to discuss it further . . .'

Branson did not see Malcolm McLaren for another five months, by which time association with the Sex Pistols carried with it the whiff of high treason . . .

To the majority of British people, the occasion of the twenty-fifth anniversary of Queen Elizabeth's ascendancy to the throne, on 5 June 1977, offered a brief respite from the prevailing air of national gloom, a rare opportunity for celebration in a Britain beset with economic and social uncertainties.

The lighting of one hundred beacons, from Jersey to the Shetland Isles, the street parties and special events and the climactic procession by the Queen along a processional route lined by one million people waving Union Jacks under a murky grey sky – all of this implied an attempt to reclaim something permanent and enduring – a sense of national pride – which had been systematically eroded by Britain's loss of standing as a world power, and by some dark and mysterious incoming tide which carried with it the flotsam of unemployment, inflation, rising crime and social decay.

The second Elizabethan Age had slumped into depression. In 1976, unemployment in Britain passed the one-million mark for the first time since the Second World War. In 1977, it stood at 1,250,600. The number of working days lost through industrial stoppages continued to rise and productivity to fall. Even the police argued for 'the right to strike'. In a final, ironic comment on what commentators now referred to as 'the British disease', television coverage of the national celebration was severely disrupted by a dispute over technicians' pay.

The most visible victims of shrinking job opportunities were the young. And the young were demanding, once again, that the world pay attention. To those at home in Jubilee week, fiddling exasperatedly with their television sets, the spectacle of their children mutilating themselves with safety-pins and chains, dressing in the black plastic sacks normally reserved for household refuse and generally conforming to all the stereotypes of what the popular press had identified as the 'punk-rock' phenomenon, was a symptom of some imponderable national malaise, and the harbinger of an awful future.

The pitched battles fought each Saturday afternoon in the Kings Road between punks and teddy-boys – the curators of Fifties sartorial and musical style – seemed a tragi-comic parody of the struggle between the forces of conservatism and the forces of chaos and change. It was a battle that was also being fought out in pop music. The spontaneity and excitement which had attended pop music's greatest flowerings – in the mid-Fifties and again in the mid-Sixties – had, once again, evaporated; the market-place was now the sole arbiter of style. Music had become increasingly splintered – into the overbearing pomposity of progressive rock, the mannered gestures and the Tin Pan Alley hokum of glam-rock, the increasingly leaden beat of disco. Rock's superstars now deigned to appear only in vast stadia, remote from their audience, dependent on banks of amplifiers and lights. Pop music had temporarily forgotten its role of addressing a young audience about its own concerns, and instead entered one of its periodic fits of mawkishness and middle-aged retrenchment, personified in the superstar of the moment – a gargantuan, bearded figure, shrouded in kaftans, precariously balanced on tiny slippers and warbling in an implausible soprano. By the end of 1976, Demis Roussos had sold more records in Britain than any other solo artist, including David Bowie and Elton John. Pop music was desperate for something: the arrival of punk brought a rude vigour which perfectly fused a musical style, a cultural statement and a political and social crisis.

That the Sex Pistols, as the principal standard-bearers of punk, should, by the time of the Silver Jubilee, have assumed the dimensions of a national menace, owed much to the manipulative skills of Malcolm McLaren. The son of a Scottish father who deserted the family home at an early age and a Jewish mother, McLaren was brought up in the middle-class London suburb of Edgware. Imaginative and headstrong, he became an art student, throwing himself wholeheartedly into all the extracurricular activities of the day, including, in 1968, organising a student occupation of his art college in Croydon with a friend, Jamie Reid.

As students, McLaren and Reid became enamoured of Situationism, a philosophy spawned in the late Fifties by a group of European artists and intellectuals which advocated the overthrow of capitalism by shock, scandal and pranks. Situationism argued that society is a 'spectacle', a false projection which masks our alienation from our true selves; it is 'culture' which supplies the spectacle, obscuring the reality of exploitation. Spectacle, it was argued, must be fought with spectacle. A typical idea abroad in Paris was to protest against the Vietnam War by floating oriental corpses, borrowed from the morgue, down the Seine with copious amounts of red dye. The true poverty, it was argued, was poverty of the imagination. The Situationists styled themselves as 'intellectual terrorists', and their ideas and slogans became central to the student uprising in Paris in 1968.

Malcolm McLaren enjoyed being an art student. So much so that he spent fully eight years in a succession of colleges before throwing himself on the tender mercies of the world. In 1972 he opened a shop in the Kings Road at first selling teddy-boy schmutter, much later, in premises renamed Sex, rubber and leather bondage clothing. His clothes business brought him increasingly into contact with the rock music world, and in 1974 McLaren moved briefly to New York where he managed the prototype glam-trash group, the New York Dolls. The partnership was not a success, and is best remembered for McLaren's ploy of persuading the group to perform onstage with a hammer and sickle banner, offending even their deeply buried atavistic feelings of patriotism. But while in New York McLaren also took note of new groups like Television and Richard Hell and the Voidoids, whose spiky crew cut and ripped and torn T-shirts and jeans, clumsily held together with safety-pins, struck McLaren as the epitome of Bohemian urban guerrilla chic.

McLaren returned to London, convinced that fashion,

music and iconography of pop culture offered the perfect medium for spectacle, subversion and profit. Now he put together his own group from bored teenagers who frequented his shop and invited his old art-school colleague Jamie Reid to join the plot. In truth, almost any quartet of disgruntled teenagers, of the barest musical competence, artfully encouraged to belch, pull faces and make rude gestures would have fitted the bill, but fate decreed in the Sex Pistols a particular exquisite chemistry of individuals. There was John Lydon, rechristened Johnny Rotten, a hunched Irish boy with a complexion like used tissue paper, a vituperative turn of phrase and a sneer made in heaven; and Steve Jones and Paul Cook, two likely lads rich with the authentic aroma of the Job Centre and remand home. The original bass-player, Glen Matlock, a chirrupy lad with dangerous aspirations to musical prowess, was quickly dropped; in his place came the infinitely more satisfactory John Ritchie, a.k.a. Sid Vicious – a simple-minded soul with no ideology save revenge, careering through life like a bad accident looking for somewhere to happen. Together this mixture of lumpen proletarian resentment and art-school manipulation lit the fuse for the first major explosion in pop music – and pop culture – for ten years.

Under McLaren's tutelage, the Pistols began playing at private parties and the occasional pub, then regularly at the 100 Club in Oxford Street, building up an excitable following and a reputation for contrived mayhem. Soon, other groups were following in their wake: the Clash, the Damned, X-Ray Spex, Siouxsie and the Banshees. At the so-called Punk Festival at the 100 Club in September 1976, a girl was struck in the eye by a flying splinter of glass. The Pistols were already banned from most established London venues; punk rock's reputation for violence was now beyond redemption.

Malcolm McLaren got short shrift when he first called on Virgin records in the summer of 1976, one stop among many in his search for a recording contract for his new protégés. Virgin were in a period of acute stagnation, desperately in need of a change. What nobody at Virgin knew was quite what form that change should take. The policy of artistic worthiness which had been pursued since *Tubular Bells*, three years before, had produced progressively diminishing returns. In fact, Virgin's best-selling album of 1976 was a collection of Mike Oldfield's first three records, packaged with a fulsomely extravagant colour brochure and entitled *Boxed*. To the record industry at large, Virgin's image remained firmly wedded to an era already passed.

In the summer of 1976, for example, a dispute between members of the group Gong over who owned the rights to the name resulted in the Virgin offices being 'occupied' by the group's followers – a motley congregation of men, women, children and animals, with the appearance of refugees from Gandalf's Garden. When the protest finally collapsed, Richard Branson stood by the door ushering out the gypsy-like throng, politely removing the records, tapes, posters and movable items of office furniture which had been secreted in robes and kaftans. It was an incident that said much of Virgin's style. At any other record company, the protesters would not have got beyond the uniformed commissionaires on the door; at no other record company would you have found a group still wearing kaftans.

Such an anachronism owed something to the belief of Simon Draper – Virgin's 'ears' – in the higher ideals of musical taste. As well as its roster of English and German progressive rock, Virgin also distributed the highly musicianly experimental jazz of the ECM and Watt labels. Draper's own favourite records of the moment were by the Brazilian guitarist Egberto Gismonti, Joni Mitchell and the virtuoso jazz pianist Keith Jarrett. By comparison, he thought the Sex Pistols were 'an indescribable noise'. Nor was Draper reassured on seeing the group perform in front of the seething, gobbing mob of self-mutations at the 100 Club in Oxford Street. The Sex Pistols were not quite 'the change' for Virgin Draper had in mind.

Richard Branson was prepared to bow to Draper's more practised musical judgement in the matter. The Sex Pistols sounded like an unholy row to him, too. So it was that in October 1976, the Pistols signed to EMI Records. 'Anarchy in the UK', the group's first single, was released on 26 November. It was greeted within Virgin by the sound of opinions being busily revised. What had sounded 'indescribable' a few months before on stage now sounded corruscatingly powerful on record. What's more, the growing climate of controversy surrounding punk had aroused Branson's instincts. No matter what the Pistols *sounded* like, he reasoned, they now made perfect commercial sense – a feeling emphatically confirmed by their confrontation with Bill Grundy. Signing the Sex Pistols, Branson reasoned, was the way to put Virgin back on the map.

The problem was how to get them. Malcolm McLaren did not arrive at the Virgin offices that December afternoon, as arranged. Nor had he ever intended to. It was not until January that EMI at last rid themselves of the Sex Pistols – 'in view of the adverse publicity generated over the last two months', as an official statement put it – and at a cost of £50,000 in settlement. McLaren then began shopping around for another label, pointedly ignoring Virgin. On 9 March the Pistols finally signed with A&M records, in a ceremony staged, for the benefit of press photographers, outside Buckingham Palace. The managing director of A&M, Derek Green, was sanguine about his controversial new signing. 'Every band is a risk,' he said, 'but in my opinion the Sex Pistols are less of a risk than most.' On 16 March Green issued another, somewhat terser statement, saying that the contract between A&M and the Sex Pistols had been terminated. Complaints from staff about the behaviour of the group at a party at A&M's office to celebrate the signing and protests from other A&M artists about the company's judgement were the reasons cited for the *volte face*. The Sex Pistols received £75,000 in compensation.

To Richard Branson, the worse the Sex Pistols' public image became, the more he wanted them. Here was the perfect opportunity to shed the stigma attached to Virgin and bring the label into the 'now'. Branson could spend ten times as much money signing half a dozen acts and never achieve the same effect. The Pistols, he believed, were 'The Rolling Stones of their generation. I was going all out to turn them into the Seventies' strongest band.' This was not, as it turned out, an accurate thesis. The Pistols' strength lay not in their future potential but in their immediate shock value. They were a highly volatile entity that would need to be properly channelled, if not contained. And Branson knew that Virgin stood a better chance of achieving that than either EMI or A&M had done. He was not answerable to shareholders. There were no major artists on Virgin whose sensibilities were likely to be offended as there had been at the Pistols' previous stopovers; no American parent company to interfere. The only reputation which worried Richard Branson was that of being the head of a record company which looked increasingly out of touch, out of time. Being spurned by Malcolm McLaren only made him want the group more. McLaren and the Sex Pistols would be a challenge. And it would be fun . . .

From the moment the Sex Pistols' contract with A&M was rescinded, Branson was on the phone to McLaren, sometimes three times a day, with the same question. 'When are you going to sign with us, Malcolm?' To Branson's irritation, McLaren prevaricated as long as possible, affecting the disinterest of an ingénue being courted by a philanderer.

McLaren too was in a quandary. While he subsequently made it appear like a carefully premeditated act of cunning, being sacked from EMI and A&M was, in fact, a disaster. Of course, it had made a bloody marvellous spectacle – not to mention £125,000 for doing absolutely nothing – but 'the boys' were growing increasingly restive at having their records, and themselves, banned. And as the Silver Jubilee drew near, the need to find a company to record the Pistols' 'commemorative' recording was becoming acute.

But Virgin was the very last label to which McLaren and Jamie Reid had wanted to sign. As the more doggedly political of the two, Reid in particular despised Richard Branson as an 'entrepreneur hippie' who had sold out everything that was exciting and subversive about the Sixties and turned it into big business. Reid found Virgin's 'hippie façade' disconcerting. With EMI or CBS you knew exactly where you stood, whether you liked it or not. It was fat-cats doing business. But with Virgin, he complained, the laid-back Sixties seediness and everybody wanting to be on first-name terms, all seemed like a ploy to lull an honest Situationist into a false sense of security. Whenever he met Branson, Reid insisted perversely on addressing him as 'Mr Branson'. In the offices of the Sex Pistols' company, Glitterbest, Branson became known as 'Mr Pickles'.

Malcolm McLaren too believed that groups and management should always be on the worst possible terms with the record company, to avoid co-option and defeat. Never believe Virgin are 'nice people', he would tell the Pistols; they're only after your money.

But for McLaren the enmity was more than ideological. Richard Branson symbolised everything he despised; the world of upper-middle-class, public-school, breadroll-throwing, cultural philistinism. It fostered in McLaren what Jamie Reid identified as 'nigh on complete hatred'. From the outset, McLaren was convinced that Branson wanted only to take the Sex Pistols away from him, 'and grind me into the ground'. But Branson too was instantly on his guard. He knew nothing about Situationism, and cared even less; but he suspected that what McLaren wanted to do was force Virgin, just as he had forced EMI and A&M, to drop them – and pay the appropriate price.

One bright May morning in 1977, Malcolm McLaren came to Branson's house in Denbigh Terrace to finalise the signing of the Sex Pistols to Virgin. The mood was cordial, almost jokey. 'You do realise what you're getting into, Richard?' asked McLaren. 'We don't want to go through that business we had with A&M. We want somebody who's going to run with us. It'll be hair-raising, but it'll be fun.'

Branson joked back. 'The question is, Malcolm, do *you* realise what you're getting into?'

That settled, the two men began to discuss plans to rush-release the Sex Pistols' first record for Virgin, a special composition to mark the Queen's Silver Jubilee. Officially entitled 'No Future', it became more popularly known as 'God Save the Queen'.

Virgin's first promotional act on signing the Sex Pistols was to organise a boat trip on the River Thames in the week of the official Jubilee celebrations, to mark the release of 'God Save the Queen'; an idea which seemed to meet everybody's requirements by being both a revolutionary gesture and a wizard prank. John Varnom booked the pleasure cruiser, fittingly named *The Elizabethan* (and which Virgin would actually buy some years later), reassuring the owner that the party was for 'some boring German synthesiser band'. In the mood of schoolboys off on an expedition to plant stinkbombs on speechday, the party set off from Westminster Pier, shadowed by two police launches. Branson and McLaren stood side by side on the upper deck, incongruous partners in crime, the contract almost comical – McLaren in drainpipes, Branson with shoulder-length hair tumbling over a multi-coloured sweater of Hobbit-like cosiness. As the boat bobbed outside the Houses of Parliament, a cacophonous version of 'God Save the Queen' echoed across the Thames to bemused sightseers. It was at that point that the police came on board, and the pleasure cruiser was ordered to return to shore. As the boat docked, police swarmed on board. 'Fascist pigs', yelled McLaren, at last creating an 'incident' worthy of the Sex Pistols' reputation. In the ensuing mêlée, McLaren, Reid and others of the Pistols camp were dragged up the gangplank and into the waiting police vans. Branson, who had been attempting to play the role of diplomat with the police, was not arrested. The incident showed the basic difference in measure of commitment to the

Pistols' ideology of subversion. While McLaren was happy, not to say eager, to be arrested, Branson was equally eager not to be. The next morning he presented himself in court to give evidence, and a character reference, on McLaren's behalf.

The release of 'God Save the Queen' caused an immediate furore. 'No pop song has ever had lyrics like these,' the *Sunday Mirror* raged sanctimoniously, helpfully reproducing them in full on its front page: 'God save the Queen/A fascist régime/Made you a moron/A potential H-bomb/God save the Queen/She ain't no human being/There ain't no future in/England's dream.' Packing ladies at the CBS factory where the record was being manufactured refused to handle it, until threatened with the sack. Television and radio advertising was banned; the BBC refused to play it, and some major retailers to stock it. On what grounds it was hard to discern. By no legal definition was the record 'obscene'; it was hardly even objectionable. But in a week in which Britain was in the self-hypnotised thrall of royalty and its traditions, any criticism carried the odium of high treason. 'But such is the new-found and disturbing power of punk that nothing can stop the disc's runaway success,' ranted the *Sunday Mirror*. Throughout Britain, thousands of teenagers, offered a rude purgative to royal overkill, chorused a noisy amen.

Yet despite selling more than 100,000 copies in its first week of release, 'God Save the Queen' reached only number two in the pop charts – Rod Stewart being at number one. Branson's suspicion that the chart had been 'fixed' to prevent the embarrassing spectacle of an anti-royalist song reaching number one during Jubilee week was lent weight by an anonymous telephone call, alleging that the British Phonographic Industry (the record companies' professional body) and the BBC had colluded to keep the record off the top of the charts. Branson was told that in the week in which the Sex Pistols might have been expected to reach number one the BPI had issued an extraordinary secret directive to the British Market Research Bureau, who compiled the charts, that all chart-return shops connected with record companies should be dropped from the weekly census of best-selling records. Virgin, the stores where most Sex Pistols records were being sold, was therefore struck off the list. One week later, the decision was reversed. But by then Virgin and the Sex Pistols had been denied their first ever number one single.

The recording contract which had been agreed between Richard Branson and Malcolm McLaren, after much protracted discussion, was, in lawyers' parlance, unusually 'live' – that is to say, open to constant reappraisal, argument and haggling. McLaren's 'plunder' of EMI and A&M was not repeated. The agreement signed on 12 May 1977 between Glitterbest and Virgin Records gave McLaren and the Pistols an initial payment of just £15,000 for the British rights for material sufficient for one Sex Pistols album, to be paid in twelve instalments. This rather meagre figure was increased by a further £50,000 one month later, when Virgin negotiated the rights to release the Pistols in all other world territories, excluding America, France and Japan.

McLaren insisted that, rather than being paid the advance in one single lump sum, an amount should be paid on the delivery of each track. The staff at Vernon Yard grew accustomed to the spectacle of Malcolm McLaren seated outside Branson's office, clutching a package of tapes under his arm. Almost from day one, the arguments over royalty rates, promotional budgets and artwork waged unceasingly. Making ever more provocative demands and outrageous gestures became an integral part of McLaren's tactics.

The initial air of reasonableness and cordiality had quickly given way to a more chameleon-like personality, shifting and dodging behind a variety of masks; one minute the crafty haberdasher, the next the erudite political activist, the next the polite, smiling business associate. Fred Vermorel, an art-college friend of McLaren's, who later wrote a book about the Sex Pistols, described him as having 'the vision of an artist, the heart of an anarchist, and the imagination of a spiv'. Sometimes Branson's phone would ring at two in the morning. It would be McLaren, intoxicated by an evening of drink and conspiracy with his lawyer, Steven Fisher, with a shopping list of demands. 'I was hoping Branson would be so tired I could beat him down, nag him into submission,' says McLaren. 'What I didn't know was that the man was an insomniac. I would go round and round on the same point, he would commiserate, pretend to understand, but never move an inch. To Richard, it was always the deal; that's what got him excited. Everything else was just water off a duck's back.'

At other times, playing back the office answering-machine first thing in the morning, Branson's secretary would be greeted by a stream of McLaren's comical invective and abuse.

One of McLaren's favourite ploys was to deliberately fly in the face of convention and logic. Coming into the Virgin offices he would make exaggeratedly friendly overtures to the post boy and the receptionist and be sullen and truculent with Branson or Simon Draper. 'It's nothing to do with business, you just don't *feel* right emotionally, Richard,' he would say, in the manner of a schoolmaster lecturing a particularly dull and inattentive pupil.

Curiously, Branson did not dislike McLaren – Malcolm's transparently roguish charm made him hard to *dislike* – but he had never trusted him from the day they had first shaken hands in Leslie Hill's office and McLaren had failed to arrive at the Virgin offices; failed to keep his promise. McLaren would be charming, interesting and warm-hearted; Branson would momentarily drop his guard, and McLaren would immediately try to exploit it. Branson came to realise that 'fair compromise was not really in Malcolm's language'. McLaren, he was convinced, was determined to get the better of him, 'and I was determined not to let him'. Malcolm liked to rattle you, catch you off-guard by making demands nobody could possibly meet. The trick was not to be rattled, but to ride along with them, at least some of the way.

McLaren's stance required an enemy to define it. It was disconcerting to his whole thesis that Branson did not behave like the enemy enough. Even when, in 1978, McLaren returned from Brazil with the news that Great Train Robber Ronnie Biggs was now 'lead singer' of the Sex Pistols and someone McLaren earnestly claimed to be the missing Nazi war criminal Martin Bormann was the new bass-guitarist, Branson took it with disarming enthusiasm. A singing Ronnie Biggs was 'a good idea'. It was McLaren's pleasure always to up the ante . . . 'And we'll call the record "Cosh the Driver", Richard.' Branson demurred at that. After yet more haggling, the title of the song was changed to 'The Biggest Blow'.

Artwork and advertisements for the Pistols records became a perennial source of conflict, a challenge to Virgin's commitment to Situationist spectacle. Jamie

Reid's graphic designs – cut-ups, like a kidnapper's ransom notes – mocked the ethos of the record industry, and the Sex Pistols' relationship with it, with a wickedly funny disrespect for politesse or law. For one single sleeve, Reid adapted the design of the American Express credit card, to depict the 'real relationships within the music industry; the record company as nothing more than a huge pump – and the band as prostitutes'. American Express won an injunction against the sleeve; copies of the record were recalled for resleeving and Virgin were ordered to pay £30,000 in legal costs. It was an ironic prelude to Richard Branson's association with American Express, some years later, advertising the credit card.

Reid reserved his most venomous attacks for Virgin and Branson. He peppered his designs with slogans which ridiculed Virgin, and then challenged the company to use them. He designed a series of posters including one of Branson himself under the caption 'No One is Innocent', and another bearing a swastika made of cannabis leaves, the Virgin logo and what had become a Sex Pistols' slogan, 'Never trust a hippie'. Branson refused to let them be used on any Virgin-owned material. There were boundaries as to how far he would go, but in his own way Branson was as much committed to creating a spectacle as McLaren and Reid, if for very different reasons. Branson was no insurrectionary. He readily acknowledged that the Pistols felt more strongly about the 'difficulties' in England than he did. Branson's views about England were more platitudinous than revolutionary; England, he would say, is 'a great place to live in, but as a great place it should carry on standing totally for democracy and people should have the absolute freedom to say what they think'.

As to offending royalty, or a significant swath of

popular opinion in releasing 'God Save the Queen', Virgin were strictly neutral – 'Like publishers. What our artists were saying was, in effect, nothing to do with us. We could have books criticising royalty, and books praising royalty. It makes no difference. To have one lone voice attacking royalty in Jubilee week seemed perfectly fair. It also happened to sell a lot of records, and was great for the company.'

To Branson, the Pistols offered an unparalleled opportunity to combine business with schoolboyish pranks – the perfect combination of a challenge and 'fun'. It was fun to watch the press perpetuating the myths of shock and outrage, and sometimes help them along by 'leaking' stories, through a compliant journalist, about the next shocking Sex Pistols record, or non-existent controversy. It was *enormous* fun to be juggling with the high explosive which had already exploded in the faces of EMI and A&M, and which the rest of the record industry had decided was too volatile to touch. As everybody at Virgin would testify, the Sex Pistols were actually, in their own screwed-up kind of way, 'sweet kids'.

Branson grew accustomed to the spectre-like figure of Sid Vicious lurching into his office unannounced to steal from his drinks cabinet, or scrounge another £5 or £10. 'Come off it, Sid,' Branson would say. 'You're a rock star now.' He began to take a liking to John Lydon, who beneath the carefully cultivated exterior of ennui, Branson recognised as being extremely bright, 'if rather lazy'. For the Sex Pistols, Richard was prepared to weather the scornful disapproval of Eve and Ted on his even occasional visits to Shamley Green.

The first Sex Pistols album, *Never Mind the Bollocks, Here's the Sex Pistols*, was released in November 1977. It immediately ran into trouble. Once again, television and radio refused to carry advertisements for the record, and in Nottingham the manager of the Virgin shop was charged under the Indecent Advertisement Act, 1899, for displaying album covers and promotional material containing the word bollocks 'in letters four inches high' in his shop window.

For Branson, the case invoked a strong sense of *déjà vu*. It was exactly the same act under which he had been prosecuted seven years before, with the Student Advisory Centre. He asked John Mortimer, once again, to defend the case in court.

Mortimer advised him to find a linguistics expert who could advise them on the meaning of the word 'bollocks'. Branson found just the man he was looking for in James Kingsley, Professor of English Studies at Nottingham University. Over the telephone, Kingsley explained to Branson that bollocks was a nickname given to priests in the eighteenth century, because of the nonsense they spoke. Hence the word had come to mean nonsense. 'By the way,' Kingsley added, 'I'm actually a priest myself. Would you like me to wear my dogcollar in court?' Branson said he thought that would be very useful.

The next day brought one of those interludes for which the English legal system should be cherished. Considering the effects of language on delicate sensibilities, John Mortimer – whose main concern had been to keep the Sex Pistols as far away from court as possible – pondered that the word Maidenhead did not appear to cause the inhabitants of that town any problems. Professor Kingsley was called and asked by prosecuting counsel, 'Are you just an expert on the word "bollocks"?' Kingsley adjusted his dogcollar meaningfully and replied that he was an expert on the English language who could speak authoritatively not only on the matter of 'bollocks' but also on 'shit' or 'fuck' if required. Thus enlightened, the magistrates dismissed the case, and English justice was served.

The success of *Never Mind the Bollocks* did nothing to heal the rift rapidly developing in the Sex Pistols camp, between McLaren and the group, and among the members of the group themselves. Johnny Rotten in particular was becoming increasingly estranged from McLaren's view of what the group should be, and resentful of McLaren's attempts to control them. Rotten had also adopted an increasingly withering view of his colleagues. Sid Vicious was notionally his 'friend', but it was obvious he was a pathetic loser. Jones and Cook were simply likeable dimwits. The whole bunch were looking more and more like liabilities. It had always been Jamie Reid's belief that the Sex Pistols should be broken up after successfully scandalising the Jubilee. In offending the most dearly held shibboleths of common decency and accepted business practice, the group had, after all, achieved what they set out to do. Making 'careers' was never in the game-plan. McLaren agreed. He had never intended the group to become pop stars – and Rotten's increasingly self-important behaviour was a worry. But McLaren had not finished with the idea of the Sex Pistols yet; he wanted to push the group further. He was now obsessed with the idea of using the Sex Pistols in a film. It was to be the cause of his downfall.

His first plan was to have the film, provisionally entitled *Who Killed Bambi?*, directed by Russ Meyer, a corpulent, moustachioed American whose films featuring pendulous-breasted women had made him an improbable recipient of cult acclaim. Meyer duly came, and went again, leaving McLaren and the Sex Pistols some thousands of dollars poorer, and with a negligible amount of film in the can.

McLaren decided to try another tack. A new face had tagged on to the Pistols party. Julien Temple was a precociously clever young film-maker, a graduate of King's College, Cambridge, and a student at the National Film School. Temple had enthusiasm, he had theories about pop culture and the importance of the teenager; above all, he had some equipment which he had borrowed from the National Film School. McLaren felt they could work together, and he started raising money on another project, to be entitled *The Great Rock 'n' Roll Swindle* – a documentary history of how McLaren and the Sex Pistols had taken the record industry for a ride. McLaren himself would star as The Swindler.

McLaren's abiding fears that Virgin were working to undermine his influence on the group had some substance. Simon Draper, in particular, realised that as the Sex Pistols began to disintegrate it was Lydon who was 'the invaluable commodity', and that Virgin should be putting some effort into cultivating a relationship with him, with an eye to the future. 'It was not a question of coming between Malcolm and John,' says Draper. 'They hated each other anyway. We had a valuable property, and it was a question of not being rowed out.' While McLaren was in Hollywood attempting to raise money for his film, Branson and John Varnom took Lydon to lunch, and over pork kebabs, persuaded him to appear on *Top of the Pops* to promote the single 'Pretty Vacant'. 'Rotten didn't want to do it,' remembers Varnom. 'But Richard said, get hold of him and we'll persuade him. I was saying, "Just think what fun it's going to be, following Cilla Black . . ." and you could just see him succumbing.' McLaren was furious when he returned. It showed the Sex Pistols were becoming 'safe'. McLaren's conviction that Branson wanted revenge, to find a way to seize control of the Pistols for good, 'and cut me off at the pass', now became an obsession.

In January 1978, the disintegration of the Sex Pistols began in earnest. Touring America for the first and last time, the group squabbled incessantly, among themselves and with McLaren, leading John Lydon finally to quit the group. To add to McLaren's troubles, the cash required to finance his film was all but gone, depleted by the Russ Meyer fiasco and the Brazilian interlude with Ronnie Biggs. Virgin were the only company that could pull him out of the hole, and it was to Virgin that McLaren now turned, cap in hand.

Richard Branson agreed to advance £200,000 to complete *The Great Rock 'n' Roll Swindle* – but on the basis that Virgin had rights not only to the film but also to recoup the money from the group's record royalties. McLaren, desperate to complete the film, had no option but to agree, thereby effectively signing away his control of the Sex Pistols' future.

He would turn this, as he turned all things, into theatre, and ultimately into myth. With great relish he would recount the story of how he had surprised Branson one morning outside his house in Denbigh Terrace. Caught him by the Arran-knit jumper, he did, and flung him against the railings, demanding money. And every week after that, he would come with a man – a big man – in a huge Mercedes, pushed all the way down Vernon Yard until the nose touched the window frames of the Virgin offices. And he and his man would take a black bin-liner and carry it upstairs and stuff it full of cash from the safe, and then carry it downstairs again on his shoulders, like Father Christmas. Six weeks this went on! Six weeks!

And forever afterwards, Richard Branson would blink and smile and say that, actually, he could not remember the incident personally and perhaps Malcolm was imagining it. And no one at Virgin could ever be found to confirm it. But it was a good yarn, just the same.

Throughout his trials with the Sex Pistols, Richard Branson had been engaged in another, even more delicate negotiation, one which promised, at last, to provide the antidote to the enduring unhappiness over his broken marriage.

It was a coincidence that, once again, Branson should have met the object of his romantic attentions at the Manor, early in 1976. The girl he had fallen in love with was named Joan Templeman. They were not, on the face of it, a likely match. Quite apart from the Pre-Raphaelite blond ringlets and blue eyes which immediately, and utterly, transfixed Branson, Joan Templeman had an air of self-contained, utterly unflappable Glaswegian common sense. Thirty years old – five years older than Richard – she carried the unmistakable air of not being easily impressed by anything, or anyone. Furthermore, she was happily married. Indeed, at the very moment at which Branson now engaged her in conversation in the Manor kitchen, her husband, Ronnie Leahy, was working in the studio next door, producing a Virgin group called Wigwam.

Joan Templeman was born and grew up in Glasgow, the daughter of a carpenter, and one of six children. In 1966 she met Ronnie Leahy, a respected musician who, for many years, played the keyboards for a Glaswegian group called Stone the Crows. Marriage to Leahy had had its ups and downs, of course; but Joan was not of a nature to play anybody false. She was not interested in Richard Branson; not interested in anybody.

A week later, however, when Branson walked into the

shop close to the Virgin offices in Portobello Road where Joan worked, selling Victorian advertising ephemera, and invited her to lunch, she accepted. He took her to his own restaurant, Duveens.

From that moment on, Richard wooed Joan with all the single-minded persistence of a deal to be clinched. Whenever her husband was away, he pressed dinner invitations on her, always in the company of friends, and thereby immune to suggestion of danger. He appeared regularly in the shop, invariably walking out with yet another purchase for which he had scant use. His Denbigh Terrace home became a shrine of tin signs advertising elixirs, tobaccos and teas.

Everywhere Joan went, Richard would appear, tipped off by mutual friends in Virgin, among whom he acquired the nickname Tag – after his constant request, 'What are you doing tonight? Seeing Joan? Mind if I tag along?'

Joan's friends did not regard Branson as a particularly eligible figure. Enforced bachelorhood had left him unkempt and ill-groomed. Sartorially, he had still to progress from desert boots to Kickers. Years of social discourse appeared to have done little to relieve his prevailing impression of awkwardness and unease, his inability to small-talk. His determination to impress Joan, to win her, made him even more tongue-tied; his usual conversational gambit was to shift from foot to foot and laugh a great deal. Joan's Scottish fluency was sufficient to fill the spaces for two.

It was a complement of total opposites. While Richard is keen on sport, Joan is utterly indifferent to it. He is intensely competitive, she is not. While he manifested his inner restlessness in a constant repertoire of ticks, gestures and an impression of perpetual motion, she radiated a stolid sense of calm. Joan's great skill, then as now, was not to be nonplussed by anything Richard did. They became the best of friends and, at length, lovers.

From the outset, Richard had said he would never encourage Joan to leave her husband; he knew the pain which a broken marriage could cause. But as the relationship deepened, so a separation between she and her husband came to seem inevitable. For some months, Joan moved in some indecision between her home and Richard's. At the beginning of 1978, she went with Ronnie to Los Angeles, where he was working with Donovan. Unbeknown to Joan, her husband had contacted Richard with a plea, 'Give me three months alone with Joan. Don't contact her, don't telephone her. And if she still wants to go with you after three months, you have my blessing.'

After two weeks in Los Angeles, Joan telephoned Richard. The bargain had evaporated. The next day she flew to New York, to join him, for good.

While Joan Templeman was in Los Angeles with her husband, playing out the last days of her marriage, Richard Branson was in Jamaica, doing business.

Virgin had been dabbling in West Indian music for three years, and again it was Chris Blackwell and Island who had been the inspiration for Virgin's involvement. Since founding Island, Blackwell had championed the cause of Jamaican music – in its different guises of ska, rock-steady, then reggae – almost single-handedly in Britain, enjoying intermittent success with artists like Millie, Jimmy Cliff and Bob and Marcia. But with Bob Marley, Blackwell at last found the performer who could escape the 'ghettoisation' to which Jamaican music had always been subjected. Marley had a revolutionary's zeal and a charismatic presence which made him an intensely romantic figure not only to the young blacks whose predicament he articulated, but also to the white rock audience. True to historical precedent, it required a white rock musician to have a hit with a black man's song – in this case Eric Clapton with 'I Shot the Sheriff' – before the breakthrough could occur; but at length Bob Marley became the first reggae superstar.

Other record companies looked enviously at Island's success – none more so than Virgin. As two independent companies, now of roughly equivalent size, they felt both a spiritual bond against the major companies such as EMI and Warners and also a natural sense of rivalry. The arrangement whereby Island pressed and distributed Virgin records had sometimes come under strain, with Virgin accusing Island of putting their own product first. To Branson, Chris Blackwell had always been something of a role-model – someone whose achievements were to be emulated, but also surpassed. If Island were having hits with reggae music, Virgin should be too.

In 1975, Branson went on an exploratory trip to Jamaica with his lawyer and friend Charles Levison. Levison had worked for Blackwell, too, and knew the Caribbean well. Branson's principal target was Peter Tosh, who had sung with Bob Marley in the Wailers. Tosh had a reputation for being difficult. According to local rumour, he had once threatened Chris Blackwell with a machete. The fact that the rumour had probably been planted by Tosh himself did nothing to diminish his fearful aspect. He treated Richard Branson with imperious disdain; twice inviting him to his home, and being pointedly out on both occasions; then declining to share his torpedo-sized spliffs when a meeting was at last arranged. He did, however, sign for Virgin, and his first solo album, *Legalize It*, was released in 1976.

But Peter Tosh did not become the superstar to challenge Bob Marley. By the time the Sex Pistols had arrived on Virgin, the initial enthusiasm for reggae among those running the label had begun to wane, but it was suddenly revived by an intriguing, and wholly unexpected, business opportunity. Towards the end of 1977, 'Greek Chris' Stylianou, Virgin's exports manager, suddenly noticed an upsurge of orders for reggae records for export to Nigeria. Quite why this should have occurred nobody could explain, but Nigerian audiences had developed a particular liking for Jamaican 'toasters' – disc-jockeys who usurped the role of singers by half scatting, half shouting over backing tracks in a style half mystical, half political, but wholly saleable. U-Roy, a toaster with only a modest following in Britain, was selling 100,000 copies of each release in Lagos. Virgin even accepted an order to manufacture a consignment of eight-track tapes, long redundant in Britain, specifically for the Nigerian market.

Richard Branson's response to this curious phenomenon was immediate. Virgin needed more reggae artists to take advantage of it. There would be an expedition to Jamaica immediately. Jumbo Van Rennen, who now worked in the A&R department and was the house authority on reggae, drew up a list of all the performers in Jamaica worth auditioning or signing, and in February 1978 a small contingent from Virgin, led by Branson, flew out to Kingston. Among them was Branson's right-hand man, Ken Berry, and also John Lydon, latterly of the Sex Pistols. Branson had decided that after his experiences in America with the Pistols, Lydon needed a holiday; a keen reggae fan, he could also help on auditions. But there was another reason for his presence. Contrary to what Malcolm McLaren believed, Lydon's departure from the Sex Pistols, and the dissolution of the group, was the last thing Richard Branson wanted. It was in Virgin's interest for the Sex Pistols to continue working together with or without McLaren. There was, Branson reasoned, more money to be made from the group's longevity. He was to spend much of his time in Jamaica fruitlessly trying to persuade Lydon to rejoin the group. They arrived in a country on the brink of civil war. Jamaica was bankrupt. Imports had virtually dried up. Cigarettes, soap, even guitarstrings, could be found only on the black market. Gunshots echoed in the languid Kingston night as henchmen of the rival 'political' parties, the People's National Party and the Jamaican Labour Party, settled territorial disputes and personal scores with a startling lack of diplomacy or discrimination.

Branson and Berry had brought with them a suitcase containing several thousands of American dollars, which was carried coolly through Customs, in defiance of the local currency regulations. It was enough to buy almost every available reggae singer on the island. Court was established in the Kingston Sheraton, and an emissary named Scubba despatched to Trenchtown to seek out those artists bearing Jumbo's seal of approval. Branson interviewed them in his hotel room, to see if they wanted a deal. They always did. Berry made out a standard record contract on the hotel typewriter and ran off photocopies. Down payments were made in cash. It spilled from the safety deposit boxes and washed over the floors of the rooms. One artist concluded his deal by standing on a cardboard box full of notes while Berry taped it up.

To the majority of performers, cash advances of any

substance were a rarity, contracts a thing only of myth. The most usual way for a musician to do business in Jamaica was through a producer, who would pay the musician a nominal sum for his work and then make his own deals with record companies: a system which traditionally guaranteed disproportionately generous returns for the producer, and next to nothing for the musician. Alerted by a grapevine of unparalleled efficiency to the presence of honkies with money, hitherto undiscovered talents began swarming in from the ghettos and down from the hills, bearing tape-recordings, even guitars, for impromptu auditions. By the end of a fortnight, Branson and Berry had signed more than a dozen acts, some good, some not, and spent over 100,000 Jamaican dollars.

Branson flew to New York, to join Joan. He felt a curious mixture of elation and unease. The delight at being finally united with Joan was tempered by a feeling of discomfort about Ronnie Leahy. Branson had fully intended to keep his word on not seeing or communicating with Joan for three months. Now he had broken it. Similarly, the satisfaction he felt over the Jamaican excursion, with its intoxicating combination of deal-making, fun and the promise of profit, was somewhat dampened by the nagging uncertainty over the future of the Sex Pistols. Lydon was adamant that under no circumstances would he rejoin the group. Furthermore, twelve months of fencing with Malcolm McLaren had taken a toll on Branson's nerves. And the New Year's greeting which McLaren had sent, scrawled on Glitterbest notepaper, saying 'Happy New Year, Richard, next year will be worse . . .' was hardly reassuring.

What Branson most felt like doing was getting away. In New York, somebody asked if he had named his company after the Virgin Islands. He hadn't, but, looking at the map, Branson could see they were within striking distance. An idea began to form in his mind. He had no idea what a tropical island cost, or even whether one was available, but it would be fun to investigate. A telephone call to London found an agent who specialised in such transactions, and an appointment was made. When Branson and Joan arrived in the Virgin Islands, they were sped effortlessly through Customs, conveyed by limousine to a private villa, and a helicopter was put at their disposal. Feeling fraudulent, but enjoying himself immensely, Branson went looking for an island. There were, in fact, two to choose from, but it was Neckar Island that took Branson's eye as he circled above it. Neckar had four beautiful beaches, abundant vegetation and wildlife – but no fresh water supply. Its last human inhabitants had been two journalists, engaged on an exercise to test their powers of self-sufficiency. They had fled the island after a week, suffering from sunburn and dehydration. But as soon as he set foot on it, Branson wanted it.

Neckar Island was owned by Lord Cobham, who had never actually set foot on it himself. He was asking £3m for it. Branson offered 250,000 dollars. The helicopter and the keys to the private villa were promptly removed; Branson rode back to the airport in a taxi. Before making the offer Branson had done some homework. Through contacts in London he found out that Lord Cobham was selling the island to finance the construction of a building in London to house an educational trust; furthermore, Cobham needed the money in a hurry. But there was one major snag to Branson's plan. Under a government order to discourage land speculation, whoever bought the island would be obliged to develop it within five years. Branson had no money for development. In order to keep

177

the island he would have to raise the money and complete building within five years. It would cost millions, but it was a challenge. Shortly after arriving back in London, Branson received a telephone call: if he could raise his offer to 300,000 dollars, Neckar Island was his. He took it.

While Branson was negotiating the purchase of his Caribbean island, the living corpse of the Sex Pistols was slowly kicking itself to final, ignominious extinction. In October 1978, Sid Vicious – whom Malcolm McLaren had described as 'never seeing a green light; it was always on red' – woke up in his room in the Chelsea Hotel, New York, to find the body of his girlfriend, Nancy Spungen, sprawled on the bathroom floor, dead from multiple knife wounds. Vicious was charged with the murder, but released on bail. Four months later, on 2 February 1979, Sid Vicious finally shot one red light too many, dying from a drug overdose, naked – so the popular press reported – and in the arms of his latest girlfriend. He was twenty-one years old.

Later that month, an action began in the High Court between John Lydon and Glitterbest, in which Lydon asked the High Court to render the management agreement void and appoint a receiver to sort out the Sex Pistols' affairs and finances. Central to Lydon's action was the allegation that McLaren had signed away the group's future record royalties to Virgin in order to finance *The Great Rock 'n' Roll Swindle*. Lydon's counsel alleged that Malcolm McLaren 'regards himself as a Svengali of these people to do whatever he cares without asking anybody else'.

The court heard that the Sex Pistols had earned £880,000 in their short career. But apart from £30,000 in the Glitterbest bank account there were no other assets left, other than future income from the film and recording contracts. The official receiver was duly ordered to exploit the film. This, at length, came under the control of Virgin, as the principal British investors, and *The Great Rock 'n' Roll Swindle* became the first production of a new company, Virgin Films. John Lydon – the punk nomenclature had been banished for good – remained contracted to Virgin with his new group, Public Image Ltd (PIL), as did Paul Cook and Steve Jones, who recorded briefly under the name the Bollock Brothers. If this constituted defeat for Malcolm McLaren, it was, perhaps, only a pyrrhic victory for Richard Branson. What Branson had wanted to do, above all else, was keep the Sex Pistols together, build a future for the group. As it was, the Pistols were not together long enough, nor did they sell sufficient records, to make the profits for Virgin which Branson had always anticipated.

Virgin did, none the less, retain all rights on the Sex Pistols', and Sid Vicious's, work for the full duration of the copyright laws, to be exploited as the company saw fit. A flow of records ensued, including a posthumous Sid Vicious album, *Sid Sings*, and sundry repackagings of those few songs which the group had actually recorded, wringing the cash cow dry, as Richard Branson later pointed out with some irony, 'in just the spirit of the Swindle Malcolm had always talked about'.

Malcolm McLaren, meanwhile, was down, but not out. He assembled another group, named Bow Wow Wow, and, again with some help from Jamie Reid, launched them as 'pirates' with a campaign in support of home-taping – which the record industry was then spending thousands of pounds declaring was 'killing music'. Bow Wow Wow did not repeat the success of the Sex Pistols.

However, in 1983, McLaren became a recording artist himself, producing an album called *Duck Rock*, which plagiarised, and brilliantly synthesised, African music and American rap and hip-hop to create a best-selling pop record. McLaren recorded *Duck Rock* for a small, independent record label called Charisma. A year later, he produced a second album, *Fans*, which did for – or unto – opera what *Duck Rock* had done for ethnic music. By then, Charisma, and the rights to Malcolm McLaren, had been sold to another British record company. In his capacity as a recording artist, McLaren visited the offices of his new holding company, and was ushered in to meet the chairman of the board as he rose from behind his desk. 'Hello again, Malcolm,' said Richard Branson.

Chapter 8

Growing Pains

In the Christmas of 1979, Richard Branson took a holiday from Virgin to go ski-ing in the Colorado resort of Aspen. The location aside, it was a holiday much like many others which Branson had taken in recent years: the party of friends consisted almost exclusively of Virgin employees – Simon Draper, Nik Powell, Ken Berry. As in previous years, the resolutions not to discuss business (it carried the threat of a fine) gave way early on the first evening. In between carousing down the powdery slopes, Branson and his colleagues could take stock of an empire that had grown almost beyond recognition in the last six years.

Virgin Records was no longer the small, struggling outsider with only a handful of artists, but an established and thriving company, vying competitively with the likes of Island and Chrysalis – and, what's more, they now had a newly-established office in America.

Virgin retail was among the top three record-shop chains in Britain, with shops in almost every major town and plans to develop a new concept in record retailing, a 'megastore', in Oxford Street, close by the site of the first ever Virgin shop. While barely profitable, retail continued to be a useful source of ready cash.

The studio division had also grown. As well as the Manor, there was now a mobile studio – the Manor Mobile – and a studio complex in West London, opened in 1978, called the Townhouse. All boasted the finest state-of-the-art recording equipment – a development largely afforded by having taken advantage of the Government's 100 per cent tax allowance on any equipment investment. To Branson, paying tax was 'a waste of money' when you could plough that money back into the company.

The music publishing company was also showing a healthy profit, particularly with the coming success of a young Newcastle songwriter, contracted to the company under the name of Gordon Sumner, but better known to the record-buying public as Sting. He had been discovered and signed to Virgin Publishing by a girl named Carol Wilson.

There was now a modest book-publishing division, concentrating mostly on pop music books. Acquiring the rights to *The Great Rock 'n' Roll Swindle* had led to the formation of what was grandly called the Film Division – although that was the only film yet within its compass. Virgin had also bought a London cinema, the Scala, specialising in 'art house' films; and a video-editing suite, called Off Line – both of which had become the particular interest of Nik Powell. It was also at Powell's suggestion that an old cinema had been acquired in Victoria, and turned, at considerable expense, into a nightclub-cum-concert hall, modelled on the Bottom Line Club in New York. The Venue, as it was called, opened on Halloween night, 1978, after a minor crisis involving fire-officers refusing to grant the appropriate permits. They relented only when Branson, who had spent three

1 Eve Huntley-Flindt, dancer, actress and pioneer of the Atlantic air routes, who stole Edward Branson's heart

2 On holiday at his grandparents' farm in Devon, the two-year-old Richard Branson takes the first steps up the ladder of success

3 A childhood that was happy and secure: Edward and Eve Branson, with Richard and eldest sister Lindi

4   Sports Day at Scaitcliffe School: a new harvest of cups for the family sideboard

5   Richard Branson, the new boy at Stowe

6   On holiday in Minorca at the age of fifteen, with sisters Lindi and Vanessa

7 Leading a post-mortem on the first issue of *Student*, in January 1968 in the basement at Connaught Square

8 Lying down in protest outside the American Embassy in Grosvenor Square, thankful that President Johnson had not, after all, wished *Student* good luck

9 & 10   In the *Student* offices, and up on the roof, at Albion Street. 'I'm Richard Branson, I'm eighteen and I run a magazine that's doing something really useful for young people'

11 The Manor House, Shipton: bought for
£30,000 in 1971, it became first of a chain of
Virgin studios

12 Marriage to Kristen Tomassi in July 1972

13 The 'Earl's Court Hippies' celebrate Richard's wedding to Kristen Tomassi.
From left: Tom Newman, Mike Armstrong, Christopher Strangeways, Simon Draper, Nik Powell and Chris Stylianou

14 Nik Powell and Richard were best man at each other's weddings, and the best of friends, until their partnership ended in 1981. Here they are at Nik's wedding

15 Branson with Mike Oldfield, the erstwhile boy-wonder on whom Virgin's first fortune had been built, at the opening of Mike Oldfield's personal Video Studio, 1985

16 Gong: champions of the Flying Teapot and the last vestiges of recherché hippie chic, to be swept aside by the onset of punk

17 An exquisite chemistry of individuals: The Sex Pistols – Sid Vicious, Steve Jones, Johnny Rotten and Paul Cook – think of England in the year of the Queen's Silver Jubilee

18 & 19 Incongruous partners in crime: Malcom McLaren, The Sex Pistols' Svengali, would-be Situationist and 'The Swindler', waged a war of wits and nerve against Branson, toasting the success of the first Pistols' album

sleepless nights preparing the club for opening, burst into tears of frustration.

And there was, at the empire's furthest perimeters, a Virgin island. The principal source of finance for all of this remained the record company. The Sex Pistols had, in part, achieved what Branson had expected of them. They had not reaped the fortune he hoped for – they had not become 'the new Rolling Stones'; but the signing had the required effect of shaking Virgin out of the torpor of the mid-Seventies. It turned the attention, and the skills, of those within the company to the younger, singles-buying music audience, and it attracted a different kind of group to the label. In one fell swoop, Virgin had acquired that most elusive of qualities, 'street credibility'; the company roster now boasted groups like Magazine, Penetration, the Members, the Skids – what was becoming known as New Wave, a marketing term used to denote almost any performer that had emerged in the aftermath of punk who did not spit in his audience's eye.

Indeed, in 1979, Virgin enjoyed its most successful year ever on the singles charts, with the Skids alone providing five consecutive hits in the Top Fifty. But it was a success that flattered to deceive. Album sales were poor. And the worst was yet to come.

The record industry in both Britain and America had gone into a worldwide recession, and Virgin were as vulnerable to its effects as anybody else. In Britain, sales of long-players dropped from 107.2m in 1978 to 92.6m in 1980. Sales of singles dropped from 88.8m to 77.8m. To a large extent, the decline was a measure of the degree to which record sales are susceptible to inflation: in times of rising prices, and tightening purses, luxury items like recorded music are among the first things people stop buying. In 1976, inflation stood at 23 per cent. By 1978, it had dropped to 8.3 per cent. But in 1979, it rose again to 13.4 per cent and in 1980 to 18 per cent. The recording industry reacted with barometric sensitivity. Pre-tax profits on UK sales for the entire industry, which had stood at 8 per cent in 1978, dropped to zero in 1979. By 1980, the industry as a whole was registering a 2 per cent loss; by 1981, a 3 per cent loss.

But if the decline reflected prevailing economic conditions, it also reflected pop music's own failure to produce records that people wanted to buy. Punk rock had had a purging effect on pop music; clearing out the old to make way for the new. Yet none of the vanguard punk groups had enjoyed significant – and, more crucially, long-standing – commercial success, not even the Sex Pistols. More importantly, punk had made a negligible impression in America, the world's largest market, where 50 per cent of all records are sold.

Virgin had long struggled to make an inroad into the American market. Ever since 1974, when Mike Oldfield's *Tubular Bells* topped the American charts, Virgin had struggled in vain to gain a foothold in that country – 'karmic retribution', as Nik Powell had it, for Virgin having reached Number One with its first ever release. Some Virgin records had continued to be released in America through licensing arrangements with Atlantic and CBS. But Branson always regarded licensing deals as unsatisfactory; in the first place, the licensee could pick and choose which records it wanted to release, and did not always have the 'emotional commitment' to making them hits. Branson and Draper were convinced that this was why acts like Oldfield and Tangerine Dream, who had been phenomenally successful in Europe, had not fared so well in America. More importantly to Branson, it meant Virgin were on a far smaller margin of any profit. Under a licensing arrangement, Virgin would receive a cash advance from the American licensee, deductible from royalties, and then only 15–18 per cent of the price of all records sold. If they were to set up their own company in America instead, and negotiate a distribution deal with an American major – just as they had done with Island when first setting up Virgin – then that profit margin could be inflated from around 18 per cent to 80 per cent. The knowledge that the larger margin was there for the taking, if you were bold enough to seize it, exercised him as much now as it had done back in 1973.

So it was that late in 1978 Ken Berry was sent to set up Virgin America. In a further echo of that first contract with Island, Branson bought the New York house of Island's managing director Chris Blackwell – a charming brownstone on Perry Street, in Greenwich Village – to use as offices.

But the American adventure proved a costly failure. Branson had not anticipated the difficulty in gaining a foothold in the American market, nor the expense. Promotional costs on Virgin's first single release alone on the new label came to around $50,000 – and it flopped; an omen of things to come. At a time when America's interest in British pop was at an all-time low, the label failed to produce one significant hit. In 1980, the office was closed, at a cost of more than £0.5m. It would be another six years before a Virgin office would open in America again. Before leaving New York, Ken Berry visited 'Black Rock', the towerblock offices of CBS, the world's largest record company, to reopen licensing discussions. With a heavy heart, Berry sat in an ante-room watching as a stream of employees were called in to be given their pink dismissal slips. It was a prophetic scene.

The recession abruptly derailed the gravy train on

which most in the record industry had ridden through the 1970s; the generous salaries, inflated expenses and trans-continental junkets. Virgin had never had the profits to squander. In 1977, Virgin recorded a profit of just £400,000. In 1978, that rose to £500,000. Salaries had never been comparable with others in the record industry; the smaller, more agreeable, 'cottage industry' atmos-phere of the company had always been held up as compensation for a parsimonious attitude to wages. Working for Virgin was fun, in a way in which working for a large, anonymous corporation such as EMI or CBS could never be. And if it entailed a degree of sacrifice, there was always the prospect of better times, just around the corner. Now it seemed as if they were postponed indefinitely. In 1980, Virgin's expansion ground to a sudden halt, as their bank, Coutts, put their foot on the brake, signalling what would develop, in the coming years, into a major crisis over banking. Since 1973, Coutts' support of Virgin had been pivoted on the cash-flow generated by *Tubular Bells*. The steady flow of money from record sales and overseas royalties had meant that Virgin had not made great demands on their overdraft facility. Whenever Coutts requested restraint, Virgin had somehow been able to achieve it. But with the industry in recession, and record sales dropping, the hitherto dependable cashflow was trickling down at an alarming rate. Furthermore, Coutts themselves were undergoing a change in policy, consolidating their busi-ness around the wealthy personal customer and shedding some of their 'high-risk' business accounts. A request by Branson for Virgin's overdraft to be extended to £3m to allow normal trading to continue was met with prevarica-tion. Coutts wanted more evidence of financial controls, 'restraint'. In an attempt to swell the accounts, Branson desperately began to call in money from abroad. The 10 × 8 notebooks, which balanced habitually on his knee or beside the telephone, and in which he scribbled details of conversations, contracts, memos to himself, became increasingly filled with lists of monies owing, from foreign licensees, publishing, club takings – a barometer of his mounting sense of urgency: 'Germany, £200,000 in deutschmarks in banking system, on way; France, £50,000 coming later this month; Portugal, £20,000 coming 14 June; Australia, 25,000 Australian dollars coming next Friday.'

In a move to consolidate the company assets, the Manor, the various office properties throughout West London and the Virgin island were revalued. Branson had already moved home, and office, to a new houseboat, the *Duende*: now the Denbigh Terrace house was sold, along with two flats in Vernon Yard and a shop in Brent Cross. The rights to all Virgin music publishing in America were extended to the licensee, Chappell Music, for a further £0.5m advance. It was like selling the family silver, but Branson believed it was necessary to maintain ownership of the family home. The one thing he always refused to consider at any time of financial uncertainty was selling any of his personal shareholding in Virgin.

As had become customary in times of financial uncertainty, Nik Powell took it upon himself to 'sort out' the accounts, as he had sorted out so much over the years, from feuding gangs in Bold Street to disruptive bank managers. Powell was the nearest thing to an orthodox businessman to be found in the Virgin offices, with an understanding of business techniques and practices – and no little amounts of jargon – studiously drawn from the American magazines to which he subscribed. It was Powell who took care of the necessary details that

Branson was too impatient to deal with – accounting, credit controls, job descriptions, compliance with Acts. Now Powell outlined a way of cutting the wages bill by almost £1m, through 'natural wastage', pay freezes but also, for the first time in Virgin's history, through redundancies. Branson and Draper drew up a list of twelve people – almost a fifth of the staff employed in the record company, Branson telling himself, with little conviction, that 'people will understand'. But people, of course, did not. The effect within Vernon Yard was one of complete shellshock. 'Nobody really knew what to do in that situation,' says Ken Berry. 'The whole Virgin approach had been that you simply don't fire people.' The number of people laid off was proportionately less than from some other record companies. But for a company which had always prided itself on its 'family' aspect it was a significant blow.

Nor was the record roster to be spared. Artists whose presence on the label was predicated on success in America were dropped, their advances written off to experience. Kevin Coyne, the longest-standing Virgin artist after Mike Oldfield, was also dropped. Virtually the entire complement of reggae artists, signed in the tropical heat of optimism eighteen months before, were dropped. The Nigerian adventure had come to an abrupt end with the arrival of a new military government and a ban on all imports.

Branson was pragmatic about the cutbacks. Pruning, he argued, was an essential part of the record business. 'You must cut your lossmakers, because they'll drain the company and ultimately bankrupt it. Sometimes a crisis focuses the attention far better than if you're doing well. You reevaluate your strengths and start again.'

Importantly, it also gave Simon Draper a chance to

start planning for the future. In September 1980 he had paid £65,000 for the British rights to the release of the first solo record by Phil Collins, the drummer from Genesis. It was an unprecedented sum for a solo album by a drummer, but Draper told his doubting colleagues that he was confident Virgin would see a return on its investment.

In pressing for cutbacks, Nik Powell also urged Draper to drop a group called the Human League from the roster. The Human League represented the coming vogue; a young group from Sheffield, much more accomplished in matters of style, presentation and business than in music, with an as yet barely formed talent for playing synthesisers. They had made one album, which had failed, partly, it was felt within the company, because they had thrown away the chance of a prestigious tour, supporting Talking Heads, by their novel plan to simply switch on their machines and tape-recorders and then sit in the auditorium with the audience and watch the show themselves. Powell believed they were a luxury Virgin could ill-afford. Draper insisted they should be retained. There was a heated argument between the two men which at length it fell to Branson to settle. Branson sided with Draper. If Simon wants to keep the Human League, he said, then he should keep them. It was a vote of faith in Draper's musical judgement rather than a demonstration of Branson's own, but the decision was the right one. The next Human League album, *Dare*, sold more than two million copies and was a major factor in digging Virgin out of its parlous financial state.

The incident was a small measure of how the balance of power, and relevance, within Virgin had shifted. As the record company, and its revenue from worldwide licensing deals, became more important, so Branson spent more time with Simon Draper and less and less with Nik Powell. No longer privy to Branson's innermost thoughts – and frequently in disagreement with them when he was – Powell's influence within Virgin began to diminish. His cautious and methodical ways, once so valuable a buffer to Richard's impetuosity, now became more and more a cause of annoyance. As Virgin's accountant, Jack Claydon, observed, Branson's attitude was to be looking ahead all the time. 'If something was a loss, he wasn't really concerned with that; somebody else could clear that up – he was already on to the next thing. He was not reckless exactly, but he certainly never stopped to consider whether that loss was too great to hamper expansion. He just got on with expansion.'

To Branson this embodied a business principle of disarming simplicity: some people, when they are in trouble, cut back and back and back until they have nothing left. The other approach is to expand. It was this principle which had saved Virgin from collapse in the wake of the Customs and Excise fine ten years before; it was the principle, Branson believed, that would now secure the company's future.

In 1981, the Virgin empire was, therefore, swollen yet further with the purchase of two more nightclubs, one called the Roof Gardens, the other, Heaven, purchased with the help of loans from the bank and monies from a foreign licensee.

The Roof Gardens had some claim to being a London landmark. Sited on the top floor of a department store in Kensington High Street, the principal feature of the club was the gardens, which had been planted, literally on the roof, some fifty years before, and grown in prodigious abundance. Formerly Derry & Toms, in the late Sixties the building became Biba's, a fashionable boutique of the day; in the Seventies, the roof club became Regine's, a watering hole of the internationally rich and idle. When, in the manner of migratory buffalo, they moved elsewhere, its owner, an Indian businessman named Ram, who had spent £2m refurbishing the club, looked for a quick sale. Branson bought it for £400,000.

The purchase of Heaven elevated eyebrows parallel to hairlines in Coutts, not least because Heaven was London's largest, and most popular, club for homosexuals. The proposal came through Branson's youngest sister, Vanessa, who had recently gone into business as an art-dealer. An artist friend wanted to sell his 50 per cent shareholding, and the second partner was open to persuasion. Branson made his way to the club – situated, by a felicitous coincidence, directly opposite Coutts's head office in the Strand – and wandered beneath the flashing strobe-lights, more fascinated than intimidated by the spectacle of 1,500 moustachioed, bejeaned and leather-clad males gyrating to the strains of 'I Want a Man'. Other businessmen, he knew, might have made their excuses and left, worried about the effect of such a purchase on their bankers, their colleagues, the City. But Branson felt quite the reverse.

Branson's awareness of homosexuality had broadened gradually. There had been homosexual behaviour at Stowe – as at most British public schools – but Branson had not participated. When running the Student Advisory Centre, he had taken telephone calls from homosexuals, assuming at first that they wished to be 'cured'. He had quickly discovered that this was not the case; the biggest problem facing gay people was the attitude of 'straight' people, and the difficulty of meeting others of like mind. It was obvious to Branson that Heaven was providing that meeting-place. Nor did it escape his attention that as well as its social role Heaven also gave access to a large group of demonstrably big spenders. To any businessman, the 'pink economy' constituted a sound investment. Branson bought Heaven for £500,000.

The acquisition of the clubs only served to inflame the disagreements between Branson and Nik Powell. Powell felt both clubs were impetuous buys which Virgin could ill-afford at a time when it was struggling out of recession. Branson, he argued, was attempting to expand at a faster rate than the resources of the company allowed. There were too many ventures for the existing management resources and expertise within the company; existing projects should become profitable before yet more were added. Board meetings grew ever more vociferous and anguished. To Branson, arguments had never been a symptom of animosity; rather, he and Powell had always argued 'like a married couple, knowing you could shout at each other and it wouldn't matter'. Sometimes one or other would misuse that privilege and perhaps shout more than was otherwise seemly, 'but the fact that we'd grown up together meant we could have our rows and know that the next day one of us would apologise, and it would all be forgotten'.

To Simon Draper, Ken Berry and the other Virgin directors, however, it was apparent that the rift was becoming unbridgeable. 'Nik didn't want to be Richard's yes-man in the company,' says Berry, 'and, frankly, he was the only person in the company with the position to be anything other than Richard's yes-man. They were just banging heads constantly. Richard was getting impatient with Nik, Nik annoyed with Richard, and everybody else was sitting around saying, What can we do about this? Nothing . . .'

At length, the dilemma was resolved in the way everybody recognised as inevitable: the marriage contract was torn up. Powell drafted a letter to Branson, laying out his areas of disagreement over company policy and raising the consideration of whether they should go forward together. Branson wrote to Powell, agreeing that the time had come for a separation. Over lunch at the Roof Gardens, an agreement was drawn up for the purchase of Powell's share in Virgin, giving him one million pounds, the Scala cinema and the video-editing suites. From these elements, Powell went on to found Palace Pictures, initially distributing videos and films, then moving into production through such films as *Mona Lisa, Company of Wolves* and *Absolute Beginners*. On the last – as on several other projects – Palace actually collaborated with Virgin, although Powell and Branson would seldom discuss these ventures personally. While their relationship managed to remain friendly they saw each other less and less in the years to come.

After ten years in partnership, Nik Powell vacated his office at Virgin in less than twenty-four hours, and Richard Branson was on his own.

The rapid expansion of the Virgin empire added fuel to the view commonly held within the music industry that Richard Branson was an ambitious, clever, acquisitive and highly idiosyncratic maverick. The withering epithet of Virgin as 'Earl's Court Hippies' was now forgotten. Yet it was clear that Branson was not properly a creature of the industry in the manner of his contemporaries. Most record-company chiefs had risen to their position by one of two ways; either they were 'record men' born and bred, who by their own taste and judgement had quietly built their own companies, or had risen through the sales and marketing ranks of some multinational to positions of prominence; or they were lawyers or accountants, practised in the art of negotiation and creative bookkeeping. Branson was neither. He was interested in the music industry only insofar as it affected Virgin. He was seldom to be found at meetings of the BPI, the industry's body, or glad-handing at functions among bowtie- and cumberbund-wearers. Some might remark disparagingly on Branson's lack of clubbishness; but most respected him, as one rival put it, 'as a successful predatory animal in the music business jungle'. In fact, Branson's almost total lack of interest in music had been an advantage. Had he been, say, Chris Blackwell at Island, he might have invested money in idiosyncratic musical favourites, to the detriment of the company's commercial fortunes. But Branson was not interested in being a gardener for art; he was interested in being successful. He was happy to let Draper make the creative decisions.

Branson was not a record man, he was an entrepreneur; and it was clear that what he wanted out of the record business were new and different opportunities. So it was that as March 1981 drew to a close, Branson telephoned Rodney Birbeck, the editor of *Music Week* – the trade 'Bible' of the British record industry – and invited him to lunch. Birbeck was surprised. His sober, professional and dependable manner, as much as his editorial position, had put him on good terms with most managing directors of most record companies, but his contacts with Branson – while always cordial – had been few. Now, as he pushed open the wooden gate leading to Branson's houseboat, and threaded his way down the overgrown towpath, Birbeck surmised that something big must be on the agenda. Just how big, he was astonished to hear.

Manoeuvring down the narrow steps into the boat, and

turning into the airy and deceptively spacious lounge, Birbeck was greeted by Branson and Al Clark, Virgin's laconic press officer, poring over a mass of paperwork. The scheme which Branson spelt out over lunch was indeed revolutionary. Virgin, he said, were planning something which would effectively wipe out the manufacture of records, tapes and home hi-fis – direct cable music. The Music Box system, as it was called, would consist of four central computer terminals, located in different parts of the country, on which would be stored every single and album ever released in Britain. Subscribers to the service required only a cable line, an amplifier, a pair of speakers and a computer pad, on which to tap out the number of their choice. Subscribers would pay a flat charge each month and receive a catalogue of available music, constantly updated. 'It beats *buying* records, eh, Rodney?' laughed Branson.

Birbeck was stunned. The scheme Branson was outlining would, Birbeck knew, effectively mean the end of the record industry as he, and anybody else, recognised it. The implications were almost too enormous to contemplate. So enormous it couldn't possibly be true – could it? In front of him, Branson was earnestly shuffling through a detailed prospectus. 'Where is the money coming from?' asked Birbeck. Branson pulled out a file and handed it to Birbeck; inside was correspondence from banks outlining weeks of discussion over preliminary financing. Of course, Branson explained, the whole scheme would be in profit very quickly: the real bonus was that under the regulations governing hospital radio, which is also transmitted by cable, Music Box would not actually be legally obliged to pay any of the standard performers' royalties. 'But we'll be prepared to give the artist something, of course,' Branson added expansively.

Birbeck reeled out into the daylight, bemused and shocked. The idea was utterly outrageous, yet also highly feasible. Cable was, after all, the buzzword of the moment in the quality newspapers; the future, it was said, of broadcasting. Among the *Music Week* staff, the general consensus was that the scheme was simply too astonishing to be true. And the more Birbeck thought of it, the clearer it became. Of course, it couldn't be true. Could it? The next day, he telephoned Al Clark, asking that *Music Week* be let in on the joke. But Clark was unequivocal when he returned the call. Richard, he said, was deeply offended that anyone should think he would lower himself to the depths of duping the editor of *Music Week*. The story was 'totally one hundred per cent'.

It duly appeared on the front cover of *Music Week* the following week: BRANSON BOMBSHELL: VIRGIN CHIEF SEEKS £20M CITY BACKING TO PUT CABLE MUSIC INTO MILLIONS OF HOMES. Astute readers might also have found a small note, placed in the magazine's gossip column, referring to the front page story and reminding readers that it was 1 April – placed there by Birbeck as a precautionary measure. But not everybody read that far. In the plush chrome and buttoned-leather offices of the record industry the story was greeted by the sound of jaws dropping incredulously. That morning Branson was inundated by telephone calls from his colleagues, accusing him of plotting to destroy them. Warner Brothers immediately set in motion its own research programme to explore the feasibility of the idea; it would run for some months before anyone realised it had been an April Fool and abandoned their research. Capital Radio offered free Music Box equipment to the first one thousand callers, and were also inundated with calls. The following day, Virgin received its first order for Music Box, from Nigeria.

Rodney Birbeck was less amused. He felt that his trust and position had been taken advantage of: that he had been made to look a fool. The dozen bottles of champagne which Branson sent, with a note 'Sorry, I had to do it', were returned to him.

Birbeck believed that Branson had played the joke as 'revenge' for a *Music Week* reporter feeding stories disparaging Branson to the satirical magazine *Private Eye* – and he was partly right. *Private Eye* was indeed an extremely sore point with Branson. The magazine had first taken note of him in his *Student* whiz-kid incarnation, when Branson had appeared in a BBC documentary entitled *Men of the Future*. Inevitably, it had been parodied in the *Eye* as *Men of the Past*, awakening in Branson the first stirrings of what became a lasting sensitivity to adverse publicity. For days afterwards, he was unable to make a telephone call without imagining he was being laughed at on the other end of the line. Lord Gnome had returned to Branson intermittently over the years, christening him 'a reptilian little shit' in stories which Branson always maintained were 'inaccuracies'. Rightly or wrongly, Branson suspected that a *Music Week* reporter had been the source of some stories (others, he suspected, had been planted by John Varnom). And revenge had been in his mind when playing the joke on *Music Week*. It was the reason he had poured so much effort, care and attention into ensuring the joke's success.

But revenge was not the whole motive: without it, the joke might have been cheaper, less elaborate, of a different kind – but there would probably have been a joke of some kind. Branson held no grudge against Rodney Birbeck. Quite the opposite. He thought Birbeck scrupulous and likeable. But the fact was that when it came to practical jokes, he regarded anybody as fair game, from the most fleeting acquaintance to the dearest friend. This was Richard Branson in his manifestation as cheerleader – a manifestation which some found charming and amusing; others intensely tiresome. It was the Richard Branson that would throw anybody in a swimming-pool – literally and metaphorically – often forgetful of the cost, be it of a junior employee's ruined wristwatch or an editor's dignity (the watch could be paid for afterwards: dignity was harder to repair); the Richard Branson that, when playing wicket-keeper in a company cricket match, would tie cotton round the bails and then 'when the batsman has been in long enough' yank them off with a roar of laughter, all the more resounding for the look of fury on the fallguy's face. Revenge was seldom, if ever, the motive in these pranks. It was Branson, the eternal child, wielding a pin at the balloon of grown-up dignity.

This may be regarded as the chairman exercising his prerogative to amuse himself; yet it is also governed by a simple and earnest desire to amuse others. It is Eve's imprecations to 'Do a turn, Ricky'. Something else which is expected of him; the most curious manifestation of *noblesse oblige*. As the host of a party, he says, you have a responsibility to amuse. And it is a characteristic of Richard Branson that wherever he is, he regards it as a party, and has usually done his best to make it such by the addition of as many people as possible. 'If there are four people in a car, Richard will always try to make it six,' says one friend. 'If he is going on holiday, the first question is "How many people can we fit in the villa?" '

This attitude became institutionalised in Virgin through the ritual of the staff outing, in which the company would take over some holiday hotel for three or four days of high jinks. This usually entailed Branson being the first to let off fire-extinguishers, initiate a food fight, or dress up in fishnet stockings and make-up for the inevitable fancy-dress party. Older, and more knowing, Virgin hands, seasoned veterans of countless swimming-pool duckings, kept their distance; but as a way of fostering a sense of belonging among staff these outings proved a powerful catalyst.

Virgin had, to a large extent, been built on Branson's abilities at man-management and manipulation – his unrivalled capacity, as one friend put it, 'to get people to do things for him, and feel that *they* are the ones who have been done a favour'. Staff accepted lower wages because Virgin seemed to be a more agreeable place to work than anywhere else in the record industry. Life was not hidebound by rules or convention. The sense of hierarchy was so subtle as to be almost non-existent. No one spoke about 'management'; it was simply Richard, Simon and Ken. Staff could feel, in that all-purpose adjective, 'involved'.

The record industry is a notoriously chauvinistic business, but almost from the outset women had been put into positions of power and seniority at Virgin. Barbara Jeffries had gone from managing the Manor to running the entire Studio Division. Women headed the International department; Sales; Production; Marketing; Promotion; Music Publishing. Carol Wilson, who had joined in Music Publishing and signed Sting's songwriting to the company (but not Sting as an artist) had developed her own label, DinDisc, under the Virgin umbrella, which in 1980 gave the company one of its best-selling artists, Orchestral Manoeuvres in the Dark. Some argued that 'equal opportunity' in this case was simply another illustration of Richard's entrepreneurial canniness. 'The theory we all had was that Richard knew very well that women worked twice as hard for half the price,' as one girl put it. But the fact remained that there were more women in positions of authority in Virgin than anywhere else in the record industry. The fact also remained that almost *everybody* in Virgin worked twice as hard for half the price.

In part, the atmosphere of almost wilful asceticism – a stoic sense of 'doing without' – that permeated the company grew unconsciously from Branson himself. His almost total indifference to the trappings of conspicuous wealth or consumption proved a subtle, yet powerful, role-model, and a disincentive to the usual gripes about status and salary. Virgin took its tone from Branson's unkempt appearance, his apparent indifference to material luxuries, the fact that his money went not towards Savile Row suits or extravagant limousines but back into the company. If Richard drove a beaten-up car, it seemed that nobody could reasonably ask for anything more themselves.

Even as the company got bigger, the familial atmosphere on which Virgin had been built in the early Seventies stayed strong, a flame that was kept alight by those who had been with Virgin since the earliest days, until it became a myth, self-perpetuating and strong enough to touch any newcomer to the organisation, strong enough to have even Richard Branson in its grip. Long after Branson had moved his office to the houseboat *Duende* and was seldom to be seen by most of the Virgin staff; long after he had ceased to know everyone by name, or even by sight, Branson himself would continue to refer to a special Virgin 'atmosphere', barely perceivable to the outside world.

Branson's readiness to delegate responsibility and encourage people in tasks for which they had no particular qualification had been important in determining the mood of the company. By turning record-packers into talent scouts, magazine salesmen into managers, Branson had paid them the compliment of saying 'I trust you'. And that trust was invariably repaid with a fierce loyalty – if not always love – to Branson himself, and to the company. Branson ignored the conventional wisdom that you do not bring friends into business, or business into friendship, and over the years there grew up around him a circle of trusted friends and advisers in the company. Those who had somehow violated the bond of trust, friendship, loyalty – for reasons they may not always be able to discern – could find themselves suddenly and inexplicably cast out into the cold. Some left, complaining that Branson demanded their soul as well as their time. Those who remained loyal could expect to be generously rewarded, in position if not always in money. With the eventual departure of Nik Powell, the inner core was built around Branson, Draper and Berry – a triumvirate whose similarity in medium-length haircuts, corduroy trousers and comfortable sweaters could, on occasion, make them look almost like brothers.

For a trusted confidant contemplating moving on, Branson could go to considerable lengths of generosity, flattery or playfulness to persuade them to stay. When, in 1978, after four years with the company, Al Clark presented himself in Branson's office to announce that he was leaving for a job with better pay and more responsibility, Branson's response was to pull a water pistol from his desk and start firing at him, grinning broadly all the while. Later that afternoon, Branson telephoned Clark's wife, pretending to be the managing director of the company to which Clark was going, and talked gibberish down the telephone. Clark capitulated and stayed with Virgin, on the grounds that idiosyncrasy and fun were worth more than conventional careerism.

Branson's standing joke that 'I believe in benevolent dictatorships – provided I'm the dictator' contained more than a germ of truth. He had always run Virgin with something of the paternalism of a nineteenth-century Lancashire mill-owner, believing himself to be mindful of the welfare of his staff, if not always fully in touch with the vicissitudes of their day-to-day existence, but certainly never tolerating any direct challenge to his authority. Unions were anathema to him. Unions meant bureaucracy and restrictive practices. In a properly run business – a sufficiently benevolent dictatorship – they should be unnecessary. That was the theory, anyway.

The occasional protests by staff through the years over pay and conditions had usually been dealt with quickly, abrasions salved and healed by the implicit belief that matters would eventually improve, if not tomorrow, then certainly by the day after – and that one was still having more fun than was to be had almost anywhere else. By 1981, however, the mood in Virgin had darkened. Figures for the twelve months ended in January 1981 showed that Virgin had traded at a loss of £900,000. The staff redundancies and the cutbacks in the artists' roster had taken their toll on everybody's morale. But among the more lowly paid members of staff there was a feeling that the sacrifices that they had been urged to make over the previous twelve months – the constraints and pay-freezes and appeals to their better nature – had not been matched by a tempering of Branson's acquisitive spirit. In the record company – the one division of the company which supported the rest – staff had been made redundant, yet money had been found to go on buying nightclubs, expand the empire. To people struggling to make ends meet, the rationale about 'expanding out of difficulties' was not easily understood.

At Vernon Yard, the complaints became more vocal. At length, a handbill was circulated, unsigned, calling for a staff meeting, without Branson, Draper or any other directors present; on the bottom was the suggestion that a vote should be taken to see if staff wished to be represented by a trades union.

There was some trepidation at the thought of even having a staff meeting at all; wasn't it, some people wondered, rather *disloyal*? But a significant body of respected people, notably from the press and A&R departments, some of whom had worked for Virgin for years, argued that the meeting should go ahead, 'For the sake,' as one person put it, 'of those who are afraid to speak up for themselves.'

To Branson, the handbill provoked feelings of complete shock and disillusionment. Didn't people realise that his door was always open? The fact that he had been unaware that there was a problem at all, and that people had grievances they felt unable to air to him privately, was, perhaps, a measure of him losing touch since moving office to the houseboat. Certainly no more flagrant invitation to anguish could have been devised than that single, small word 'union'. He would talk to them.

On the allotted day, some forty people crowded into an upstairs office at Vernon Yard. Branson stood beside Simon Draper, visibly shaking, his face set in a grim mask. 'I can't tell you,' he began, 'how sad I am that people have felt the need to have a meeting, without Simon and I being present. It's a strange experience for me . . .' He paused, as if gathering breath for an ascent up a steep mountainside. 'I've always felt in the past that if anyone had a problem, they could always come to me and talk about it, and there haven't been many problems that we haven't been able to solve that way.'

It had, he said, been a very tough year, and times were tight. 'But that said, if people feel the way they do, if you don't think I have your best interests at heart, if we aren't all pulling together as one, then I have personally failed. If the time has come when Virgin needs a union for people's grievances to be redressed and their rights upheld, then it would almost not be worth me going on, and I will pack up and get out.'

Among some of the staff there now swelled feelings of awkwardness, embarrassment, even incredulity. For Richard Branson was clearly upset, sniffing hard and wiping at his face with his sleeve. Some swore they saw tears. People coughed, shuffled and looked away. Nobody could have dreamt of introducing the subject of a union now; for some mysterious reason, even the feelings of righteous indignation about pay and conditions had given way to distinct pangs of guilt.

'But, Richard,' a voice came from the floor. 'There's people here on just forty quid a week. Do you know the cost of rent, groceries, even a pint of milk? This isn't about changing the company; what people want is more money . . .'

The word brought a change over Branson's countenance; a glimmer of something like light, as if to say, Money? Is that all it is? Just money . . . The meeting broke up in disarray.

The next day an announcement was made to staff. A number of people would have their wages reviewed immediately, and the wage structure would be altered so that people on the lowest wages would get proportionately higher increases. Furthermore, there would be regular staff meetings from then on. And for a while there were, until staff no longer bothered turning up for them, and the practice was quietly abandoned. The whole episode had been an education for all, with one revealing truth emerging among many. Richard Branson actually *didn't* know the price of a pint of milk.

From the outset, Joan Templeman had some difficulty growing accustomed to the fact that living with Richard Branson seldom meant actually being alone with him. Branson's living arrangements had always been a movable feast, a reflection of the lack of boundaries between his work and private life. The house in Denbigh Terrace, which was his home during and after his marriage to Kristen Tomassi, had been progressively colonised by the office; Nik Powell took over the first floor; board meetings were conducted in the lounge; paperwork spilled into the bedrooms. When, late in 1978, Kristen and her boyfriend Kevin Ayers announced that they were leaving England to live in Spain, Branson took the opportunity to buy Ayers' houseboat, the *Duende*, moored on the Regents Canal, a short distance from his old boat. Branson's relationship with his former wife remained highly civilised. He and Kristen kept in touch; Joan and Kristen became friends. Some years later, when Kristen fell in love with a German architect named Axel Langer, he and Branson became partners in the ownership of a hotel in Majorca.

Joan had no wish to live in Denbigh Terrace, a house filled with all Branson's memories and few of her own, and the pair moved in together on the *Duende*. Conditions on the boat were cosy, not to say cramped, reflecting Branson's absorption in work and his somewhat bemusing sense of priorities. There were any number of telephones and a photocopier, but no washing-machine.

With things being tight at work it was necessary to set an example, he explained to Joan, as she set off yet again for the launderette.

Early in 1980, Joan announced that she was pregnant. Branson was less than enthusiastic. 'The thing is,' he confessed to his assistant Penni Pike, 'I haven't got my career together yet.' She could hardly believe her ears. 'Richard, you're twenty-nine years old, you've got everything you wanted and more than you need; you're ready for children.' But the thought of a child, and the responsibility it would entail, continued to panic Branson. To Joan, he confessed that he was 'not sure' so often that at one point she left the boat, determined to have the child on her own. Branson spent a frantic evening phoning around friends until he found her, and persuaded her to return.

In the summer, while Branson was away in Europe on business, Joan, now six months pregnant, returned to Scotland for a holiday. Whilst in Fort William she was taken ill with stomach pains. Doctors diagnosed appendicitis and she was operated on. Branson flew back from Europe and they went to a house near Inverness, where Richard's sister Lindi was staying, for Joan to convalesce. But within days she went into labour. Joan was told that the baby would be unlikely to survive, but she was advised to give birth naturally, to avoid gynaecological problems that might affect her capacity to have children in the future. The baby, a girl, three months premature and perilously fragile, died four days later.

The death of the child deeply affected both of them. But at the age of thirty-five Joan was determined to get pregnant again as soon as possible. Slowly, Branson's continuing fear of the responsibility which a child would bring began to evaporate. But again the pregnancy was not without drama.

Six weeks before the baby was due, Branson attended a dinner at the Venue. It was a long evening, and he arrived home at two in the morning, much the worse for wear. Shortly after falling into bed, he was awakened by an urgent voice in his ear, 'Richard. It's happening.' Feeling one step from death, Branson dragged himself out to the car and drove quickly through the early morning traffic to the hospital in Wimbledon. At the hospital, the doctor examined Joan and said, 'You look fine'; the verdict on Branson was less optimistic. 'You look absolutely dreadful,' said the doctor. 'Take two aspirins, go to bed, and we'll wake you when we need you.' An hour later, he awoke to find three figures clustered around his bed, dressed in white and wearing face masks. For a moment he thought he had been in a terrible accident. The next minute, he was clutching Joan's hand as she gave birth to a daughter. 'Because she was premature, as they were pulling at this thing I was thinking, "Don't touch . . .", and one worries that something might go wrong, and then there's this tremendous sense of relief, and elation and exhaustion. And it is the most incredible thing.'

As anyone but Richard himself might have predicted, the palpable, screaming existence of his daughter, Holly, assuaged whatever doubts he might have had about his readiness for parenthood. 'I think he was quite shocked at how much you could love something when Holly was born,' says his sister Vanessa. 'I don't think anyone had warned him about how overwhelming that feeling of love can be.'

On a bitterly cold November day, Richard collected Joan and the small, pale, vulnerable bundle and brought them home to the boat. The central heating was fixed at ninety degrees. Through the night feeds, he sat transfixed, preparing endless cups of tea. Parenthood began to impose its own time-honoured and inexorable pattern.

It was not in Richard Branson's instincts to look back, but occasionally – just occasionally – he thought about *Student*, and what it might have been.

In his own mind, Richard Branson had never fully abandoned journalism. An inveterate reader of newspapers, his understanding of what constitutes 'a good story' had been put to some use over the years in the cause of promoting his own artists, not least the Sex Pistols. But the thought of returning to publishing had not seriously entered his head until the spring of 1981, when his attention suddenly focused on an industrial dispute afflicting *Time Out* magazine and its proprietor Tony Elliott.

Elliott was a man cut, in many ways, from a similar bolt of cloth to Branson. He too had been educated at Stowe – although he was three years older – and like Branson he turned an understanding of Sixties culture to profitable advantage. Elliott had founded *Time Out* in 1968 as a duplicated broadsheet guide to London's 'alternative' events. With its listings of all-night movies, 'happenings' and a news section of political agitation that once moved Mick Jagger to remark that wading through it to find out what was showing at the NFT was 'like crossing a picket line', *Time Out* became as much a fixture of London bedsit life as the latest Mike Oldfield or Sex Pistols record. Just like Branson, Elliott had run his business with a curious mixture of post-hippie idealism and proprietorial *droit de seigneur*; for many years, all staff, from the postboy to the editor, were paid the same amount. But in May 1981 the contradictions finally became irreconcilable when Elliott insisted on his right to hire prestigious journalists at 'appropriate salaries'. The staff revolted, Elliott locked them out of the *Time Out* offices, and the magazine vanished from the newsstands.

Elliott's predicament was watched with some interest from the houseboat *Duende*. Richard Branson had long admired the simplicity and effectiveness of the *Time Out* concept. It was, in many ways, the magazine *Student* might have become under different circumstances. In 1978, Elliott approached Branson with a view to tying up a New York version of *Time Out* with Virgin's American office. At that time Branson said no. But as the *Time Out* dispute gathered steam, he telephoned Elliott with another proposition. 'It's clear from what you've said in the papers that you're determined to have a full blown lock-out and deal with the union problem once and for all,' Branson said. 'That means you're going to be off the streets for quite a while.'

'It looks like it,' said Elliott.

'Then why don't we look at this scenario?' said Branson. 'I'll start a publication to fill the gap – let's call it *Stepping Out* – which could possibly be free. I'll run that for as long as you're off the streets, and then, when you've solved your problems, I'll close *Stepping Out* and we'll do *Time Out* together.'

The following weekend, Elliott went to the Manor to meet Branson and discuss the proposition further, but after some thought he turned it down. He felt he knew Branson well enough to surmise that it would not evolve into an equal partnership, because Branson would be bound to 'over-interfere'. Furthermore, there was a marked difference in 'ethos'. Elliott thought Branson rather straight: 'I had a suspicion he would want people like George Melly in as columnists.'

Branson was nonplussed by Elliott's refusal; in fact, it

constituted the perfect challenge. If Elliott did not want a partner, he would have a rival. Branson had long felt that the greatest drawback to *Time Out* was its left-wing politics. He would start his own listings magazine, *Event*, without a picket line – metaphorical or real.

The project was greeted with some antagonism among his Virgin colleagues. Simon Draper thought it a bad idea, but realised that argument was futile. It was almost the last item of discussion with Nik Powell before Powell's departure. Powell had no argument with the principle of starting a magazine, or even over the amount of money it would cost, but he felt that Branson was treading on sensitive political ground in attempting to take advantage of somebody else's industrial dispute. But, more than anybody, Powell recognised that whatever the business opportunities *Event* presented, it was also Branson's way of exorcising the journalistic instincts – the excitement of chasing stories and airing issues – which had been thwarted by the failure of *Student*.

Branson spared no expense in getting *Event* off the ground. He plundered the opposition and hired Pearce Marchbank, a designer whose covers had done so much to establish the identity of *Time Out* on newsstands, as co-editor, along with Al Clark. He commissioned an expensive advertising campaign. At a launch party, at Heaven, he took two platefuls of celebratory cake and, with a gesture of proprietorial confidence that Rupert Murdoch or Robert Maxwell would have been hard put to match, flung them in the faces of his two editors.

But *Event* was already doomed, through a congruence of misfortune and misjudgement. Branson conceived *Event* to fill a gap; it would, he maintained, be a general entertainment and listings magazine, without the strident political polemic of *Time Out*. He believed the dispute at

Time Out would not alter the magazine's spirit. Even when *Time Out* returned to the stands, those readers tired of the magazine's 'agit-prop' news coverage and of film reviews dense with Marxist dialectic, would surely switch to *Event*. The belief – fallacious, as it turned out – in the unique selling points of *Event* lulled everybody on the magazine into a false sense of security. What Branson did not envisage was that the dissenting faction of the *Time Out* staff would leave to produce their own magazine, *City Limits*, run on the cooperative principles eschewed by Tony Elliott; and that *Time Out* would return to the streets largely shorn of its radical bent – in fact, very much the magazine Branson wished *Event* to be.

The first new-look *Time Out* appeared on 18 September 1981; the first *City Limits* a fortnight later. The first issue of *Event* appeared on 2 October; by then, as Branson admits, 'Our reason for existence had already vanished.' Lacking the long-established authority of *Time Out*, or the political commitment of *City Limits*, *Event* fell awkwardly between both stools.

Branson's role in any Virgin project was traditionally to set it up and leave it be, getting involved only when things went wrong. But from the outset he had felt jittery about *Event*: it was not a project that he could trust to a dependable partner, as he could trust the record company to Simon Draper. The obvious fact that *Event* was not working, his instincts to protect his investment, but also the awakening of his latent enthusiasm for the business of running a magazine, all drew Branson deeper into the quicksand which *Event* became.

The magazine's initial circulation of 50,000 was, by now, on an inexorable downward spiral. By January, it was just 18,000. Branson's response was to try and cut overheads. Redundancies were made; the magazine was reduced in size; the number of colour pages were cut back and eventually eliminated altogether – measures that lent an impression of panic and fast-reducing circumstances to the operation. By then, Pearce Marchbank had resigned in an acrimonious row over money. 'Richard didn't understand magazine publishing,' he says. 'He thought it was like a record – that you go to Number One immediately. He didn't understand that you have to throw away a million pounds in the first year in order to establish a readership and the faith of advertisers.'

But for Branson a quick death had become preferable to the prospect of prolonged agony. *Event* had become too much of a drain on both his time and the resources of the rest of the Virgin Group. 'We lost heart over it,' he says. After four more months, and two more editors, Branson closed the magazine, with a sense of something like relief.

The project had been wrong-footed from the outset. Initially conceived to capitalise on *Time Out* being off the streets, it was clearly a mistake to sit back and allow *Time Out* to return first. There were question marks too over Branson's choice of his editorial team. Marchbank was, first and foremost, a designer, not a journalist; Al Clark had some journalistic experience, but not as an editor; nobody had any great confidence in the man Branson had appointed as publisher, Greg Thain. Branson himself was torn between a belief that the magazine needed more of his time, and not having the time to give it. He remained convinced that if he could have spent ten hours a day working on *Event*, 'wining and dining advertisers and so on', the magazine could have been saved. But there was never the time to put the theory to the test.

Failing, as he would say, is not important, 'just as long as you've done everything you possibly can to avoid it'. As it was, the failure of *Event* cost Richard Branson more than £750,000. The cost to his pride was not so easily calculated. He had closed down businesses before, but never so publicly, and the fact that it was a project so dear to his heart wounded even more. To close one magazine is unlucky; but to close two casts serious doubts on your capabilities as a publisher. Shortly before *Event* closed, Branson made one last telephone call to Tony Elliott. 'Tony,' he said, 'I've made an awful lot of cash from the Human League. I could put it into *Event*, or I could give it to you for *Time Out* . . .' It was a gesture of bravado rather than a serious business proposition. But Elliott turned him down anyway.

There was nothing for Branson to do now but cut his losses, and trust to a return of the Branson luck. No one could have predicted it would soon arrive in the form of a boy dressed as a woman, and calling himself George . . .

Chapter 9

Litigation and Consolidation

In April 1982, a Task Force of warships and marines set sail from British ports to dispute with a tin-pot dictatorship the ownership of a territory on the other side of the world, of which many Britons had never before heard. Where were the Falkland Islands anyway?

By June, when the war was over, the Falklands had entered the British vocabulary: a word with mixed connotations of heroism, waste, duplicity, valour and a desperate, atavistic yearning for national pride. The 'Falklands factor' would be seen as a principal reason for the Conservatives' unexpectedly good showing in the local council elections that year, and, too, for the return of Margaret Thatcher for a second term as prime minister at the General Election of 1983. It was 'the Falklands spirit', Mrs Thatcher said, that would make Britain great again.

This yearning for former glories was already manifest in a particular kind of sentimentality and nostalgia. The wedding in 1981 between the heir to the throne and a nursery-school helper had confirmed the elevation of the Royal Family in the popular imagination to a singular hybrid of deity and soap-opera. The enormous popularity on television, and on film, of *Brideshead Revisited* and *Chariots of Fire*, suggested a nation looking collectively over its shoulder towards the cosy certainties of the past. Perhaps, together, these totems could banish the modern-day spectres of inflation and spending cuts; of strike action that endangered hospital patients or people whose houses were on fire; of lying politicians and rampaging football hooligans; of the seemingly irreversible rise in unemployment, and the terrible inner-city disturbances of the summer of 1981, from which the country was still reeling, and which had brought a suddenly sinister resonance to otherwise neighbourly sounding places. Toxteth, Brixton, Handsworth.

Pop music mirrored the mood of Britain's desperation – and its barely expressed hopes – in a curious way. The new groups who were in the charts, even as the British Task Force made its way across the Atlantic – Duran Duran, ABC, Spandau Ballet – suggested that, of all things, fun was once again back in fashion. After the *film noir* of punk had come the escapist musical spectacular of 'the new pop', demonstrated in a wild flamboyance which banished the austerity of punk rock to the shadows. In the gloom of a London club called Blitz, the person who would define this new sensibility above all others, the club's sometime cloakroom attendant, a young boy called George O'Dowd, caught sight of his reflection in the mirror, applied his make-up – as he would put it, 'to remove all the hideousness' – and plotted how he might acquire the only worthwhile currency left: fame. Such flamboyance is a familiar response of popular culture to recession: consider Hollywood in the Thirties. Yet it also signified, at another level, how pop music was responding to the undercurrents of the new mood of the country, and the pronouncements of an insistent, steely-haired woman in a blue twin-set about a sleeker, leaner Britain, built on the cut and thrust of the free market; unfettered competition; standing, as it was frequently said, on one's own two feet.

In fact, the pop industry has always embodied what were now coming to be known as 'Thatcherite' values: highly competitive, determined by 'market forces', with no grants, no subsidies, negligible government interference. There is no more exacting a yardstick of free-market principles than the pop charts, where the successful bask unashamedly in the spotlight and conspicuously consume the fruits of their success, while scant sympathy is expended on the failures. The difference now was that while once the significant body of musicians had attempted – or affected – to snub those values, they now embraced them.

Paradoxically, the example of Malcolm McLaren and the Sex Pistols – pop music's last true anarchists, and *Investors Review*'s 'Young Businessman of the Year' in 1977 – was an abiding influence on the new manners. The film *The Great Rock 'n' Roll Swindle* provided a blueprint for embezzlement to a rising breed of would-be McLarens – notwithstanding the irony that the erstwhile Swindler's tract was distributed on film and video by his most bitter adversaries, Virgin. Indeed, that only underlined the moral: pop music could be playful, and possibly even subversive, but nobody could pretend any more that it was anything but business. To the coming generation of performers, pop was no longer expected to mean anything other than what it represented on the surface; it was as if pop music's aspirations towards deeper meanings and truths had been exhausted; social realism was distanced by irony and a conscious manipulation of artifice. A tyranny of 'style' was born.

'Credibility' now meant working with the right video producer, clothes designer and hair stylist. Groups spoke of 'strategies' and making 'career moves'; the jargon of the Harvard Business School had banished forever the Utopian clichés of Woodstock, and the anarchist ones of punk. Irony piled upon irony in the shape of one group of the Virgin roster, Heaven 17, whose 'image' portrayed them as pony-tailed businessmen in executive 'power' suits. Everybody had an 'image' now. Even punk, once the rhetoric about dole queues, anarchy and Sten guns in Knightsbridge had been exhausted, had become just one more uniform to be hung on the clothesrail of British pop culture, to be dusted down nostalgically on anniversaries.

The rise of the pop video was an important element in the growing supremacy of style over substance. The video had originally come into use as a promotional device – a way for a group to receive television coverage, in Britain and abroad, without the expensive and time-consuming necessity of travel, hotel bills, etc. A few, more adventurous, performers had spotted the creative potential of the medium, and were busy conceptualising music for video as well as disc. But in the main videos were, simply, advertisements for records. That changed in 1981, with the arrival in America of MTV – the cable television station which broadcast music videos twenty-four hours a day to a rapt teenage audience. MTV asserted the primacy of the new medium of pop video, and once again, through ready access, made British pop fashionable, and saleable, in America. It also made the pop video an industry in itself, with its own cast of producers, directors, cameramen, technicians and so on. The video quickly became a mandatory part of the pop star's armoury; no performer, no matter how well established, could afford to ignore it; the simple truth was that without a video a record stood less chance of becoming a hit. And a strong video, projecting the right image for a performer, could turn the most indifferent song into a smash, and the performer into a star.

To a generation of prospective pop stars, the video offered new possibilities of benediction. No longer did one have to sound right, one need only look right – or, at the very least, *different*. From the nightclubs of London there surfaced a person called Steve Strange, a burly Welsh boy whose only demonstrable skill lay in concealing his prosaic origins beneath make-up and fancy dress. Strange's achievement in parlaying this modest qualification into a highly visible career in fashion magazines, pop videos and records was a potent example to those, like George O'Dowd, whose most ardent infatuation was with their self-image.

The coming of MTV, and the growing importance of the pop video, also sowed the first seeds of future developments within Virgin. The pop video had become a commodity saleable to the public. From the need to produce videos of Virgin artists came the idea of distributing them on a commercial basis as well as through their own distribution company; and within two years Virgin were busily developing their own, European version of MTV, Music Box.

The reshaping of Virgin's musical policy over the past three years, under Simon Draper's direction, had positioned the record label perfectly to capitalise on the new developments in pop The failure of *Event* magazine had been offset – and ultimately subsidised – by two great successes in 1981. The Human League and Phil Collins embodied two distinct strands of the pop music that would come to dominate the charts. The Human League's snappy pop songs, drum machines and synthesisers were the embodiment of 'electro-pop', the new teenage esperanto; while Collins' sleek, craftsmanlike records were the perfect palliative for an older generation of listeners, turned off by punk rock, whose interest in pop music would be rekindled by the coming phenomenon of the compact disc. The Human League's *Dare* album sold 1.8m copies around the world in its first year of release. And Collins' *Face Value* also became a million-seller. Both records were auguries of things to come. With Collins, the Human League, Japan, Simple Minds, Heaven 17 (whose two pony-tailed members had previously been in the Human League), Virgin began to swamp the pop charts.

Meanwhile, George O'Dowd, the former Blitz cloakroom attendant, had been making some progress of his own towards the altar of fame. He had become the singer with a group which was exciting some interest among the A&R men and women of London's record companies, including Steve Lewis, the head of Virgin's music publishing company. Lewis impressed upon Simon Draper the need for Virgin to sign the group, Culture Club, and their lead singer – now rechristened Boy George. They signed with Virgin early in 1982. Within a year, Boy George was the biggest pop star in the world.

With British pop music once again in the ascendant, Richard Branson set off to America to sell Virgin artists, with an optimism that almost banished the memory of his company's disastrous American adventure of two years before. Branson had made countless such sales trips over the years, and it was not a task he relished. In fact, he had come to find it degrading, having to adopt the demeanour and the practices of a door-to-door brush salesman to A&R men, long bored by the entreaties of managers, artists and agents to hear their 'product'. He had become inured to the long, solitary vigils in hotel rooms awaiting the return telephone calls; learnt the art of never leaving one's name and telephone number more than once, because 'it makes you look desperate'.

These trips would proceed on the basis that Richard Branson's lack of musical expertise was less of a liability than Simon Draper's lack of salesmanship. Having been primed by Draper back in the hotel room on who played or produced what, Branson would present himself with a box of tapes and play just one track by each artist; enough to whet the appetite, but not so much as to test his customer's patience – or indeed Branson's own musical knowledge. To executives more accustomed to the slick, desk-pounding, hustling and screaming school of salesmanship, Branson's gauche, schoolboy manner and his abashed confessions that 'actually, I'm not sure who produced this one' proved appealing, particularly when allied with the offer to license yet another curious collection of British haircuts whom their competitors were anxious to sign.

Returning from one trip, where they had licensed the material of three groups to different American record labels, Branson and Draper were greeted at Heathrow Airport by a girl brandishing a questionnaire: Where have you been? How did you fly? Did you do any business in America? And, she added jokingly, did you make any money? Branson and Draper smiled broadly at each other. 'Just $1.5m,' said Branson.

The renewed popularity of British music in America only made Branson more determined than ever that Virgin should, once again, have their own operation in the States. Indeed, he was determined that Virgin should, one day, have their own offices throughout the world, with all their licensing deals changed to distribution arrangements.

The closure of the American office was a temporary set-back; attention was now turned to Europe. Only one other British record company – EMI – had ever taken the step of setting up their own operations in Europe. Only a handful of British companies were of a size to contemplate it, and among them there existed a curious air of parochialism, of not wanting to venture into foreign-language recordings, or markets which were unfamiliar. But Branson's attitude was simplicity itself. 'You just take the margin you're paying somebody else; make sure your overheads didn't come out to more than that, and you can't lose.'

In 1981, Virgin set up their first overseas operation, in France. The occasion was celebrated at a hotel in Normandy, where local sales representatives were treated to a screening of *The Great Rock 'n' Roll Swindle*. Somebody, not informed of Branson's excitable nature, had made the mistake of arranging the buffet luncheon around an open-air swimming-pool; within minutes, waiters, guests and chairs were all in the pool. Virgin were banned from the hotel for life.

However, the French adventure established a successful formula. In all the countries across Europe, the most likely individuals handling Virgin material for the licensee in that country were approached to set up the new local Virgin office. Unhappy about losing 80 per cent of their profits on Virgin acts, but unwilling to surrender 10–20 per cent, most foreign companies accepted the switch from being licensees to being distributors. With committed and knowledgeable staff in each country, Virgin set about a policy of signing local acts as well. Performers such as Richard Cocciante, Sandra, Renaud and Telephone mean little to British audiences, but in their own countries – Italy, Germany and France – they were stars, selling enormous quantities of records. By 1986, almost 75 per cent of Virgin's overall business was being generated by its foreign subsidiaries.

Foreign expansion also gave fresh vigour to Branson's powers of hyperbole. Staff in Virgin's international department grew to accept the fact of opening *Music Week* to read that Virgin now had offices in fifteen countries (a slight exaggeration), and would shortly open in a further five (It's the first we've heard of it, Richard has to be kidding!). These pronouncements became, in time, self-fulfilling prophesies.

The expansion of the Virgin operation, the sharp influx of profits (the loss of £900,000 reported at the beginning of 1981 had been turned into a profit of £1.5m by the beginning of 1982), and the more aggressive attitude of performers to selling themselves had all put Virgin in a more competitive milieu and frame of mind. The record industry is actually subject to a very simple application of market forces. When a group is unknown, the advantage lies with the record company in signing them on the company's terms. What confounds that argument is if the group can inflate its value before signing with anybody, either on its musical merits, or by 'hyping' a reputation. By hyping through shock value alone Malcolm McLaren had provided a model with the Sex Pistols and in his wake came a new wave of manager-entrepreneurs who recognised that the process of 'selling' a performer began long before you signed a record contract. By creating demand for the group among record companies you could provoke an auction which would push up your advance (signing-on fee) by tens of thousands of pounds, and your royalty percentages by two or three 'points'. After that, it was your lawyer against theirs.

For record companies, it now became a question of who could pay the most money to secure the most in-demand acts. This appealed to Branson's competitive instincts. From 1979 onwards, most of the negotiations on record deals, and all the practical day-to-day details of the record company, had been handled by Simon Draper, as managing director, and Ken Berry, as the company's all-purpose troubleshooter. Branson's absence had made office life more predictable, less exciting, but Virgin had become a better record company. As Draper put it, 'Richard liked instant excitement; let's go for it, negotiate, and then if the record wasn't out in three weeks, he'd lose interest.' However, there was nothing to stimulate Branson's interest more than the prospect of a good contract race against a rival company – Chrysalis, Polydor or CBS.

Branson's increasing celebrity, albeit still confined to the music industry, had become a selling point in itself. Other record companies offered long, fattening lunches in over-priced restaurants as part of the deal-making process. Virgin had their own method. To walk the overgrown towpath to Branson's barge, bang your head as you descended the small, brass-railed ladder and step over the pile of nappies; to be served stir-fried vegetables and noodles, fresh orange juice and Perrier; to be treated to a private exposition of what were becoming the most famous teeth in the record industry – to attain these was a sign that a group was truly regarded as important.

On one occasion it was a group called the Fine Young Cannibals who made the journey, to discuss Virgin's offer for the rights to their song-publishing. Another company had offered an identical amount; to the group there was little to choose between them. After some deliberation, the group made a proposal, 'We'll sign with you,' they said, 'if you throw in a Steinway Grand piano, non-recoupable.'

Branson thought for a moment. 'That's about £5,000. I'll tell you what, why don't we toss for the piano?'

Amid great deliberation, the coin was tossed. Branson won.

'But,' he said, 'you can have the piano anyway.'

In any contractual negotiation with a record company, a good lawyer had become as important to a performer as a good tune, or a good haircut. Historically, the advantage in record contracts had lain on the industry's side. Venality was rife; the precedent of even groups as illustrious as the Beatles and the Stones signing to contracts which gave them only a penny a record had become legendary: at the end of the Sixties, Allen Klein had achieved notoriety for his dexterous accounting abilities, working for both groups in the role of both 'finder' – extracting hidden royalties from the record company for the group – and 'taker' – extracting them from the group for himself.

Entertainment had become the growth area for the legal profession during the 1970s, as more and more lawyers sought to capitalise on the growing awareness of pop groups about the inequities of the world they inhabited. The entrance of lawyers changed the pattern. No longer did record companies set a contractual agenda which the young, naive performer was obliged to follow. Armed with a lawyer, an artist could, theoretically, get a contract that was equal to – or, at a push, even greater than – his worth. Relations between performer and record companies became more combative, with legal action, or the recurrent threat of it, the principal weaponry.

Many of these exchanges followed a predictable pattern. A group signs with a record company at a modest royalty rate, in direct proportion to their lowly status and their impatience to become stars. Suddenly they become successful. Their immediate wish is either to improve the terms of their contract, or, failing that, to leave the company and go elsewhere. In more severe cases, the performer awakes, as if from a deep sleep, to realise that he has been cheated of his just desserts. To lawyers the challenge became how to find loopholes in existing contracts, through which their clients could either escape, or drive a series of new demands. A number of test cases through the Seventies had established precedents for what courts would and would not accept as 'fair' in existing contracts. It became clear, for example, that a contract signed without the artist having had independent legal advice was virtually unenforceable. And a further principle was established – that of 'conflict of interest', in which a manager who advises an artist to sign with his own record and music publishing companies can hardly be said to be acting impartially, or necessarily in the best interests of his client.

For years, Virgin had been largely untroubled by litigation. Relations with the four hundred or so different acts that had passed through the company had been, for the most part, harmonious. And such arguments as there were had been settled without recourse to the courts. Which was why the writ which arrived on the desk of Virgin's lawyer, Stephen Navin, in September 1979 from solicitors representing Gordon Matthew Sumner, came as a particular shock.

'Sting', as Sumner was better known to the record-buying public, had been signed to Virgin music publishing as a complete unknown in 1976. This meant that Virgin had the right to publish his songs, but no rights on Sting himself as a performer: his group, the Police, were signed as recording artists to A&M. In the past three years, as his star had risen, Sting had become an important asset in Virgin's publishing catalogue. Now he was issuing a writ which alleged that Virgin had made 'fraudulent use of a dominant position' in their dealings with him, and claimed damages and a reversion of all his songwriting copyrights.

Richard Branson regarded it as vital that Virgin should win the case. It was the first time that an artist had taken the company to court. It was not only Virgin's reputation that was being challenged – Branson had no doubt that the contract signed with Sting was fair; but if a court ruled otherwise it could set a precedent which other acts, and their lawyers, would be looking to exploit. It was unfortunate then that Virgin's case should be complicated by, and ultimately hinge upon, another, far less public, contractual dispute.

Sting, as a songwriter, had been signed to Virgin by the head of the publishing division, Carol Wilson. It was Wilson who had discovered the singer as an unknown in his native Newcastle, playing with a local group called Last Exit. Under her direction, and with Virgin money, Sting had recorded a series of demos which had led to his association with the Police, a recording contract with A&M and, ultimately, the hit parade.

The arrangement Sting had signed with Virgin had been for a 50–50 split, rising to 60–40 in Sting's favour after two years. It was a standard contract for an unknown songwriter, but as the Police began to enjoy enormous success, so Sting's value in the market-place rose. Virgin offered to improve the deal still further to a 75-25 split, but Miles Copeland, Sting's manager, flatly refused, ostensibly because Virgin were asking for the length of the contract to be extended to include the publishing rights to more albums. To Carol Wilson, however, it became fairly obvious that Copeland wanted to sign Sting's publishing to his own company. Sting and Carol Wilson had remained friends throughout the negotiations. In fact it was she who had advised him to get a second opinion on the matter, from a lawyer. He did – and a writ was issued against Virgin shortly afterwards.

For Wilson, Sting's success, and the prodigious royalties it had earned for Virgin, was merely one feather in an increasingly crowded cap. Not only did Wilson have a good 'pair of ears', in musicbiz speak, but she was also a formidable negotiator, tenacious in the pursuit of acts she wanted to sign, and in fighting her corner over day-to-day interdepartmental matters. Simon Draper took to calling her 'She who must be obeyed' – if not to her face. She also got on well with Branson; she had become one of the 'inner circle' at Virgin, invited on ski-ing holidays and country weekends, utterly trusted within her own sphere; a model, in fact, of the Virgin ethos of somebody being given responsibility and rising to it.

In 1979, she and Branson began talking about establishing an independent label, which Wilson would head, working under the aegis of Virgin and to be called DinDisc. It was verbally agreed between them that as well as a salary she should have 15 per cent of the company to Virgin's 85. Negotiations over the final contract were still going on as the first DinDisc releases appeared. Martha and the Muffins and Orchestral Manoeuvres in the Dark, both Wilson discoveries, came and went in the charts – and still negotiations dragged on. Each party was now becoming increasingly impatient with the other. Wilson had employed a lawyer who, according to Simon Draper, was 'well known in the record industry for never being able to conclude an agreement'. At one meeting, Branson became so exasperated that he walked off his own boat and paced up and down the towpath outside to cool down. But Carol Wilson believed that it was Branson who was 'stalling' over giving her any control in the company. At one point, she discussed the position with Simon Draper. Draper, after all, was in a not dissimilar position himself, as a 15-per-cent shareholder of Virgin. 'Look, Carol,' he said. 'In the end it's a matter of trust. As a minority shareholder you're in no position to get anything out of Richard. You either trust that he is going to do things fairly or you don't.' But Wilson felt aggrieved. She had, by then, been with Virgin for six years, and brought the company much success, in particular during a time of economic crisis for Virgin. In 1980, Orchestral Manoeuvres in the Dark, a DinDisc act, had given the company their biggest selling album of an otherwise disastrous year. Wilson felt she deserved more.

By now, at Virgin's instigation, negotiations had taken a turn in another direction. Rather than a shareholding, it was proposed that Wilson should be on an 'over-ride royalty', whereby she would be paid a royalty for every record sold. It was a scheme that promised more immediate profits for Wilson, based on results, but entailed sacrificing any control of the company. Wilson agreed. It was settled that Branson would give her the signed contract at the Roof Gardens, where all the directors of Virgin were meeting for a Christmas dinner. Wilson arrived at the table, as arranged, but the contract did not. 'It's in the car,' said Branson. 'I'll sign it tomorrow.' Coldly, Wilson turned on her heel, walked out of the restaurant – and out of Virgin.

Her resignation became official in January 1982, with a £25,000 settlement from Virgin. Wilson says there was a condition on the settlement – that she should agree to give evidence in the impending case of *Gordon Sumner* v. *Virgin*. She refused to sign, but was paid the settlement anyway.

Wilson's reputation as a talent scout ensured that she was not out in the cold for long. A plan to go into business with Chris Blackwell at Island did not materialise; but she did agree to operate a new company, Inter-Disc, under the aegis of CBS. It was only when she began to spend time at CBS's corporate headquarters that Wilson realised just how congenial the atmosphere at Virgin had been by comparison – particularly for a highly motivated woman. By record industry standards, she felt, Virgin was a haven for 'oddballs' – she and Richard Branson both. So when Branson contacted her to see whether they could resume negotiations, Wilson agreed. The deal that was eventually signed in April 1982 was, in essence, the deal that had not quite been signed at Christmas 1981, giving Wilson an over-ride, but no percentage of the company. Within hours of signing, however, she began to have doubts. Her arrangement with CBS would have given her a 100-per-cent shareholding in her own company. If she was running the same company for Virgin, shouldn't she have some shareholding in it? The next day she went back to Branson and asked if he would renegotiate along the lines of the original Virgin proposition, for an 85–15 split in the shareholding. Both Simon Draper and Ken Berry had been vehement in their opposition to Branson even contemplating rehiring Wilson, and advised him to now tear up the contract and be done with it. For his part, Branson was within his rights to insist that Wilson abide by the contract she had signed, but he agreed to renegotiate.

It was a delicious quirk of fate that this situation should have arisen even as the legal action with Sting loomed on the near horizon. For Wilson, as both she and Branson were acutely aware, was a key figure in Virgin's defence.

The importance of the case, and the fact that Virgin's public reputation was at stake, had driven Branson to take an active role in preparing Virgin's defence, rather than simply entrusting it to his lawyers. In a week of feverish detective work, he amassed a dossier on the publishing arrangements of Sting's manager, Miles Copeland. What he discovered was rather surprising. The standard agreement which Copeland's company had with such acts as Caravan, the Climax Blues Band, Wishbone Ash and Squeeze was for a 50–50 split – a worse arrangement than the one Copeland had encouraged Sting to sue Branson over. To Branson, it was evidence of 'the worst kind of hypocrisy', and proof of the relative fairness of the Virgin contract.

The crux of Sting's accusation, however, was that he had suffered from 'inequality of bargaining power' – which is to say, that he had not had proper legal advice when signing the deal, and had been taken advantage of by Virgin. In fact, as he later admitted in court, he had been represented by a lawyer from Newcastle at the time of signing to Virgin: not a music-business lawyer, it was true, but a lawyer none the less. Carol Wilson was a potentially important witness on this point. After all, she had signed Sting in the first place (she had even given him a list of music-business lawyers to consult at the time, but he had used the Newcastle lawyer because he was cheaper). And she had been party to every stage of his renegotiations. She and Sting were still on good terms – they actually sat beside each other throughout the court case, exchanging pleasantries. Without her testimony, Virgin's lawyer, Stephen Navin, believed that Virgin's case could look 'a bit pathetic'. It was important, everybody in the Virgin camp agreed, to keep Carol Wilson sweet.

Wilson too recognised her value to Virgin's defence. Her renegotiations with Branson over her contract now became a question of who was using whom. Wilson suspected that Virgin were simply 'stringing her along' on her promise to give testimony on their behalf. Could that even have been why Branson had invited her back in the first place? Branson, meanwhile, suspected that she was trying to 'blackmail' Virgin into bringing her renegotiations to a hasty and favourable conclusion. Wasn't that why she had asked to renegotiate after signing the contract? But without Wilson as what he termed 'a reliable witness', could a favourable outcome of the Sting case be assured?

By now, the case of *Sumner* v. *Virgin* had dragged on in the law courts for eleven days, with the two parties holding each other up in the centre of the ring like panting heavyweights, while the legal fees gushed forth like blood from the wounds. The case had already cost Virgin alone more than £100,000. Counsel on both sides were pressing for a settlement; to go on would be futile. In a feverish rush, an agreement was finally drawn up in the corridors outside the court room, under which Virgin were entitled to one more album of Sting's songs (*Synchronicity*) and also retained the 'exploitation' rights on existing material for a further eight to ten years. But Sting's royalty rate was increased, and backdated, giving him an immediate cash payment of some £100,000. It was a pyrrhic victory for both sides. Ironically, Carol Wilson had not, after all, been called upon to give testimony. But neither had the rancour of the last weeks been dissolved.

A week after the case finished, Wilson received a letter from Branson saying that the contract which she had actually signed some three months before was now binding. There would be no more renegotiation. Wilson was furious. But Branson was in no mood for reconciliation. Virgin, he claimed, had been precipitated into a compromise with Sting largely because their key witness was unreliable. 'We felt that if she was going to turn on those sort of tactics we were not going to be gentlemanly about it, and that she should just get on and do the job.' But Carol Wilson never did go back to Virgin. Branson held her to contract for five more months, preventing her from working anywhere else, until he decided it was unreasonable to hold her any longer, and she was at last able to find work elsewhere in the record industry.

As is invariably the case in such matters, the only people to profit from the entire episode were the lawyers. The irony was that two years later Copeland and Branson were once again on cordial terms, their differences momentarily forgotten, while they discussed a possible business deal together. Richard Branson and Carol Wilson, on the other hand, have not spoken since.

Business and friendship can often make for strained bedfellows – as the experience of the man who had made Virgin's first fortune also proved.

The past ten years had been a long, strange and often

puzzling journey for Mike Oldfield. His first response to the enormous success of *Tubular Bells* was to undergo a minor nervous breakdown. Craving isolation, he moved to the depths of Herefordshire. He expressed interest in few things in life beyond music, and the purchase of a series of improbably fast and expensive motor cars. He ventured forth to London, and the offices of Virgin, only rarely, to sit silently under the desk of Richard Branson's secretary, Alison, while she arranged test drives of the latest Italian roadsters.

Oldfield's friendship with Richard Branson remained one of the few absolutes of his life. He continued to idolise Branson; and Branson, in turn, to protect Oldfield. But Branson's role as Oldfield's manager was now made somewhat problematic by the musician's recalcitrant attitude. He produced records at his own unhurried pace; he refused to tour, give interviews, or engage in any sort of promotion. His recreational hours were invariably spent either driving at great speed down country lanes or in the public bars of Herefordshire, engaged in uncomplicated conversations with local farmers.

The possible paradox of having Branson as both his manager and the head of his record company did not occur to Oldfield until 1976. By then, he had made three albums for Virgin, all of which had sold enormous quantities, but the contract which he signed in 1972 had not been reviewed. That contract was for ten albums, which, at Oldfield's work rate, could amount to fifteen to twenty years' work. And while a 5 per cent royalty rate might have been fair in 1972, times had changed. It had not escaped Oldfield's attention that even young, inexperienced artists signing to Virgin were commanding 3 or 4 per cent more than he was. Tom Newman, who had managed the Manor and been so instrumental in the creation of *Tubular Bells*, was among those urging Oldfield to seek an improved arrangement. But Mike, says Newman, was 'frightened of his own shadow'. He would certainly never challenge Branson.

However, Oldfield did get himself a lawyer, and after negotiation with Virgin, an amendment to his contract was signed in April 1977, increasing his royalty rate to 8 per cent. Oldfield himself asked Branson to carry on as his manager, which Branson agreed to do for a new rate – Oldfield would pay him one barrel of beer a year.

The following year, Oldfield underwent Exegesis, the then fashionable and expensive 'therapy' in which people are shouted at and humiliated in front of a group, and then convinced by 'brainwashing' techniques that they actually feel better for it. Oldfield emerged a new man. From being a painfully shy, diffident recluse, he suddenly metamorphosed into a garrulous and sometimes painfully overbearing extrovert.

The first indication that Richard Branson had of his young protégé's dramatic metamorphosis came with a telephone call. Wide-eyed and dazzled from his epiphany, Oldfield announced that he was to marry the daughter of his Exegesis instructor and Richard must be best man. Branson had grown accustomed to Oldfield's eccentricities; but even by past standards this seemed positively lunatic. 'You've known her less than a week, Mike,' he protested. 'Wouldn't it be better to wait?'

'No, no,' said Oldfield. 'I want to get married now – tomorrow, as soon as possible. You've got to organise it, Richard.'

With a distinct feeling of foreboding, Branson arranged a date at Kensington registry office. On the allotted day, he and Joan arrived at the office for a ten o'clock wedding, carrying with them a gift of two enormous chairs of the type popular with minor African potentates. There was no sign of Oldfield and his bride-to-be. For two hours Richard and Joan sat in the potentates' chairs on the pavement outside the registry office, watching the conveyor belt of marriages go by. By the time Oldfield and his bride-to-be at last arrived, Joan and Richard had fallen to speculating which of the marriages would end in divorce.

Wedded at last, Oldfield and his new wife waved goodbye. Twenty-four hours later, he was on the telephone again to Branson with another request. 'Richard, can you arrange a divorce?'

Oldfield's marriage lasted for just two weeks, requiring lawyers and a large sum of money to bring it to a conclusion satisfactory to the bride. However, the effects of Exegesis lasted somewhat longer. Having once decried 'commercialism' in all its forms, Oldfield now embraced it: he recorded a disco song, 'Not Guilty', and, for reasons that were not altogether clear, was photographed for the music papers posing naked as Rodin's Thinker. And, for the first time ever, he announced that he would be touring – not alone, not even with a small, manageable and economically viable ensemble, but with an enormous entourage, including a choir of young schoolgirls.

The tour, unsurprisingly, lost money; both Oldfield's own, and some £250,000 which Virgin had put up for tour support. It also marked the end of Branson's role as manager; at his suggestion, Oldfield took on somebody else to supervise the tour. The friendship between Branson and Oldfield had been based initially on dependence and protectiveness – mutual need, and mutual gratitude. Without the cement of regular meetings or contact, they gradually began to drift apart.

Oldfield grew increasingly unhappy. A new manager

and a new accountant had alerted him to the alarming fact that, notwithstanding his private plane, home recording studio and sports cars, he was short of money. The more he thought about it, the more he felt that the contract he had renegotiated with Virgin had not gone far enough. Furthermore, he felt that Virgin were being distinctly 'unhelpful' towards him these days. Once upon a time he had instant access to anyone in the office; now he would telephone and be put on hold. The musical policy of the label had changed – Oldfield thought punk rock 'absolutely disgusting music' – and it was as if he was no longer important to the label which he had done so much to build. The final humiliation came when Branson and Draper flew out to Munich to see Oldfield perform in concert and bring him up to date on the current situation. After the concert, Branson explained how difficult it was to sell Oldfield's music in America; indeed, the only way Virgin had been able to find an American distributor for his records at all was on the back of a deal made for a new group on the label, XTC – precisely the kind of music Oldfield abhorred. 'I wasn't getting any respect, any money; I couldn't even get hold of Richard when I wanted to, so I decided to put my foot down and straighten things out. I got a new lawyer and said, I just want out.'

In July 1981, a firm of lawyers acting for Mike Oldfield issued a writ against Virgin for 'repudiation', claiming that the original contract, signed in 1972, was not valid. Branson was shocked by the claim. In the first place he disputed the contention of Oldfield's lawyer that the original, 1972 contract was unfair. Record companies, he argued, make their profits by taking risks on unknown acts, which are signed for modest royalty rates. Oldfield's initial deal had been a fair reflection of the market-place at the time. Furthermore, every other record company in London had turned Oldfield down. Virgin, it could be argued, had given him a chance when nobody else would. With the 1977 renegotiation, Branson argued, a new royalty had been set which Oldfield and his lawyer at the time had considered fair. Now here was another set of lawyers coming along and saying, 'I think I can do better for you than that.' In other words, trying it on . . .

Nor could it have occurred at a worse time. In mid-1981 Virgin was doing badly; the company had made redundancies and the roster was being cut back. Branson felt in no mood to be conciliatory, let alone generous – even to Oldfield. 'Mike,' he complained to Draper, 'is richer than the label is. Sometimes you have to put your foot down and say no, a contract is a contract.' This, he felt, was very much one of those times.

Underlying his bullishness was a feeling of incredulity that Oldfield, one of his oldest friends, should be taking such a step at all, and that Oldfield could have drifted so far away from him without Branson having read the warning signs. 'Mike is being put up to this by his lawyer,' he told friends. But Mike wasn't. For Oldfield, exacting a satisfactory arrangement with Virgin had become a point of principle, inextricably entwined with his feelings for the man whom he had long regarded as friend and protector, and his need to prove something to himself: 'It had got to a point where I said I can't respect myself unless I'm prepared to stand up and fight Richard. I was quite prepared to go to court. I knew that I would probably lose the case if I did, and lose everything, but for my own personal esteem I needed to actually make that stand.'

The argument ground on for almost two years, in a mood of escalating resentment and bitterness. Oldfield refused even to speak to the person he had once idolised. Stephen Navin was urging that the case should be allowed to go to court: Virgin, he argued, were on solid ground. But Branson was very reluctant to go that far. The thought of facing his old friend, and the man on whom Virgin's fortunes had been largely built, across a courtroom was too upsetting. A contract may be a contract, but Branson was now coming round to the belated realisation that a suitable gesture to Oldfield much earlier on in his career – increasing his royalty rate after *Tubular Bells*, for example – could have prevented all this ugliness. An independent manager would have been fighting on behalf of his artist for just such a concession; but for a manager who owned the record company, that meant arguing against himself.

Life, Branson reasoned, was too short to make enemies. At a final lawyers' meeting, it was at last agreed that Oldfield's royalties should be increased, in varying amounts according to territories. He also received a large sum of money, which included all the commission Richard Branson had ever earned as his manager. In return, Oldfield agreed to add three more albums to his Virgin contract. The final, symbolic point on which Branson relented was in giving Oldfield an increased royalty on all future sales of *Tubular Bells*. As they toasted the agreement in champagne, and Oldfield and Branson shook hands, somebody pointed out that it was exactly ten years since *Tubular Bells* had first entered the charts. In time, Branson and Oldfield even became close friends again.

This was, as far as anyone could remember, the first, and last, occasion on which Richard Branson had allowed sentiment to interfere with business.

To everyone in Virgin who had met him, it was only a matter of time before George O'Dowd proved to the world at large what he already believed, they suspected, and a not inconsiderable advance was banking on – the fact that he was a star. The first two singles released by Culture Club failed. There was no panic, no consternation. All they had to do was wait. Then, in October 1982 came 'Do You Really Want to Hurt Me'. It went immediately to Number One. The group's fourth single, 'Karma Chameleon', became the best-selling single of 1983, selling 1.3m copies in Britain alone.

Yet, beguiling as these songs may have been, there was little doubt that the success of Culture Club was based largely on the curious popular appeal of Boy George himself. The spectacle of a beautiful boy in a dress and dreadlocks confiding to the nation's media that he preferred 'a cup of tea' to sex appeared both to arouse the public appetite for sexual frisson and deflate it with humour, honesty and a curious sort of innocence. He was all things to all people: to *The Times Literary Supplement* he was 'striking a sincere blow for one of the oldest traditions of them all: genuine, unself-conscious self-expression'. To the tabloid newspapers he was 'Naughty Boy George', one minute 'a poof with muscles', the next 'laying off love for seven months'. To the frock-coated bankers at Coutts he was a welcome asset in the account of a perennially trying customer.

Culture Club's first album, *Kissing To Be Clever*, was released in October 1982. It went on to sell four million copies around the world, the lion's share, it was noted with some satisfaction with Virgin, in territories where Virgin had their own label. The second album, *Colour By Numbers*, went on to sell ten million.

The arrival of Culture Club, allied to the successes of

the Human League, Phil Collins, Japan, Simple Minds and others, released vast reservoirs of cash into the Virgin account. By the end of 1982, the company turnover was £48.6m, and the profits had risen to £2m. By the end of 1983, as the worldwide royalties from Culture Club and others poured in, the turnover had risen to £94m and profits to £11.4m.

Richard Branson now headed an empire that encompassed some fifty different companies, incorporating records, studios, nightclubs, video production and distribution, film-making, book-publishing and property. There was a company developing games; another developing an instrument called the Synthaxe; for reasons which nobody could quite discern, there was a company dedicated to the servicing of air-conditioners, and another, called Top Nosh, selling food around industrial estates.

And yet, for all its size, this remained an unusual sort of an empire, not consolidated, in the customary imperial manner, in some glossy West End towerblock but scattered around Notting Hill in a random assortment of properties, in varying states of ramshackle informality. Virgin did not place much store by superficial appearances. The record company had now moved from Vernon Yard to larger premises, beyond the canal, railway tracks and council estates. But still the boxes continued to pile up in reception and the feeling of overcrowding persisted. Only the haircuts had changed. The head office was now located in a converted Victorian property on the litter-strewn thoroughfare of Ladbroke Grove, opposite a particularly combative Irish pub. Other outposts included converted industrial premises beside the canal, for the film division, and two minute mews houses on the Portobello Road, for whoever needed them. In all of this there existed an air of the cottage industry, with an informality that, consciously or not, took its measure from the example of its chairman, who continued to live and work – now with the added impedimenta of potties and baby-gates – on a houseboat on the Regents Canal; who drove a second-hand Volvo; and who had not long come into possession of a washing-machine.

But the appearance of modesty was somewhat misleading. Branson also had his own Virgin island; and he and Joan had acquired a country house for weekends, a short distance from the Manor Studios. But he insisted on continuing to live on the houseboat *Duende*, despite Joan's pleadings to find somewhere with more room to accommodate the needs of their growing daughter Holly. It was not until early in 1984 that Branson was finally persuaded to stop living on the houseboat, by his doctor, after he had contracted a severe case of pneumonia. Joan found an imposing, double-fronted house in Notting Hill Gate and the family moved in. Branson, however, continued to work on the boat.

Out of the apparent random chaos of the Virgin organisation, a business philosophy – almost an entrepreneurial blueprint – could be discerned. By situating each company in its own – albeit small and determinedly unglamorous premises – overheads were kept to a minimum, but, more important, a familial atmosphere was created among staff. As the record company had grown, it too had been broken down into smaller units: DinDisc had been a model for two more affiliated labels, 10 and Siren. The greater number of small companies you have, Branson reasoned, the greater number of people to whom you can give responsibility; 'encouraging entrepreneurship', as he put it, under the umbrella of Virgin.

In setting up any new project, Branson's abiding objective had been – in what was fast becoming his favourite phrase – to 'protect the downside'. It had become his belief that a good entrepreneur is not the person who takes the biggest risks but the one who learns to spot the safest bets. Virgin had grown through a series of developments that business schools call 'vertical integration', but which Branson saw as just common sense. The progression from selling records by mail-order to retailing in shops, to running a record label, studios, publishing company – all was perfectly logical and obvious, allowing Branson and his colleagues to expand in the business they knew best. Indeed, it was on those occasions when Branson had invested in projects not obviously related to the pop milieu that the losses had been greatest; clothes, restaurants, *Event* magazine. Top Nosh and air-conditioning servicing were shortly to go the same way.

That was why Simon Draper was appalled, horrified and dumbstruck when Richard Branson telephoned him at home one Sunday evening in March 1984, gushing enthusiasm for another idea.

'Simon,' he laughed down the phone. 'What do you think of starting an airline?'

Chapter 10

Virgin Atlantic

It had not occurred to Richard Branson, even in his wildest dreams, to own an airline. So the message that a Mr Randolph Fields had telephoned to see if he was interested in buying one only mildly excited his curiosity. He deflected the call. When Fields persevered, Branson told his assistant Penni Pike to ask him if he would send 'something on paper'. The dossier outlining how Richard Branson might conquer the North Atlantic air-routes arrived the next day.

He took it away with him for the weekend, to his home in Oxfordshire. It was a cold, wet February; and Branson spent most of the weekend in front of the blazing log fire, reading. Fields, he learned, owned a 'paper' airline, British Atlantic, which had applied for a licence to fly from Gatwick to Newark airport, New York, on an air 'frequency' which had been vacant since the collapse of Laker Airways two years before. Fields had spent some months, and a modest amount of money, examining the feasibility of a new transatlantic airline; he had approached several key figures who had been with Laker Airways and solicited their interest; he had begun to make enquiries about purchasing an aircraft. All he needed was Richard Branson's money.

As Branson would have been the first to acknowledge, common sense dictated that he avoid it at all costs. He knew nothing about airlines, and even less about Randolph Fields. It was nothing to do with the record industry, or entertainment of any sort, and thus a radical departure from the Virgin principle of expanding into related fields. Furthermore, the investments necessary to make an airline work could, theoretically, drag Virgin to bankruptcy. And yet, the more Branson thought about Fields's scheme, the more feasible – and attractive – it began to look. By Sunday evening, what had seemed utterly ludicrous a mere forty-eight hours before, had taken on almost tangible form in his mind. The first person Branson telephoned on Monday morning was Randolph Fields. Within a week they had agreed, in principle, to be partners. Virgin were going into the air line business.

Randolph Fields was thirty-one years old and a barrister by profession. A short, somewhat corpulent man, he wore dark, double-breasted suits of discreet quality. A brown kisscurl fell over his forehead; he chortled often, showing the sly, boyish grin and the self-satisfied air of one who had been told once too often that he was a lovable rascal. Fields had been born in America and had moved to Britain as a child. He had been expelled from grammar school at the age of sixteen, manufactured tie-dye T-shirts, and then worked in the refreshment kiosk in the monkey-house at London Zoo, where he had the distinction of organising the first strike (of staff, not animals) in the zoo's history. Finally, deciding to 'get serious about life', he had enrolled to study law at the Polytechnic of Central London. His contemporaries remember him as 'Dear Randy', the epitome of the slick student politician. He qualified as a barrister in 1980 and within a year was an attorney-at-law in commercial insurance litigation which he claimed was making him £500,000 a year.

The idea of starting an airline had come to him on the demise of Laker Airways in February 1982. Fields's first scheme had been to capitalise on the aftermath of the Falklands conflict, by operating a service between Gatwick and Port Stanley. That was modified to running a business-class only service to New York. He had discussions with a company called Travel Trust to back his project and, in December 1983, had applied to the British Civil Aviation Authority (CAA) for a licence to operate a service between London and New York. This application was refused, but he was told by the CAA that there was an opening on the route if he wished to re-apply for a licence. Fields now began thinking along the lines of a low-budget operation – and of a possible investor with the money, and the push, to satisfy the requirements of the CAA, and get the airline aloft. Virgin, he thought, fitted the bill. Furthermore, he felt a curious bond with Branson. 'Like Richard,' he said, 'I've always been considered precocious too.'

Branson did not warm to Fields's initial concept of a 100-per-cent business-class service between London and New York; that, he felt, was 'not the right image from Virgin's point of view'. But a cut-price airline, along the lines of Laker, certainly would be. People Express, the American carrier which had, to a certain extent, inherited the mantle of Laker's 'Skytrain', was a proven success, but research showed that the transatlantic market was big enough to support two cut-price carriers. And, after all, discounting was what Virgin had been built on. It just added further proof to Branson's growing conviction that Virgin and the airline business were made for each other. Now all he had to do was convince his colleagues in the company of the fact.

Ever since the departure of Nik Powell, it had fallen to Simon Draper and Ken Berry to perform the function of attempting, where necessary, to temper Richard Branson's more fanciful, grandiose and outlandish schemes. For Draper, the principle of expanding only into related fields, where Virgin had at least a margin of experience and expertise, was sacrosanct. Draper had tried to veto *Event*, and been proved right; he had tried to veto Top Nosh, and been proved right on that too. But Branson could be obstinate when he wanted to be. He would listen to advice, but invariably trust to instinct. It had let him down badly on some occasions, but, on balance, nobody could deny that it had served him extremely well.

Draper was appalled when Branson telephoned him from Oxford on the Sunday evening, bubbling with enthusiasm for his new project. Draper interrupted him in mid-flow: 'I think you're a megalomaniac, Richard. I don't want to be in the airline business. I don't want to know. This is the beginning of the end of our relationship if you do this.' Branson was taken aback by his vehemence. But while Draper might protest against the idea – while he might fulminate against his partner risking the hard-earned profits of the record company, the fruits of years of work and tears on a hare-brained scheme to run an airline – he also knew that there was little he could actually do to stop it. Branson, after all, owned 85 per cent of Virgin. The point at which Draper categorically said 'You can't do this' would be the point at which he would have to leave. 'That's what owning 85 per cent of the company is all about . . .' Draper reasoned. '. . . Doing what you want.'

Ken Berry too was deeply sceptical. Of the three men, Berry was the most innately conservative and cautious; thorough and conscientious, his ability to explore every nook and cranny of a record deal exceeded even Branson's. Berry knew the record business backwards, and he also knew that this was what Virgin's success had been built on. Buying an airline seemed foolhardy and unnecessarily ostentatious: it affronted his sense of proportion.

But Branson swept all objections aside. It was a risk, certainly, but an acceptable one, within the strictures of his maxim about 'protecting the downside'. He promised Draper and Berry that he would not stake the existence of Virgin on the airline. On the basis of Fields's figures, if certain guidelines were adhered to rigorously, Branson estimated that it would cost Virgin £20m a year to run the airline, but the most they stood to lose by 'cutting and running' at any time was £2m. Flying at full capacity – which was highly unlikely – the airline could show a $9m profit in its first year. It would need to be flying with 70 per cent capacity to break even; for every percent above that it would make $250,000.

Nor, Branson had now convinced himself, was an airline that far removed from the principle of expanding into related businesses. The people who would fly a Virgin airline were the same young, mobile, relatively affluent people who had been buying records by Virgin artists in Virgin record stores for years. Latterly, they would have been reading Virgin books, watching Virgin videos and Virgin films. Virgin had long ago ceased to be simply in the music business; it was now in that most Eighties of concepts, the *lifestyle* business.

Branson was faced with an immediate, and critical,

choice. Virgin Atlantic, as the new airline was to be called, would need to become airborne within the next three to four months, to take advantage of the summer traffic and generate the necessary cash reserves to see it through the fallow winter months. Failing that, it would have to wait another twelve months. Branson had no interest in waiting. He would attempt the impossible and set up an airline from scratch in three months. The fact that he knew absolutely nothing about the airline business was neither here nor there. He would educate himself – fast; and there was no better place to start than with the sorry tale of Freddie Laker.

Randolph Fields had already recruited to the nascent operation two former Laker executives, Roy Gardner, who later became Virgin Atlantic's chief executive, and David Tait, who was appointed head of the American operation. Both had worked closely with Laker; been witness to – and victims of – his downfall; both had much to say about the pitfalls Branson should, at all costs, avoid.

Branson already knew enough about Laker, his entrepreneurial flair, his reputation as the champion of 'the ordinary man' in air travel, to regard him as something of a hero. Laker was a highly charismatic individual; a self-made man who had built his airplane business on a visionary self-determination and zeal, a refusal to take no for an answer – all qualities which Branson fancied he could sympathise with. But Laker, like all tragic heroes, had his fatal flaw, hubris. Simply, he had been carried away on the potency of his own vision, and come to believe himself infallible.

He had launched Laker Airways saying it would be a tight operation with no more than six planes and a staff of 120. Thus established as a low-risk business, flying under contract for package-holiday firms, Laker had promptly assumed all the risk by buying out his two biggest customers. Then in June 1971, he had launched Skytrain – the first ever low-budget, no-frills service between London and New York. He was so confident of his own sense of destiny that he had bought 3 DC-10s before the US government had even approved the Skytrain service. He made £2m profit in his first year. Intoxicated by success, he then ordered eight DC-10s and ten Airbuses in rapid succession, saddling himself with a debt of £350m. His fundamental mistake was not only to buy all his planes, but to buy them only on borrowed money. He borrowed £150m to buy his planes from McDonnell Douglas and Airbus Industrie, and each year he had to find the cash to repay the instalments as well as paying the interest. With wafer-thin profit margins, this meant he had to keep his planes to full capacity if he were to meet his debts, which he was never able to do. The final nail in Laker's coffin came in the winter of 1981 when the big transatlantic carriers, including British Airways, cut their fares to match Laker's. It was the end of 'the people's champion'. The only fight Laker would have with the big airlines thereafter was in the American courts, suing them under the anti-trust laws for driving him out of business.

Another factor in Laker's downfall had been currency. He had bought his planes in dollars, so the falling value of the pound had made his repayments all the more expensive. Virgin, as Branson well knew, could not afford to buy an aircraft outright; nor would it be wise to do so. By leasing he could not only spread the payments, but either enjoy for himself the benefit of a 100 per cent tax write-off on the asset of the plane in the first year, or come to some arrangement with a financier, who would

build the tax deduction into the price. The very first
words which Branson scribbled in his diary as he began
his researches were, 'If we go out of business, must get
out of plane deal – three months' notice preferably.'

By the end of two weeks, Branson had the following
locked firmly in his mind: the airline would not be an all
business-class service – but it would combine an economy
section with a first-class section at business-class prices.
The aircraft should be a 747, not a DC-10, in order to
carry freight as well as passengers. And it should be
leased, not bought, and the purchasing agreement should
be protected against swings in currency.

In April, Freddie Laker himself came to lunch on
Branson's boat, to recount once again the story of his
own downfall for the benefit of his would-be successor.
At the end of lunch, Branson said in a faltering voice that
there was something he had been thinking of doing, and
he wanted to ask Laker how he would feel about it. Still
unsure whether or not it was appropriate, he said that he
would like to name Virgin's first plane *Spirit of Sir
Freddie*. Laker flushed slightly and fell silent. At length,
he looked up and quietly thanked Branson. Of course, he
said, he was flattered by the suggestion, but it would be a
mistake. 'It's best to break with the past,' he said. Laker
knew only too well that the name which had once been an
asset in the world of aviation was now a liability.

The public hearing of Virgin Atlantic's application for a
licence to fly between Gatwick and Newark was scheduled to begin at the Holborn offices of the Civil Aviation
Authority (CAA: the regulatory body of the airline
industry) on 1 March. Three days before the CAA hearing, the new Virgin Atlantic Airways was launched publicly at Maxims restaurant in London, with the requisite

drum-banging to ensure the media paid full attention to Branson's claim that there were '250,000 people who do not yet travel to New York, but would if the price was right'. As a publicity exercise, however, its main target was not the public at all, but the CAA. 'We felt it was important to let them know beforehand that the public would welcome another airline,' as Branson put it.

As the man with some previous experience of CAA hearings, it was Randolph Fields who arrived at Civil Aviation House in Kingsway, London, on the first day of the hearing to present the case for the newly inaugurated Virgin Atlantic Airways. Branson was not present, but his personal lawyer, Colin Howes, sat through the hearing with a sinking heart. Fields's presentation was rambling, discursive and, at times, Howes thought, 'over emotional'. It was clear the licensing panel were not impressed. Howes reported back to Branson that evening with the advice that 'you'd better be there yourself tomorrow'.

Howes's fears were well-founded. Having already turned down Fields's first licence application in December 1983, Raymond Colegate, the CAA's commercial director and the chairman of the licensing panel, was 'deeply sceptical' of Fields's ability to get the project airborne. But the arrival of Richard Branson changed Colegate's view. Branson, he felt, had just what the airline needed – money. Presenting himself at Holborn the next day – without a tie, the panel's secretary noted disapprovingly – Branson assured the CAA that Virgin would guarantee the airline up to £3.5m.

When the lawyer representing British Caledonian Airways, who were opposing Virgin's application, remarked that Virgin would need 'a lot of groups on *Top of the Pops*' to afford to run an airline, Branson promptly retorted that Virgin's £11.4m profits in 1983 were actually more than twice those of British Caledonian. A month later, the CAA notified Virgin of their decision. The airline had permission to fly.

Being granted a CAA licence was, however, only the beginning. Branson had drawn up what was to become known as the 'Million List' – the number of things that had to be taken care of in the next three months before the airline could fly.

At the new airline's operational headquarters – a small warehouse at Lowfield Heath, near Gatwick – recruitment of aircrews began. There were some three hundred cabin attendants to be found, and trained from scratch. British Airways' recent decision to lower the optional retirement age for their pilots, however, meant there was a sudden surplus in the airline business of highly experienced pilots, still hungry to fly: Virgin's first flightcrews had the highest number of flying hours of any British airline. There was a complex web of landing and departure agreements to be negotiated with the British Airports Authority: maintenance and service contracts to be drawn up. There was the provision of food, drink, in-flight entertainment and duty-free goods, and the printing of tickets. Branson, in a moment of impulse, decided to do away with the convention of describing passengers as first class or economy; instead baggage stickers were printed for 'Upper Class', 'Middle Class' and 'Riff Raff'. Older, wiser heads in the organisation prevailed upon him to stick with 'Economy'.

And then, of course, there was the aircraft.

Ever since filing his first application as British Atlantic, Randolph Fields had been scouring the world looking for aircraft of the right type and price. His search had led him, at length, to the headquarters of the Boeing aircraft corporation in Seattle, where row upon row of second-hand aircraft of every size and specification sat awaiting scrutiny. Responsibility for disposing of this fleet, which Boeing employees had nicknamed 'The Aluminium Cloud', had fallen to one of the company's most experienced salesmen, R.Q. Wilson – a tall, cadaverous man whose Brooks Brothers suits, and the ostentatious flashes of gold at his wrist, cuff and spectacle-rims actually belied a distinctly English politesse and gentility. When Richard Branson took over negotiations from Fields in March, Wilson and a team of Boeing executives and lawyers flew to Britain, installed themselves in the Carlton Towers hotel in Knightsbridge and prepared to make a killing. One of Virgin's lawyers returned to his office after a preliminary meeting with the news that 'there are two American piranha fish in that hotel, waiting to eat Virgin up . . .'

The deal that was eventually drawn up between Boeing and Virgin was of a complexity unprecedented even in R.Q. Wilson's considerable experience. Who had killed whom at the end of the day was hard to tell. Tactics which Branson had developed in negotiating the fine points of recording contracts were now amplified in the more complex arena of aircraft negotiation. Wilson found it agreeably 'refreshing' to face a customer not across a football-field-sized desk in a corporate head-quarters but bobbing gently up and down in a houseboat on the Regents Canal, or over a pleasant weekend in Branson's Oxford home.

The deal agreed was structured to put two parties between Virgin and Boeing: one was Barclays Bank, who actually bought the plane in cash, and took advantage of the tax allowances available; they then leased the aircraft (on a UK Tax Lease) to Chemco Equipment Finance (a subsidiary of the American Chemical Bank), who in turn subleased it (on an Operating Lease) to Virgin Atlantic. Chemical Bank guaranteed Chemco's obligation to Barclays; and the obligations of Virgin Atlantic to Chemco were guaranteed by the Virgin Group and County Bank. The safety net for the Virgin Group was the 'buy-back' clause – an option for Virgin to return the aircraft to Boeing at the end of the first, second or third years, if required; and for Virgin to retain the 'outside' value of the plane. This meant that if the plane increased in value, Virgin were the beneficiaries; while if it decreased in value, Virgin were protected by a fixed-price agreement. Boeing fought to have that clause removed; Branson, equally tenaciously, insisted it should be retained. At length, Boeing conceded the point, leaving Bob Wilson to lament that 'it was easier to sell a fleet of aircraft to United Airlines, than to sell one to Virgin'.

As a final safeguard on their position, Chemco insisted on Virgin Atlantic taking out a forward-currency contract to protect the buy-back agreement against fluctuations in the pound against the dollar – and to protect themselves if Virgin defaulted or went bust. If Virgin pulled out, Chemco would be left with an obligation to pay Barclays £16.8m in sterling. But the asset in the deal – i.e. the aircraft – was valued in dollars. If the dollar fell, the sterling value of the plane could have dropped below £16.8m. The 'insurance policy' would ensure that there would be a matched sum delivered come 15 July 1985. The exchange rate at the time the contract was signed was 1.45 dollars to the pound. Branson crossed his fingers that sterling would hold firm. The negotiations for the purchase of the aircraft culminated in the offices of the London lawyers, Freshfields, with representatives of five companies and some six different law firms clustered around a table in the conference room. At the end of it all, Virgin had agreed to pay a total of $31m dollars, spread over ten years, for their first aircraft.

The plane Virgin bought was a 747-200 series, with one previous, careful owner, Aeroleneas Argentinas, and only 19,000 flying hours on the clock. Bob Wilson was so confident that the deal would go through that some weeks before it was even completed he had given authorisation for the work to begin at the Boeing factory in Seattle to modify the aircraft to British CAA regulations and finish it in the red and grey Virgin livery.

With permission granted to operate a service out of Britain, Virgin now looked to America for permission from the American regulatory bodies, the Civil Aeronautics Board and the Federal Aviation Authority, to fly into that country. This would not prove so easy.

The airline world is built on a fine web of international agreements, with each government vying to protect the interests of its own airlines, as well as of international passengers. It was unfortunate for Virgin that in applying for 'exemption' to fly into America they should have walked into a simmering row between the American and British governments over the British refusal to allow PanAm to operate a third frequency across the Atlantic. Virgin's application was just the bargaining chip the Americans had been looking for. Under international agreements the Americans were obliged to notify Virgin within sixty days whether exemption would be given. Under the bilateral agreement there was a clear case for the Americans to admit a British carrier to 'balance' People Express. It was almost unthinkable that the Americans would refuse outright to grant the exemption, but it quickly became clear that they would prevaricate for as long as possible.

After discussions with American Department of Transportation officials, Branson's Washington lawyers advised him that although there was no clear indication that Virgin's application would be 'held hostage' to the demands of PanAm, 'the US team certainly has these issues at the forefront of their decision-making process'.

One US DOT official, Matt Scocozza, had even suggested that Virgin 'might wish to mention to British aviation officials the benefits to UK carriers from flexibility in the next round of bilateral negotiations, scheduled to begin in August' – in other words, lean on the British government on the American government's behalf. And while Scocozza was optimistic that Virgin's request would eventually be granted, he warned that 'it would not be easy', and encouraged Virgin to exert pressure on 'decisionmakers'.

Meanwhile, Virgin's application became the subject of intense lobbying by British government officials in Washington. The British were emphatic that Virgin's application and the question of PanAm's third frequency were unrelated. Branson himself was assured by British officials that the government were wholly on his side, and that there would be 'an unholy row' if Virgin was not flying on 22 June. Branson was fully aware that even if the Americans decided to grant permission, it was likely that it would not be given until a day or two before the flight – retaliatory treatment for the way the British government had delayed until the eleventh hour and fifty-ninth minute permission for People Express to fly into Britain. And he was right. The CAB did not grant the necessary exemption until 19 June – three days before the first plane was due to land at Newark.

By then, Branson already had an alternative tactic in mind. If the Americans refused permission to land, he said, he would simply take off anyway and embarrass them into giving landing permission from above Newark airport.

The delay effectively hindered the setting up of the American end of the Virgin operation. David Tait had arrived in New York in March, with the instructions to 'set up an airline; we'll be sending you a 747 a day in three months' time'. He moved into the Greenwich Village brownstone which had once housed Virgin's American record company operation and hastily recruited staff. Now he was faced with the problem of how to promote an airline which was forbidden under US law to sell tickets or advertise its service until the CAB and Federal Aviation Authority had given their approval. Tait and his advertising agents hit on an idea for generic advertising, of filling the skies above New York with a message done by 'skytyping' – a development of sky-writing in which five light aircraft, working on computer synchronicity, puff dots into the sky to form letters sixty feet high. A suitable 'teaser' message was devised, and the aircraft booked for Memorial Day weekend, traditionally the first holiday of the year when New Yorkers take to the beaches and the parks.

That day, the aircraft wheeled above Manhattan in tight formation, pumping out their message, thrown into relief against a clear blue sky with vivid clarity, WAIT FOR THE ENGLISH . . . It was at that point that the planes vanished into the solitary cloud in the sky, leaving all of New York craning their necks, scratching their heads and asking 'What the hell is an ENGLISH VIRGI . . . ?'

The airline business gave Richard Branson a challenge

which, in recent years, the record industry had been unable to provide. And he attacked it with a relish and enthusiasm which surprised even himself. Whether Branson had taken over Virgin Atlantic or it had overtaken him was difficult to tell. Between March and June 1984, he worked harder than he had ever worked in his life. He negotiated the purchase of a plane, and the acquisition of a licence, he flirted with domestic politics, and international diplomacy. And he thoroughly enjoyed every minute of it. Even the minutiae of the airline business obsessed him more than the minutiae of the record business ever had. He fussed over what kind of headphones to use on the aircraft, approved uniforms and checked menus. Getting the airline up and flying – proving wrong everyone who had doubted him – became an obsession.

Of one thing Branson was certain: if the airline was to succeed, it needed to be sold to the public, and to the media – and sold hard. Virgin's future competitors – PanAm, British Airways, British Caledonian – all had huge advertising budgets, running into millions of pounds, to attract customers. Virgin could never compete with that. Another way would need to be found.

What other companies fancifully referred to as 'corporate public relations' had hardly been an issue at Virgin up till now. The record industry, of course, runs on hyperbole, and Virgin Records, like any other, had a press office feeding stories to the music or national press when it profited them to do so, and doing their utmost to keep the press at bay when it didn't. Branson understood media manipulation as well as anybody, and had much enjoyed helping to orchestrate the on-going controversy around the Sex Pistols once they had signed to Virgin. But this had never required him to put himself in the spotlight. Few people outside the record industry knew who Richard Branson was. Indeed, Branson had often gone out of his way to avoid newspaper or television interviews. In part this was due to an acute awareness of his own awkwardness as a speaker; the stuttering circumlocutions, the ers and ahs, leading inexorably to a pained silence, or the word that always hung there like a tail, 'Anyway . . .' The memories of public humiliation, all those years ago, on the steps of University College, London, with Tariq Ali and Daniel Cohn-Bendit remained fresh in the mind. And so too, for some curious reason, did an injunction from his father many, many years before: if you want to be happy, keep out of the public eye.

With the launch of the airline, however, Branson decided that things would have to change. He would put privacy to one side, and consciously set out to become what Freddie Laker had been: his company's most visible and effective public relations asset. The requirement of spreading the name of Virgin in Britain, but also in America, shaped Branson's life from that point on.

To help publicise the launch of the airline, Branson had taken on the services of Tony Brainsby, a man whose hyperventilated style of press-arousal on behalf of such clients as Paul McCartney had made him a small legend in the pop world. It was Brainsby's idea for Richard Branson to arrive at the inaugural press conference wearing a brown leather aviator's helmet, *à la* Biggles, in an attempt to lend the launching of an international airline something of the savour of a *Boys Own* adventure. But it quickly became apparent to the practised eye of Brainsby that Branson required little advice in the matter of public relations – or, for that matter, in dressing up. The exhibitionist streak that had been confined to fancy-dress parties at Virgin's weekends away now found full public licence; Richard Branson embarked on a sort of alternative career in fancy dress that would see him, over the years, photographed in airline captain's uniform, as Peter Pan, Spider Man, City Gent and, on one occasion and for reasons that were never entirely clear, in the bath, wearing only bubbles and a cunningly placed newspaper.

Nor did Branson's social awkwardness prove quite the liability he had feared. Indeed, it became something of an asset in formulating a public persona. For Branson did not appear pompous, overbearing, practised or City-Slicker smooth in the manner of other captains of industry. In fact, you could hardly believe he was a businessman at all. Businessmen simply did not become *celebrities*. Newspapers actually seemed to find the gauche, schoolboyish manner, the ubiquitous sloppy sweaters – a clothing preference that Branson subtly exploited as a sort of trademark – all rather charming. His naturalness made a refreshing change; there were no obstructive minders or ghastly PR men surrounding Branson. He was disarmingly available, with a natural propensity for generating what Randolph Fields called 'free ink'. If a journalist wished to talk to Richard Branson, he simply telephoned; not only did Branson invariably take the call, but he treated the journalist with civility. Journalists liked that. The trick of public relations, Branson discovered, was not to pretend to be something you were not, but simply to project what you were on to a larger canvas.

Colin Howes, Branson's lawyer, perhaps recognised better than most that Branson was in a period of significant transition. In conversations snatched in the backs of taxis between meetings, and in office anterooms, Branson spoke about the process of turning himself into a public figure if the airline were to succeed, fully aware of the consequences. On one occasion, they clambered out of a taxi in Oxford Street. On the other side of the road, outside the HMV record shop a horde of young girls mobbed a limousine, carrying members of the group Duran Duran to a personal appearance. Branson and Howes walked past the scene, ignored. Howes thought it a prescient occasion. Unlikely as it was that Richard Branson would ever have quite the impact on teenage sensibilities of Duran Duran, the days he could walk down a busy London street totally unrecognised were surely numbered.

On 19 June, three days before the inaugural flight of Virgin Atlantic's Gatwick to New York service, Richard Branson flew by helicopter from the Midlands to Gatwick airport, in the company of two other passengers, the cricketers Ian Botham and Viv Richards. En route, the helicopter flew over Stowe School. Looking down, Branson could see a cricket match in progress in the grounds. He had not been back to Stowe since the day he left, almost seventeen years before. Now, in a mood of heady exhilaration, a delicious scenario flashed in his mind; the school drop-out, on the way to take delivery of his own Jumbo Jet, literally dropping back in during a First XI cricket match with two of the most celebrated test cricketers in the world in tow. The expression on the faces of the boys – and the masters – of Stowe would be a joy to behold . . . but the helicopter flew on.

The 747 was waiting on the runway, in pristine white livery, the Virgin name emblazoned on the tailfin in red. Branson was as awed as anyone could expect to be at the first sight of their own Jumbo Jet. It was barely four months since Randolph Fields had first approached him with the idea of starting an airline. Now he had one. It was all quite ludicrous after all.

That afternoon, the plane sped down the runway, on the flight of inspection for the air-operator's certificate. It was the 'one millionth' item on the list, but now, surely, a mere formality. On board the plane was the entire staff of Virgin Atlantic Airways. Branson himself was seated next to a CAA inspector. But as the plane climbed in a steep curve above the Sussex countryside it was rocked by a sudden explosion. Looking out of the window, Branson saw flames streaming momentarily from an engine; then the plane righted itself and flew on. He could feel the blood draining down to his shoes. The CAA inspector put his arm round Branson in an avuncular manner. 'Don't worry, Richard, these things happen.'

Only when the plane landed was it discovered that there had been a compressor-blade failure in one of the engines. It would need to be replaced overnight, in time for another test flight – and, because insurance cover only became active on the granting of a certificate, it would cost £600,000 to do it. Relieved that he had an airplane at all, Branson received the news with a wan smile. There was a reporter and a photographer from the *Financial Times* waiting to interview Branson as he touched down. They had seen and photographed everything that had happened. Branson did not need them to tell him the damage that could be done to the airline's reputation by a story appearing about engine failure on the day before the inaugural flight. 'Don't worry,' said the reporter. 'We're not really that kind of paper.' The photographer pulled his roll of film from the camera and held it up to the light. Branson almost wept in gratitude.

Two days later, journalists, television crews, a smattering of 'celebrities', and even some paying passengers were loaded on to the plane for its inaugural flight. As the 747 coasted down the runway for take-off, a voice announced to passengers that, following the lead of some American airlines, passengers would be shown the view of take-off from the cockpit. The backs of the heads of the first and second officer and engineer flashed on the video screens. As the plane soared up, all three turned round: Ian Botham, Viv Richards and Branson himself. It was not the sort of gag one would have expected from Lord King, and it set a certain tone . . .

Virgin Atlantic's 747 flew the ocean fuelled by some seventy crates of champagne. The pilot's only problem en route was the need to constantly readjust the trim to cope with the numbers of people rolling towards the front of the aircraft. Richard Branson gave some hundred press interviews, sipping discreetly at his champagne, acutely conscious of being, in his own phrase, 'on duty', while the majority of passengers, blissfully unaware of the dramas of the last forty-eight hours – or the last four months – drank themselves into a condition of happy oblivion. In this sense, it was the perfectly orchestrated media event. Fleet Street journalists require a modest range of incentives to make them feel agreeably disposed towards something, and the maiden flight (on a plane which had been named the *Maiden Voyager*) was warmly and comprehensively reported in almost every national daily and Sunday newspaper.

On the return journey, Branson, utterly spent and exhausted by the events of the last four months, slept a deep and dreamless sleep. Midway across the Atlantic, the 747 was struck by lightning. It bucked wildly in the night sky, as if deciding whether or not Richard Branson had been lucky enough already, then righted itself and plied on through the night sky, swift and inviolate.

★ ★ ★

When Richard Branson returned from New York some-what hungover and in a state of weary exhilaration, there was a visitor waiting at his London home to see him.

Chris Rashbrook, the manager of Virgin's account at Coutts Bank, had hoped to avoid this meeting, but over the previous week circumstances had made an unpleasant and embarrassing task unavoidable. For some time, Coutts had been considering an application from Virgin to increase their overdraft facility above the previously agreed limit of £4m. The previous week, Virgin had requested immediate permission to go over the facility by some £200,000, to meet short-term outgoings for the airline (to pay, in fact, for the engine which had expired on the air-operator's test flight). The application had been subject to long and disapproving scrutiny at Coutts. The bank had made no secret of their dismay over Virgin's venture into airlines. For a company with Virgin's limited borrowing power the venture seemed foolhardy, not to say suicidal – notwithstanding Branson's protesta-tions about 'protecting the downside'. But that was not all. In the last year Virgin had invested some £4m in their first major film project, *Electric Dreams*; more money was now being poured into yet another, a new version of George Orwell's book *Nineteen Eighty-Four*. When would it end?

Rashbrook broke the news as delicately as he could. He had come, he said, to give Branson a message. Coutts had considered Virgin's request to exceed their overdraft by £200,000 over the next seven days. And had decided to refuse it. If Virgin exceeded their overdraft by so much as £25, the cheque would, alas, be returned marked 'refer to drawer'. In a word, bounced.

'This is an absolute farce,' Branson said. Coutts had

been informed that a cheque for $6m was expected at any moment from MGM films in America – payment for the distribution rights of *Electric Dreams*. The company had made a proper request to extend its facility.

'You're telling me that it's official Coutts policy to bounce a cheque on one of the ten biggest private companies in Britain?'

Rashbrook nodded silently.

Branson felt indignant. Virgin had shown a profit of more than £11m in the last year. At an absolute minimum, the worth of the company must be £100m (in fact, within the next two years it would be worth £250m). And yet Coutts were threatening to bounce cheques of £25! In fact, Branson should have known it was coming. Virgin and Coutts had long been growing apart. From the earliest days of *Student* magazine, Coutts had indulged the idiosyncrasies of Branson's banking practices with bemused aplomb. They had raised only the most discreet eyebrow at the bedraggled urchins who queued to deposit the takings from the magazine and mail-order; at the implausible schemes for manor-house recording studios and sundry businesses of a bizzareness beyond the bank's mannered comprehension. The Bransons, after all, had banked with Coutts for generations. Richard was one of 'us' – after a fashion. But, in recent years, the relationship had outgrown even that important bond. Virgin were now a commercial concern, trading with a flair, and a lack of convention, that tested Coutts's nerve and understanding. Such assets as Virgin had were almost meaningless: not the bricks and mortar so reassuring on the balance sheet, but the more nebulous assets of music and publishing copyrights – tangible enough, perhaps, to people who understood the music business, and knew that at any given moment Virgin could raise millions if they so chose; less comprehensible to a bank where customers were still greeted by frock-coated doormen.

Branson's attitude to his bank had always veered between naivety, respect – and evasiveness. He no longer approached his bank manager with the trepidation of an errant sixth-former being summoned before a housemaster; indeed, he no longer approached his bank manager at *all* if he could help it. He had always preferred to leave that to Nik Powell, or the man who had joined Virgin as financial director on Powell's departure, Terry Baughan. The prospect of changing banks had been discussed before. But changing banks, as Branson was prone to saying, 'is a bit like changing your parents for a new set. When you've been with the same bank since you were thirteen, you somehow feel they will grow up with you.' This was patently no longer the case.

Branson brought the conversation with Rashbrook to a perfunctory close. 'I'm sorry,' he said, 'but you are not welcome in my house. I'd rather you left.'

He then telephoned Ken Berry, to begin the task of urgently calling in money from abroad. It was a depressing reprise of a familiar refrain: scouring for deposits in banks in France and Germany; outstanding royalties from Greece and Scandinavia. Berry, Branson knew, would salvage the situation in the short term. The long-term solution would have to wait.

Randolph Fields had taken to describing the relationship between him and Richard Branson as 'very magical'. 'It's what the Americans call "synergy",' he gushed to the *Sunday Times*, a week before the inaugural Virgin Atlantic flight. 'Richard and I understand each other perfectly.'

The fact that Branson had not a clue what 'synergy' meant was just one sign that he found the understanding between them somewhat less than 'magical'. 'Exhausting', 'frustrating', 'maddening' – all of these things, perhaps; but 'magical'? No.

Indeed, from the outset, relations with 'Dear Randy' had been somewhat strained. The original agreement, signed on 4 April, between the Virgin Group and Fields Investments, Fields's holding company, gave Virgin 75 per cent equity in the new Virgin Atlantic Airways to Fields's 25 per cent. But it also guaranteed Fields equal say in the running of the company, by the expedient of comprising the board of four directors. Two 'A' directors would come from Virgin Group, balanced by two 'B' directors – Fields and another director nominated by him. As president of the company, Branson would not have a seat on the board. That agreement had been signed only after acrimonious debates about the size of Fields's shareholding (Fields had originally wanted 50 per cent), and the payment to him of £250,000 – the amount of money he had spent on laying the foundations of the airline before meeting Branson. At one stage, Fields had threatened to pull out of the arrangement altogether and find a new partner, until the CAA made it clear that Fields would not have a licence without Virgin's involvement.

The agreement drawn up between Branson and Fields in April 1984 gave Fields, as chairman, responsibility for the day-to-day running of the airline, while Branson, as president, considered the broader picture. Fields set up new offices in London's West End – in Woodstock Street – with the reservations and booking staff. Branson continued, as ever, to work from the houseboat. But the arrangement was not a recipe for happiness. Fields privately resented the way in which Branson had taken responsibility for the purchase of the first Virgin aircraft; while Branson, for his part, grew increasingly alarmed at the way in which his new partner appeared to be running the rest of the company.

In early June, while Fields was away in New York, a deputation approached Branson from the Woodstock Street offices, with a litany of complaints. Bookings, reservations, staffing . . . just about everything, they claimed, was in a state of total chaos. Branson brought in a travel consultant, Douglas Paul, from Virgin's own travel agency subsidiary, All Star Travel, to report on the situation. With barely a week to go before the maiden flight, Paul's report made alarming reading. He reported that the situation at Woodstock Street was 'far worse than was previously imagined', and that 'the prevailing background chaos could have severe effects on the future successful operations of Virgin Atlantic'.

Ticketing was 'desperate'. Operating problems with the computer reservations system had resulted in a backlog of 10,000 bookings needing to be rechecked, making it impossible to tell who had and had not paid for tickets. In all the confusion, it was quite possible that some people would be flying on Virgin Atlantic for nothing. Paul then addressed the matter of Fields's man-management. Staff had been employed, he claimed, who were grossly inexperienced and 'who would not be in a position to question or disagree with any actions being taken by Randolph Fields'. Most 'appeared to be frightened of the man'. The commercial manager had admitted he obtained the job 'because he knew Randolph's brother', and was 'totally out of his depth'. Morale, Paul went on, was at a 'frighteningly low level'.

'I cannot understand how or why Randolph Fields has been allowed to permit such a situation when the whole of the Virgin Group is at stake if Virgin Atlantic is not a success.' This, clearly, was melodrama, but the point was made.

At a strained board meeting held on 18 June, four days before take-off, Douglas Paul's report on the reservations situation was read out and it was agreed that Fields should leave the Woodstock Street offices immediately and relinquish personal control of the reservations. Branson began to assemble a dossier on his chairman's activities. It included a memorandum from David Tait, in charge of American operations – and originally a Fields appointee – urging that Fields 'be restrained from any further involvement in Virgin Atlantic's North American operation'. Tait had already resigned after a row with Fields, only withdrawing his resignation after Branson had pleaded with him to stay on.

By this time, Branson and the other Virgin Group directors were of one opinion, Randolph Fields must be got rid of. In formulating the original agreement with Fields, Branson had ensured a clause be written in stipulating that, under the Articles, Virgin as the majority shareholder had the right to appoint more than two 'A' directors, and thereby gain a majority of the board, if it was 'not satisfied with the financial position, or the management position of the company'. Confident that there was enough evidence to support the move, Branson now appointed himself to the board as an 'A' director, giving the Virgin Group a three to two majority over Fields.

To Fields it was clear what was happening. Having grabbed the idea of the airline with both hands, Branson was now trying to squeeze him out of the operation altogether. In July, Fields sought an injunction, restraining Virgin Atlantic from 'terminating or altering' its agreement with him and restraining Branson from acting as a director. In a sworn affidavit, Fields alleged that Branson and the Virgin Group had 'merely treated [Virgin Atlantic Airways] as just another subsidiary without any proper regard for the contractual arrangements entered into in April 1984'. He went on: 'The truth of the matter is that Mr Branson and the Virgin Group appear to be determined to get the company exclusively for themselves and to exclude me from it. That is their real motivation for this litigation.'

The injunction was subsequently lifted by the court, effectively endorsing Branson's appointment as director and leaving the way open for the Virgin Group directors to exercise full and unhindered control of the airline. However, the court did restrain Virgin from terminating or altering the terms of Fields's service agreements. Even this, however, was only a partial reprieve for Fields. In September, Virgin and Fields finally agreed that his contract should be terminated, and a sum of £125,000 was agreed in compensation. He did, however, continue to remain a director and shareholder in Virgin Atlantic until an agreement was reached in 1985 to buy out his shareholding.

Branson was unrepentant about Fields's departure. It was not, he would say, a reflection of his – Richard Branson's – inability to enter into equal partnership with anybody. 'I would love to be in partnership with someone who would do all the work, and leave me 50 per cent. But it gets frustrating when you think the other person isn't delivering, or is endangering our interest. And that was the situation with Randolph.' The nuts and bolts of running an airline were not necessarily Fields's strength, Branson said, 'but conceptually, he was very good'. The fact that Fields had arrived out of the blue, managed to sell Branson the basic idea of an airline and walked away six months later on his way to a million pounds ... that was evidence of a particular sort of skill which Richard Branson could appreciate. Branson did not have to like Randolph Fields, but, in a curious sort of way, he admired him.

Richard Branson had always known that, sooner or later, he would have to face the possibility of a price war with the big transatlantic carriers. Everyone from Sir Freddie Laker to the CAA warned him it was likely, and Branson had taken what measures he could to prevent it happening.

In June 1984, shortly before Virgin's inaugural flight, he sought a meeting with the Government's Secretary of State for Transport, Nicholas Ridley. What Branson was looking for was nothing short of government protection. He expressed to Ridley his fears that, come the winter months, when payloads on the North Atlantic dropped alarmingly, the big airlines could very easily get together to squeeze Virgin out of the market-place, in the same way they had squeezed out Laker. The government should bear in mind that Virgin did not have permission to fly 95 per cent of the routes around the world; it was unfair for British Airways to fly a 'loss leader' on the one route where Virgin did have permission. When there was *prima facie* evidence of an airline cutting the price on one route simply to take a competitor out of the market, then there should be machinery compelling that airline to cut prices on all its other routes. That way, protection could be extended to small airlines, such as Virgin, in the winter months, enabling them to lower fares in the summer months. 'We believe in competition,' Branson told Ridley, 'but having a bleeding competition with a blood bank isn't fair competition.'

Branson realised the difficulty of trying to influence a Tory minister, whom he suspected was fairly sceptical about the idea of government interference at all. But Ridley was cordial and interested in what Branson had to say. Even if he did politely turn down Branson's parting offer of a seat on Virgin's inaugural flight – for obvious reasons.

The crisis Branson had been expecting broke in October, when British Airways dropped the price of their cheapest return ticket on the London–New York route from £278 to £259 – only £1 more than Virgin – and began selling tickets 'subject to government confirmation'. The same day, the other major transatlantic carriers, PanAm and TWA, rushed to match them. Branson protested loudly to whoever would listen: the Virgin fare was a 'realistic' one, which reflected his airline's lower overheads. The new fares proposed by the big airlines, however, were not realistic at all, but 'predatory' – designed simply to put Virgin out of business.

The outbreak of price warfare put the British government in an ideological dilemma. In theory, the government was pledged to promote more competition among airlines, with the aim of reducing fares and generating more services. To be seen to be defending Virgin against attack by the big airlines would be a contradiction of this. But more pragmatically, the British government was hamstrung by its aviation agreements with America, and the fears of debilitating legal consequences if it allowed a price war to break out.

The ill-feeling between the British and American governments which had led to the delay in granting Virgin an exemption to fly into the States back in June now resurfaced. At the heart of the disagreement was the air-traffic agreement between the two countries, known as the

Bermuda Two Agreement, which had been signed in 1977. This agreement, arrived at in a period of relative stability in international air travel, had been thrown into question with the arrival – and more pertinently, the collapse – of Freddie Laker's cut-price service. Laker's liquidators had taken the opportunity under American law to pursue an anti-trust suit, seeking up to £1 billion in damages against British Airways and others, claiming that through 'predatory' fare-cutting they had driven Laker out of business. Britain argued that British Airways should not be included in any anti-trust action because, under the Bermuda Two Agreement, British carriers should be excluded from the effects of US domestic law.

The new fare reductions filed by British Airways, in response to Virgin and People Express, and the matching fares filed by the other big airlines, therefore worried the British government. Branson's fierce attack on 'predatory pricing' carried with it the implied threat of another anti-trust suit against British Airways in the American courts. And the implications of that as the government readied itself for the privatisation of British Airways were too horrific to contemplate. The government were not reassured to learn that Branson had been in consultation with Robert Beckman, the New York lawyer who was fighting the anti-trust action on Laker's behalf. Beckman had indeed contacted Branson to see if he could advise him on the taking of anti-trust action, but the offer had not been taken up. The only consultations now were with Beckman's market research consultancy over anodyne questions of marketing.

The British government now sought assurances from the Americans that British Airways, and other UK airlines, would be safe from anti-trust action if the new fare proposals were accepted. The Americans refused, arguing that granting immunity from US domestic law to one section of commerce would create immense constitutional difficulties in other areas. On 18 October, therefore, the British government turned down the new fare proposals from American operators, while the CAA rejected British Airways' request. Branson himself said that he welcomed the ruling, if it accepted that the fare proposals were predatory, but that he was 'obviously disturbed' if the decision had been taken as a political move to stop Virgin applying in the US courts for remedies under the anti-trust laws.

In fact, the government's action caused chaos. Some 100,000 tickets had already been sold at the new, low fare, in Britain and America, before the government ruling. On 30 October, faced with the prospect of chaotic and unpleasant scenes at airports if ticket-holders were asked to pay a surcharge, the Transport Secretary, Nicholas Ridley, performed an about-turn, and allowed a moratorium on the cheap tickets sold up to 18 October. Seven thousand people who had bought tickets at the cheap rate in the following week were obliged to pay a surcharge.

However, the principle of resisting fare cuts – for whatever reason – had been maintained. Ray Colegate of the CAA continued to argue that his authority had moved to block British Airways on the principle of 'infant firm protection'. 'One intervenes to protect competition, to ensure so far as one can that competition continues to exist in the marketplace.' But it was not, as it proved, an effective measure. The CAA had allowed British Airways to introduce a low-cost Latesaver fare on the Boston route. In the event, PanAm, which did not serve Boston, seized the opportunity to introduce a London–New York–Boston ticket, in order to fly to New

York on the lower Boston fare. The result was that all New York fares could now be reduced, bringing them to a level only slightly above that of Virgin's competing New York fare, and fares on the Boston route were adjusted to match the New York level. This time, Colegate told Branson that there was nothing more the CAA could do, and that Branson was 'on his own' from then on. Virgin subsequently filed its own, even lower fare to New York.

The cut and thrust over pricing proved a salutary experience for Virgin Atlantic and Richard Branson. The international airline business is a fiercely combative arena, where competitors enjoy nothing more than slitting each other's throats; Virgin's tribulations showed the difficulties in allowing it to be governed by free market principles. Branson's feeling that 'competition is good for the consumer if fares come down, but not good if it puts us out of business' constituted a political education of sorts. Competing in the free market of air fares had catapulted Branson into the rarefied area of government policy and international relations, and helped to define what had hitherto been purely instinctive beliefs in a more rigid ideological context. The fact that Virgin Atlantic had won the licence to fly the Atlantic in the first place was, he said, a brave move on the part of the Civil Aviation Authority, given the Laker experience, but also a measure of government policy. 'There is no way we would have got in under a Labour government.'

Big business and politics, he had now discovered for himself, were inseparable bedfellows – a lesson he learnt with increasing frequency in the years to come. The shift of Richard Branson from the hazy and ill-defined politics of idealism to the politics of pragmatism had begun in earnest.

By the end of 1984, Virgin Atlantic seemed well and truly airborne. The airline had withstood the predatory pricing moves of its competitors, and overcome its early loss. It had been running at more than 90 per cent capacity through the peak season, and weathered the lean winter months to show a profit of more than £250,000. Emboldened by the success on the North Atlantic, Virgin now introduced a short-haul service to Maastricht, in Holland, with an initial fare of £19 one-way, using a plane leased from British Island Airways. The service also proved a modest success, and Branson began exploring the possibility of flying to Dublin, and to Miami, on a route which had not been taken up by a British carrier since the collapse of Laker.

Everything pointed to the fact that something at an extremely high altitude looked favourably on Branson's endeavours. Only a bolt out of the blue could stop him now.

It came at eleven o'clock on the morning of 18 April, when Chemical Bank in New York telephoned Branson with some unexpected news. A crisp voice informed him that the arrangement between Chemical and Virgin over the financing of Virgin's aircraft was to be terminated forthwith, and the aircraft given back to Boeing. Branson was staggered. What the hell was going on? Virgin's payments had all been made on time, and as far as he was aware there was no problem at all. What he did not know was that Chemical had run into massive internal problems. The New York headquarters of Chemical had discovered that the deal their leasing arm, based in London, had negotiated with Virgin could technically be regarded as an infringement of New York banking law, through theoretically leaving Chemical with unlimited liability if the Virgin Group were to suddenly collapse. It was not Virgin's responsibility, but from Chemical's head-quarters in New York, the instruction went out to terminate a number of existing contracts negotiated by the London office – Virgin's among them.

The news was deeply worrying for Branson. Whatever happened, the Virgin Group was secure, but the airline, 500 jobs, everything that had been built up over the last eighteen months, was suddenly in jeopardy through no fault of anyone at Virgin. Furthermore, if Chemical did hand back the plane to Boeing, it would be at an effective cost to Virgin of a further $10m – the amount by which the plane's value had increased in the time Virgin had owned it.

If Chemical attempted to terminate the deal, Branson threatened, then Virgin would sue for that $10m, plus damages. Within two hours, a representative from Harbottle and Lewis, the lawyers retained by Branson, was at the High Court in London getting an injunction to stop Chemical handing back the plane to Boeing. The possibility of the action being leaked to the press – with the ensuing headlines screaming BRANSON AIRLINE COLLAPSE – did nothing to calm Branson's nerves. But to his enormous relief the story never got out.

The injunction began a saga that was to run for two months, as Virgin scrabbled to find another bank to take over the role played in the lease agreement by Chemical. After much negotiation, Security Pacific eventually agreed to take Chemical's place in the leasing arrangement, securing the future of the airline – at least, until more permanent financing could be worked out. However, there was still one more thing to worry about: the currency protection deal which Virgin had entered into at the beginning of the aircraft negotiation. When Virgin had entered into the deal, the dollar rate stood at 1.45 to the pound. But by January the pound had dropped in value to 1.05. This was not good news. The currency deal expired in July; if the exchange rate remained the same, Virgin would be obliged to pay £6m, to make up the difference. This would not affect the finances of Virgin Group at all. The £6m would be paid for by the sale of the aircraft, but that would mean the end of the airline.

For the next four months, Branson watched the exchange rate with uncommon interest and trepidation, until the pound at last began to climb penny by agonising penny against the dollar. By February, the potential loss to Virgin was down to £4m. As the commitment came due in July, the exchange rate had climbed above $1.40 to the pound, leaving Virgin with a loss of £0.5m. That, thought Branson, was affordable.

To the passengers in the skies over the Atlantic drinking free champagne to celebrate the first anniversary of Virgin Atlantic, oblivious to all the dramas which had unfolded to keep them airborne, it probably would have seemed a bargain.

Chapter 11

Sound and Vision

The day on which the most powerful man in the record business threatened to blow Richard Branson's aircraft out of the sky, to destroy his business, his life, just about everything, actually started pleasantly enough . . .

Richard Branson was sitting in the garden of his Oxfordshire home when Walter Yetnikoff rang. Branson had come to relish his weekends in the country. It had always been his practice to escape from London on Fridays whenever possible. For years, the Manor, Virgin's Oxfordshire recording studio, had doubled as a retreat, but the perpetual presence of rock bands, the ever-present reminders of work, had obliged Branson and Joan to find a country home that was properly their own. The home they found was a mere two miles from the Manor, across rolling pasture; a sprawling and picturesque stone-built farmhouse set in eight acres of land. The River Cherwell flowed past the bottom of the garden, a home to black Australian swans and a small colony of otters, fenced in for protection. At the back of the house, behind a screen of trees, a pasture had been cleared to accommodate a cricket pitch, where a local XI played regularly. The house did not bring solitude – the weekends were invariably shared with friends and business acquaintances – but at least the quality of congestion was of Branson's and Joan's own choosing.

That June weekend in 1984, a few days before Virgin Atlantic's inaugural flight to America, a small party of guests from Europe gathered at the house – the heads of Virgin operations in France, Germany and the Benelux countries. Branson bubbled with enthusiasm for the airline; for the others, the principal topic of conversation was the apparently unstoppable rise of Culture Club.

Virgin Atlantic was not quite 'the airline that Boy George paid for', as popular newspaper mythology already had it, but nobody could deny that the singer had made a considerable difference to the company's fortunes. The Boy George phenomenon had swept through every country in Europe, and then the world; in less than two years, Culture Club had sold almost twenty-five million singles and albums. America had found the idiosyncratic charms of George particularly irresistible. Boy George lookalikes, Boy George dolls, admittance to the charmed circle of chat-show guests – George, as *Rolling Stone* put it, had won 'the Liberace vote' – an allusion to which he would later pay oblique homage when, in early 1984, Culture Club won the Grammy Award for Best Newcomers. 'America,' said George on receiving his award, 'you have taste, style and you know a good drag queen when you see one.'

Walter Yetnikoff had not risen to be chairman of CBS Records America by recognising good drag queens but by recognising good business propositions and, in pop music, on present reckoning, Boy George was just about the best business proposition there was. CBS had licensed Virgin acts in America on and off for several years, but none had been as successful as George, and Yetnikoff was determined to keep him for as long as possible. But the harmonious relationship between Virgin and CBS, locked in an embrace of mutual profitability around the mascarra'd arriviste from South London, was now in some jeopardy.

In the last twelve months, Virgin had made their first, tentative moves into full-scale feature films with two productions: a modestly budgeted film called *Secret Places*, and the more ambitious *Electric Dreams*. A story of young love and computer-technology, *Electric Dreams* was symptomatic of the coming generation of Hollywood films to which a soundtrack laden with pop hits was deemed crucial. The presence of two tracks by Culture Club was an insurance policy for the soundtrack's success, but posed a potential problem. As exclusive licensees of Culture Club's output in America, CBS had indicated that they would be prepared to release the soundtrack. The film was nearing completion when Walter Yetnikoff made a suggestion: as CBS were releasing *Electric Dreams*, perhaps Virgin would care to consider extending the Culture Club contract by a further two albums? Branson declined: plans for Virgin's own American label were now under way and Branson wanted to ensure that Culture Club were not contracted to anybody else when it was launched. CBS put their suggestion another way. They would not be releasing *Electric Dreams* unless the Culture Club contract was extended by another two albums. Branson was furious. As Yetnikoff well knew, the box-office potential of *Electric Dreams*, the movie, depended greatly on having hit songs from the soundtrack on the radio and on MTV at the time of release; what CBS were doing, Branson complained, was unethical.

Richard Branson reflected on his position as he now

left his guests in the garden and made his way into the house to take the telephone call. Walter Yetnikoff's voice crackled down the line from America. The conversation was brief. Walter did not like being accused of unethical behaviour; furthermore, he wanted to come to an agreement over the Culture Club albums. If no agreement was forthcoming he had another vision of the future: Branson's new Virgin aircraft would drop out of the sky; his house would be taken over; his business ruined. 'And,' he railed, 'I wanna telex by midnight.'

'Are you joking, Walter?' asked Branson. Walter was not joking. Rather, he was in the grip of a fury that even from a distance of some 3,000 miles Branson could tell was real and uncontrollable. He replaced the receiver and went out, blinking in the sunshine, to rejoin his friends, joking and laughing on the lawn. To be threatened with virtual extinction by the most powerful record executive in the world was, he supposed, some sort of imprimatur of arrival.

When Walter Yetnikoff telephoned, Richard Branson could joke that Virgin was probably the only film production company in Britain with a 100 per cent Oscar-winning record.

The film, *A Shocking Accident* – a narrative short based on Graham Greene's darkly comic short story about a man being killed by a falling pig – had won Hollywood's highest accolade for its producer. Virgin's investment of just £15,000 was all that was required to top up the £45,000 loan the producers had already secured from the National Film Finance Corporation. The ease with which the film was made – not to mention the Oscar – was a misleading omen.

It was characteristic of Richard Branson's belief in

giving people a chance, that Virgin's film business was being run by Al Clark and Robert Devereux: two men with absolutely no experience in film-making or production, of whom only one had anything more than a passing knowledge of the subject. Al Clark was one of the longest-standing employees at Virgin, having joined the company as press officer in 1974, shortly after the move to Vernon Yard. Over the years, Clark's laconic manner, and his relish for anecdotes, had made him a popular and, to Branson, invaluable, figure, equally eloquent in espousing Mike Oldfield or the Sex Pistols to the press. But Clark's principal love was film. In 1981, following his unhappy experience of editing, and quickly resigning from *Event*, Clark had gone on to write a book about Raymond Chandler and Hollywood. He returned to Virgin as 'creative director' – a position which Branson had invented on the spot to woo him back, and which transpired to mean editing the rock and film yearbooks for Virgin's book publishing company. After a year, he became head of production for the fledgling film company, under Robert Devereux.

Being married to Richard Branson's sister had certainly been no hindrance in Devereux's rise within Virgin, but neither, Branson always insisted, had it been a particular help. It was Devereux's ability to consistently beat Branson at chess which Branson said had initially led him to invite Devereux to join Virgin. Devereux went from a position in the marketing department at the publishing firm Macmillan to becoming head of Virgin Books. By scrapping the idea of a fiction list and concentrating on the publication of low-budget 'quickies', primarily on rock music, Devereux took the book-publishing arm from loss to profit within eighteen months, before moving over to take charge of video and films.

Clark and Devereux began hunting for film 'properties' for distribution at the American film market in 1983, looking specifically for low-budget, independent films that would benefit from specialist handling. But fifteen minutes in a darkened viewing room with *A Night to Dismember* or *Death at the Vatican* proved dispiriting.

Instead, Clark went ahead on a number of limited-investment English co-productions: *A Shocking Accident*, *Secret Places* and a film called *Loose Connections*, directed by Richard Eyre and produced by Simon Perry. Perry already had three-quarters of the funds in place through the NFFC, and the 100 per cent tax write-off to which Virgin were entitled in their first year of production made that a profitable, as well as an artistically rewarding, investment.

But ironically the company's first major production was found not by Clark or Devereux, but by Richard Branson. *Electric Dreams* had been brought to Branson by a young director called Steve Barron. Barron had made his name as one of the rising lights of the pop-video business, with credits including Michael Jackson's 'Billie Jean' and several videos for Virgin artists such as the Human League, Japan and the Skids. His production company, Limelight, eventually grew to be the largest video production house in the world. Barron's sister, Siobhan, lived with Simon Draper, and gradually Barron had been drawn into Richard Branson's circle of friends, holidaying in the Caribbean and Minorca, a keen and competitive partner for Branson at tennis and golf.

Barron had a film property; a script which had been shown to him by an American writer and producer named Rusty Lemorande, whose most recent job had been working on Barbra Streisand's *Yentl* – a film on which Barron's mother, Zelda, had been script-supervisor. Lemorande's script, entitled *Electric Dreams*, cleverly wedded the elements of computer technology, rock music, metaphysics and young love into an entertaining, if soft-centred, yarn. Barron was excited by the script and after some deliberation discussed it with Branson. Over the course of ten minutes Barron sketched the outline of the film and its relationship in both artistic and marketing terms to pop music. 'How much will it cost?' asked Branson. Barron sucked in his breath 'About £4–5m,' he said.

'Will it work?' asked Branson.

'Er . . . I think so,' said Barron.

'Then let's do it,' said Branson. He did not get round to reading the script.

Branson's immediate priority was to find a buyer for the American distribution rights, to guarantee as much of Virgin's investment as possible – the film world's usual way of 'protecting the downside'. Universal, Warners and Paramount all expressed varying degrees of interest, but it was MGM which seemed most keen. MGM's chief executive, Frank Yablans, was one of a vanishing breed of Hollywood czars. He had once been head of Paramount Pictures, then a successful independent producer, before being invited to head MGM and pull the studio out of its doldrums. Yablans was hungry for a film that would tap the youthful market of which Hollywood was in perpetual pursuit, and *Electric Dreams* a film plugged directly into the video arcade/MTV sensibility of American teenagers, if ever there was one – seemed just the one to do it.

In the spring of 1983, Yablans came to London and invited Branson and Rusty Lemorande – who was now co-producing the film – to dinner at Annabels for a preliminary meeting. Branson collected Lemorande from his hotel in his recently acquired vintage Humber convertible car. Driving along the Bayswater Road, the car ran out of petrol. 'Got any cash on you, Rusty?' Branson asked, setting off in search of a petrol station. Lemorande thought it charming. 'This is what these crazy English moguls are like; they run around with holes in their socks and no money in their pocket.'

Frank Yablans was a different kind of mogul altogether. He sat across from Branson and Lemorande in the velvet-upholstered gloom of Annabels, short, squat and immaculately groomed, his head almost totally bald but for a small tonsure on the crown, and slightly pointed, giving the impression of a small but potentially lethal battering ram. Beside him sat a large man in a snakeskin suit who said very little.

Branson fidgeted throughout the meeting, 'like a brilliant kid trying to play an adult game', thought Lemorande, as Yablans enthused about *Electric Dreams* and what MGM could do for distribution. The more Yablans talked, the more obvious it became how badly he needed the film. MGM and Universal were by now the only two companies in the bidding. Universal had offered $2m dollars. Branson turned them down, saying he wanted $6m. It was an absurd demand – almost the total budget for the film, when a third as much would have been regarded as reasonable. But Branson was both intoxicated by the novelty of dealing with Hollywood and nervous about the extent of Virgin's financial commitment. The truth was, he needed all the money he could get from America, and instinct told him that somebody would pay it – and that somebody would be Frank Yablans. MGM offered $2.5m, Universal dropped out, but still Branson stuck on $6m. It seemed that the more he dug his heels in the more determined Yablans became to have the film at almost any cost. At length, to Branson's astonishment and delight, MGM agreed to the full asking price. It was the largest deal for a 'negative pick-up' (a film made outside the studio, and before shooting had begun) of a foreign film MGM had ever made.

But Branson's bullishness had not made the arrangement an altogether harmonious one. While Yablans had agreed to Virgin's asking price – he needed the film badly, or thought he did – he felt that he had been taken advantage of by being stung for almost the full production cost. Now, as the film neared completion, he began to make Branson sweat. The deal had changed, he said; as MGM had paid the full amount for the film, they now wanted world rights. Branson might have a contract, but Yablans still had the cheque. This was the last thing Branson needed. The £4m Virgin had already spent to make the film had put an acute strain on the company bank balance. Coutts, Virgin's bank, were pressurising for strict financial controls and were making meaningful examinations of Virgin's overdraft facility. Only after Robert Devereux had flown out to Los Angeles to plead for clemency did Yablans relent, paying the cheque in return for some foreign rights on the film.

Nor was the discomfiture over, however, for either Branson or Yablans. From the outset, a strong soundtrack had been crucial to the film's success, and when Culture Club agreed to contribute to the soundtrack album everyone's spirits soared. But the argument between Walter Yetnikoff and Branson over Culture Club's American contract had sent them plummeting again. Frank Yablans was as angry as anyone. A hit soundtrack was an invaluable trailer for the movie; and, for whatever reasons, Branson was failing to deliver it on time. Branson pleaded with Yablans to delay release of the film until the problem of the soundtrack could be resolved, but Yablans was already locked into theatre schedules across America. *Electric Dreams* opened in Los Angeles with no soundtrack album in view.

For Walter Yetnikoff, the explosion over the telephone to Branson had been forgotten. The matter had now passed into the hands of lawyers and subordinates, who were inching painfully towards a rapprochement.

The delay in releasing the soundtrack was no less vexing for Rusty Lemorande, the film's writer and co-producer. Lemorande had no idea of the rights and wrongs of the Culture Club wrangle; as far as he was concerned, it was Branson and Yetnikoff having 'a pissing contest; two guys trying to see who could piss furthest' – and he was just one of the innocent parties caught in the spray. But ironically, Lemorande was better placed than almost anybody to intervene. He was close friends with Barbra Streisand and not only was Streisand a CBS recording artist, but Walter Yetnikoff 'worshipped the ground she walked on'.

Within a week of Lemorande telephoning Yetnikoff, the *Electric Dreams* album was on the CBS release schedule. It was too late, however, to do anything to arrest the disappearance of *Electric Dreams*. The film was not the blockbuster MGM, and Virgin, had hoped it would be, although over the next five years, on film and video, it did recoup some £8.6m. CBS and Virgin enjoyed modest success with the soundtrack, but Walter Yetnikoff lost his battle to secure more Culture Club albums.

For Richard Branson it was a salutary baptism into the vagaries of movie-making. Sometimes, he reflected, you can strike a deal which is too good to be true; even 'too good for your own good'; perhaps that was the case in his original agreement with Yablans – and Yablans had punished him for it. As Virgin's next project was to prove, financing a film is seldom so easy, and while the film business is where one may make the best of friends, one may also make the most implacable of enemies.

The relationship between Virgin and Simon Perry had produced a modest and likeable film in *Loose Connections*, but also a warm friendship. A softly spoken, bearded man of forty, Perry exuded an air of quiet intelligence and capability which endeared him to Al Clark, Robert Devereux and to Branson himself.

While Branson wrestled to complete *Electric Dreams*, Perry and his partner, the director Mike Radford, had acquired a new property. In October 1983, through their production company, Umbrella Films, Perry and Radford bought the film rights to George Orwell's *Nineteen Eighty-Four* from a Chicago lawyer named Marvin Rosenblum.

Orwell's allegorical novel about totalitarianism had been filmed twice in the past, but it presented a particular challenge to be made in the year after which the book was named. Orwell had not, of course, intended his book as prophecy but as an allegory drawn from his view of Soviet Russia in the year in which the book was written – 1948. If Big Brother had a single model, it was Stalin. And yet prophecy is what it none the less seemed to have become; a yardstick by which could be measured the erosions of privacy and liberty, the corruption and degradation of language and the insidious encroachment of state power into our lives. There was no doubt that *Nineteen Eighty-Four* would be a timely and an important film; but Perry and Radford knew that if it were to have any pertinence it would have to be 'turned round' – from concept to finished print – in under twelve months; a tall order for anybody. In a state of high excitement, Mike Radford had drafted a working script within five weeks. It was obvious that the film needed one, committed financier if it was to be made in the available time. Perry had initially approached EMI and Rank; but over a breakfast with Al Clark and Robert Devereux at Devereux's Notting Hill house in November 1983 the idea of Virgin financing the film was raised, by Devereux. The deal was concluded a few days later at the London Film Festival, where *Loose Connections* was the closing film. It had the air of a double celebration.

John Hurt, the outstanding British actor who had first made his name playing Quentin Crisp in the television adaptation of *The Naked Civil Servant*, immediately agreed to play the leading role of Winston Smith.

Perry's preliminary costings – his 'guesstimate' – had reckoned a budget for the film of £1.9m. That rose to £2.5m, but it quickly became apparent in pre-production that even this was wildly optimistic. It was left to Al Clark to explain the situation to Richard Branson; for £2.5m Virgin would have a reasonable film, with something of the production values of a superior made-for-television movie. A better and more saleable film would now cost £3.7m. Branson's initial reaction was to opt for the lower budget. It took a long and skilful pitch by Clark to persuade him of the wisdom of the second option, and then only with the condition of built-in 'deferments' in respect of Marvin Rosenblum's rights agreement, a third of Perry's fee as producer and the entire fee for Umbrella Films. In total, Perry and his company deferred £100,000 to be paid only when the film went into profit. These deferments meant that the £3.7m budget constituted an investment of some £3m in real terms for Virgin. Radford's fee as director remained intact.

Shooting began, on the £3.7m budget, on 2 April 1984, in a disused railway yard in the shadows of Battersea power station, before moving to Twickenham studios. Almost immediately, the film ran into trouble. For Perry, the challenge of shooting fast, and recreating Orwell's world on a shoestring – albeit a very long shoestring – was proving increasingly problematic. After five weeks he informed Clark that the budget had now been revised upwards by another £70,000. Clark was concerned, but kept the information to himself. By shaving this and condensing that, Perry assured him, a reduction would be shown as the weeks went on. Meanwhile, Richard Branson had been attempting to sell *Nineteen Eighty-Four* in America. It was unusual for a film to proceed without some sort of guarantee of American distribution, but time was of the essence. However, Branson was running into insurmountable problems in interesting American studios in a film where the overwhelming colour was grey, and the hero ended up a crushed and beaten pawn of the system. Everyone that Branson and Devereux met with began by applauding the film's virtues, but concluded with the same reservation: wasn't it the tiniest bit depressing? Couldn't Radford come up with an 'up-beat' ending – something along the lines of the 1954 film of the book, perhaps, where Winston and Julia are reunited on the astral plane? The need for an American sale became more acute, and it also became obvious that this time there would be no Frank Yablans to pick up the whole tab. MGM, savouring the taste of revenge, had been the first to pass on the film as 'too esoteric'.

For Radford and Perry, a happy ending, of any sort,

was looking increasingly remote. Under increasing pressure, Perry had fallen out with two of his key production personnel. The accountant, John Bigland, was the first to go, and the production manager, Bill Kirk, resigned shortly afterwards. Perry explained to Clark that they were 'too stuck in their ways'; this was a fast, complicated film that needed to be made in flexible circumstances; you needed people who knew how to juggle. They were replaced by two reliable industry 'troubleshooters' – John Davis and Jack Smith – fresh from work on the latest James Bond film, *Never Say Never Again*. But the truth of the matter was that, almost by the hour, the film was now soaring way beyond budget.

On the night of 18 May, shooting commenced at the Alexandra Palace on the most difficult scene in the film – the 'hate rally' in Victory Square. In the production office, deep in the bowels of the building, John Davis and Jack Smith were uncovering a chilling scene of their own. Close scrutiny of the accounts revealed that if *Nineteen Eighty-Four* was to be completed on schedule another £1.8m would have to be added to the budget.

The next morning, Al Clark returned from the Cannes Film Festival, where he had been promoting the film, to be told the news. In a state of some anxiety, Clark spent the next twenty-four hours checking the figures before coming to the inevitable, and depressing, conclusion that Branson would have to be told.

There was no doubt in Clark's mind that Perry would – and indeed should – be sacked from the film, and a 'troubleshooting' producer be appointed in his place who would not only scythe through the budget but would also respect the rights of the investors. Having pleaded with Branson in the first instance for Perry's budget to be increased from £1.9m to £3.7m, Clark was now in no mood to be charitable to the producer. Perry's attitude was penitent, contrite and fulsomely apologetic when he and Clark met with Branson on the houseboat the next day. Perry, too, was fully expecting to be sacked. But to both his and Clark's astonishment Branson did no such thing. Scribbling rapid calculations in his notebook, he asked evenly if there was any way expenditure could be cut back, and the film still completed to standard. Perry threw up his hands. 'Richard, I promise you I've made all the economies I can. And everything had been deferred, except for Mike Radford's fee.' Branson struggled to contain his temper. 'I'm not going to fire you,' he said, 'because I know you've had a difficult time. Above all, we shouldn't prevent Mike from making the film to the best of his abilities. We'll just have to go with it.' Perry could hardly believe what he was hearing. He was only too aware that had this been Hollywood and not the Regents Canal he would have been dusting himself off on the pavement by now. But Branson was behaving like 'a sweetheart'.

It was only after Perry had left the boat that Branson exploded. 'I was as angry as I've ever been in my life.' Perry, he felt, had behaved 'unbelievably irresponsibly' in allowing the budget to climb unchecked. At Universal, Paramount or Warners, another £1.8m on the budget would hardly have occasioned a blink. But this wasn't Hollywood. With the airline barely aloft, and Coutts clamping down on Virgin's loan facility, the company was already in a precipitous financial condition. Perry's carelessness and extravagance was putting the whole company at stake. *Nineteen Eighty-Four* was fast becoming Virgin's *Heaven's Gate*. As far as Branson was concerned, a producer's responsibility is to bring a film in within budget – that is his complete responsibility, no matter what the director requires for the artistic and creative side. The producer costs the film to raise the investment, and thereafter he is working on trust to keep the film within budget. 'But there is a danger when you have a film which is a potential masterpiece that people don't worry about whether the film is going to make profits, or whether the financiers can afford it.' Perry, he believed, was 'guilty of wanting to create a masterpiece' – an objective with which Branson could sympathise, 'but not when it was in danger of damaging Virgin almost irreparably'. Branson felt in an impossible position. What had been originally proposed as a £1.9m project had climbed to £5.5m, but if Virgin were to recoup any of their investment there was no alternative but to swallow hard and cough up the money. It was not a position he relished, or would ever forgive.

Branson's immediate priority now was to ensure that as much of the investment as possible could be recouped by a strong – which was to say, profitable – soundtrack album. David Bowie had already been approached, and expressed enthusiasm for the project, but his asking price of £1m, to include just one vocal track for release as a single, was too high. Other names were discussed – the Human League, Brian Eno and Thomas Dolby – but no agreement reached. Meanwhile, an experienced film composer, Dominic Muldownie, who had written some incidental music for the film, was asked to provide a full score, as a fail-safe measure. Then, in July, Branson announced that he had signed the Eurythmics to provide the music. There was only one problem: the Eurythmics were on a tour, which they would not complete until one week before the dubbing of the *Nineteen Eighty-Four* score was due to begin. And, for tax reasons, they would not be returning to Britain: they would prepare the soundtrack in Nassau, in the Bahamas.

Radford was incredulous. He was not opposed to the Eurythmics in principle, but nobody could be expected to record a film score in such hurried circumstances, without seeing the film or meeting the director. Reluctantly, he agreed to send film rushes to Nassau and spoke at length to Dave Stewart and Annie Lennox on the telephone. The music filtered back almost on a daily basis. At the end of a week, the completed score was dubbed on to a print and Branson, Perry, Clark, Radford and staff from Virgin Records gathered in a viewing theatre to pass judgement. Perry and Radford were unequivocal: the music was 'awful. It has absolutely nothing to do with the film,' protested Radford. Even the unflappable Al Clark admitted to being 'rather unsettled by it'. Muldownie's soundtrack may have been dour and undistinctive, but at least it was thematically consistent with the film; the Eurythmics' strident electro-pop bore all the hallmarks of having been conceived in haste, and rang incongruously with the painfully poignant and elegiac mood of Radford's film. Simon Draper and Robert Devereux both felt the soundtrack was at the very least adequate to the film's needs. Artistically, opinion was divided: commercially, there was only one obvious choice to be made. Branson was insistent. 'You should listen to the record people's verdict; they know about these things.'

But Radford and Perry were not placated by the commercial prospects or otherwise of the Eurythmics' record. Unless the Muldownie soundtrack was used, Perry said, he and Radford would disown the film altogether. Branson was faced with a dilemma. If he used the Eurythmics' score for the press previews and press conference, he risked the damaging publicity of a public row before the film even opened. But if he did not use the

Eurythmics' score, he had no commercially viable sound-track with which to promote the film – and there would be a further £600,000 loss on the fee paid to the Eurythmics themselves. Anyway, Branson was beginning to feel bloody-minded. He had paid for the film; he should have the right to choose what music to put on it. His frustration and anger at Perry and Radford grew almost by the hour. None the less, he wrote to Mike Radford suggesting a compromise: the press previews and the actual premier itself would feature Muldownie's music. In the meantime, he would do some instant market-research tests on the Eurythmics' music; if this showed that the music had 'a negative effect' on the film he would think again. If it did not, he would go ahead with the Eurythmics. If that was the case, however, it would be his, Branson's, decision and nobody else's, and he asked that there should be 'no public denunciations' of the film by Radford and Perry, 'as we would never speak foul of anybody going over budget'.

Nineteen Eighty-Four opened at the Odeon Haymarket in October 1984, with the music of Dominic Muldownie. Talking to reporters afterwards, Simon Perry and Mike Radford paid tribute to Richard Branson's support and vision. What they did not realise was that, even as they spoke, another print of the film was being prepared for general distribution – with the Eurythmics' soundtrack. The market-research tests, held at a series of sneak previews in front of specially selected audiences, had revealed no antipathy to the Eurythmics' music. Richard Branson had moved to secure his investment. And it was that version of the film which was seen by audiences throughout Britain, and most of the world. Ironically, in Germany, the Muldownie soundtrack was used, due to technical problems; and in France, too, where Radford invoked the French law of *droit d'auteur* to insist on the film being exhibited to his criteria.

The relationship between Branson and Perry and Radford now began to freeze. In November, Mike Radford attended the ceremony for the Evening Standard Film Awards, where *Nineteen Eighty-Four* was named as Best British Film of the Year. In his acceptance speech, Radford departed dramatically from the usual text of pleasantries and tributes. 'The film for which I have won this award is not the film now playing in the cinemas,' he told a shocked audience. 'That film has a soundtrack foisted on it by Virgin and the Eurythmics against my wishes.' Richard Branson was not in the audience to hear Radford's outburst, but Robert Devereux and his wife Vanessa – Branson's sister – were. By the end, tears were streaming down Vanessa's face. Pulling her to her feet, Devereux beat a path to the door, through a thicket of newspaper reporters. In fact, it had not been a spur of the moment gesture by Radford. The speech was planned and, on arriving at the Inn on the Park for the ceremony, Radford had even given a television interview, for transmission later that night, as if the presentation had already been made, and commenting on the speech which he had yet to deliver. Only as he took his seat in the darkened banqueting suite, after giving the television interview, did he begin to have serious doubts over what he was about to say, but by then he was already committed to the course.

Certainly Richard Branson was not pleased to be publicly criticised by Radford, but years in the record business had made Branson both respectful and understanding of artistry. But he remained unshakeable in his belief that it is one hundred per cent the producer's responsibility to bring the film in on budget. It was for

Simon Perry that Branson harboured a lingering resentment and antagonism.

In October, an item appeared in the William Hickey column of the *Daily Express*, talking of the 'almighty row' which had broken out between Branson and Perry over *Nineteen Eighty-Four*. In it, Perry was quoted as saying that Branson had been unable to sell the film in America due to 'inexperience', and that Branson had told 'a tissue of lies' about the budget going over. Branson, meanwhile, criticised Perry for running up 'three times' the original budget. A certain piquancy was added to this exchange of unpleasantries by the fact that the Hickey story was written by the wife of one of Branson's closest legal advisers. It was not that lawyer, however, who advised Branson to sue Perry for libel. Perry insisted he had been misquoted in the piece and threatened to bring a further action against the *Daily Express*. The case did not come to court, but it did result in Perry and the *Express* making a joint contribution to a charity of Branson's choice. Perry lost a further £15,000 in legal fees.

The case had barely been resolved when, in March 1985, Branson took his place at a table with Joan, Al Clark and Clark's female companion for a BAFTA awards dinner at a London hotel. Midway through the evening, the party was interrupted when Simon Perry appeared at the table to exchange pleasantries with Clark's companion. Branson regarded him coldly. 'Can you please leave this table,' he said. 'I just don't want to sit at the same table as you. Please, just go away.' The chilled politeness of the request was more telling than if he had launched himself across the table at Perry's throat. Perry quietly left without a word. When Clark's companion came to Perry's defence, Branson said nothing, but rose from the table and vanished, to spend the rest of the evening brooding alone. Neither Joan nor Al Clark had ever seen Richard Branson snub anyone before. It was an anodyne enough incident in itself, but the effect was curiously, and lingeringly, shocking . . .

Nineteen Eighty-Four marked the zenith of Virgin's involvement in film production. In 1985, Virgin were co-financiers of *Absolute Beginners* – Julien Temple's adaptation of Colin MacInnes's novel, rendered in the style of Vincente Minnelli on amphetamines – with Goldcrest and Palace Pictures, the company run by Branson's old partner, Nik Powell. Despite an astonishing amount of hype – or perhaps because of it – the film was a critical and commercial flop, although Virgin recouped their investment. But commitment to new productions began to diminish. As Virgin moved towards flotation on the stockmarket, in 1986, it was decided to stop production altogether and concentrate on distribution. A far less risky business.

By that time, most of the interests of Virgin Visions, as the film division had been called, were already being consolidated in the development of cable and satellite television operations. Like a number of people in the communications industry, Branson and Robert Devereux had followed the fortunes of MTV, the American 24-hour rock-video cable operation, with interest. MTV had put on ten million subscribers in its first two years of operation in America, by the ploy of inviting a series of pop stars to push their faces into the camera and bawl 'AH WANT MAH EM TEE VEE' in the manner of a particularly fractious baby being parted from its mother's breast. It became a clarion call for television brats across America.

But the number of households wired for cable in Britain are few in comparison with the United States. It was apparent to Branson and Devereux that investing in developing cable in Britain would not be viable: any investment must be geared in the short term to making programmes for the European market, where cable was already widespread. In 1982, Virgin announced the setting up of their own cable music operation Cable Music. They were joining an already crowded field; Thorn-EMI had formed Music Box, and Yorkshire Television, Music Vision. It was immediately obvious that the market was not big enough to accommodate three competing systems. Within a matter of months Virgin had merged their operation with Yorkshire TV's to form The Music Channel. They had produced only pilot programmes before there was another merger with the remaining competitor, Thorn. Under the new configuration, renamed The Music Channel Ltd, Thorn held a 50 per cent shareholding, Virgin 45 per cent and Yorkshire 5 per cent. Thorn already had a contract to produce some music programming for Rupert Murdoch's satellite TV operation, SkyChannel. But in 1984, the new consortium began transmitting their programme entitled *Music Box* on its own signal to 40,000 homes in Holland, Finland and Britain. In its combination of pop videos, concerts and somnambulistic 'interviews' with the stars, *Music Box* aped the format established by MTV, and thinly modified it for European consumption. By the beginning of 1986, the channel was transmitting twenty-four hours a day to some three million homes across Europe.

By this time, Thorn's commitment to cable television was beginning to wane. The company had been in disarray for some time, incurring huge losses in both its record and film divisions, and simply could not afford to sustain the investment in cable; which had become, in short, a liability. Virgin had already invested £3m in the operation, and Branson was prepared for a further two years' investment before seeing some return. The news Thorn wanted out did not necessarily dismay him, particularly if it meant that Virgin could buy out Thorn's share in the company for a reasonable price, and then sell it on. The clause in the original contract holding that Virgin had first refusal on Thorn shares was a distinct advantage.

Branson knew that if he acquired Thorn's shares, he would find a ready buyer in Granada, the television rental company. Granada had been looking for a way into the European cable market since 1983, when they had considered investing in their own music channel, in rivalry to the then independent operations of Thorn, Virgin and Yorkshire. Ironically, the man who had advised them against that, on the grounds that the market was already too congested, was Charles Levison – the lawyer who many years before had advised Richard Branson on his earliest contracts with European record distributors and gone on to represent Virgin's interests in America, but was now acting as an independent broadcasting consultant. (He subsequently became managing director of *Music Box*.) Granada, however, had never lost interest in buying into cable, and now approached Virgin to explore the possibilities. Branson knew that if Thorn were to learn of Granada's interest it could undermine his bargaining power in buying them out, and force up the price – even though Thorn themselves were unable to sell their shareholding to anyone else. So it was that, under conditions of some secrecy, and no little haste, in January 1986, Richard Branson agreed to pay Thorn the total of £1 for their shares in The Music Channel Ltd. Five days later, in a deal concluded in the Marble Arch flat of Alex Bernstein, the chairman of Granada, Virgin sold on a little over half the Thorn shares – for which Virgin had paid some 60p – for a total of £3.5m. Yorkshire paid a further £1m to increase their shareholding. In less than a week Richard Branson had turned an investment of just £1 into a profit of just over £4.5m, and launched Virgin into the big league of global communications.

Chapter 12

Challenger

Each year, Virgin held an open day at Goodwood motor-racing circuit, at which staff were given the opportunity to indulge their fantasies by putting high-speed saloon cars through their paces on the track. There was no more enthusiastic participant than Richard Branson. Speeding fines decorated Branson's driving licence; for Joan, the weekly escape from London, up the motorway to Oxford, was the equivalent of a white-knuckle ride.

One year Stefan Johansson, the Grand Prix driver, was the guest at Goodwood. After two circuits with Branson, each taking it in turns driving, Johansson gave his verdict back in the pits. 'Your boss,' he said. 'He's got a lot of balls, but no bloody skill.'

Johansson might also have added that Branson had a lot of luck. Everybody has their own fund of favourite stories and anecdotes which, like holiday snapshots, are taken out from time to time for reappraisal. Branson's collection contains more than its fair share of reminiscence about scrapes with disaster, narrowly averted, near misses and close shaves: there is the story about accidentally taking off in a microlight aircraft without knowing how to land it; another about tumbling out of control down a steep ski slope and being saved by his ski-stick catching in a rabbit hole. There was hardly a person of his acquaintance who could not add to the list. Steve Barron told a story of how he and Branson were on Neckar Island, clambering over slippery rocks, when Branson attempted to leap a gully some six feet across, with a forty-foot drop on to rocks below. But Branson slipped as he jumped, throwing him off balance. Instinctively clutching at the air, by extraordinary good fortune he ended up forming a 'bridge' across the gully with his outflung hands, and Barron was able to help him to safety. Branson was cut and bruised, but made light of the accident; Barron was convinced that anyone else would have been killed. 'Richard,' he would say, 'has the luck of the devil.' But then, everybody said that.

The Goodwood motor-racing days were the idea of Simon Draper and Rod Vickery, both keen enthusiasts of motor sport. They had even mused on the possibilities of Virgin becoming involved in motor-racing sponsorship. But the idea was never put seriously to Branson. His interest was in flinging cars around a track himself, not in paying for somebody else to do it.

Vickery in particular had become friends with members of the Toleman Grand Prix racing team. The Toleman Group had built its fortune through the 1970s as the largest car-delivery company in Britain. The company had diversified into motor sport as both a hobby and an investment. But when Bob Toleman was killed in an accident, his brother, and the company's chairman, Ted, stopped motor-racing and switched his interest to racing off-shore powerboats, in the process acquiring the controlling interest in a boat-building company specialising in the manufacture of catamarans called Cougar-Marine.

One of the founders of Cougar was a brilliant marine

designer named James Beard who died tragically of leukaemia in 1981. It was Beard who had given Ted Toleman the idea of racing one of the Cougar catamarans across the Atlantic in a bid to win the Blue Riband – the trophy for the fastest transatlantic crossing for which the great Atlantic liners had once competed. Winning the trophy would not only be priceless publicity for Cougar-Marine and Toleman: more importantly, it would provide an unparalleled 'shopwindow' to demonstrate the feasibility of the catamaran as a sea-going, as well as inshore boat, and put it in line for the most lucrative commercial and military markets, as a gun- or missile-carrying vessel.

Enthused by the challenge, Toleman began to assemble a team that included Chay Blyth – Britain's most famous yachtsman, whose achievements included a single-handed circumnavigation of the globe from east to west, against the prevailing currents – and the television presenter Noel Edmonds, who also raced off-shore power-boats as a hobby. All that Toleman now required was a sponsor with some £1.5m to invest to make the project a reality.

Richard Branson had never been on a powerboat in his life. But the idea had immediate appeal when it was first put to him at a meeting with Rod Vickery and a representative from Toleman, Chris Witty. It would be the perfect vehicle to fulfil what had become one of Branson's principal obsessions – getting as much publicity as possible for the airline, particularly in America. It would also be enormous fun. The idea of racing across the Atlantic in a powerboat appealed to the schoolboy in Branson; while the prospect of winning the Blue Riband, and with it the Hales Trophy, carried a distinctly romantic savour.

The tradition of the fastest ship across the Atlantic

flying the Blue Riband from its mast had begun in 1838, firstly with the cargo and passenger-carrying clippers and 'steam packets', then with the enormous floating palaces which plied between America and Europe before the advent of commercial air travel. The Hales Trophy – four feet high, made of gold-plated solid silver, and mounted on an onyx base – was inaugurated in 1935 by Harold K. Hales, a retired Midlands businessman, former Member of Parliament and ship enthusiast, who died – with poignant irony – rowing a skiff across the River Thames. The trophy had been in America, in the New York Maritime Museum, since 1952, when it had been won by the steam ship *United States*. In bestowing the trophy, Harold Hales had spoken of his 'long cherished ambition to present a trophy for international competition, to be held by the ship making the quickest transatlantic passage' and of 'ocean greyhounds of revolutionary design, cleaving their paths to New York and back again'. As Branson was to discover, exactly what Harold Hales meant by the word 'ship' – and what did, or did not, constitute an 'ocean greyhound' – would be a matter of sore conjecture in the year to come.

In winning the Blue Riband, the *SS United States* had covered the 2,949 nautical miles from the Ambrose Light Tower, at the entrance to New York harbour, to the Bishops Rock Lighthouse, off the Scilly Isles, in three days, ten hours and forty minutes – at an average speed of 35.59 knots. This was achieved without once disturbing the equilibrium of the passengers dining off silver service in the first-class accommodation.

By comparison, *Virgin Challenger 1*, as the boat built by Cougar-Marine was subsequently named, was little more than a floating propulsion unit, with the barest of creature comforts grafted on. A mere sixty-five feet in length, the vessel was powered by two 2000-h.p. diesel engines, built by the West German company MTU. With each engine burning seventy-four gallons per hour at full power, space had to be found for 3,440 gallons of fuel, plus a further 200 gallons as reserve. Even that would not be enough to carry the boat all the way across the Atlantic. Instead, it would need to leapfrog between refuelling stops – one off Halifax, Nova Scotia, and a second on the Grand Banks off Newfoundland. A third refuelling vessel would put out from the Scilly Isles, to a point six hundred miles into the Atlantic, leaving the *Virgin Challenger* to straddle the central section of 1,000 miles without a stop.

Branson agreed that Virgin would pay £350,000 towards the cost of the boat and a further £150,000 towards advertising and public relations. Other costs would be offset by subsidiary sponsorships. Virgin Atlantic already spent £10.9m a year with Esso on aviation fuel. Over lunch with the board of directors of Esso, and its chairman Archie Foster, Branson spelt out his requirements for three refuelling vessels and all the fuel for the crossing. It would, he assured them, be an investment generously repaid in publicity. 'We'll have the name BP plastered all over the boat, the refuelling vessels, and clearly visible on television,' he promised – then slid theatrically under the table in embarrassment. Reassured that, in fact, there would be no free publicity for their rival, Esso agreed to come in.

Ted Toleman, the man who would captain the Blue Riband attempt, was a different kind of extrovert from Richard Branson. Both wore beards of the kind favoured by Elizabethan pirate adventurers, but there the similarity ended. Toleman's silver hair rose upwards in a plume; a gold medallion hung on a chain round his neck; a Ferrari and a Rolls-Royce were to be found parked in the drive of his country house. If Branson still bore the self-effacing traces of the Surrey stockbroker belt, where money is taken for granted, Toleman evoked the flashy aura of certain parts of Essex where it is treated as a novelty. Toleman had raced cars at Le Mans and powerboats around the world and had been five times UK powerboat champion. He relished the thought of having his name in the record books for the fastest crossing of the Atlantic.

Chris Witty, who handled the public relations for Toleman's motor-racing team, recognised Branson's growing skill at self-publicity, and the media's susceptibility to it. Witty had initiated the approach to Virgin in the first place, but none the less cautioned Toleman that things might not turn out as he expected, and that the transatlantic challenge 'could become the Virgin show'. Ted Toleman checked slightly at that, but the rest of the Cougar board were keen, and the show went ahead. Branson announced his involvement in the project by taking 400 journalists up in the Virgin Atlantic Jumbo Jet for a low-level flight over the Bishops Rock Lighthouse, and then conducting a press conference while dressed as Long John Silver with a parrot on his shoulder. Few of those reporting the event found room to mention that the project had been initiated by Ted Toleman.

It was an omen of things to come. As the attempt on the Atlantic record drew nearer, it was Branson to whom the television and newspaper reporters invariably addressed their questions, not Toleman, no matter how much Branson tried to bring him into the picture. It was irritating for Toleman. He had brought the idea to Branson, not the other way around; and he was captaining the vessel. The constant references to 'Richard Branson's Atlantic challenge' began to get under his skin.

Toleman was discovering that in the land of the publicity-seeker, the man who actually pays the bills is king. The cost of Branson funding the project was Toleman's surrendering the press coverage which he had craved – and quite possibly deserved – for himself. As the *Virgin Challenger* neared completion at Cougar-Marine's yard, there were squabbles amongst staff about the size and placement of company names on the boat. Two weeks before the event, in a bid to assert authority, Toleman ordered a shirt for himself marked 'Skipper'. Everyone else in the crew, including Branson and Blyth, wore unmarked shirts.

The final crew was to be Toleman; Branson; Blyth; Dag Pike, a former merchant seaman and an expert on navigation; two Royal Marines, Steve Goodwill and Chris Duggan; a Royal Navy engineer, Nobby Clarke; Steve Ridgeway, the project manager; and Peter Macann, a presenter for the BBC's *Tomorrow's World* programme who would be making a film on the voyage.

At the end of July, the team flew to America to await a clear 'weather window' when the attempt could be made. Branson had a particular reason for hoping the wait would not be too long: Joan was pregnant; the moment of birth drawing ever nearer. The likelihood was that the voyage would be completed well before the birth. But then began a frustrating series of delays as the departure was put back due to heavy seas, thick fog and icebergs en route.

While the rest of the crew waited for the weather to change, Branson flew back and forth between New York and London twice in a week to see Joan and to monitor business. On the second trip, he flew north to Scotland, where the annual Virgin staff weekend party was being held. No sooner had he arrived than he was told that the

Challenger was once again on stand-by, necessitating his flying straight back to America. He was already feeling 'completely and utterly knackered' by the time the *Virgin Atlantic Challenger* slipped its mooring in the New York Yacht Club and pulled into the East Hudson River to begin the 3,000-mile journey to Britain. It was mid-day, Monday 12 August.

The *Challenger* headed out in choppy waters, maintaining a good speed riding ahead of further bad weather conditions. At the first refuelling ship off Newfoundland, a slight blockage in the fuel pumps delayed them for almost two hours. By the time the *Challenger* was underway, the storm was almost upon them, whipping the waters into a churning sea of foam. As the *Challenger* gathered speed, a voice crackled through on the radio. It was Branson's mother, Eve, with the news that Joan had given birth to a son. His elation at the news dissipated any feelings of tiredness, or apprehension about the voyage: the bottle of champagne which had been brought on board to celebrate crossing the finishing line was now cracked open. It afforded everyone a last touch of jollity as the storm began to engulf them. It also ensured that good champagne did not go to waste . . .

The next thirty-six hours were among the most uncomfortable any of the crew had ever experienced, as *Challenger* fought its way through the churning seas at speeds of up to forty knots. Every wave created an impact which each crew member could feel in a jarring shudder from feet to neck. There was no escaping the physical discomfort. Attempting to sit in the airline-style seats one was likely to be thrown out, unless strapped in, in which case one was subjected to a violent chafing on the ribcage and the kidneys. Branson made the mistake of trying to crawl into the solitary bunk to sleep, and spent twenty minutes being bounced violently between base and ceiling before managing to crawl free, battered and bruised. There was little for the crew to do but set the boat on automatic steering and hang on as best they could.

The storm at last abated, leaving everyone spent and exhausted.

The boat had by now been at sea for three days, Bishops Rock was just 250 miles away and the record was in sight. Five hours from home, and with eight hours in hand, a mood of elation gripped the *Challenger*. On the radio, Branson conducted two celebratory interviews, in anticipation of crossing the line well within record time. Then, with just 138 miles to go, the *Challenger* rode a wave and came down with a crash; a shudder ran through the boat. It had struck a piece of floating debris, tearing a gaping hole in the hull through which water now gushed unchecked. The crew now donned wetsuits and lifejackets. Dag Pike tried to put out a verbal Mayday signal, but the radio had flooded; the automatic Mayday was activated instead. Peter Macann was cursing; having spent the entire journey fighting to keep his camera straight in the wildly bucking craft, he had been rewarded by the camera jamming at the most crucial moment of all and the whole of his film stock being lost in the heaving sea. On deck, the two liferafts were put over the side and, one by one, the crew slipped into the water and pulled themselves on to the rafts.

Bobbing violently in the heavy Atlantic swell, they watched as the *Challenger* quickly turned turtle and sank below the waves, leaving only the tip of her prow visible, like a tombstone planted in the sea. On the liferaft the crew clung together shivering, but thankful to be alive. The violent pitching of the waves was, if anything, even more uncomfortable than it had been in the worst moments on board *Challenger*. Several people were continuously sick over the sides. It was the moment for the fitting gesture: Branson started singing 'Summer Holiday'. Not everybody thought it was fitting, but all picked up the refrain.

It was two hours before they were finally plucked from the sea by a passenger-carrying banana boat, the *Geestbay*, on its way to the Caribbean. They were greeted by passengers dressed in dinner jackets and evening dresses, about to sit down for dinner. The crew of the *Challenger*, still in their wetsuits, accepted an invitation to dine. At the table, an elderly woman produced a copy of an English newspaper from the previous day. 'And that,' she said, pointing to a front page photograph, 'is your new son.'

Branson was now summoned to the radio. A salvage boat was in the area. Would he give permission for them to go ahead and attempt to retrieve the *Challenger*? Branson said yes, and returned to the table.

'Wonderful news, Chay,' he enthused to Blyth. 'There's a salvage boat on its way.' Blyth looked at him incredulously. 'You bloody fool, Richard. Haven't you read your insurance policy? You'll never get any money back if they go and pull out the boat.'

An RAF Sea King helicopter lifted the weary crew off the container ship and flew them to St Mary's in the Isles of Scilly. The relief at being safe and warm was now giving way to feelings of bitter disappointment. They had done everything possible, in the face of the worst possible weather conditions, only to be cheated by a stray piece of flotsam. The words 'never again' had been heard frequently as the *Challenger* bucked through the storms, battering and bruising its crew – but that was now forgotten. There was no doubt that they would do it again. The inquest afterwards raised the inevitable question about the role which the services had played in what was, after all, a private enterprise. The forces offer a standard explanation at such times. The RAF Nimrod was on Atlantic patrol anyway; the Sea King's job is air-sea rescue; and being called out to emergencies constitutes useful training. All of which is perfectly true, but still leaves the nagging suspicion that they help, above all, because they rather enjoy it. Branson's offer to pay the bill for the rescue was politely declined, and he donated £10,000 to the Royal National Lifeboat Institution instead.

The *Virgin Atlantic Challenger* had not brought the Blue Riband or the Hales Trophy back to Britain, but in its other purpose – as a publicity exercise – the project had been remarkably effective. To have failed so agonisingly, and so spectacularly, was arguably more interesting to the media and the general public than succeeding would have been. Sinking brought the adventure the savour of heroic failure (and Britain likes a heroic failure even more than a consummate success), and seemed to confirm that it was not as easy as people might have imagined it was. As an exercise in publicising Virgin, the airline and Branson himself, it had exceeded Branson's wildest expectations. And come in well within budget. Chay Blyth's worries about the insurance were unfounded. By the time the salvage ship arrived at the *Challenger*, the boat was below water and unsalvageable. Branson was therefore able to recover the insurance. The great Atlantic challenge had cost Virgin next to nothing.

In the wake of the *Challenger* crossing, the creation of Richard Branson's public persona continued apace. His teeth, revealed in the ubiquitous Branson smile, were among the most recognisable in Britain – second only to Shergar and Esther Rantzen, as the humorist Stephen Pile pointed out. Pile speculated that the entire Virgin empire was built on Branson flinging his arms outward in a celebratory gesture and flashing those teeth at the cameras. If the tooth fairy were to steal into Branson's room after nightfall and whip them out, the whole shooting match would be over.

Advertisers now clamoured for Branson to endorse their products, as well as his own. He was filmed in the bath reading the *Guardian* newspaper – one of a series of public figures chosen to reflect the paper's tone as discerning, liberal-minded and tasteful. Branson was indeed an avid reader of the *Guardian* at the time – although he subsequently changed to the *Independent*.

Most interesting of all, however, was the choice of Branson to advertise the American Express credit card. The company had apparently forgotten that they had once sued Branson for illegal use of their logo on a Sex Pistols record sleeve.

The market research conducted by American Express into the effectiveness of the campaign featuring Branson provided an intriguing insight into Branson's 'image' – as perceived both by the public, and by marketing men. The perception of Branson as having come from 'rags to riches', being a self-made man, was very strong. He was seen as being endearingly roguish, a 'kind of Arthur Daley-ish' figure who could 'talk his way out of anything'. The report stated that to those questioned in the sample, 'The key, and most attractive image dimension of Branson concerned the lifestyle with which he was associated and could choose to participate in *if he wished to do so*, and the lifestyle that Branson *himself* preferred to lead. The image of glamorous jet-setting and endless socialising was one that *surrounded* Branson as part of the Virgin publicity machine, but was in fact divorced from the *real* Branson. Thus, Branson and the image of glamour were not fused as one, but led a distinctly symbiotic existence.' Behind this gobbledegook lay an interesting perception. Branson, the suggestion was, had money but did not flaunt it; could choose any sort of existence he liked, yet plumped for a relatively simple one. As one respondent to the survey put it, 'He doesn't seem to be a jet-setter. I think he probably keeps himself to himself, sitting on his houseboat drinking champagne.' The remark showed how potent the mythology of Richard Branson as 'hippie entrepreneur' had become. But while it was true that Branson did not live as ostentatious a life as some of Virgin's artists, the days of austerity were long past. A more accurate picture of Branson's life was conveyed in a glossy brochure for Fiat cars, which dropped through the letterboxes of selected homes in Britain in 1986, rhapsodising at length on 'the style of Richard Branson' – the country house, the Virgin island, the 1949 Humber Super-Snipe. Branson did not even drive a Fiat.

That Branson should have been perceived so strongly as a self-made man was also telling, for, while Branson himself had not been rich as a young man, his background was far from being underprivileged. Yet to the public at large, Branson suggested utter classlessness – an important factor in a society built on subliminal class antagonisms. Leaving public school at the age of sixteen and going into the world had stripped Branson of the more obvious brandings of his caste. Both his parents, and his sisters, spoke with an enunciation which left no doubt as to their social origins – a fact which in his late teens, at a time when he was most set against his parents', and particularly Eve's, political views, had been a source of embarrassment to him – an embarrassment which he, in turn, would later feel somewhat ashamed of. Now, in voice, manner and bearing, Branson appeared to have materialised from the broad and indefinable swath of the 'middle classes'; a child, not of the privileged caste but of the meritocracy. It had born in him a curious indifference to social rank in others, and to the normal conventions of social climbing. A visitor to the boat had once over- heard Branson dismissing an invitation to a dinner where he would be introduced to the Duke of Edinburgh as if it were an invitation to the launch of a new ball-point pen. It was not a gesture of republicanism; there were simply more important things to do. Increasingly, however, Branson found himself party to the official function, where business acumen as well as protocol demanded his presence; official dinners with eminent persons; recep- tions with the Prime Minister and in the company of cabinet ministers. Margaret Thatcher, it was said, looked favourably upon Branson's endeavours. His vigorous entrepreneurial flair was, after all, precisely what the Conservative government was committed to; there was much about Richard Branson that Mrs Thatcher could understand and respond to – even if there was much which she could not.

Friends who had known Branson in an earlier incarna- tion found it somewhat implausible, not to say innately amusing, that the erstwhile editor of *Student*, and a man whose usual response to any menu was to hand it to the person next to him and ask them to order for him, was now invited to Kensington Palace to dine with Prince and Princess Michael of Kent. Any possibility of Branson being 'corrupted' by moving in the circles of minor royalty were kept firmly in check by Joan, whose response on returning home from the palace was to remark that she was glad she didn't have to live like that.

But, to a large extent, the image of Branson leading a life devoid of grandeur and ostentation was true. In fact, he had shaped for himself a life which revolved around his two abiding passions; his work and his family. A daily routine had asserted itself: a series of meetings on the houseboat, perhaps a business lunch (prepared by a Cordon Bleu cook); an unending stream of telephone calls, parried by his long-standing personal assistant Penni Pike and two other aides. As soon as the day allowed, Branson would return to the family home, a ten-minute drive away, off Ladbroke Grove, to be with Joan and the children.

Branson's momentary enthusiasm for naming his new-born son Chay, after his *Challenger* colleague, had been firmly over-ruled by Joan. Instead, he was named Sam. Amidst the comfortable clutter of family life, work continued. While Branson played the telephone and took the occasional meeting in one lounge, Joan occupied another, with a revolving cast of family and friends, creating all the easy, companionable domesticity of a Glasgow tenement. Sometimes, Branson would hardly emerge at all: one night, Ian Howes, an old friend since the early days of *Student*, but who now lived in the Lake District, came to visit. Howes sat in one room talking with Joan, fussing over the new-born Sam, while Richard sat in the other, fielding an unending stream of calls long into the night. Howes eventually left, having enjoyed a pleasant evening, but given up on the prospect of talking to his old friend.

On an exultantly warm and sunny Saturday in July 1985,

millions of people around the world joined hands, in a figurative sense, to help the starving of Africa. Bob Geldof's messianic and obsessive campaign to alleviate the terrible suffering of the African famine belt had involved him bullying, browbeating and morally black-mailing politicians, pop stars, businessmen and the public at large into the service of the dispossessed. It was an act of supreme humanity, and heroism, which had touched everybody by example. (Richard Branson too had quietly got involved in famine relief through Oxfam by supplying and organising the transportation of food and medical supplies.)

Geldof's action had shamed the British government – by exposing its relative inactivity. Margaret Thatcher had refused to waive VAT on the Band Aid record, and the government had subsequently refused to recognise Geldof in the Honours List at a time when he was being seriously spoken of as a candidate for the Nobel Peace Prize. To those of a mind to read between the lines, Geldof's initiative unconsciously and quietly underlined a growing truth, that as governments pledged to the principles of the free market, of 'non-interventionism', surrendered the notion of state responsibility, in all manner of areas, it now lay in the hands of interested individuals to take up that responsibility.

But it also invoked the power of the personality as a political lever. Geldof had a charisma which any politician would envy. He had the full weight of moral imperative on his side – which virtually no politician could claim. He galvanised the conjunction of the youth constituency and political and humanitarian sentiment. 'The Geldof Factor' as a synonym for harnessing youthful enthusiasm became a consideration of which politicians of all shades became suddenly mindful.

Richard Branson's interest in politics had always been a matter of instinct rather than theory. As a young man, he hewed closely to the liberal ideas which had been championed in the basement at Albion Street and which had resulted, as the Seventies wore on, in a not uncommon feeling of dissatisfaction with the parties on both sides of the political divide. Branson was a great admirer of Roy Jenkins. When Jenkins was in the wilderness of the European Parliament in Brussels in the late Seventies, Branson, in a totally uncharacteristic gesture, actually wrote to him suggesting that he should come back to lead another, centrist political party in Britain. It can be safely assumed that Jenkins was not specifically answering Branson's call when he returned to Britain to help to set up the SDP, as one of the Gang of Four, but the party had the support of Branson, at least in spirit. (When, however, some years later, he was approached by the party's treasurer, David Sainsbury, for funds, Branson refused on the grounds that he observed strict political neutrality.) Branson's social instincts had always been – and indeed remained – somewhere near the centre, even as his economic instincts had veered if not towards what was conventionally regarded as the right, then certainly towards the politics of the free market. 'Economically Mrs Thatcher's got it about right,' he would tell friends. 'The dead wood needed to be trimmed. But there's a lot of room in this government for a more caring attitude.'

He was therefore surprised at the beginning of May 1986 to receive a telephone call asking if he would meet Kenneth Baker, the government's Secretary of State for the Environment, at his office. Branson left the meeting an hour later contemplating an invitation to head a new scheme with the twin aim of both improving the environment and reducing unemployment.

The scheme had grown out of a report into environmental improvement and the unemployed by two voluntary groups, the British Trust Conservation Volunteers (BTCV) and the Dartington Institute. The new scheme – provisionally named Operation Facelift – would bring together a number of conservation groups already funded through the government special grants programme – BTCV, Friends of the Earth, Civic Trust, Community Service Volunteers – under one umbrella. Money would be made available through the Community Programme – a long-standing government programme under which the long-term unemployed are given training for a year – to give work to some 5,000 unemployed people on a whole range of schemes designed to enhance the environment. These would include the restoration and rehabilitation of derelict buildings, canals and towpaths; tree-planting and garden schemes.

It was Kenneth Baker's idea to approach Richard Branson. What the scheme needed, the minister explained, was someone to give it identity, focus and flair: a figurehead – but an active one – who could inspire both committee members and, equally importantly, the young people the scheme was designed to help.

There were two ways of considering this. Either it was an imaginative initiative by the government to enlist a youthful, energetic and successful businessman in helping to solve a national problem. Or it was an opportunistic piece of window-dressing, using a vaguely youth-orientated figure as an Elastoplast to cover the chronic disease of unemployment. Branson took the more positive view. To him, the environmental aspect was interesting, but not as interesting as the possibility of helping to create jobs among the young. There is nothing more destructive of the spirit, he would say, than having nothing to wake up for in the morning.

Branson agreed provisionally to take on the task for one year, but with certain assurances – that the scheme itself would not be 'a twelve-month wonder', but constituted a long-term commitment on the part of the Department of the Environment; and that it should be – *and be seen to be* – totally neutral politically, free from government or departmental interference. Before agreeing to accept the role, Branson consulted with David Owen of the SDP, David Steel of the Liberal Party, and met with George Cunningham, Labour's spokesman on the environment. The fact that all gave their qualified approval to the scheme was a factor in Branson accepting, although both Steel and Owen expressed fears – presciently, as it happened – that the public might perceive Branson's involvement as a personal endorsement of the Conservative Party.

Branson's decision was not greeted with unanimous approval by the Virgin board. One of his colleagues pondered that 'perhaps it was the incipient scoutmaster in him' that had persuaded Branson to accept the role. Don Cruickshank, the quietly spoken yet unmistakably steely Scotsman whom Branson had appointed as his group managing director, thought it would be a distraction at a time when Virgin were making preparatory moves for flotation on the Stock Market.

Ken Berry's worries were more complex, but equally prescient. Association with the project, he felt, would tar Branson with the brush of politics; it would be seen as a Conservative Party project, no matter how much Branson fought against it; and charismatic figure that he was, Branson was leaving himself open to be used by politicians. The political spectre would return to haunt

Branson throughout the campaign. While some local authorities – whose cooperation was fundamental to the success of all the UK 2000 schemes – regarded Branson as the embodiment of a new British spirit of motivation and achievement, others regarded him as a Thatcher tool. In visiting schemes up and down the country, Branson's response to any scepticism was to ignore it, greeting town mayors, Tory and Labour councillors and trades union officials with equal perfunctory politeness, always more comfortable talking to the young people employed by the schemes, swinging a shovel or pushing a wheelbarrow. To comment about politics, he would say, was 'counter-productive'.

UK 2000 was just the sort of scheme he would have expected any government – Tory, Labour or Alliance – to back. 'Nobody out of work should be forced to do anything, but work should be available for them to do, and that is how I saw UK 2000.' The longer he spent working on UK 2000, the more convinced Branson became in his belief that every person out of work should have the opportunity to take up a place on the Community Programme at the very least. The amount of money it would cost the government would be no more than it was already spending on Social Security, but that money would be circulated back into the British economy and would have the double effect of restoring pride and dignity to the unemployed, and environmental beauty to the community. It was a drum that Branson continued to beat whenever he met government ministers such as Lord Young and Norman Fowler. In November 1987, the number of Community Programme places was increased by a further 200,000.

His engagement in UK 2000 was to prove an education for Branson in many ways. He came to realise, for example, that the 'political process' was not something necessarily enacted in parliament; that it also meant being seated next to Douglas Hurd at a dinner party, and seizing the opportunity to lament the financial capping on the Community Programme – or stress the wisdom of deregulation in the television industry – in between conversations about children, seat-belts and what Boy George is *really* like. Branson was not overawed by position or protocol; if he wanted to talk to a government minister, he picked up the telephone and asked if he could make an appointment – an enthusiasm and ingenuousness which could cut through red tape, but lead those with more experience to observe that once in the ministerial presence Branson did not always ask the right questions, or correctly decode the cryptic, mandarin utterances he was receiving.

Shortly after beginning work on UK 2000 Branson was approached by a junior minister in the government requesting a meeting, and duly presented himself at the minister's office. After a brief exchange about the environment and unemployment, the minister said he had something else he would like to discuss; would Branson mind coming down to his car? Puzzled, Branson agreed, and they made their way outside to a chauffeur driven limousine. As the car set off through the London streets, the minister finally came to the point. 'The fact is,' he said, 'I also play in a pop group, part-time. Would you mind listening to a tape?' The tape was slotted into the cassette machine, and for the next thirty minutes Branson counselled the minister on a career in pop music. At the end of the excursion, Branson took the tape and said he would see what he could do. The matter was never mentioned again. The notion of public service was growing in Branson almost by the day.

★　★　★

From the outset, as others had predicted, UK 2000, and Branson's role in it, was blighted by misunderstanding. The first public notice of the campaign came in the *Sunday Telegraph*, published in the week that Branson was in the Scilly Isles on a courtesy visit to thank the islanders for the help they had given during the *Challenger* attempt. The *Telegraph*'s story stated, quite incorrectly, that the new scheme was an anti-litter, Keep Britain Tidy campaign, prompted by Mrs Thatcher's recent visit to Israel and her Pauline revelation that Tel Aviv was cleaner than the road to Heathrow Airport. The leak to the *Telegraph* had clearly come from Downing Street, and Kenneth Baker for one was said to be furious: the Prime Minister had 'hijacked' his project to make capital for her own personal obsession.

Branson too was perplexed, particularly when a photographer from the *Sun* newspaper arrived in the Scilly Isles by helicopter carrying a broom as a prop; the first swallow in what became an increasingly tedious and irritating summer of 'Minister for Litter' cartoons and headlines. The misunderstanding was particularly galling to Branson, who had an acute sensitivity about his public persona which could sometimes border on the obsessive.

The relationship between the media and the 'celebrities' they create is a curious one. Branson had consciously set out to build himself into a public figure in order to 'sell' Virgin, rather than having this role thrust unwittingly upon him. Furthermore, it was a role he clearly enjoyed. And the media had been largely complicit in creating it. Branson was 'good copy'; colourful, likeable and invariably available, at least on the end of a telephone, for a quote.

But Branson knew better than most that the press are

notoriously fickle creatures, as likely to bite the hands of those that feed them stories as they are to lick them. Some people take adverse publicity with a shrug, reason that it will be forgotten by the day after next and move on to the next matter in hand. To Branson, however, one thing was paramount. 'The most important thing in my life is my reputation,' he would say. And he was fiercely protective of it. Press management became something of a vocation with him, attempting to tickle the temperamental beast of Fleet Street behind the ears with one hand and keep its teeth at bay with a stick held in the other. Any piece of adverse press coverage, no matter how small or insignificant, was viewed as potentially damaging and swiftly answered, either with a telephone call or a letter to the editor – sometimes from his lawyers.

In 1984, Branson stopped an edition of the American magazine *Rolling Stone* being published in Britain because an otherwise flattering profile contained the allegation that he had once sold bootleg copies of his own artists' records, thereby cheating them of royalties. The claim had in fact been made by a manager, and former associate, of Branson's with a particularly mischievous disposition. *Rolling Stone* were obliged to print a full retraction in the next issue.

That was an obvious example of acting swiftly to stamp out a potentially damaging story. But even stories that were not potentially libellous – in fact not libellous at all – could come to occupy a disproportionate amount of Branson's time. In 1987, when the first interim accounts were published since Virgin had been floated on the Stock Market, the *Financial Times* Lex column published a less than flattering piece about Virgin's performance. Branson was angry, and summoned Don Cruickshank to help deal with it. After numerous exchanges of telephone calls and correspondence, taking up the best part of a full day's work for both men, the most the *Financial Times* would concede was the publication of a letter in reply. It was hardly a cost-effective exercise, but it was an indication of Branson's determination never to have anything adverse on the record – even when a more effective ploy might have been to have a quiet word in the ear of the editor of the Lex column.

At other times, however, Branson's handling of the press, his way of getting reporters on his side, could be masterly. During National Environment Week in 1987, Branson travelled by train to Wigan to inaugurate a new UK 2000 scheme, with a retinue of journalists in tow. En route, he mentioned to one reporter from a Fleet Street news agency that after nine months he had found the chairmanship of UK 2000 more arduous than he had expected and sometimes felt like packing it in. It was an off-the-cuff remark, half intended in jest, but the reporter duly ducked off the train at the first stop and telephoned his wire service. By the time Branson arrived at Wigan, the story was already abroad that he was to 'resign', necessitating his issuing a hasty and embarrassing denial. When the reporter responsible for the story caught up with the party later in the day, Branson flattered him with his attention, making play with a piece of rope, as if to hang him; then entreating him to a quiet chat on the train back to London. The reporter left the train, head buzzing with the story of some new Virgin scheme to be duly filed the next day. A potentially difficult situation had been defused, and a hitherto 'neutral' reporter had become an ally.

Even before the first *Challenger* attempt, the New York Maritime Museum, which had housed the Hales Trophy since 1952, when it had been won by the *SS United States*, stated that it would refuse to hand over the trophy in the event of *Challenger* breaking the record. Hales, the museum said, had meant it for 'ocean liners, not toy boats'. Stung by the remark, Branson had initiated an exercise to prove that Hales would have approved of the *Challenger* attempts (a belief subsequently corroborated by the wife of Hales's son), and that the trophy could, legally, be brought back to Britain if a second *Challenger* attempt were to be successful. Branson had not been short of expert advice following the first attempt, and all of it pointed to one conclusion: a monohull craft would be preferable to a catamaran. Branson agreed, but where did this leave Ted Toleman?

Cougar-Marine did not build monohulls, and were anyway now more interested in developing a boat for the Americas Cup. Toleman was in two minds. He wanted to make the trip, but it would effectively have meant him buying sponsorship – and a seat – on a boat built by a company other than his own. The board of Cougar-Marine would not accept that, and Toleman stepped down.

The task of designing the new boat fell to Sonny Levi, a marine designer of thirty-five years' experience; and of building it to Brooke Marine, a recently denationalised shipyard in Lowestoft. Levi designed a boat in the classic 'delta' shape, marginally larger than *Challenger*, but with the same type of turbo-charged diesel engines, again provided by MTU. This time, there would be more room for fuel and the crew would be smaller – six, instead of nine. Branson was now captain, with a crew consisting of Chay Blyth, Peter Macann (again filming for the BBC), Dag Pike and Steve Ridgeway. The sixth member was to be Pete Downie, but he unfortunately broke a leg during sea trials off the South Coast, giving rise to an incident that confirmed Branson's growing celebrity. The *Challenger* put back in at Plymouth; as Branson and the crew gingerly carried Downie down the gangplank towards an ambulance, their path was blocked by holidaymakers jostling Branson for his autograph. Downie was replaced by Eckhard Rastig, an engineer on loan from MTU. Esso again agreed to provide all fuel and the first two refuelling facilities; this time, however, the Irish Navy offered to provide the third refuelling vessel. It would, they reasoned, be a good publicity exercise for them too.

At 6 a.m. local time on 15 July 1986, *Challenger II* slipped out of New York harbour, the Manhattan skyline clarifying in the early morning light like a photographic print, then receding to a blur as the boat sped out into the open sea.

The first leg of the voyage was uneventful, the only disturbance coming after two and a half hours with the sudden appearance of a whale, surfacing fifty yards ahead, causing the boat to swerve to avoid a collision. After a rendezvous with the first refuelling vessel (RV), some twenty miles outside the Halifax harbour, the *Challenger* left behind the last sight of land. The boat hurtled on through the darkness, barely reducing its speed from 50 to 42 knots, guided solely by radar – an eerie and unsettling experience which Branson likened to driving a fast car while blindfolded.

The following morning *Challenger II* passed unscathed through the stretch of water known as Iceberg Alley and through thick patches of fog. The boat was ahead of schedule, fostering a buoyancy among the crew which disguised the growing feelings of fatigue. At the second refuelling stop everything again went according to plan.

After a forty-minute stop, the boat kicked into life . . . then suddenly thick black clouds of smoke plumed from the exhausts and the engine stuttered to a halt. Engineer Rastig disappeared below decks to check the engines and reappeared with alarming news: the fuel filters were full of water. The filters were drained, and an abortive attempt made to restart the engines. Again the filters were checked, and again found to be full of water. Somehow the fuel supply from the RV2 was being contaminated, even as the fuel was being pumped on board the *Challenger*. The tanks were now drained of as much fuel as possible, in readiness for refuelling. It was reckoned that for every 12.5 tonnes of fuel taken on board there were some four tonnes of water.

With fresh fuel on board, the engines were restarted, but again ground to a halt. The process of draining and refuelling continued for more than seven hours, eating into the *Challenger*'s precious time margin and straining relations between the boat's crew and the captain of RV2 to breaking point. Rastig had been joined below decks by the refuelling engineer from RV2, Steve Lawes. When the *Challenger* at last got under way it was with Lawes on board as seventh crew member, working with Rastig in the cauldron below deck, drenched in diesel oil as they constantly drained and replaced fuel filters in an attempt to keep the engines – and the attempt – alive.

It quickly became apparent that without more filters the voyage would come to an abrupt halt somewhere in mid-Atlantic. A message was sent out to London control, strings were discreetly tugged and within an hour an RAF Nimrod was setting out from Britain carrying spare filters, to be dropped by parachute in the *Challenger*'s path. The weather had now worsened, and the *Challenger* was fighting hard against a heavy swell to make up the lost time. Through sheeting rain the third, and last, RV – the Irish Navy boat *Aiofe* – loomed into view. The refuelling line snaked between the two boats and a dinghy put out from the *Aiofe*, carrying pots of hot Irish stew. The attempt on the Blue Riband was rapidly assuming the dimensions of an international relief mission.

With boat and crew refuelled, the *Challenger* now set off on the final leg, and a race against the clock. Because of the deteriorating weather conditions, London control had plotted a new route, twenty-five miles longer, but avoiding the worst conditions, steering the boat away from the atrocious into the merely awful. The incessant battering from the weather, the inability of the boat to make headway against the heavy swell and the nagging worry of the fuel filters – still being changed every hour by Rastig and Lawes – had all taken their toll; everybody was now frozen into a limbo of utter exhaustion. But with just four hundred miles to run, the weather at last began to change. Within an hour the conditions were almost idyllic as the *Challenger* sped towards Bishops Rock at its top speed of 50 knots. At the point at which the previous year's attempt had foundered, the boat fell silent; nobody now dared to speak of the record being broken. But at last, three miles out, the slim needle of the Bishops Rock Lighthouse came into view. A small flight of helicopters now appeared in the sky, to escort the *Challenger* towards home, and a greeting by an armada of small boats. At 18.43 GMT, *Challenger II* sped past the finishing line and puttered to a halt as the crew at last gave up the fight against the fuel filters. The Atlantic crossing had been completed in 80 hours, 31 minutes – clipping the previous record by 2 hours and 9 minutes.

The reception accorded to this feat was, by any standards, extraordinary. News of Branson's achievement was immediately flashed on British television, for the benefit of the millions of viewers watching the World Cup final from Mexico. The evening news bulletins on all TV channels led with the story, giving copious exposure to the spectacle of team members in the London control centre, uniformly dressed in Virgin T-shirts, popping open bottles of champagne. It was an achievement which seemed to strike a chord deep in the national *Zeitgeist*, and Richard Branson was momentarily akin to a folk hero.

Whether this was first and foremost a triumph of man's ingenuity and fortitude against the elements, or a public relations coup of unprecedented proportions, it was difficult to tell. The answer was actually something of both. In an earlier age, any expeditionary challenge was the prerogative of the wealthy; and so it remains. But the fact that such an event is nowadays governed as much by the imperatives of marketing as of adventure does not detract from the achievement itself.

A week later, *Challenger II* sailed up the River Thames, the Blue Riband flying aloft, and passed under Tower Bridge raised in salute. On deck beside Richard Branson stood the Prime Minister, Margaret Thatcher. The official British governmental stamp of approval upon his activities was now complete. Even within Virgin, some pondered the consequences of that with foreboding. For Branson it was a moment to savour.

Not even the refusal of the New York Maritime Museum to surrender the Hales Trophy to Branson's 'toy boat' could cast him down. After contemplating suing them, Branson came up with another idea. The Maritime Museum could keep their trophy. He would inaugurate a trophy of his own.

Chapter 13

The Boy and the City

For Boy George, the first sweet taste of fame had turned sour. Things had begun to go persistently, and dangerously, wrong.

At first, success had brought something hitherto absent from George O'Dowd's life – stability. In stardom, bathed in the warm glow of recognition and admiration, he found something to temporarily assuage the feelings of profound insecurity which had been with him since childhood. From the moment George's star began to rise, he was an incessant presence at the Virgin offices, geeing up record-pluggers, arranging video sessions, patiently tackling the growing mountain of fan mail. Gone was the frenetic nightclubbing of his past life; in its place came hard work, discipline and chastening pronouncements against drugs and the warning that anyone associated with the group, in any capacity, who indulged would be immediately fired. He also had a steady boyfriend – Culture Club's drummer, Jon Moss.

But George had always been hungry for fame, and once it arrived he became addicted to it. As the Culture Club phenomenon grew, he took to telephoning the Virgin offices from wherever he happened to be in the world, demanding that his press clippings be read over the telephone to him – an increasingly time-consuming, and expensive, task as his popularity spread.

The sheer volume of press coverage of his activities at first astonished, then alarmed his publicity handlers at Virgin, for George wilfully made himself as available to journalists as possible, in defiance of a fundamental truth of celebrity – that it depends on the maintenance of mystique. He began to discover that modern fame is an entity dangerously susceptible to the laws of gravity. Where once he could depend on being noticed, photographed, talked and written about – when everything he said or did had been seized on for its novelty and humour value – he now began to suffer criticism from the press; worse yet, he was ignored.

Even the seemingly indefatigable ardour of the fans began to wear thin. 'The Medal Song', released for Christmas 1984, became the first Culture Club single since 'Do you Really Want to Hurt me?', two years before, not to reach the Top Twenty.

Complacency and discord beset Culture Club. George's relationship with Jon Moss ended, over Moss's relationship with a girl. George grew increasingly depressed. Everything seemed to be going wrong. Fame had brought him many things, but none of them compensated for the old, familiar feelings of anxiety he had always tried to suppress. It was like banging and banging on a door and it finally swinging open, only to admit you into a room exactly like the one you had just left. In Paris, for the fashion shows, George was the centre of attention among models, designers, hangers-on. In a nightclub, somebody palmed him a packet of heroin, which he snorted for the first time. He was violently sick, but not discouraged. Within a month, he was taking up to a gram a week. Soon it was more.

Concern over George's behaviour, and condition, began to spread – through Culture Club, his management and those closest to him at Virgin. For George was beginning to screw up; turning up late for recording dates, or cancelling them altogether; crying off with 'laryngitis'. When a pop star begins to display the symptoms of becoming a drug addict it puts two things in jeopardy: his health and his career. There are likely to be any number of parties with a vested interest in getting him better, for any number of motives. Similarly, any number of people will adopt a statue-like pose in the face of the problem, fearful of rocking the boat, or incurring the star's – their benefactor's – disapproval.

When Richard Branson first heard of George's problem he immediately sought to intervene. George was not the first Virgin artist to have been troubled by drugs. There had been the horrible death of Sid Vicious, of course; and later, Malcolm Owen, the lead singer of another Virgin group, the Ruts, had also died of heroin abuse. Branson hardly knew Owen; but while the death of Sid Vicious had surprised no one, it had affected Branson for its rank stupidity and inevitability – the way in which everyone had stood on the sidelines watching a tragic and inadequate young boy, deluded into believing himself a 'star', quite literally, kill himself. Help, the offshoot of the Student Advisory Centre, which Branson had continued to fund quietly over the years, had treated any number of drug addicts. And when the brother of a long-standing Virgin employee and a friend of Branson and Joan, became addicted to heroin, Branson paid for the treatment which cured him. It was not long after the deaths of Vicious and Malcolm Owen that yet another Virgin-signed artist, Keith Levene, the bass-player with Public Image, also developed a heroin problem. This time,

Virgin took responsibility. Tessa Watts, who was in charge of the company's promotion department, knew Meg Paterson, the Scottish doctor who had pioneered a treatment by which limited electrical charges are passed through the addict's body. A small, elderly and determined lady, Paterson had faced stringent criticism from the medical establishment over her treatment, but it had been employed to apparently successful effect by a number of pop celebrities, notably Eric Clapton and Pete Townsend. Branson had acquired a second houseboat, moored next to the *Duende*, and Levene was moved in there to be treated over a period of weeks by Meg Paterson. Twice he disappeared from the boat, twice he was brought back, but the treatment was successful.

Now Branson consulted Paterson again over the subject of George. Branson and Boy George had met only briefly before. These days, Branson had almost no direct contact with the day-to-day running of the label – that was Simon Draper's and Ken Berry's responsibility; he had not been involved in the signing of George, nor in shaping the development of his career. But the general consternation now being felt within Virgin at George's condition warranted personal intervention. In April 1986, Branson wrote to the Villa Cimarrone, in Ochos Rios, Jamaica, where George had retreated to 'get away from it all':

> Although we don't know each other enormously well, I believe we have held a lot of respect for each other over the years, and therefore I hope you will give this letter some thought. If the situation was to be reversed one day – and I know how easy that could be – I should appreciate a similar note from you.

It's beginning to become plain to everyone around you that you have a problem (which you are not willing to acknowledge). So clear that one newspaper is now offering £50,000 to anyone who can prove it. You believe you have this problem under control, but it's patently not true. For instance, last week you threw away the TV [appearance] in Holland, your management have just cancelled the most important TV in Italy in case the same thing happened again, etc. etc. Your dealings with people are irrational.

You have a chance of being right back at the top and it would be such a ridiculous waste if you chuck everything away now. Anyway, what or what not it does to your career is one thing, but what it does to you is what really matters.

We have had two of our artists who killed themselves, and others who effectively did the same, and before it's too late I'd like to suggest you acknowledge you have a problem and let us help you do something about it.

Boy George did not reply to the letter. And it would be three months before he responded to Branson's plea. But Branson was correct in believing that a Fleet Street witchhunt was closing in on George. In July, the *Sun* finally emblazoned the story on their front page in letters two inches high – JUNKIE GEORGE HAS 8 WEEKS TO LIVE. The source was George's brother David, who had told the story, he explained, in a bid to jolt the singer to his senses.

For George, events now began to move at a bewildering pace. On the day the *Sun* story was published, he appeared on the *News at Ten* in an attempt to deny it. At his London home reporters camped on the doorstep and eavesdropped at the windows. For four days, George dodged and ducked to no avail. On the fifth day, he vanished.

Even as George struggled to evade reporters, Richard Branson received a telephone call from George's boyfriend, an Irishman named Michael Dunne, as unobtrusive as George was flamboyant, asking whether Branson could now arrange a meeting with Meg Paterson. That same evening, under a cloak of secrecy, Branson drove George, Michael, Meg Paterson and her son down to his home in Oxfordshire so that treatment could begin immediately. Nobody else was informed; not George's family, his management company, friends, nor anyone else in Virgin. Meg Paterson had emphasised that George should be as isolated from pressure as possible if the treatment were to have any chance of success. For a short while, the subterfuge was successful; Paterson was able to continue her black box treatment undisturbed and George began to show the first signs of responding to it.

But in the press the hue and cry for George had also become a clamour for retribution and a demand for 'action' from the police. Three days after George's arrival in Oxfordshire, a squad of detectives engaged in Operation Culture raided his mews house in London. No drugs were found on the premises, but on the following day the police announced that they were now looking for George himself. Branson immediately contacted the police and told them, in confidence, that George was in his care and under medical supervision. Branson said he would appreciate it if the police did not tell anybody where he was. 'Since he had done nothing illegal, there was no reason why they should be involved.'

The police agreed to the request, but the pressure from outside was growing and it was clearly a secret that could not be kept. That evening Branson received a telephone call warning him that the *Daily Mail* intended to publish a story the following morning attacking him for 'hiding' George from the police. Branson immediately contacted the editor of the *Mail*, Sir David English, to complain, and the story was instead modified to suggest that the police had succumbed to Branson's 'influence'.

To the press, Branson now held the key to George's whereabouts, and it was not long before reporters and photographers were camped outside Branson's Oxfordshire home. Inside, a dazed, weary and weakened George maintained his sense of irony. He scribbled a message to the pack at the gate, and held it up to the window. MORAL MAJORITY – HAVE YOU COME TO RETURN MY GRACE!!, it read.

Alerted by telephone, Richard Branson drove down from London that afternoon. Parking his car some distance from his home, he cut across the fields and slipped into his house by the back door. The others were waiting. In the gathering dusk, Branson led the small and motley group of people – George, Michael, Meg and her son – on hands and knees back across the lawn and through the brambled undergrowth (here the controversial doctor was given a lift on the back of the so-called 'Minister for Litter') to arrive at last at a car waiting in a graveyard. A friend drove Boy George and the doctor away. Branson drove his car to his home, as if arriving there for the first time that day, walked up to waiting pressmen at the gate and invited them inside for a drink.

George was taken to the house of Culture Club's guitarist, Roy Hay, for the treatment to continue, and it was there that he was arrested two days later and charged with possession of heroin, on the basis of his own confession. To Branson the implications of this were doubly alarming. 'George had gone voluntarily for treatment. If every addict thought the police were going to arrest them after they'd gone for care, none of them would.' The press, Branson believed, had been largely responsible for the police action: George was being penalised less for what he had done than for who he was.

The interruption in George's treatment effectively quashed whatever beneficial effects it was having. The continual harassment by the press and the ordeal of arrest by the police had put him back where he had started. He began to take methadone – a prescribed heroin substitute – but supplemented with a variety of illicit drugs. His life was now set, seemingly inexorably, on a calamitous course.

In early August, Michael Rudetsky, a session musician whom George had met in New York, arrived in London to begin work on George's solo album. Less than forty-eight hours after arrival, he was found dead of a drugs overdose in George's Hampstead home. George was not on the premises at the time, and there was no suggestion he had been taking drugs with Rudetsky (although Rudetsky's parents subsequently filed a multi-million dollar lawsuit claiming he was responsible for their son's death).

In the desperate hope that work would prove a palliative, George was now shuttled off to the Caribbean island of Montserrat to begin recording a solo album. Virgin were called upon to provide guarantees to the local government that George was carrying only prescribed tranquillisers. Simon Draper had the presence of mind to ensure that the cost of the venture was set against future royalties. Nobody was taking any chances now.

In fact, the Caribbean trip partially restored George, but in London again he slipped back into trouble.

20 The signing of Phil Collins as a solo artist in 1981 marked a significant turning-point at a time when Virgin were in crisis

21 Do you know me? Branson's teddy-boy disguise for the premiere of the film *Absolute Beginners* does not fool Joan Templeman or his parents

22 One of the few occasions when Branson took a proprietorial interest in a Virgin film, visiting the set of *Nineteen Eighty-Four* to meet Suzanna Hamilton, John Hurt and Richard Burton

23 & 24 With cricketers Viv Richards and Ian Botham, whose appearance as 'captain' and 'first officer' on the maiden Virgin Atlantic flight caused hilarity among the passengers (*below*), including (from left) Penni Pike, Branson, Joan Templeman and daughter Holly

25 Fuelled with champagne (*below*), passengers of varying degrees of 'celebrity', including David Frost, Clement Freud and Holly Johnson, of Frankie Goes to Hollywood, find their feet in New York after the maiden Virgin Atlantic flight

26 The teeth, the sweater, the houseboat. By 1984, the components of the Branson myth were fixed in the public imagination

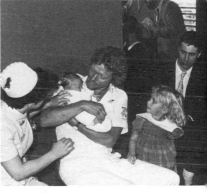

27 & 28 The end of a challenge: (*left*) the bow of the *Virgin Atlantic Challenger I* marks a watery grave for the first attempt on the Blue Riband in 1985. But (*above*) a first meeting with his new-born son, Sam, provides ample consolation for Richard Branson

29 Exultation in the Scilly Isles as *Challenger II* finally captures the Blue Riband in 1986. The Americans, however, refused to surrender the Hales Trophy

30 & 31 Bob Geldof (*left*) shares a ride in *Challenger II* up the river Thames, while (*below*) Prime Minister Margaret Thatcher shares the moment of public glory

32 Branson lending his weight to the UK 2000 campaign

33 At home in Notting Hill, celebrating son Sam's birthday, with Joan and daughter Holly

34 Boy George, the star who, more than any other, paved the way for Virgin's fortune, seen here before things started to go horribly wrong

35 Learning to skydive above the Hampshire countryside, moments before Branson – and Virgin's share price – made a perilous fall

36 The moment of truth as the *Virgin Atlantic Flyer* touches down in the Irish Sea after its epic flight from America, and Richard Branson jumps

37 Branson and Lord King brush shoulders at an airline awards dinner. 'If Richard Branson had worn a pair of steel rimmed glasses and shaved off his beard, I would have taken him seriously', said King. Not doing so was to prove fatal

38   Alex Ritchie, Richard Branson and Per Lindstrand pose in front of *Global Challenger* before taking off from Morocco in January 1997 for their short-lived round-the-world balloon attempt

39   Branson took on the Inter-City West Coast Main Line franchise in 1997 in another major expansion of the Virgin business

Richard Branson was, by now, receiving almost daily reports on his progress. George, he was told by Michael Dunne, was taking tablets 'as if they are Smarties. He's happy and joking, but taking loads. I don't want to see him destroying himself. His luck is going to run out. He's bent on destruction; lying to himself, and the people who do really care about him he rejects.'

As George's condition fluctuated, Branson continued to explore possible avenues of cure. He contacted Harry Eves, the director of Broadreach House, a clinic in Exeter that practised the Minnesota method of addiction treatment, who told him that if George continued mixing prescribed and illegal drugs he would soon be dead.

In early October, George himself telephoned saying he needed Branson's help. In a newspaper interview he had been quoted as criticising Meg Paterson. Branson asked him to come to the boat that afternoon, then telephoned the clinic in Exeter and arranged for a private plane to ferry Harry Eves to London immediately. The plane was delayed by fog, but that evening Branson and Eves went to George's house in St John's Wood. Branson wrote in his diary that George 'sang us three of his new songs, but looked as close to death as anyone could look'. He also agreed to be admitted to Broadreach House on the following Monday, but it was yet another appointment he would never keep.

Eves suggested that emotional blackmail might be required to cut through the addict's curtain of absorption in the drug and his craving for it: Branson might threaten to hold back release of his album, for example; even threaten to turn him over to the police. With George's father, Gerry O'Dowd, Branson even began to lay plans to kidnap George and force him to have treatment. The idea was hastily ruled out by lawyers. But at ministerial meetings, drinks parties and business lunches, Branson began dropping the suggestion to whoever would listen that some legislation was required whereby heroin addicts could be admitted to clinics for treatment, against their will if necessary. In the end, none of this was of much consequence to Boy George. It would be another two months – and require the death of his young friend Mark Golding from a drugs overdose as a catalyst – before George finally kicked his drug addiction himself, through an odd, but effective, mixture of painful withdrawal, tranquillisers and Buddhist chanting.

Branson was rewarded for his efforts by an article in the *Sun* newspaper in November, in which George was quoted as saying that Branson had helped him only 'to get a knighthood'. It was an intemperate remark, made while George was still under the influence of prescribed, and non-prescribed drugs, and he later apologised to Branson for it. Six months later, Branson and George met again, in Basle, Switzerland, where both had gone to appear on the same television programme. George had pulled himself back to the top, 'coming out' in triumph at the British Phonographic Industry Awards and reaching Number One with his comeback record, 'Everything I Own'.

Branson was preparing to fly the Atlantic in a balloon. After filming, a small, and somewhat curious, party retired to a restaurant: George, his manager Tony Gordon, and his make-up artist, Branson, a handful of Virgin's local staff and another signing to the label, the veteran singer Roy Orbison. The talk was of politics; Margaret Thatcher's hairstyle; how to repair the damage done to George's career in America; and of Branson's forthcoming balloon attempt.

'Just make sure you pay my royalties before you go . . .' said George.

'What about a bet?' said Branson. 'Double them if I don't make it. We won't pay you any if I do . . .'

The table broke into laughter. George's party left first. Branson rose, and he and the singer squeezed hands. Nothing more was necessary.

Through the summer of 1984, as Boy George's fortunes began to change from bad to worse, Richard Branson pondered the increasingly vexing question of what was to become of Virgin.

It had long been clear to Branson that the rate of growth he had in mind for Virgin could not be achieved out of the company's generated cashflow and what Coutts Bank was prepared to lend (which was not, as it happened, very much). It was time for Virgin to become a public company. But before that could happen, Virgin's increasingly complicated financial dealings needed unravelling and a more systematised set of controls brought to bear. It was also apparent that the people to do it would not be found from within the company but would have to be appointed from outside.

In August 1984, Branson appointed Don Cruickshank as Virgin's new managing director. Cruickshank was a quietly spoken Scotsman in his early forties whose prematurely grey hair framed a face remarkably unmarked by the lines of care or age. An intense and highly ambitious man, he had been financial director of the *Sunday Times* in the years when the newspaper was owned by Lord Thomson and edited by Harold Evans, where he had been regarded as a clever theoretician, but lacking the assassin's disposition in dealings with the trades unions over the issues which led to the *Times'* one-year shut-down in 1979 and the eventual takeover of Times Newspapers by Rupert Murdoch in 1981. Party to the consortium which unsuccessfully attempted to block Murdoch's takeover, Cruickshank left to work for Pearson-Longman and then for Goldcrest Pictures. It was the film producer David Puttnam, a mutual acquaintance, who had recommended him to Branson.

Cruickshank brought with him a new financial director. Trevor Abbott had formerly been with MAM – the entertainment company that had originally been built by Gordon Mills on the fortunes he made from Gilbert O'Sullivan, Tom Jones and Engelbert Humperdinck. Abbott's youthful countenance and somewhat vague and preoccupied manner – the impression that at any moment he might produce a half-eaten toffee-apple or something cooked up with his chemistry set from his suit pockets – belied an extremely alert and imaginative financial brain. Both he and Cruickshank were businessmen of a more orthodox stripe than anybody else in Virgin, with a demeanour, not to say a style of suiting that would inspire confidence in the City. Their arrival in key positions confirmed that the 'cottage industry' days of Virgin were over. Older hands in the company might still wax sentimental about Virgin's 'family' atmosphere and look back wistfully to a time when everybody knew everybody else, but Virgin was now one of Britain's largest private companies, on line in 1986 to show a turnover of £188.6m and a profit of £19.1m. There was nothing cottage-industry-like about that.

Don Cruickshank had quickly proved himself to be a clever and tenacious operator. Arriving at the height of the dispute with Randolph Fields over Virgin Atlantic Airways, he had assumed the role of Branson's surrogate in the boardroom battles which saw off Fields altogether.

Cruickshank's fundamental, and most pressing role, however, was to prepare Virgin for Stock Market flotation.

To this end, he set about streamlining Virgin's myriad companies into three separate divisions: Music (records, song publishing, studios, etc.); Vision (cable, film, etc.); and Retail. At Cruickshank's instigation, peripheral businesses, such as the air-conditioning servicing and the Top Nosh food line had been discarded. If Virgin was to appeal to the City's institutional investors, it should be seen to be as sleek, profitable and safe – as unencumbered with volatile or high-risk businesses – as possible. To this end, it was decided that the airline – a high-risk company in City eyes – should be instituted as a separate company, Voyager, which would be privately owned by Branson. Voyager would also include Virgin's travel agency, development and manufacture of the Synthaxe musical instrument and the nightclubs. Ownership of Britain's largest gay meeting-place was not necessarily regarded as an asset in the city.

Meanwhile, Trevor Abbott was attempting to unravel what he bluntly regarded as 'a pig's ear' of Virgin's financial operation. To Abbott's mind, the company had been living on a shoestring: to have achieved a turnover of £94m and profits of £11.4m on an overdraft facility which veered between £3m and £4m, as the company had done in 1984, was both extraordinary and a joke. Living largely by cashflow made Virgin permanently vulnerable to the threat of overtrading, particularly at those months of the year – April and November – when it faced vast outgoings on artists' royalty payments.

The visit of Chris Rashbrook, the manager of Virgin's account at Coutts, on the day on which Branson returned from Virgin Atlantic's maiden flight to New York had emphasised the strained relationships between Coutts and Virgin and the pressing need to get alternative banking arrangements in place.

Coutts had long been encouraging Branson to sell part

of his personal shareholding in Virgin as a way of raising capital. But Branson was intent on holding off any dissipation of his shareholding for as long as possible until the company was in the best possible position for public flotation. On 30 May 1985 Coutts wrote to Virgin confirming that the company's overdraft facility stood at £4m and adding, 'As you are aware, we shall expect to see a private placing of new shares or loan stock to provide a capital injection of £15m before October 1985. These monies required to meet the substantial outgoings envisaged at that time, with the flotation of the group being scheduled for the spring of 1986 to provide further funds . . .'

In fact, Virgin had already started discussions with the merchant bankers Morgan Grenfell about a limited private placing of shares, prior to flotation on the Stock Exchange. But in June Virgin informed Coutts that they were now seeking alternative banking arrangements elsewhere. Branson and Cruickshank had been in discussions with Barclays over transferring the Virgin business, but that negotiation had fallen down over Virgin's refusal to accept two non-executive directors of Barclays' choice on the Virgin board. Abbott now set about negotiating with a consortium of banks, persuading them that the Virgin accounts were not 'being done on the back of an envelope' and that Virgin's cashflow – and profits – over the past twelve months was a realistic reflection of the company's strengths and future potential.

The continuing negotiations over new banking facilities did nothing to ease the relationship with Coutts. One morning in July, Abbott was summoned from a Virgin management meeting at the Kensington Hilton Hotel to a telephone call from Coutts saying that a number of cheques had been issued on Virgin's account, and that

£250,000 would need to be deposited by one p.m. that day if they were to be cleared. Abbott spent a frantic two hours shuffling monies from one account to another and calling in overseas debts to cover the transaction.

A fortnight later, on 25 July, there was an even more acute crisis when Abbott was informed that in order to contain Virgin's borrowings within the £4m overdraft limit, Coutts had returned five cheques totalling £420,029 marked 'refer to drawer'.

On this occasion an embarrassed Abbott was obliged to concoct a hasty fiction for creditors that there had been 'a bit of a muddle' over who had permission to sign cheques. A reputation that their bank was 'rubberising' cheques was the last thing Virgin needed. It was an exasperating, not to say ludicrous, situation. Coutts were refusing to extend an overdraft beyond £4m on a company that within eighteen months would be valued at some £250m. By November, however, the new banking arrangements were in place. Instead of Coutts, Virgin now had arrangements with no less than six banks and an overdraft facility which had risen from £4m to £30m. Within a year it would be double that. Everything was now ready for flotation.

The Conservative Party manifesto for the general election of 1979 had made only scant reference to the subject of privatisation. But by 1983, when the government was returned to power by a substantial majority, the importance of privatisation as a central plank in Margaret Thatcher's economic and political ideology had become manifest.

The share issues in British Telecom in November 1984 and the Trustee Savings Bank in October 1986 has fostered a hitherto unparalleled public awareness of share-ownership as some sort of glorified national sweepstake – like a housewife's flutter on the Derby – which would reach its zenith in the British Gas issue and the massive government advertising campaign to 'Tell Sid'. Between 1983 and 1987 (immediately prior to the flotation of BP), share ownership in Britain leapt from 5 per cent of the population to 19 per cent. The long-term political implications of this were clear; under the banner of 'popular capitalism' the government were creating a new share-owning constituency who would henceforth have their own reasons for keeping at bay any political party committed to renationalisation.

Richard Branson had been an enthusiastic supporter of the drive to privatise. In the issue of the British Telecom shares, Branson acted as honest broker, purchasing shares on behalf of Virgin employees, the majority of whom sold them immediately afterwards, making some £300 profit. So successful was this that the offer was repeated on the TSB and the British Gas flotations.

'Popular capitalism', the 'free market', the 'Big Bang' of City deregulation had all become buzz-words of the times. It was as if among those in work the acquisition of money, and with it profligate consumerism, had gained a new patina of acceptability; or rather, shed the old one of disrepute. Implicit in Thatcherism was the coded message that the 'Haves' no longer feel guilty about the having. Business was good. Profit was good, for all stood to profit from the creation of wealth. At its most extreme it was an ethic that had spawned its own mythological character: the 'Yuppies' had emerged as the new exemplar of self-interest and being 'on the make'; clad in 'power-suits', bearing the totems of accessory fetishism, clambering into fast cars bought on the profits of dawn raids on the Stock Markets of New York and Tokyo and roaring back to their warehouse conversions in the new developers' utopia of Docklands.

This was not an ethic which Richard Branson wholeheartedly embraced. Branson too believed that 'wealth creation' was the answer to Britain's economic problems. But not the only answer. For if Branson, in many ways, embodied the practices of the new Toryism with its emphasis on enterprise and its belief that 'trade' was not beyond the pale, then he also retained much of the old Tory sensibility, the belief that success and privilege brought with it a modicum of obligation. The more he travelled around Britain visiting UK 2000 projects, the more convinced Branson became that business had a social as well as an economic role – even if, at this stage, he could not be sure quite how to put it into practice.

If people thought of Branson as a businessman at all it was as a businessman of an unorthodox stripe – if somewhat less unorthodox than he used to be. The association with UK 2000, and the benediction from Margaret Thatcher, had both conspired to make him seem more an Establishment figure than ever. Simon Draper was told that the deciding reason why Elvis Costello, the highly regarded singer-songwriter, had turned down an offer to sign with Virgin was because of Branson's links with Mrs Thatcher and her appearance beside him on the bridge of the *Challenger*. Market research conducted in Virgin Retail about 'customer perceptions' (nowadays, nobody just licked their finger and stuck it up in the air) suggested that the young people buying records in Virgin stores no longer perceived Richard Branson as 'one of us', but as 'one of them'. But what was lost in the 'consumer-warmth' side of the business, as one Virgin executive reasoned, was gained at the 'macroeconomic clout' end.

Branson was ubiquitous. In his public speeches after the *Challenger* crossing, Chay Blyth had taken to telling a story about his erstwhile captain in which Branson hails a taxi and instructs the driver to take him to Billingsgate. 'Give us a clue, guv . . .' says the cabbie, scrutinising his passenger's face in the rear-view mirror. '*Atlantic Challenger* . . . ?' says Branson. 'UK 2000? Virgin Airline? Boy George . . . ?' 'No, no, no,' says the driver. 'Give us a clue how to get to Billingsgate . . .' The point being, there was nobody in Britain who did not recognise Richard Branson.

In 1986, he was voted both the best-dressed man in Britain and the worst; one of the nation's '100 most handsome men'; the Jammy Bastard of the Year (an award made by Robertson's the jam company); and the Communicator of the Year – an award which caused much private hilarity to Branson himself, and to anyone who had ever sat through one of his speeches. Had he smoked a pipe he would probably have been Pipesmoker of the Year, too. Of more significance to Branson himself was the clutch of business awards won by Virgin, including the Company of the Year Award for 1985, given by the *Sunday Telegraph*, Lloyds Bank and the CBI.

For Virgin, the record business was thriving and the company was now set on its most ambitious expansion yet. The débâcle of the retreat from America in 1980 had continued to rankle; as had the frustration of seeing Virgin artists such as Culture Club and the Human League having enormous hits in America under licence to other companies. For two years, Branson and Simon Draper had been manoeuvring the right circumstances to try again; now, with an investment of more than ten million pounds, Virgin opened their own

American division, with headquarters in Los Angeles. Jordan Harris and Jeff Ayeroff were put in charge of the new label. Harris had been head of A&R at A&M records in Hollywood, in which capacity he had 'broken' such Virgin acts as Simple Minds and the Human League on the American charts. Ayeroff had been creative director of both A&M and Warners, planning campaigns on such artists as Madonna and the Police.

In April 1987, Virgin America had its first Number One single, with its first release by a hitherto unknown English group called Cutting Crew. The American office had also made its first direct signing – Steve Winwood. It was almost fourteen years since Branson had asked Winwood if he would play at the first ever public performance of *Tubular Bells*. Now Winwood was the winner of no less than five Grammy awards. Luring him away from Island Records, and his American company Warners, was a coup for Virgin, if one achieved at no little cost. Record business gossip had it that Winwood's deal was worth $13m to him, with a royalty rate of a hefty 18 per cent.

The Music Division remained Virgin's principal 'cash-cow', yet Vision had now become the fastest growing of all Virgin's activities. The production of feature films had been wound down; it was too volatile and speculative an enterprise to entertain Stock Market confidence. In 1986, Virgin Books was sold to W.H. Allen, in return for a 20 per cent interest in the company (Virgin subsequently bought out W.H. Allen a year later). Vision now concentrated on film and video distribution, and the field which Branson and Robert Devereux, the managing director of the Vision arm, had decided was the future – cable and satellite television. Virgin remained majority shareholder in Music Box and also a major shareholder in Superchannel, the twenty-four hour cable television service which broadcasts throughout Europe. And in the early part of 1986 Virgin became the leading partner in a company called British Satellite Broadcasting (BSB) – a consortium which also included Granada, Pearson-Longman and Anglia Television – which won the franchise to operate Britain's direct broadcasting satellite, beaming three more television channels into Britain from 1989.

In fifteen years, Virgin had come from nothing to being one of Britain's largest private companies. Now, as the advertisements which began to appear on television screens in October 1986, showing a City businessman jiving under a Walkman, would have it – came the step from The Rock Market to The Stock Market.

The private placing of a small percentage of Virgin shares with financial institutions – the prelude to Stock Market flotation – went better than expected. Virgin's merchant bankers Morgan Grenfell, and their stockbrokers Rowe & Pitman, had set an expected target of £10m. In fact, £25m was raised from twenty institutions. It was an encouraging start for a company trading primarily in what the City regards as the volatile, unpredictable – if not altogether incomprehensible – world of pop music.

At the behest of his City advisers, Branson had brought two non-executive directors on to the Virgin board – a move intended partly to bring more business experience to the company, but also as a necessary 'window-dressing', to help win the confidence of City investors. Rowe & Pitman recommended Cob Stenham, formerly the financial director of Unilever, now the European head of Bankers Trust, and a highly respected figure in the City. Sir Philip Harris, the head of the Harris-Queensway chain of carpeting and furniture stores, was invited to join the board after Branson had met him at a social function. Branson hoped that Harris could lend expertise on Virgin's retailing business, which was continuing to perform in a disappointingly desultory fashion. Don Cruickshank brought an approach to Virgin honed through the customs of business management. His view of what he described as 'the topography' of Virgin, and its possibilities, was very different from Branson's. Branson's vision of the company was largely shaped by the individuals around him – some of whom, like Draper, Berry and Rod Vickery, had been friends for years – and a series of constantly changing priorities, determined by his own impulses and interests; Cruickshank's vision was of accountability and responsibility – to shareholders, institutional investors, banks – which would come with flotation.

Cruickshank was not old-style Virgin material: he did not go on Caribbean holidays, ski or join the 'boys' club'. He read Proust, ate in rather expensive French restaurants, worried about his teenage children's education and generally kept himself to himself. There were middle-level executives in the record company who had never met him at all.

Yet in a curious way he and Branson provided a workable complement to each other. Branson recognised him as the foil he had always needed – the voice of responsibility and fine, nitpicking detail, which long ago had been Nik Powell; and which Draper and Berry had fulfilled in the record company, but not across Branson's activities as a whole.

For his part, Cruickshank was both intrigued and charmed by the lack of convention in Branson's thinking, as well as his manner. He noticed that Branson had a self-confidence which prevented him being embarrassed by his own lack of knowledge. The fact that the financial advisers might privately turn their noses up at the thought of the chairman of a £250m company not knowing what 'earnings per share' meant – and Branson did not know before embarking on flotation – simply did not occur to Branson. The same naïvety gave rise to the cheerleader's ability which could convince anybody from pop stars to institutional investors that it might just be worth tagging along for the ride, in the expectancy – not to say the hope – that as long as he had the general idea, the details would be filled in later . . .

But there was a paradox at work here. The relaxed, affable and devil-may-care demeanour which had made Branson, and Virgin, a household name was the very thing that made the financial institutions cautious of him and the company. His adeptness at publicising Virgin, and by extension himself, had, in the word to which he had lately become so partial, its 'downside'. City analysts who studied the company before the launch, and who made their recommendations to financial institutions, acknowledged that Branson had acted wisely in bringing in Cruickshank and Abbott – solid men with experience of the leisure industry who had arrested Virgin's hand-to-mouth financial forecasting. They were precisely the sort of executive with which the City could identify. Branson was not. Turning up in multi-coloured sweaters and open-neck shirts on television chat shows was 'colourful'; turning up at City meetings in the same outfit was bad form. Racing powerboats across the Atlantic, or abseiling down the side of Centrepoint in a Spiderman outfit for charity was exciting to behold; but the City likes chairmen firmly anchored to their mahogany desks.

Furthermore, Branson's reputation for impetuosity, and for having a low boredom threshold, travelled before him. In the run-up to flotation, he was apt to walk out in the middle of the highly complex and protracted discussions with bankers over taxation and the share issue to make telephone calls. Even before flotation, other Virgin executives had been called upon to mollify the company's new consortium of banks, bemused by Branson's announcements about new routes, new aircraft, and reassure them that, in fact, Virgin operated a stringent set of checks and balances. Branson's will and determination had built Virgin from nothing: he had listened to the advice of those around him, and then gone ahead and done what he was going to do anyway. That was one thing in a private company, but quite another in a public one, where the chairman and board were answerable to shareholders. Would Branson actually listen to what his other executives had to say now? As the analysts pondered the questions, Cruickshank and Abbott did their utmost to 'run interference'.

Branson and his team worked assiduously to 'sell' Virgin to the institutions before the launch. In seminar and conference rooms, on the top of City towerblocks, the Virgin pitch was made to the analysts and investors – the insurance companies and pension funds who decide a company's value and whether it is worth investing their money in. It was a curious scene. Audiences of soberly suited men and women sitting expectantly as the strains of *Tubular Bells* percolated gently through the atmosphere as a prelude to a recitation of sales figures and profits, comparative performance ratios and percentage growth expectations. From a presidential-style podium, Branson and Cruickshank read addresses which had been carefully tailored to emphasise the points the City would like to hear: that 40 per cent of turnover in records came not from new releases, but from back catalogue (that means stability); that in France, 40 per cent of turnover came from French artists (if Boy George died tomorrow it would not mean the collapse of Virgin).

Roger Seelig, who was orchestrating the Virgin issue on behalf of Morgan Grenfell, had advised that Virgin should go to the market by 'tender' offer. In this, the company's share price is set not by the seller but by the market demand. It is an effective ploy in a buoyant, or 'bull', market, where the expectation is that the share price will continue to rise; a way of maximising the income from what is expected to be a popular issue. Everybody was confident that there would be no short-age of private investors – swept up in the enthusiasm of share issues in general, and Virgin's in particular – who would wish to take part, if only in the expectation of being able to sell their shares quickly as the price rose in the aftermath of the issue, as had been the case with Telecom and TSB. But there was still some lingering doubt about the enthusiasm of institutional investors, who would bring a more long-term stability to the issue.

Only two British record companies were already listed on the Stock Market: the long-established Thorn-EMI, and Chrysalis, who had come to the market the year before. But Chrysalis's performance had not lived up to the analysts' expectations, adding weight to the more general reservations the City was feeling about the record business – that it was founded not on the concrete and recognisable assets which spell safety to the City, but on the more ephemeral equation of artistic talent and public taste. In its pre-launch campaign, Virgin had emphasised the company's strength in breadth. But among analysts there were still caveats, particularly about the investment required to get the American operation up and running, and the baffling inability of Retail to deliver substantial profits.

Nor do the financial institutions particularly favour the method of sale by tender: firstly, it involves too much work, pricing the company themselves instead of having it done for them; without a price for the share, and therefore a total valuation of the company, they have no idea of what percentage of the company they will eventually own. Secondly, it fosters the lingering suspicion that the company will 'take the cream off the market' – close the price as high as possible, with as much money in their own coffers, but leaving a torpid 'aftermarket' in the shares. On the Virgin board, opinion was divided as to whether to sell by tender at all. But the principal problem was that neither Seelig, nor anybody else, could actually price the company's shares. They would let the investors decide.

The minimum tender price for offers was set at 120p. On 13 November, the day on which the offer closed, private investors queued outside Virgin's City bank with their applications. For Branson, shaking hands with those in line, it was an emotional moment. He had built Virgin from nothing: the lines of people wanting to invest in the company was a testament to his achievement. He was, he said, 'humbled' at the response. In his excitement that morning he had somehow managed to put on odd shoes.

The next morning, however, the mood was less buoyant. At 8.30 a.m., Branson, Cruickshank, Abbott, Roger Seelig of Morgan Grenfell and Nick Verey of the stockbrokers Rowe & Pitman met to examine the computer print-outs of the bids and fix a share price. Virgin had received some 100,000 applications, with bids ranging from the minimum 120p up to 200p. The demand from the public was the highest of any flotation outside the government's privatisation programme. But uptake among institutions was particularly disappointing. The small-time, private investors had supported Richard Branson in droves; but the City had rebuffed him.

All at the meeting were agreed that whatever price was set should allow sufficient margin for a lively 'aftermarket' in the shares. The computer graph suggested that there were enough bids to fix the price at between 160p and 165p – just. But Nick Verey argued that that was too high. He urged that the price should be set at 140p. Branson had hoped that it would be higher, but he remained sanguine, acknowledging that, above all, a price should be set that was not exploitive, 'and at which everybody could make a profit if they chose to sell'. 140p it was. The share issue priced Virgin at £240m. Branson himself retained a fraction under 55 per cent of the company, Simon Draper 9 per cent. Branson raised some £21m gross from the issue, virtually all of which went straight into the Voyager company and Virgin Atlantic Airways.

But the lingering lack of confidence in the share among institutional investors affected the aftermarket for Virgin shares. For two days after the issue the price hovered at 140p, then dropped to 136p. On reflection, the Virgin board decided, 130–135p would have been the right price. Thus began an up-and-down fluctuation in the share price – rising to 180p, dropping to 160p, rising, dropping – which mirrored Virgin's perennially uneasy relationship with the City.

Curiously, the fluctuation in the share price was by no means an accurate reflection of Virgin's efficiency and profitability. The reservations the City had expressed at the time of the issue about Virgin's rate of growth were unfounded. At the end of its first year's trading as a public company, Virgin recorded a profit of £31m, on a turnover of £250m – exceeding the most optimistic analysts' expectations.

Yet they continued to retain a sense of bemusement about Virgin, or at least the way in which the company was embodied in Richard Branson himself. Branson's appetite for activity, and the sheer breadth of his interests, raised questions. If a man is running a private airline and refurbishing Britain's environment, with the best will in the world, how much time is he actually devoting to running his public company and protecting the interests of his shareholders? To a large extent, whatever unease existed between Branson and the City was largely a question of style. Even his non-executive directors, accustomed to a more formal approach to business, found Virgin's ways disconcerting – the fact that board meetings, for example, were held not in a board room but in the lounge of Branson's home (although sometimes Sir Philip Harris played host in his Cadogan Square flat).

Harris had warmed to Branson on first meeting him and had been intrigued by the challenge of joining the Virgin board – to the incredulity of his more straitlaced City friends. Harris too was a self-made man who had left school at fifteen and built his empire on native wit, shrewdness and hard work. He could recognise the same qualities in Branson. But Harris's own empire had run into trouble; it had grown beyond his capacity to personally control its every aspect as Harris had become more and more preoccupied with extramural activities – notably charity fund-raising. He had taken his eye off the ball. And he feared that Branson was in danger of doing the same thing.

Branson faced a double-edged sword. In most people's

minds, Richard Branson *was* Virgin. The truth of the matter was that this was no longer the case. Virgin was a public company with shareholders and executive officers. It could run on its own without Branson. Having sold the notion that the company was built on his entrepreneurial zeal and enthusiasm, it was now necessary to emphasise the notion that in fact Virgin had always been run by Branson delegating responsibility and that now, more than ever, while valuable, he was not indispensable. And there was a side of him that no amount of caution urged by his board of directors could contain. It was this side that now announced that he was embarking on his most hazardous enterprise yet.

Chapter 14

Balloons

Richard Branson had found freedom – or the next best thing to it. Two thousand feet above the earth, with only the sound of the wind in his ears, he floated over the Spanish countryside feeling a heady mixture of utter tranquillity and exhilaration. The world had never before seemed so still and peaceful.

For the first time in his life, Branson was flying a hot-air balloon, solo. In just a few months he would be flying another one – across the Atlantic ocean.

The last few days in Spain had been extremely fruitful. For some eight hours each day, in perfect weather conditions, Branson had been airborne, being coached in the rudiments of ballooning; by night he had pored over meteorological and navigational charts. Swept up in his new enthusiasm, he had proved the model student. While Branson applied himself to his studies, his new partner, Per Lindstrand, had engaged in a quite different exercise – ascending to altitudes of 39,000 feet in a prototype of the special pressurised capsule in which he and Branson were to make their attempt on the Atlantic crossing.

At thirty-eight, Per Lindstrand was already recognised as a brilliant aeronautical engineer and one of the leading

363

balloonists in the world when he first enquired whether Branson might, perhaps, be interested in flying the Atlantic in a hot-air balloon. And, of course, pay for it.

Lindstrand trained as a pilot in the Swedish Air Force, then worked as a project engineer on high-altitude aircraft-testing. An expert balloonist and free-fall parachutist, he had already been involved in the setting of two world records, piloting the balloons from which the world altitude record for parachuting, and the world altitude record for hang-gliding had been set.

In 1975, Lindstrand left Sweden for Britain, to build up a business developing and manufacturing hot-air balloons. His company, Thunder & Colt, had manufactured two promotional balloons for Virgin Atlantic, including one in the shape of a Jumbo Jet.

Branson received Lindstrand's proposal with immediate enthusiasm. Learning to fly a hot-air balloon would be a marvellous adventure in itself, to become one of the first men to fly across the Atlantic in one would be more marvellous still. Nor was the element of danger a deterrent. Branson did not believe in taking unnecessary risks with his life; but neither did he believe in caution unnecessarily circumscribing his enjoyment – and ballooning was something he was coming to enjoy a lot.

There was also, of course, the publicity element to consider. The *Challenger* crossing had proved one-thousand-fold the economic worth of such a project in publicising the airline, Branson himself and by implication the entire Virgin Group in the run-up to flotation on the Stock Market. Flying a balloon across the Atlantic was an even more appropriate way of publicising the airline – particularly in America – than piloting a power-boat had been. Public interest – which is to say, media interest – in such a project would be enormous, Branson reasoned. The Virgin publicity machine would make sure of it.

There had been seventeen attempts to cross the Atlantic by helium-filled balloon – but only three of them were successful. The first was in 1978, when the American balloon Double Eagle flew from Maine to Miserey in France in five days. Two more successful crossings followed, including an extraordinary solo flight from Maine to Savona, Italy, by a retired US Air Force colonel, Joe Kittinger. To cross by hot-air balloon, however, had always been thought impossible because of the enormous amount of propane gas that would need to be burned to keep the balloon aloft. But Per Lindstrand was convinced the attempt could be made by using another energy source – natural light from the sun, trapped in a double-skinned envelope (or balloon) which would allow infra-red absorption in one direction and prevent heat-loss in another. By travelling at very high altitudes, with the crew secured in a pressurised capsule, Lindstrand theorised, such a balloon could do what had never been done before – ride the jet stream across the Atlantic, at speeds of up to 120 knots. In theory, the 3,500-mile journey could be completed in three to four days.

The balloon which Lindstrand designed for him and Branson to attempt the crossing would be the largest hot-air balloon ever built. The envelope itself would be made of 12 miles of material, measuring 170 feet across and with a capacity of 2.3m cubic feet when fully inflated – large enough to swallow a Jumbo Jet. It would stand 196 feet tall – higher than Nelson's column, and would be capable of lifting a payload of 12,500 kilogrammes – the equivalent of a double-decker London bus.

Eight propane gas-burners would launch the balloon, and keep it aloft at night, but by day the lift would come from the fabric of the envelope itself. In order to maximise the natural energy source of daylight, the attempt would be made on, or as near as possible to, 21 June – the longest day of the year.

Richard Branson realised that he had inherited not only a balloon adventure but a private vendetta in January, when at the press conference at the Royal Aeronautical Society to announce the balloon attempt, a small, bony-faced man stood up in the body of the hall, waved a piece of paper towards the dais and issued a challenge. Would Richard Branson turn his balloon trip into a transatlantic race?

Don Cameron was one of Britain's foremost balloonists. He had attempted to cross the Atlantic once before, in a helium-filled balloon, in 1978, coming to grief a mere 100 nautical miles short of the French coast. He had been planning another attempt ever since. More to the point, he had long been Britain's foremost balloon manufacturer – until, that is, the rise of Lindstrand's Thunder & Colt company. In recent years, Thunder & Colt had quietly stolen a march on their longer-established rivals, and the British market was now divided equally between them, with rivalry for the lucrative foreign markets fierce. Branson had stumbled into the middle of a private feud.

In fact, Cameron's challenge to a race was always a non-starter. He believed a crossing from the American mainland was impossible, and refused to alter his plans to leave from Newfoundland – a distance some 800 miles less. Branson was phlegmatic about Cameron's intervention. 'We are not in a race,' he said. 'We are both doing our own thing. But any wagers are off.' However, Lindstrand was personally infuriated, not by the challenge but by the fact that it had been specifically addressed not to him and Thunder & Colt but to Branson and Virgin. Cameron, Lindstrand believed, was climbing on to the Virgin bandwagon to extract as much publicity as possible for his own attempt, and his sponsors Zanussi. As the months passed, Cameron adeptly dramatised the contest as a morality play: the might, and the marketing, of the Virgin organisation versus the plucky gentleman-adventurer – himself. A drama in which pluck was to suffer a fatal blow when Cameron's balloon collapsed on its launch site in Newfoundland, never to be heard of again.

In February 1987, as Branson applied himself assiduously to the study of navigation and meteorology, a series of alarming advertisements appeared on British television screens.

The government education campaign on AIDS struck fear into the heart of everyone, if only temporarily, and no less Richard Branson than anyone else. What sort of world would his own children, Holly and Sam, be inheriting? Branson wondered. As did many people, he turned his mind afresh to that small pharmaceutical item, the object of so much adolescent mirth and embarrassment, now hailed as the potential saviour of lives – the condom. In fact, Branson knew quite a lot about condoms. Some eighteen months earlier – long before the AIDS scare had reached near epidemic proportions – Branson had been invited to take over a brand of contraceptives called Jiffy. It was no more, and no less, than a business proposition, to which he had given momentary consideration. The International Rubber Company, manufacturers of Durex, enjoyed a 95 per cent monopoly of the British market: there was room for a competitor, particularly one marketed correctly to appeal to the young. Branson had

367

even raised the topic one day at a family gathering. 'Oh, Ricky . . .' His mother Eve greeted the idea with thinly veiled distaste. 'When are you going to do something useful with your life?'

The idea was dropped. But the government campaign on AIDS set Branson thinking again. He had grown up in a period of comparative sexual freedom – the Sixties – which clearly was now over. His children would not enjoy the same untroubled freedoms; at worst, they would always be at risk; at best, troubled and confused about sex. To Branson, it was clear from all the evidence, and his own common sense, that the threat of AIDS would not stop people making love. But while the government campaign had been horribly effective in alerting people to the existence of AIDS, it had done next to nothing to promote what medical opinion agreed was the most effective prevention, short of chastity – the wearing of condoms.

Shortly after the government campaign, Branson contacted the health minister, Norman Fowler, and asked for a private meeting. Would it not be possible, Branson asked, for the government to make condoms widely available free of charge? Virgin would be prepared to help in the publicity and distribution in any way they could. But Fowler told him that the cost to the government of free contraceptives would be prohibitive. Branson went away and gave the matter some thought. Even if free condoms were out, they should be made much more widely available, and at a lower price, and that availability should be reinforced with a campaign designed to remove the stigma of using them.

The idea of Virgin manufacturing and selling condoms as a business enterprise was quickly discarded. The most effective way to get across the message of wearing condoms – the only way, Branson believed, in which it would be treated with the seriousness he was convinced it warranted – was for the whole exercise to be organised as a charitable trust, completely independent of Virgin, the public company. Branson had devised a way of doing it. With £5m from his own share premium he would personally underwrite the costs of manufacturing and advertising the condoms, which would be marketed under the name Mates. This seed money would be returned to him if and when the launch costs were covered, but the entire operation would be completely non-profitmaking. All monies would go back into health education and research on AIDS, and to help sufferers from the disease.

Branson appointed a director to administer the project, John Jackson, who had been chief executive with the pharmaceutical and cosmetics company, Cheeseborough Ponds. He also approached Anita Roddick, chairwoman of the Body Shop chain, to see if she would be interested in joining forces as a trustee. Roddick embraced the idea with gusto and ideas for future projects for the Healthcare Foundation began to snowball: the manufacture and distribution of essential medicines at cost price, undercutting the enormous profits made by the drug companies, screening facilities for cervical cancer; the treatment of drug addiction and alcoholism. Branson saw it as the working model of the principle of 'enlightened capitalism'. Successful companies such as Virgin had a moral responsibility to give something back to society. One way was simply to give money to charity; another was to use your business skills to generate money for organisations that need it by underwriting charitable ventures to tackle issues which arguably should be the responsibility of government, but which it is either unable – or disinclined – to take responsibility for. If large organisations would undertake to underwrite, and operate, just one company on a charitable basis, a whole range of social and medical needs could be met.

For Branson, the campaign turned into a personal obsession: he became an evangelist of the condom. He was in no doubt that AIDS posed the most serious threat to world health, and that contraceptives were the most effective way of stopping its spread. He was a moral pragmatist: the argument that the best way of stopping the spread of AIDS was to foster the moral precepts of abstinence, chastity or self-denial did not strike him as realistic. Branson was, in this sense, very much a child of the Sixties. He had enjoyed a number of sexual relationships in his youth, and nothing would convince him that young people in the 1980s would not wish to do the same thing – or convince him that it was not perfectly natural. He rationalised bluntly, 'You're never going to stop people making love. And I don't see why people shouldn't have four or five relationships before settling down – although the media would crucify me for saying so.'

Branson's zeal for combating AIDS met with a more sanguine response from his colleagues within Virgin. His oldest friends, Simon Draper and Ken Berry, both sighed quietly, but kept their own counsel; they had trodden a similar path before. But the non-executive directors, Sir Philip Harris and Cob Stenham, argued vociferously that it was potentially damaging for the Virgin name to be associated with as controversial and emotive a subject as AIDS and the marketing of condoms. If Branson had to have his project, at least call it something other than Virgin Healthcare. Don Cruickshank too was concerned that shareholders would be confused and worried, and think that it was their money, not Branson's own, that was being put at risk. Theoretically, under the Articles of

Virgin, the public company, Branson was not allowed to use the name Virgin at all without the majority approval of the board. After much debate, it was finally agreed that the name Virgin should be dropped and that it should be called simply the Healthcare Foundation. The name of the company distributing and marketing condoms was changed to Mates Healthcare Ltd.

That was not the limit of the Virgin board's objections, however. One director in particular objected vehemently to the scheme on moral grounds. Wasn't such a scheme simply endorsing promiscuity rather than fighting AIDS? It was an argument that Branson would meet with increasing ferocity in the months ahead, along with the renewed suggestion that it would be politic to divest himself of ownership of the gay club Heaven. Too close an association with the gay community at a time like this could be a liability. Branson brushed all the objections aside. Gay people had enough problems as it was, without him shutting down or selling out Heaven. It was a point of principle. And the Mates scheme would go ahead. Whatever his critics inside and outside Virgin might think, Branson *believed* passionately in the Mates campaign. It had galvanised his enthusiasm in a way no business project had done since the launch of the airline almost three years before. The mixture of business and philanthropy satisfied all his instincts and, he thought, set some sort of precedent for the direction his life would go in the future.

Within fourteen weeks of the launch on 10 November 1987, forty million Mates had been sold (the total sale of condoms in Great Britain in 1986 had been 120 million). And Branson was predicting that in 1988 sales of Mates would raise £5m for AIDS education and care.

Branson's involvement in the Mates campaign exacerbated the fears of his directors about the time he was spending away from Virgin matters. The ballooning expedition in Toledo in January was followed by another in Kenya. Ironically, when Branson first announced the balloon trip publicly, contrary to the expectations of his directors, the price of Virgin shares had actually risen. But in May a television documentary about the preparations for the transatlantic flight showed Branson practising free-fall parachuting – and pulling the wrong ripcord. Only quick thinking by his instructor, yanking at the cord of his emergency parachute, prevented Branson plummeting to his death. On the day after the programme was shown, Virgin's shares also plummeted, by 15p – knocking some £15m off the value of the company.

The near-fatal mishap unsettled more than Virgin's share price. Branson took to replaying a video of the incident to friends, with a nervous chuckle of disbelief at how close he had come to death. The thought of something going terribly wrong with the balloon at high altitude, and of being forced to free-fall out of trouble became a fear almost tantamount to phobia.

On a weekend at the beginning of June, Branson visited the Thunder & Colt factory in Oswestry, Shropshire, to examine the balloon capsule and begin preliminary tests on communication equipment. Resting on runners in the empty, cold factory, the capsule looked less like a piece of sophisticated technology than a figment of the imagination of Jules Verne – an aluminium boiler, flanked by six pairs of fuel tanks, with a fragile trelliswork of steel tubing aloft to support the propane gas-burners, navigational equipment and the engine that would generate electricity and maintain pressurisation. Inside, in an area barely eight feet wide and twenty-four feet in circumference, two reclining airline-style seats in Virgin livery were set side-by-side, each with its own desk-top and instrument-panel, to control the craft's navigation, communication and life-support systems: satellite navigation; Decca navigation; storm-scop (for monitoring electrical activity in the air); high frequency receiver; two VHF and one HF radios; one transponder; Omega Navigation System; oxygen and carbon-dioxide monitors. A perspex dome in the roof gave 360 degree vision around the craft, and access to the equipment above. The capsule had taken seven men, working under the direction of the project manager Tom Barrow, about 18,000 man hours to design and construct. Its navigation and communication systems were as sophisticated as those to be found on one of Branson's Jumbo Jets. 'It just cost eighty times less,' said Barrow.

Over the weekend, Barrow and Lindstrand briefed Branson on the coming voyage. The balloon would fly at a maximum of 28,000 feet, high enough to catch the jet stream blowing from west to east; but below the flight-path of civil aircraft. Wind speeds across the Atlantic can vary enormously within a band of two thousand feet. The balloon would cross the Atlantic by 'playing' the air streams, manoeuvring up and down to ride the fastest currents and avoid bad weather storms: the chances of a balloon of that size surviving a thunderstorm were almost nil. The most serious navigational difficulty would arise some two-thirds of the way across the Atlantic, when the balloon would have to negotiate two giant 'gears' of wind. A fraction too far north, and the winds would carry them towards Iceland and beyond; too far south, and they would be circling the Azores. Getting it right, said Barrow, was 'like rolling a ballbearing between two magnets'. In the event of an emergency at high altitude they would parachute out. If the balloon ditched in the ocean, flotation collars around the capsule would keep it buoyant. 'And what if they don't inflate?' asked Branson. 'You get your money back on them,' said Barrow.

But the most perilous aspect of the trip would be the landing. Because of air thermals, landing should be attempted only at dawn or dusk. Nobody had ever brought down a balloon of that size before. In fact, it would be less a landing, more of a 'controlled crash'. With a wind gusting through it at ground level, the balloon would have an inertia of 70 tons; it would, in Lindstrand's disquieting analogy, be 'like a freewheeling battle tank without any brakes'. The most important pieces of equipment on board, therefore, were the explosive bolts that would release the envelope from the capsule at the moment of impact with ground or water.

At the end of that weekend, Barrow gave a final briefing. As the project director, he said, he reserved the right to abort the flight for whatever reasons he felt fit. If the balloon was not ready to fly, or if either Branson or Lindstrand developed health problems.

'Does that include mental instability?' joked Branson.

'No,' deadpanned Barrow. 'That's a prerequisite for making the flight. If you're not half nuts and scared to death, you shouldn't be getting into that balloon at all.'

In the few days before he left Britain for America, Richard Branson began receiving a stream of telephone calls and messages, from friends he had not seen for years, business acquaintances of old. The tidings of good luck conspired to give the uncomfortable impression of his life passing before his eyes.

The reality of what he was undertaking was at last coming home to him. His best friends had made it quite clear to him that they thought it a lunatic enterprise, an unnecessary risk. His family put on a brave face. Joan quickly realised the impossibility of dissuading him, but decided that the experience would be too traumatic to witness at first hand and that she would stay in England with the children when he made the attempt. His parents, Ted and Eve, were deeply anxious privately, but stood steadfastly beside him, as they had at every turn in his life: always the first to arrive at any Branson function, and always the last to leave. The one factor which had never been in question in Richard Branson's life was the love and loyalty of his family.

The apprehension of others did nothing to reassure Branson himself. Ever since the near-fatal incident with the parachute, the more he thought about the balloon flight, the less he relished it. In fact, he definitely met at least half of Tom Barrow's criteria for getting into the balloon: he was scared to death. Surely there were other – perhaps safer – adventures that would prove as challenging as this one? If, in the final days before the planned departure of the balloon, an opportunity to back down gracefully had presented itself, then it is quite possible that Richard Branson would have taken it. But no such opportunity came. Only a telephone call, summoning him to America. The weather prediction was good. The balloon would go up in two days' time. A Jumbo Jet carried Branson, and his parents, to Boston airport. At immigration, the large, black official scrutinised Branson's passport.

'You here on business or pleasure?'

'Well . . .' Branson paused, thinking how best to put it. 'Business or pleasure . . .'

'Well, actually, I'm here to fly a hot-air balloon across the Atlantic . . .'

'That right?' The Customs man stamped the passport without batting an eyelid.

A small private aircraft carried the party north, to Maine. The site chosen for the launch was at a ski resort called Sugarloaf Mountain. Set in the middle of a thickly wooded forest, and ringed by mountains, it provided a perfectly sheltered spot. It quickly became a circus of television crews, newspaper reporters, holidaymakers and balloon enthusiasts – veterans of previous attempts on the Atlantic; phlegmatic men wearing gold-rimmed spectacles and mechanics' caps, all of whom appeared to be called Doc or Bob. It became apparent that one of these was to be central in the unfolding drama – the project meteorologist, Bob Rice. On his word, and his alone, would the balloon rise or stay grounded. He did not control the weather. That was God's department. But Rice quickly came to be regarded as His emissary on earth.

On the morning after Branson's arrival, Rice made his first pronouncement. The balloon would not be taking off the next day, after all, because of unsuitable weather conditions. While the balloon would be carrying enough fuel for a flight of a hundred hours, the preferred estimate was sixty hours. Under present conditions, it would be airborne for seventy-five hours. Safe, but not safe enough.

So began a pattern. Each morning Branson, Lindstrand and the press would gather in the suite of rooms designated as operations control to hear Bob Rice announce that the balloon would not, after all, be taking off on the following day.

Publicly, the balloon team expressed disappointment. Privately, everyone breathed an enormous sigh of relief. There was much fine-tuning still to be done to the capsule itself. Sundry pieces of ancillary equipment, of varying degrees of importance, had still not arrived from Britain. And if Per Lindstrand was in a full state of readiness for the flight, it was clear that Richard Branson was not.

Keeping Branson's concentration on the project had proved a problem. There was an irony here. Just as Virgin's directors complained that it was impossible to keep his concentration focused on business without it wandering off to the balloon, so the balloon team voiced disquiet about Branson not concentrating enough on learning all that was required for the trip. It had long been apparent to his closest friends and associates that he was habitually incapable of concentrating on any one thing for very long. Nor did he have a natural mechanical aptitude; as one of the crew put it, at the age of fifteen or sixteen when some boys are figuring out how a car engine works, Richard was probably buying and selling them for a profit.

For the last eighteen months, Per Lindstrand had devoted his energies to almost nothing but the balloon. It had become his life. For the past nine months, it had been only a part of Branson's, along with Virgin, UK 2000, Mates . . .

Branson was spreading himself dangerously thin. But in this case it could be his life that was at stake. Ballooning across the Atlantic would not be a joy-ride. It would require enormous reserves of courage and stamina. There was no doubt that Branson had both. But there would be no opportunity for improvisation if at 27,000 feet Lindstrand suddenly passed out and Branson was left in control of the craft on his own. Branson was not half as familiar with the capsule and its procedures as he should have been. The delay in take-off afforded a vital opportunity for Branson to be force-fed as much necessary learning as possible. From the outset, the project had been a challenge to Branson's temperament in more ways than one. As someone accustomed to making his own decisions and to getting his own way, Branson had had to subordinate his temperament to Lindstrand's in the manner of a pupil to a teacher. And the teacher now became a rigid disciplinarian.

If the delay gave breathing space, it also created a problem with the attendant circus of newspaper and television crews. As the launch was postponed yet again, from Tuesday to Thursday – possibly – the need to keep the press amused, and to keep the story 'alive', became more pressing, the value of the media to the enterprise ever more disproportionately exaggerated. Branson's unfailing accommodating attitude to the press began to irritate Lindstrand. 'Radio and television, the faintest scent of it,' he sighed with the merest whiff of amused indulgence as Branson was called to yet another interview. 'It's like an addict with morphine . . .'

In fact, as a public relations exercise, it was already clear that the balloon trip was a bargain. Virgin had invested some $750,000 in sponsorship. But by the time subsidiary sponsors, paying £25,000 apiece, had been considered, along with the £100,000 which TVS were paying for the rights to film the project, Virgin's on-line costs would only amount to some £200,000.

Among the facilities laid on for the media was a mobile satellite truck, and Virgin's own television crew, on hand to feed a constant supply of pictures and reports to any local or national television station in America who wanted to pick it up. This was also used by the BBC and ITN to feed pictures directly back to London and provide a 'live' link for Branson to appear on *Wogan* twice in one week. The value of this particular investment was incalculable. For the American networks to have sent their own trucks and crews to the site would have been prohibitively expensive. By offering the networks free coverage, Virgin were considerably increasing the possibility of the flight preparations – and the flight itself – gaining maximum coverage. No longer do you set up shop, cross your fingers and hope the world's media come to you. Rather, you provide all the facilities to make your story available to them, saving them money – and winning yourself kudos – in the process. The impact which coverage of the balloon trip made on what his American advisers had taken to describing as Branson's 'celebrity profile' was similarly incalculable. Branson, it was said, as if describing some prototype of aeronautical engineering, had at last broken the Johnny Carson barrier.

'We've been ringing American television shows for three years. A year ago we could hardly get him arrested outside the studios. Now they're ringing us,' said one PR person. Even before the balloon had left the ground, Virgin's promotional staff were pronouncing the project a success in marketing terms. By Branson's own estimate, by the end of the flight the Virgin name had been given the equivalent of approximately £25m-worth of free advertising.

To Branson himself, however, the constant intrusion of the press at last became less an addiction, more an irritation – as much for the way in which the media themselves began to depict the balloon trip as simply a media event, caught as they were in the double-bind of acknowledging that Branson was creating something that was quite genuinely 'news', yet suspicious of being used to publicise Virgin at the same time. The suggestion that the balloon trip was nothing but a glorified publicity stunt incensed him. Certainly, he had sought as much publicity for Virgin Atlantic from the venture as he could possibly get – and if you are doing that, he reasoned, you should do it properly. But it was the challenge that was paramount. Virgin had not simply bought publicity; they were also funding an extraordinary technical and engineering achievement, which, if successful, would have very real practical applications for communications and meteorology in the future. The balloon trip was a manifestation of man's spirit of enquiry and adventure at its most noble – as well as being a lot of fun. It had caught the imagination of the world. And he was not about to risk his life simply for the sake of publicity.

Branson had been waiting at Sugarloaf Mountain for six days when Bob Rice announced that weather conditions would not be favourable in 'the foreseeable future'. On the same day, Branson learned that his hitherto secret plans for Mates had been leaked to the press. He flew back to London to a press conference – and jokes about his imminent plans to fly the biggest condom in the world across the Atlantic. A week later, another call summoned him back to America. The weather pattern had changed. The balloon would go up in two days' time. Bob Rice almost promised as much.

Back at Sugarloaf, the bond between Branson and Lindstrand now began to cement in earnest. The media interviews were pushed aside, and the two men spent hours sequestered in their hotel suite, poring over charts, plans and instruction manuals. Branson had become the model student, constantly revising all he could be required to know: navigation, meteorology, basic physics; how to strap on a parachute, liferaft and dinghy while blindfolded. For hours he and Lindstrand sat in the capsule, until every switch, dial and item of equipment was intimately familiar to them. Branson's confidence in the project, and most noticeably in his own ability to master every one of the complex and detailed procedures involved in flying the capsule, grew visibly. He was as ready as he was ever going to be.

On Wednesday, the day before the Virgin Atlantic Flyer balloon was scheduled to take off, two lawyers arrived at the door of Richard Branson's hotel suite and were ushered inside. They left an hour later, carrying a signed copy of Branson's last will and testament. That morning, the capsule was tipped on its side, resting on a yellow inflatable cushion, in a position to be attached to the envelope itself. Gingerly, the folded envelope was taken from its container, unfurled and spread across the green. Inflating the balloon was always going to be one of the most hazardous aspects of the entire operation. It could be inflated once, and only once. A tear, a snag on a tree or piece of equipment and the whole project could be aborted. It required nothing less than absolute calm.

Throughout the day, the wind gusted across the launch site, rippling the yards of silver and black fabric laid out on the green. In his customarily oracular fashion, Bob Rice had predicted that the wind would drop to zero at ground level some time between eight and nine p.m. enabling inflation to begin by ten. At eight p.m. the pine trees could be seen bowing in a stiff breeze; then, suddenly, the wind stilled and the small helium balloon tethered at the site stood as perpendicular as a church steeple.

As darkness descended, inflation of the envelope began. At three a.m. on the Thursday morning, the car carrying Branson and Lindstrand from their hotel moved slowly through the darkness towards the site, a blue light flashing on its roof. The night sky was perfectly still and quiet. The car turned a corner, from behind a screen of trees, before sloping down to the site. 'Christ!' Branson breathed. 'Can you stop the car?' What he saw made his heart suddenly beat faster. In front of them, the balloon filled their entire field of vision; picked out by spotlights, vast and eerie, an enormous shining black orb strained on its tether, as below it the burners breathed fire into its gaping mouth. Orange-suited figures swarmed purposefully around its base, and disembodied voices echoed from the public-address system through the woodland. Nobody spoke as the car edged forward slowly, to be engulfed in a tide of pointing cameras and lights and jabbering voices.

With the first glimmer of dawn painting an orange rim along the mountain range to the east, the countdown began. As the heat of the burners gained in intensity, the balloon with Branson and Lindstrand in it lifted inches from the ground, then hovered, checked in its progress by the ballast of sandbags hanging from its sides. Around it, hands tugged at the guy lines to set the balloon free. Then suddenly something went wrong. A line had snagged around two fuel tanks and, with pulling, brought them crashing to the ground. The capsule rocked slightly, keeled as if about to plunge to the ground, then righted itself and rose slowly upwards. It skirted the trees, hung in the air and then, as if pushed by a giant finger, rolled across the crimson sky, like a giant ballbearing, glinting in the strengthening sun.

In the capsule, Branson and Lindstrand were totally unaware of the momentary crisis below, unaware even that they had taken off at all until Branson stuck his head out of the observation dome to wave goodbye and saw that they were 150 feet above the ground and rising fast. Within ninety minutes they were rising through 25,000 to 26,000 feet and cruising at a speed of 75 knots.

Within six hours they had covered 420 nautical miles (500 statute miles), and the balloon was skimming through the sky at an incredible 110–120 knots, a mote in the jet stream, straining to climb higher still as the solar skin yielded to the warmth of the sun. Branson and Lindstrand grinned at each other in disbelief. Things were going better than either of them had dared to hope. There was no sound, no untoward movement in the capsule. They were aware of the extraordinary sensation of being cradled in the sky; utterly safe and secure. Far below, the land slipped quickly by, like scenery being wound across a stage; on every side it was shining blue into infinity. Branson got a start when he looked behind the capsule and could see a plume of white smoke trailing across the sky behind them. For a moment he thought the balloon was on fire, then realised it was simply a vapour trail caused by the balloon arriving in the bitterly cold air at 27,000 feet. Between Halifax, Nova Scotia, and St John's, Newfoundland, there was a sudden jerk and the balloon pulled upwards. For a fleeting moment, Lindstrand thought they had collided with something, but a few seconds later the radio crackled with a message from a passing Concorde. The plane had flown by 28,000 feet above, but in the thin atmosphere its sonic boom shockwave had shaken the balloon like a giant hand. Three more Concordes would pass by in the course of the flight, but all radioed in advance.

Ten hours into the flight, they plotted their position as 914 miles from the launch site; the hot-air balloon long-distance record had been broken with ease.

Then came trouble. Two hundred miles off Gander, the balloon hit a low pressure front – the giant 'gears' of wind that could pull it off-course either north or south, and which had brought previous Atlantic attempts to grief. Bob Rice had been emphatic: however rough it gets, stick at 27,000 feet and the air-stream will carry the balloon through. It was pitch black outside the portholes; snow beat against the capsule and the buffeting wind sent nervous tremors through the envelope. Below, Lindstrand could see clear air. He took the balloon gently down. All was seductively calm. At that moment, he realised the mistake which previous pilots had made and pulled the balloon back to 27,000 feet. He radioed his position back to Rice. Change altitude again, Rice said, and I'll never talk to you again. For the next three hours the balloon bucked and keeled in the currents; the feelings of exhilarated disbelief had now given way to apprehension as both men concentrated intently on maintaining the balloon's stability. Then, suddenly, they broke through into brilliant sunshine. If the balloon could survive that, Lindstrand thought, it could survive anything.

They were now more than halfway across the Atlantic, having used only one tank of fuel, travelling at speeds of up to 140 m.p.h. which no balloonist had ever experienced before.

Throughout the night, and into the following morning, a procession of passenger jets flew past, out of sight, but within radio distance. The Virgin Atlantic Jumbo Jet carrying the balloon's launch and recovery crew and the two pilots' families back to Britain descended 4,000 feet to fly a figure of eight around the balloon. In the capsule, Eve Branson's voice came crackling over the receiver with a laugh. 'Can't you go any faster, Ricky?'

The performance of the balloon's 'double skin' solar

power had been a problem in the last way either pilot expected. Lindstrand had been confident the double skin of the envelope would keep the capsule aloft during the daylight hours. He had not expected it to perform quite as well as it did, straining upwards, as if reaching for some congruence with the source of its energy and life. It had required careful 'venting' of the flap at the top of the envelope, to maintain a constant altitude. But three hours from the coast of Ireland, the capsule suddenly started climbing upwards, out of Lindstrand's control. He pulled quickly at the vent, but still the balloon continued to climb. A snagged wire was preventing it opening. At 60,000 feet, starved of oxygen, the engine would go down, the cabin would depressurise and they would be in serious trouble. Both quickly donned parachutes and prepared to abandon the capsule, but miraculously the fault rectified itself, and the balloon slowly descended below 30,000 feet.

They were, by now, within sight of land. At 2.33 p.m. on the afternoon of Friday 3 July the balloon crossed the coast of Ireland, over Donegal. They had been airborne for just 29 hours and 23 minutes.

They began to consider the prospects for landing. The astonishing speed of their journey across the Atlantic had created an unforeseen problem; only two double fuel tanks had been used during the flight; three full tanks were still attached to the capsule. These would have to be jettisoned before landing to minimise the risk of an explosion. But how to get rid of them was a problem. Below them was a solid base of cloud; to drop the tanks by parachute was to risk inadvertently hitting something, or someone. Even dropping them in water would be like laying mines. The two men decided they would descend gently, deposit the tanks on land and climb on towards the Scottish mainland. Lindstrand ignited the burners and began shooting bursts of hot air into the envelope to control its rate of descent. Through the break in the cloud, they could see Londonderry airfield, but ahead there was only open farmland. Only as Lindstrand brought the balloon down did he realise the difficulty of the manoeuvre. The wind was much faster at ground level than he had anticipated; the balloon bucked through the air out of control as the ground appeared to rush up at them, to arrive with a bone-jarring thump. 'Fucking hell, Per, what's happening?' Branson shouted. 'Hang on, Richard, we're going up . . .' The balloon tore across a field, gouging and skimming the grass, then veered upwards, missing the top of a barn by feet, and climbed sharply away, leaving its remaining fuel canisters buried in the grass below. There had been no need to jettison the tanks; they had been torn off in the impact.

Stripped of the weight of the surplus fuel, the balloon soared sharply upwards. Branson and Lindstrand were both shaken by the incident. The impact had knocked out all electrical power in the balloon; the lights were dead; more importantly, so was the radio. Branson wanted to turn on the emergency beacons each man carried in his pocket, but Lindstrand argued against it; it would only make everyone more anxious. They were going to bring the balloon down. Branson switched his on anyway, but it too was dead. Everything was going horribly wrong.

Through the porthole they could see the Mull of Kintyre, and the mountainous outcrop of the Isle of Arran, under a grey blanket of drizzle. A light aircraft flew past trailing a banner, 'Well done, Richard Brandon.' Even his name had gone wrong.

The two men hastily considered their predicament.

Wind speed was higher than they had expected, and carrying them on a north-easterly trajectory; if they carried on they could be swept miles off the coast the other side of Aberdeen by the time darkness fell. A ground landing was much too unpredictable. Lindstrand's analogy of a battle tank without brakes had become all too apt. The damage to houses, the balloon, themselves, could be horrible. Instead, they would try to bring it down now, on a beach if possible, or near one. Lindstrand began venting the balloon envelope, bringing the craft down. They had rehearsed the procedure for such a landing countless times in their heads. Lindstrand would push the two red ignition buttons to fire the explosive bolts and release the balloon envelope from the capsule. If the envelope remained attached to the capsule, it would either drag it uncontrollably across the sea or turn the capsule into a submarine, dragging it below the waves with its weight, and almost certainly drowning them. If all went according to plan, however, the balloon would be released, leaving the capsule to float safely on the water until they were collected.

The capsule bounced on the water with a resounding thump, shaking them both. Lindstrand punched frantically at the ignition buttons for the explosive bolts. 'Christ! They haven't gone off. Get out, Richard! Get out.' Lindstrand prised off the canopy, and clambered on to the top of the capsule, Branson hard on his heels. The capsule was skidding and bouncing along the tops of the waves like a stone, skimmed by a giant hand, the envelope flapping and billowing ahead. Then Lindstrand was shouting 'Jump Richard, for God's sake jump' – and he was gone. Branson pulled himself to the edge of the rail and looked down. The balloon was rising upwards like an express elevator: 75, 100, 200, 500 feet above the water. It was too late to jump now. Looking down on to the grey water he could see no sign of Lindstrand. Surely he could not have survived a jump from that height; surely he was dead. 'Oh Christ, oh Christ . . .' Branson clambered back through the roof into the capsule, slumped in a seat, and tugged at the handle of the burners to give himself time to think. The balloon was ascending at what seemed to be an astounding rate, into thick cloud. Above him the burners gave off a thin and watery light. Branson realised he was finding it hard to breathe. That meant he had risen further and faster than he thought. He pulled his oxygen mask on and took several deep breaths to calm himself. Think, Richard, think. He would parachute out. That's what he would do. Branson strapped on his parachute and his liferaft and clambered back on to the roof of the capsule. Was this going to be it? For a fleeting moment, Branson believed he was about to die. Curiously, the thought did not frighten him or alarm him. Rather, he looked at it quizzically, as if watching himself from a distance. It was not true what they said about your life flashing in front of your eyes. You did not think of your father cradling you in his arms as a baby, or your mother on the finishing line at school sports day, shouting 'Come on Ricky . . .' You did not think about your friends, or lovers or Joan and the children, or Boy George, Margaret Thatcher, share issues, business deals, condoms or even whether or not God was looking after you. You didn't think of anything when you were about to die. Only of how ludicrous it seemed when there was so much to live for. Only of how much you wanted to live, and what you needed to do to ensure your survival.

He pulled himself back into the capsule, found a pencil and paper and scribbled a note, to his family. 'I love you.' Then he clambered back out again.

The metal on the capsule roof was freezing cold and damp to the touch. Branson shivered. He felt very, very alone. Peering over the edge he could see only thick mist. It was impossible to tell whether he was over land or water, but he thought that somewhere he could hear the chatter of helicopter rotor blades. He did not want to jump. He suddenly remembered his parachute training; a warm spring day above the Hampshire countryside, pulling the wrong cord and suddenly dropping out of control, to be yanked to safety by a hand tugging at his side. A feeling of nausea came into his throat. He had to jump. But wait. Supposing he jumped, landed in water, and wasn't seen. Wouldn't everybody assume that he and Per were still in the balloon? Nobody would be looking for them in the sea. Per would drown, if he hadn't drowned already. He would drown too. It made more sense to stay with the balloon; that is what the rescue services would be watching. He must bring it down himself, then he could tell them where to look for Per; then they would both be safe. Shivering, Branson pulled himself back inside the capsule. How long had he been up here by himself. Ten minutes? Twenty? It seemed like an hour. Branson settled himself into his seat. He was breathing evenly now, tugging at the levers which controlled the burners, venting the balloon. Everything according to procedure.

The balloon was descending slowly now; the cloud thinning. And then it was clear. Below, riding the waves like a bathtub toy, Branson could see a ship – a Navy ship. And there was a helicopter. And another. Branson took off his parachute and checked his lifevest and pulled himself back on to the capsule roof. The water rushed up towards him. Richard Branson looked into the void. And jumped.

Chapter 15

Virgin's War and Peace

Richard Branson was lifted from the Irish Sea by a Royal Navy Sea King helicopter: Per Lindstrand was picked up by a fisherman in a rubber dinghy after two hours spent in the freezing water; the two men were transported to Kilmarnock hospital, and released later that night, exhausted but otherwise healthy.

Assuring all and sundry that the balloon trip marked the end of his adventures and the beginning of a new chapter of sobriety and responsibility, anchored to his desk as chairman of a public company, Branson turned his mind to other activities.

In January 1988 he flew to Moscow as a guest of the Soviet government, to be welcomed in the new spirit of *glasnost*. One of Britain's foremost capitalists slept in the bed once used by Lenin, and negotiated a partnership to bring British holidaymakers to a specially appointed 'Virgin' hotel in the Russian resort of Yalta. He was subsequently made the first ever non-Russian director of Intourist, the official Soviet tourist body. Not reported in the press were further negotiations for the Healthcare Foundation to supply 300 million condoms to Russia on a non-profit basis, to be paid for not in Russian currency, but in oil.

In April, taking advantage of the government-sanctioned takeover of British Caledonian Airways by British Airways, Branson applied for the licence to fly routes which had hitherto been flown by BCal. Virgin subsequently secured the licences to fly to Los Angeles, JFK New York, and Tokyo. Buoyed by a £10m profit recorded by the airline in 1987–88, Branson laid plans to begin the services by the middle of 1989.

In June, Virgin announced the impending sale of seventy record shops to W.H. Smith for £24m. The sale eliminated all Virgin retail outlets of less than 3,000 square feet. Henceforth, Virgin would concentrate solely on the development of the Megastores.

But Branson was beginning to rethink the future of the company in a more dramatic fashion. In July, he made an announcement that shocked Virgin's shareholders. He was preparing to buy back the company he had sold them less than two years before.

Virgin's flotation on the Stock Market had not been the success Branson had hoped for. Even taking into account the effect of Black Monday on the market as a whole, the Virgin share price had continued to perform disappointingly. To Branson this was evidence of a suspicion that he had harboured even as the company was going to the Stock Market – that the City simply didn't understand Virgin's business, and was unable to mark the shares at a price Branson considered commensurate with the company's performance, and its potential.

The City, he complained increasingly vociferously to friends, didn't understand the nature of the music business; more importantly it didn't understand entrepreneurialism – or at least his particular style of it. 'Being an entrepreneur and the chairman of a public company just doesn't mix,' he said.

While City investors had urged the company to go for short-term profits, Branson preferred to take the longer view. The setting up of independent Virgin companies in Japan and America was a case in point. Virgin had been trying to establish a secure toehold in America for years. Flush with money from the public issue, the obvious solution would have been simply to take over an existing American company, thereby incorporating its previous profits into Virgin's balance sheets. Instead, Branson's preferred tactic was to spend almost £10m starting a new Virgin company from scratch, investing in new staff, new premises and a completely fresh roster of artists.

To Branson, it was a question of his personal judgement, and the lengths to which his City investors were prepared to back it. In the wake of the Stock Market crash, and the City's sanguine view of any business regarded as 'unpredictable', this was not as far as Branson would have liked.

There was another thing to consider, of course. Branson was not the only person to be disappointed by the performance of the Virgin shares. There were some 40,000 small shareholders who had placed their trust, and their savings, in the company – many of them friends or employees of Branson. They were feeling pretty disappointed too. Branson decided that in buying back the company, nobody would be offered less for their shares than they had originally paid. Negotiations were set in place for £200m worth of bank loans to finance the privatisation.

The decision afforded a sense of relief to Branson and his fellow directors on the board. Functioning as a public company had proved a stifling experience, incompatible with the spirit in which the Virgin empire had been built. It was not as simple as swapping casual jumpers for suits and ties. For the previous eighteen months, Branson had felt buttoned-up in other ways; constrained and uncomfortable. The feeling of liberation as the privatisation got underway was intoxicating.

In May 1989, the first Virgin flight took off for Tokyo, carrying 300 passengers, including the Secretary of State for Trade and Industry, Lord Young. For Branson, it was the further cementing of links with Japan. Among the round of tea ceremonies, the visits to Kabuki theatre and Sumo wrestling, the endless exchange of gifts and pleasantries, and the ornate rituals of politesse, Branson had opened negotiations with the Japanese communications Fujisankei – Japan's largest owner of television, newspaper and radio interests – to take a stake in Virgin records.

The deal was finalised in October, Fujisankei taking a 25.1 per cent stake in Virgin, worth £115m. It was the biggest equity investment by a Japanese company in Britain ever, eclipsing the acquisition by Honda of a 20 per cent stake in Rover Group, the British Aerospace subsidiary. Branson's long-standing reluctance to dilute in any way his own control over the business and take on partners was beginning to undergo a subtle sea change. In the wake of buying the company back from the Stock Market, a new strategy had been devised for growth – to take limited partnerships. Finance director Trevor Abbott declared that Virgin would be swapping 40,000-odd shareholders for a few close partners, as the company embarked on a strategy of joint ventures to bring in the capital no longer available from outside shareholders in a public company.

The Fujisankei deal had the immediate benefit of paying off some of the bank loans taken out to buy Virgin back from the Stock Market. Furthermore, it would arm Virgin for a strenuous battle to maintain its standing in an increasingly competitive market-place.

Throughout the late Eighties, the trend in the record industry had been the gradual erosion of independent labels, and the growing dominance of the Big Five: Thorn-EMI of Britain; Polygram, a subsidiary of the Dutch group Philips; Time-Warner in America; Sony of Japan: and the Bertelsmann company of West Germany. Companies like Virgin which had been founded in the late Sixties and early Seventies had begun to vanish one by one. First Chrysalis was absorbed by Thorn-EMI. Then Polygram paid £200m to take over Island Records, owned by Branson's old friend and business adversary Chris Blackwell. Shortly afterwards, Polygram paid a further $500m for the American-owned label A&M. The deal with Fujisankei not only provided money in the bank to help repel any predatory moves on Virgin from any of the Big Five, but also gave access to the full promotional benefits of Fujisankei's enormous empire in Japan.

In fact, there had been another offer on the Virgin table. One of the Big Five had offered $100m more than Fujisankei for a 25 per cent stake in Virgin, but with the condition that they should distribute Virgin product throughout the world and have a major say in how the company was run. To Branson it would have been the beginning of the end. He was not ready to relinquish control of Virgin. Not yet, at least.

But still, the trend towards partnership and dispersal continued. In 1989 Virgin Vision was sold to an American company, Management Company Entertainment

Group, for $83m – a price which probably over-estimated the true value of the company. The publishing company W.H. Allen, which had been acquired in 1987, was closed down in 1990 (although Virgin books continued).

In May 1990, the Japanese hotel group Seibu Saison paid £36m to take a 10 per cent stake in the airline holding company, Voyager. And a month later, Virgin entered into a fifty-fifty arrangement with a Japanese retail company, Marui, to open the first Virgin megastore in Tokyo.

In 1988, Branson had shed the smaller Virgin record shops to W.H. Smith, in order to concentrate on the Megastores. But at the end of 1991, as high street retailing slumped to its lowest levels for years, it was announced that W.H. Smith had paid around £20m for a half share in the Megastores. By the end of 1991, Virgin would be entwined in some eighteen joint ventures around the world.

It was no coincidence that the most significant of these should be with Japanese companies. Branson did not share the suspicion with which many Western businessmen seemed to view the Japanese. The best response to Japanese incursions into Western markets was not despair, he reasoned, but pragmatism: the Japanese might be tough negotiators, but it was up to Western businessmen to do business with them and strike the best possible deals.

Branson found much to admire in the Japanese. Japanese companies display a loyalty to their staff which Branson thought exemplary; and they display the same loyalty to their friends and business partners. So, Fujisankei, he believed, offered him something which the cautious – and suspicious – investors of the London Stock Market never had: a long-term financial commitment to

Virgin, without the impediment of managerial interference or conditions. It was as close to a guarantee of independence as Virgin would find.

During negotiations, one of the Fujisankei executives had expressed it thus: 'Do you want a Japanese wife, or a Western wife? Japanese wife far more docile than Western wife.' Branson chose a Japanese wife.

The blossoming relationship between Virgin and Japan was to be celebrated in typical style. In October 1989, Branson again flew to Tokyo, this time to announce that having conquered the Atlantic in a hot-air balloon, he and Lindstrand would now be turning their attention to the Pacific, attempting to fly from Japan to America.

Richard Branson's first thought after the successful crossing of the Atlantic by hot-air balloon was 'never again'. If the first twenty-seven hours had been among the most exhilarating of his life, the last three had certainly been the most terrifying. No more. That's what he told Joan, his family, his friends, his colleagues, the media. But that had been eighteen months before. Times had changed. 'It's like anything,' he reasoned. 'You're apt to forget the bad moments and only remember the good ones; nature is wonderful like that.'

Quite apart from anything else, he *enjoyed* sticking his neck out, whether in business or in a hot-air balloon. 'I'm in a position now where I don't need to be doing most of the things I do,' he said, 'but I feel I should do them. One of the things I've learned about myself is that the satisfaction I get from testing myself on the boating and balloon trips has been a great part of my life. I've had enormous satisfaction from those things – not just the event itself, but everything that goes into it, the planning, the learning, the people you're working with. I simply enjoy it.'

In fact, within a month of being fished out of the Irish Sea, Per Lindstrand had started drawing up designs for a new capsule and envelope that could carry him and Branson across the Pacific.

Among Branson's family and close friends the old familiar fears began to resurface. Joan had long given up arguing. These exploits brought out the best and worst in Branson; they tested his physical courage, his enterprise and his fortitude; but they also brought out the irresponsible schoolboy in him – going in to each project with the minimum preparation, as if these were some sort of Corinthian sporting occasions rather than life-or-death risks, seemed to have become almost an article of faith – and showed the most selfish side of his nature, deaf, as he was, to the entreaties of those closest to him.

What was the point? friends asked. He'd already proved his courage, daring, resourcefulness – or recklessness. He'd met quite enough 'challenges'; and whatever value these had had in publicity terms, they certainly weren't worth losing his life for. The new project scared the wits out of his family and friends, and sent a tremor of nervousness through the entire Virgin organisation. What was the point?

The point was clear enough. First Branson wanted to fly the Pacific because, like Mount Everest, it was there. Secondly because it was fun. Thirdly, the publicity value of such an exercise, in a country where Virgin had real ambitions for expansion, was enormous. The project was to be underwritten by a Japanese soft-drinks manufacturer with the improbable name of Pocari Sweat; and the ties with Fujisankei would ensure media saturation of the event in Japan.

Furthermore, the trip would provide an opportunity for Branson to publicise some of his interests in the environment, and promote awareness in Japan of environmental problems in the Pacific basin. The project adopted a scientific expedition from Cambridge University, exploring ways of preserving the Indonesian rainforests, under threat from Japanese exploitation. And to this particular cause, Branson added two more: whaling and ivory, both areas in which the Japanese were prime culprits.

Branson had become a popular figure in Japan: the businessman as celebrity. His shaggy haircut and loud sweaters were a source of delighted curiosity; his diffident, polite manner could sometimes threaten to out-humble even the Japanese themselves – world masters of the art. Now, as if to prove that he was not only wildly eccentric, but also quite possibly mad, he was about to risk hara-kiri by flying off in a hot-air balloon. Heads of multi-million dollar companies in Japan simply did not do that sort of thing. It was all very strange. And the Japanese loved him for it.

Crossing the Atlantic, Branson and Lindstrand had flown a total of 3,075 miles, from Sugarloaf Mountain in Maine to the coast of Scotland. The new *Pacific Flyer* would be attempting a journey of some 6,200 miles, from Miyakonojo, on the southern Japanese island of Kyushu, to its expected landing point in Northern California, Flying at altitudes of up to 38,000 feet, and at speeds of up to 200 m.p.h., they expected to be airborne for four days. Everything about the *Pacific Flyer* was larger – but not much. The balloon envelope was double-skinned, 2.6 million cubic feet, and required 27 miles of fabric to manufacture. When inflated it would stand 196 feet in height – one and a half times as tall as Nelson's Column.

And while the capsule for the Atlantic flight had been approximately the size of a broom-cupboard, more or less confining the two aeronauts to their seats for the whole flight, the capsule of the *Pacific Flyer* did at least afford some mobility, with sufficient space between the two aircraft seats to stretch out on the floor and sleep. In the event, there would be no opportunity to take advantage of this luxury.

Strapped in their seats, both men would be surrounded by banks of switches, dials and valves. Food and medical supplies would be stored in six containers under the capsule floor; the two men would subsist on a diet, specially designed in space programmes, to minimise bodily waste and – they would subsequently discover – any hint of flavour.

The capsule was flanked by six fuel tanks loaded with propane, feeding the twelve burners mounted on the roof of the capsule. Tom Barrow, whose calm leadership of the team had proved so invaluable on the Atlantic flight, would not be present for the Pacific one. Barrow had set up his own airship company in California, and he and Lindstrand were on strained terms. Instead the support team would be led by Mike Kendrick, an experienced balloonist who, most recently, had been organising balloon flights in Egypt for one of Branson's subsidiary companies. However, the same navigation and meteorological team had been retained from the Atlantic flight, headed by the phlegmatic veterans Doc Wiley and Bob Rice, whom Branson had taken to referring to as 'the voice of God'. They would be based on the American – or 'receiving' – end of the trip.

At first glance, the launch site at Miyakonojo, where the team arrived in November 1989 to make their final preparations for the flight, seemed perfect; a baseball park, looking not unlike a Roman amphitheatre, ringed by hills, and, in the far distance, Mount Tajachiko where, as legend had it, the grandson of the Sun Goddess descended to earth to create a divine race – the genesis of Japan. But, notwithstanding its beauty and its mythic connotations, the site proved a miscalculation: the winds coming down off the mountainsides each morning would make inflation of the balloon a precarious business.

To the townspeople of Miyakonojo, the circus of the balloon launch was both a thrilling and puzzling spectacle. Miyakonojo welcomed the aeronauts with flags, flowers, official speeches. The mayor, grateful for the way his small town was being put on the map, invoked the legend of Mount Tajachiko, and described Branson as 'a modern god who is about to ascend into the sky'.

On the allotted day of the take-off, thousands of people gathered in bitterly cold weather to await the inflation of the balloon. But the winds off the mountain were unrelenting. The take-off was postponed, and Branson addressed the crowds to thank them, apologise and suggest they come back next day.

The following day the winds settled, and the balloon was inflated, to the astonishment and delight of the crowd. Branson and Lindstrand arrived on site, keyed up and ready for take-off, and walked around the capsule, gazing upwards into the huge balloon billowing above them. To their astonishment, pieces of the balloon's inner skin suddenly started raining down like snowflakes onto the burners below. The envelope had been laid out on the ground overnight for some hours before inflation, and frost had attacked the inner lining, which had now started to break up in the heat of the warm air from the burners. The fact that it had happened half an hour before the scheduled lift-off, rather than half an hour after it, was some consolation, but there was nothing else to do but call the flight off. Once again, Branson found himself apologising to the assembled crowd, and promised that he and Lindstrand would be back next year.

Joan had chosen not to be in Japan for the launch. Instead, she and the two children, along with Branson's eldest sister Lindi and her husband Robin, had arranged to leave London by plane for Los Angeles at around the same time the balloon was scheduled to go up. Halfway across the Atlantic, the captain of the aircraft picked up the news from Japan on his radio. A steward informed Joan that the balloon flight had been aborted. The tension drained out of her face. 'Thank God for that,' she sighed, and ordered champagne.

To Branson, the failure to lift off was a profoundly deflating experience. The build-up to the event had been enormous; now everybody felt cheated, frustrated and somewhat foolish. While Lindstrand supervised the winding-down on the operations in Japan, Branson flew alone to Los Angeles, where the American operations centre had been set up on an airfield in Santa Monica. A hangar had been given over to a press and hospitality centre, with direct TV links to the site in Japan, and copious amounts of food and drink. But the anticipated celebration as the balloon soared into the sky had fallen somewhat flat. Branson painstakingly thanked the team that had worked on the project, putting as brave a face as he could on his disappointment.

The following day, he took Joan and the children to Disneyland. He might not have been able to fly the balloon, but the Pirates of the Caribbean was almost as much fun, and considerably safer.

At Christmas 1989 Richard and Joan Templeman were

married, on the island of Neckar, after some twelve years of living together. They returned to a new home, in the pleasant and leafy West London neighbourhood of Holland Park, about a mile – and a world – away from their previous house in Oxford Gardens, at the ramshackle end of Ladbroke Grove. The new property had cost some £3.5m: it was a magnificent four-storey, double-fronted house, in a quiet street backing on to Holland Park itself. The Swiss ambassador was a neighbour; on the opposite side of the road lived an Arab potentate, the front of his house regularly patrolled by chunky-looking men in dark suits.

No expense had been spared on the house. There was a swimming-pool and jacuzzi installed downstairs, adjacent to the breakfast room and kitchen. The top floor had been turned into a huge lounge and games room, with a full-size pool table, and furniture specially imported from Bali. Friends agreed that it was very beautiful, of course, but was such opulence and grandeur quite Richard's style? Oxford Gardens had been very much a comfortable, cosy family home: Holland Park felt like a palace.

For the first few months after moving in Branson padded over the new carpets and in and out of the enormous rooms looking somewhat lost, and not a little uncomfortable. Joan's pleasure in the new house was also somewhat dampened when shortly after moving in, she awoke one night to find an intruder who had broken in despite the battery of expensive security devices. He escaped with Branson in hot pursuit. The incident sounded a small note of unease. This was one of the things that more conspicuous affluence brought with it: the need for security cameras at the door, the worries about being a target. But the house had the advantage of being big enough to double as an office not only for

Branson himself, but also for his team of secretaries. And, at last, there was an enormous oak dining-table large enough to accommodate a board meeting.

Business was flourishing. In one week in June 1990, Virgin Atlantic was voted Airline of the Year in the magazine *Executive Traveller*. Virgin records had the number one record in America by Maxi Priest. Virgin retailing opened the largest record shop in Japan. Branson himself flew as a passenger with the RAF Red Arrows, and travelled to the Russian space centre outside Moscow to meet a cosmonaut, with a view to a proposed round-the-world balloon trip. In the same week the *Daily Mirror* published an account of Branson dressed in stockings and a suspender belt at an office party under the heading 'Branson the Virgin Queen Goes Wild In Drag'.

Time had done little to quieten Branson's frenetic schedule, nor, it seemed, the popular interest in his life. Yet Branson himself was feeling increasingly restless and dissatisfied. In July 1990 he flew back to Neckar for a fortieth birthday party in the company of a few close friends. It was a happy occasion, though an anniversary which Branson had been contemplating with some trepidation. It is an unusual man who can pass the milestone of forty without some reflection on what he has achieved in his life. There could be no question that Branson's material achievements were considerable, but wasn't there more to life than that? From as early an age as he could remember, Branson had been under the charge to 'do something useful'. Now he was forty: he had built Virgin into a company with interests straddling the globe. He was fighting for the survival of his airline in a vicious fare war with British Airways. He had a beautiful and loving wife and children. But still Branson felt unaccountably restless.

Then on 1 August, Iraq invaded Kuwait. The invasion brought a new figure of demonology out of the wings and onto the main stage of world politics. Saddam Hussein – the second Hitler, according to the less temperate headline writers and columnists.

The invasion of Kuwait sounded alarm bells in the West. Not only was Saddam violating the sovereign status of another country, albeit one of almost feudal corruption and injustice, he was also threatening oil supplies that were essential to the West. The United Nations condemned the invasion, and issued an ultimatum to Iraq to leave the occupied territories or risk war. An alliance of troops from some forty different countries, led by the Americans and the British, took up position in Saudi Arabia, facing off against the massed ranks of the Iraqi army across the desert sand.

The conflict fascinated Branson. He had never visited Kuwait or Iraq but he had been to neighbouring Jordan, as a guest of King Hussein and his American-born wife, Queen Noor. They had first met in London, shortly after Branson's transatlantic balloon crossing. The king and queen had expressed an interest in ballooning, and Branson had obliged them by taking a balloon over to Jordan. They had subsequently met in London, and some four months before the Iraqi invasion, Branson and the king had been guests at a dinner at Chequers, the Prime Minister's country residence, hosted by Margaret Thatcher and the Foreign Secretary, Douglas Hurd.

King Hussein's friendship with Saddam, and his refusal to condemn Iraq's invasion of Kuwait, would make him an increasingly unpopular and vilified figure in the West. But Branson would remain loyal to his friend. The invasion of Kuwait sent migrant workers from Pakistan, Sri Lanka and other Arab countries fleeing over the border into Jordan. Branson wrote to King Hussein, commiserating with his position, and offering to help in whatever way he could.

The West's anger at Saddam was compounded by his treatment of foreign nationals who happened to be living in Iraq or in Kuwait at the time of the invasion: they were arrested. 'Guests of the Iraqi government', said Saddam; 'Victims of international terrorist blackmail', said the West. The plight of the hostages went straight to the hearts of people in Britain, watching the developments unfold night by night on their television screens.

Branson was no less moved, as he sat at home in Holland Park watching the news of Saddam Hussein's announcement that he would allow women and children to leave Iraq. Just as he had been seized with an impulse some five years earlier on watching a television documentary on AIDS to get involved, to do something, so now Branson felt compelled to some sort of action. Would Saddam's offer still be good in two or three days' time? Branson's first thought was fly the hostages home immediately.

That night Branson went down to the Gatwick offices of Virgin and started putting together his own task force. In a lather of activity and impatience he contacted the Foreign Office, and Harold 'Hookey' Walker, the British ambassador in Baghdad. He then spoke to the Iraqi embassy in London in an attempt to gain permission to take off to, and land in, Iraq. In frustration, it was decided to file a flight plan. A phone call to the Iraqi ambassador in Paris confirmed that permission would be given to land in Baghdad.

The preparations and permissions were somewhat premature. The Iraqis did not, in the event, give permission for any aircraft to land in Baghdad. The hostages were to be carried in convoy to Amman, to be collected from there.

That same weekend, Branson received a telephone call from Queen Noor in Jordan, in reply to his letter. The refugee situation was grave, she said; camps had been set up along the border between Jordan and Kuwait, but food, medicines and blankets were in short supply. The climate was hot by day, freezing cold by night and she feared that people would start dying within three days if shelter was not provided. Branson promised he would do what he could. That same day he contacted his friend David Sainsbury, of the supermarket family, who agreed to donate rice. He then contacted William Waldegrave at the Foreign Office – a sometime tennis partner – who promised to organise the provision of blankets. A public appeal was launched, and a flight was arranged into Amman for the following Tuesday.

The first plane arrived in Amman carrying about 44,000 blankets which were unloaded to make ready for its payload of women and children. Branson was asked at a press conference why he was only carrying out Western nationals: why not the refugees in the makeshift camps along the Jordanian border, whose needs were, if anything, even more acute? Branson was taken to a refugee camp by helicopter, so he could see the situation for himself. It was obvious that repatriation was a desperate priority.

But even in the matter of evacuation, national sensitivities were very much to the fore. There were women and children of all nationalities clamouring to leave Amman. Virgin offered to carry as many people as its 747 would take. But the ambassadors of both Egypt and France declined to let nationals from their respective countries board the Virgin plane.

Branson accused the French ambassador of prevaricating; a French plane would not be in Jordan for another forty-eight hours. But to be seen to be flying the flag had clearly become a matter of some importance. Lord King of British Airways quickly declared his willingness to make BA planes available to collect hostages, deliver supplies and repatriate refugees, and was said to be so angry that Virgin had stolen a march on BA by landing in Amman first that he berated a government minister, asking, 'Has Virgin become part of the Foreign Office?' Keen to make it clear that BA were also doing their bit, King later appeared at Heathrow Airport to personally greet the first hostages to be flown home in a BA plane.

The first Virgin flight from Amman carried home fifty-seven British women and children, and thirty-five people of other nationalities. Branson arrived back in London feeling tired but elated, fired with a sense of purpose. He immediately began lobbying the British government to give money to the International Organisation of Migration to help repatriate the 150,000 refugees in Jordan. Over the next three weeks, following a green light from Lynda Chalker, the Overseas Development minister, Branson would organise the flight of eight aircraft – two Virgin planes, and six chartered craft – into Jordan, carrying some 400 tonnes of food and supplies.

The events in the Gulf had a galvanising effect on Richard Branson. Two months before he had been bored, distracted, depressed, wondering whether to sell all or part of Virgin; wondering what to do with his life. Such deliberations were now forced to the back of his mind; the mood of doubt and self-reflection evaporated in the heat of enthusiasm for the job in hand.

'When the invasion of Kuwait took place, it just occurred to me that in the same way as the Mates campaign had been one response to the crisis of AIDS. Perhaps somebody outside politics might be able to make a contribution in the Gulf,' he said. 'Why not bring entrepreneurial skills to a situation like this, rather than just using them to build another company?' The remark was a measure of just how much Branson, and his circumstances, had changed. Running the airline had pulled him into an orbit infinitely more rarefied than the music business. He was now on first-name terms with government ministers, and heads of state; a figure of opinion and, it now transpired, of influence.

Not everybody thought his motives entirely altruistic. The accusation that Branson had used the hostage crisis for his own purposes was aired in some newspaper editorials. One member of the Gulf relatives support group accused him of turning the airlift into 'a sick publicity stunt'.

Branson was deeply hurt by the criticism. It was true he had been photographed in front of the Virgin plane before it left for Amman, but that, he insisted, was not instigated by him as a publicity stunt or for his own personal glory; it was at the request of the assembled newspaper photographers. 'The press were there at Gatwick, begging for just one picture, one picture,' he explained, 'so I agreed to them taking a picture of the volunteer crew down at the plane; and then, of course, they asked "Can you join them, Richard?" and I agreed, which was a big mistake . . .'

It was a perennial puzzle to Branson. He could never quite understand the apparent paradox whereby any public figures doing something for themselves – buying a new house, boosting their own fortune, taking a new mistress or toyboy – receives acres of approving copy in the newspapers, while anybody doing anything for others is immediately open to accusations of selfishness.

'If I go out to promote one of my companies, to make lots of money, I never get criticised for that,' he said. 'But if anybody tries to do anything positive they get criticised. It was the same for Bob Geldof. There are some things that don't need publicity, but we were appealing to the nation to send in blankets for refugees. And you've got to use yourself to do that.'

The first airlifts had brought home virtually all of the women and children who had been caught in Kuwait or Iraq. But the fate of the men continued to hang in the balance as the volume of rhetoric grew ever more intense, the prospects for peace less likely. Many of the hostages, it was known, had been sent to military installations, factories and other likely targets for allied bombs in the eventuality of war. No guarantees existed for their physical condition. Many were known to be sick, suffering from illnesses that required regular treatment or particular medications.

Frank Hessey, a rest-home proprietor in Blackpool, had a sister Maureen and brother-in-law Tony Wilbraham in Iraq. Wilbraham was suffering from lung cancer, and had only a matter of months to live. From the moment the Iraqi invasion had started, Hessey had been petitioning anybody who would listen, to free his brother-in-law and the other hostages who were ill and in desperate need of proper medical treatment. He had approached the Foreign Office, the Iraqi ambassadors in Britain and France, even the Iraqi government in Baghdad.

He had also contacted Richard Branson, and the former prime minister Edward Heath, who had emerged from the shadows of the Conservative back benches to play an increasingly vocal role in the public debate over the Gulf. Heath's emphasis on finding a diplomatic solution to the crisis had angered some elements of the press, who were growing increasingly jingoistic at the prospect of war, but Hessey had been impressed by Heath's position, and his refusal to brand Saddam 'a second Hitler'.

Hessey suggested to Branson that an incentive could be offered to the Iraqis to release the sick hostages: medical supplies that were much needed in Iraq. Branson spoke with the Foreign Office to see whether carrying medicines into Iraq would contravene United Nations sanctions, and to gauge their response to the idea of flying in medicines and flying out sick hostages.

The Foreign Office were sanguine. The British government, Branson was told, could never be seen to support any action which could be construed as 'buying out hostages'. But neither would they seek to stand in Branson's way if he went ahead under his own steam, and the idea could well work. 'After all,' said one official drily, 'it's not good PR for the Iraqis to have cancer cases dying in their hospitals.'

Early in September, Branson went back to Amman alone, as a guest at the palace of King Hussein. He felt acutely that this was one of the most important times in his life, a turning point, after which things could never be quite the same. The criticism he had received still rankled. Branson had never been particularly self-reflective, but now, as he sat in his room in Hussein's palace in Amman, pondering on the events of the last few weeks, he felt moved to write in his notebook.

What are my motives for doing this? Is there any truth in the jibes? One month ago I was doing an interview for *Vanity Fair* and I was at an all-time low: I seemed to have run out of a purpose for life;

411

I'd proved myself to myself in many areas. I'd just turned forty and was seeking new challenges. I was even considering selling up everything except the airline, getting smaller and concentrating on one business venture, but also to have the time to use my business skills to concentrate on issues where I felt I could help. I thought I could get more self-satisfaction this way.

Do I need recognition for this? I don't think so. In order to campaign on many issues you need to use yourself. The situation with the refugees has now been arrested, and by not speaking out it might not have been. How often can one use the press this way in one small country like England without losing one's appeal to the public? It should be a hint that if one was doing it for personal glory then one won't be able to do it at all.

Branson spent the weekend in Amman in a frenzy of activity. He visited refugee camps with Queen Noor, to see for himself how the provisions which had been raised in Britain were being used. He had meetings with the Jordanian Minister of the Interior and his deputies. He wrote letters to refugee organisations and telephoned foreign embassies, attempting to get a full list of all the foreign nationals classified as 'sick and disabled' who were being held in Iraq. He spent an evening with King Hussein, in a study where photographs of the king with Saddam Hussein, and with Margaret Thatcher, stood side by side on the table. Hussein's conversation ranged over the Palestinian problem, the delicacy of his own position as a friend of both Saddam and the West, and his personal difficulties in holding Jordan together in such a tense period. The king's conciliatory stance towards Saddam Hussein, his insistence that the conflict was not as simple as the Western governments and media made it out to be, had made him a target of vilification in some sections of the British press; but Branson retained a great admiration for him. He thought King Hussein was 'a great ruler', greatly misunderstood.

They spoke about the plight of the sick British hostages, and the possibilities of their release. King Hussein said he would do what he could to help. That night, Branson wrote a letter to Saddam, offering to fly medicines into Iraq, and pleading for the sick hostages to be released so that they could be returned to Britain on the same plane. The letter was personally translated into Arabic by King Hussein, who appended a note telling Saddam of his friendship with Branson, and asking for Branson's plea to be given serious consideration.

On his return to London, Branson was contacted by Edward Heath. Heath had agreed to take up Frank Hessey's case, and to negotiate the release of the sick hostages. Branson briefed him on what had happened in Amman, and confirmed that a Virgin plane would be available if it was needed.

Hessey himself contacted Izat Ibrahim, the Iraqi Minister for Plenipotentiary in London, who indicated that Heath was an intermediary respected by the Iraqis. Ibrahim visited Heath at his home in Salisbury. Hessey then contacted William Waldegrave at the Foreign Office who, according to him, 'expressed encouragement' over Heath's role as intermediary. Branson also contacted Waldegrave, to see if the government would make some contribution towards the cost of the flight – perhaps as much as it would have cost to fly a military plane to Iraq and back. Waldegrave told Branson he was nervous about the British government being seen to pay for it, lest the world believe that the government had set it up in the first place. If the flight went ahead, Waldegrave emphasised, it must be seen to be the work of 'public-spirited individuals', not the government; furthermore, the government could offer no protection, and no guarantees, if the Virgin flight was, for any reason, stranded in Iraq.

Publicly, Mrs Thatcher was being cool about Edward Heath's overtures towards Saddam Hussein, and anxious to dissociate herself from any errands to Iraq, merciful or otherwise. Privately, her ministers seemed to be endorsing the flight, while doing their utmost not to be seen to be doing so. The inevitable argument eventually burst into public view in October, when Foreign Secretary Douglas Hurd denied Edward Heath's assertion that it was Hurd who had asked him to go to Baghdad. To Frank Hessey, the government's position was plain enough. 'They wanted it done,' he said, 'but not to be seen to be doing it themselves. They wanted someone else to do it: Richard Branson, Ted Heath and myself.'

On 20 October, Edward Heath arrived in Baghdad, having flown via Amman, to begin talks with Saddam Hussein. He carried with him a list of some two hundred people said to qualify as sick or elderly. In tense negotiations over the next two days, these names would be haggled and argued over like poker chips. How sick was a sick man? Did cancer qualify? A perforated eardrum? A sprained ankle?

On 23 October a Virgin 747 left Gatwick for Iraq, carrying a team of medical personnel, stretchers, heart defibrillators and respiratory equipment. Frank Hessey and his wife Diana were also on board. The plane was not, however, carrying medicines for Iraq.

'I've just had a call from Margaret Thatcher,' Branson joked over the public address system as the plane banked

over the English countryside. 'She assures me she wants
to see Ted Heath home and she won't bomb Baghdad
while we're there.'

Darkness was descending as the 747 flew into Baghdad
airport. The plane taxied to a halt, and the door swung
open to reveal not the anticipated soldiers and government officials, but a handful of mechanics and airport
officials, looking embarrassed and unsure what to do
next. Branson ordered a tray of coffees for the 'reception
committee', which were accepted with guarded gratitude.
A stewardess brought a tray of choc-ices, and they were
eaten in silence. After almost an hour, the British visitors
were let off the plane and ushered into the airport, utterly
deserted, eerily quiet. Harold Walker, the British ambassador to Iraq, looking almost supernaturally phlegmatic
in the face of extraordinary pressure, shook Branson's
hand, and exchanged a few words with the Hesseys.
There had been a hold-up. Nobody knew how many
hostages were to be released as a result of the talks, or
when they would arrive. The plane would have to wait.

In the airport's VIP lounge, under portraits of Saddam
Hussein, Iraqi officials proffered orange juices and polite
smiles. At last, word came that the hostages had arrived
at the airport. One by one they filed on to the plane, at
two and three minute intervals, to be met by Branson
with a handshake and a glass of champagne. Some were
led to their seats by stewardesses; some to stretchers.
Tony Wilbraham and his wife Maureen came on board,
completely unaware that they had their own private
family welcoming committee. 'You're always bloody late,
you two . . .' said Frank Hessey, stepping forward, his
arms outstretched, a catch in his voice. There was a
moment of suspected disbelief, then floods of tears.

Edward Heath was the last to come aboard, to a

chorus of cheers. The discussions and haggling over numbers had settled at a disappointingly low figure – only thirty-three men, five women, two children (and two dogs). But they were free.

The plane flew home on champagne, with Heath and Branson being lauded as heroes. At Gatwick, Edward Heath played the role of elder statesman to perfection, speaking with dignity about the task accomplished, declining to be photographed with the attendant chorus of jubilant, grateful hostages – and contemplating with some satisfaction, no doubt, the discomfort which the plaudits surrounding his achievement in the next morning's papers would inflict on Margaret Thatcher.

Richard Branson dodged the scrum. As the pack of journalists descended on the hostages to hear their stories of horror and deliverance from the hands of Saddam, Branson slipped quietly through the crowd and into a waiting car to be driven away, without a comment.

The excitement of the 'freedom flight' to Iraq; his time in Amman; the contribution which Virgin had made to relieving the plight of the refugees in Jordan – all of this had left Richard Branson in a state of some exhilaration.

To Branson, Virgin's part in the Gulf conflict was a vindication of his beliefs about the role private companies could play in public affairs. The collection and distribution of blankets, foods and medicines to the refugees in Jordan; the help and advice which had been given in running the camps, was an example, he believed, of how entrepreneurial skills could be usefully turned to crisis management on a large scale. It confirmed his growing belief that successful companies had a responsibility to use their expertise for the benefit of the community at large, not only for themselves.

It had replenished Branson's appetite for good works. Although he had severed his connection with UK 2000 and the Mates campaign had also petered out, by the time the Virgin Healthcare Foundation sold Mates to Ansell, the company who actually manufactured the condoms, 100,000 vending machines had been installed at sites where there had been nothing before and the company had 25 per cent of the market, breaking the monopoly of Durex. And the Foundation continued to retain a small royalty which went towards health education.

However, the Healthcare Foundation remained active in the other areas. Branson had a new bugbear now: cigarette smoking. In January of 1990, the Healthcare Foundation donated £100,000 towards the launch of a lobby group called Parents Against Tobacco. Branson's enthusiasm for the new campaign had been galvanised by his 'revulsion and embarrassment' at watching a commercial on the Virgin in-flight programme glamourising cigarette smoking for a captive audience of young children. Whether smoking cigarettes or flying hot-air balloons, adults had the right to choose their own risks, he reasoned, but he wanted no part in encouraging children to smoke. Cigarette advertising on Virgin flights and in the in-flight magazine was banned forthwith. Branson then began lobbying leading industrialists and bankers, asking for their help in a scheme to raise £100m in government and private money to 'buy out' all the tobacco companies' sponsorship in sporting programmes.

Twenty-two years before, Richard Branson had sold advertising for *Student* with the breathless litany, 'I'm Richard Branson, I'm eighteen and I run a magazine that's doing something really useful for young people . . .' Nowadays, his profile as a public figure was somewhat higher, his network of connections somewhat more extensive; yet his powers and manner of persuasion remained essentially the same, whether he was calling William Waldegrave at home on a Sunday morning begging for blankets for Jordan, or phoning Marmaduke Hussey, chairman both of the BBC and of the Royal Marsden Hospital, to point out the paradox of BBC televising events sponsored by tobacco companies while the Royal Marsden specialised in cancer treatment. Now, as then, Branson was relentless in his enthusiasm, shameless in his persistence, if it was for what he regarded as a worthy cause.

In December of 1990, as the clock on the Allied ultimatum to Saddam Hussein continued to tick down, Richard Branson and Per Lindstrand arrived back in Miyakonojo to renew their assault on the Pacific ocean by hot-air balloon. The disappointment of the first aborted attempt, where thousands of local people had gathered in near freezing temperatures only to watch the tragi-comic spectacle of the balloon starting to fall apart, had apparently done nothing to diminish their enthusiasm. The site in the shadow of Mount Tajachiko was once again crowded with sightseers, reporters and television crews, as the capsule and the new balloon envelope were made ready.

Pocari Sweat, the unfortunately named Japanese drinks manufacturer, had renewed their commitment to sponsorship, to the tune of £1m – and with the same proviso, that the balloon must achieve an altitude of 30,000 feet, and get within American territorial waters, for all the money to be paid. The aborted attempt of the previous year had been a costly, as well as a frustrating, failure.

Pocari Sweat wanted a copper-bottomed insurance

policy. But Branson took no such precautions. He had made no attempt to take out additional insurance on his own life, although while he was away Trevor Abbott, Virgin's financial director, quietly took out a policy, largely to reassure Virgin's banks that if anything happened to Branson, the company had financial stability.

The timing of the launch had been carefully chosen to take maximum advantage of the jet stream across the Pacific. This is formed when cold air coming down from the north meets the warmer air coming up from the south. The jet is at its strongest from early October to March, but because 1990 had been an unusually mild year, the jet had been slow to form. For almost a fortnight, Branson, Lindstrand, the launch crew, the newspaper and television reporters, waited and waited for the winds to come: to no avail. Finally, the flight was postponed until after Christmas.

Branson and his family flew to Indonesia for two weeks' relaxation. A Japanese balloonist, Fumio Niwa, was also making an attempt on the Pacific, but by helium balloon. A spirit of friendly encouragement had grown up between Branson and Lindstrand and the Japanese aeronaut, with exchanges of greetings and information. But when Branson arrived back in Japan from Indonesia, it was to learn that Niwa was dead. He had taken off the previous day, but come down in the sea after only a few hours. It had taken the Japanese rescue services almost seventeen hours to reach the ditched craft just 260 miles off the Japanese coast, by which time Niwa had died of exposure.

The *Pacific Flyer* team set to readying their balloon capsule in a sober mood. The eyes of the world, however, were elsewhere.

The Allied forces' ultimatum to Saddam Hussein to

withdraw from Kuwait had expired on 15 January. The expectation of an Allied invasion of Iraq and occupied Kuwait was growing by the hour. Air-traffic permissions for the balloon flight also expired on 15 January. Branson and Lindstrand had agreed that if war broke out before the balloon could be launched, they would abandon the flight; otherwise, they would go. Both were tired of waiting. The flight had lost much of its value as a publicity exercise for Virgin and Lindstrand's balloon company, Thunder & Colt. The aborted attempt some fifteen months before had been front-page news. This time, the combination of a looming war, and a proper reticence on the part of the Virgin publicity machine, meant that few people in Britain or America were even aware that the attempt was about to take place (although the fascination of the Japanese media for the event seemed undiminished, war or no war). But the simple fact was that nobody could face the prospect of yet another postponement. The people of Miyakonojo had been the very model of helpfulness and hospitality, but to have had to come back a *third* time would have stretched everybody's patience beyond breaking-point.

Plans were made to launch the balloon on Sunday 13 January. But the day before, it was obvious that the surface weather would block an inflation. By the next day, the forecast for the jet stream across the Pacific for an entry into Oregon looked good, but a high wind on the ground again prevented inflation.

For the 15th, the only cloud on the horizon was war. At 2.30 that morning, Branson and Lindstrand arrived at the launch site. Speeches were made, white doves released, and Branson and Lindstrand clambered into the capsule. At 5 a.m., the biggest hot-air balloon in the world began its slow, graceful ascent into the skies over Miyakonojo.

The idea was to gain altitude and manoeuvre into the jet stream as soon as possible. But the subtropical jet proved a less accommodating host than its Atlantic cousin. Gaining altitude, the balloon took a vicious buffeting. More than once, wind-shear tossed the envelope back out of the jet, the ferocity of the wind completely extinguishing the flames from the propane burner. Struggling to maintain an altitude around 27,000 feet was a physically and emotionally taxing experience, but it was imperative to jump on 'the moving pavement' of the jet stream as soon as possible – it would be moving even faster further over the Pacific, and jumping onto it then would be that much more difficult. Indeed, at times the balloon would be carried along at speeds of up to 260 m.p.h.

After seven hours' buffeting, Lindstrand announced that it was time to change fuel tanks and jettison the empty tank for the sharks. Both men pulled on their oxygen masks, and strapped themselves into their seats. Lindstrand armed the release mechanism, while Branson trained the external cameras onto the tank, to film it falling away from the capsule. Lindstrand hit the switch. There was an unusually loud bang, and a tremendous lurch, as the entire capsule tilted violently at an angle of 45 degrees. Through his TV monitor, Branson could see what appeared to be a large chunk of the capsule spiralling away towards the sea, some 30,000 feet below.

'Per . . .' Branson had trouble getting the words out. 'This didn't happen when we crossed the Atlantic . . .'

Such was the angle of the capsule that while a few moments before, Lindstrand had been seated *beside* him, Branson now had to tilt his head downwards to see his friend. Cups, papers, pens – anything not battened down – had scattered on the floor. Branson noticed that Lindstrand had turned quite white.

Lindstrand eased himself into the dome of the capsule and peered out. To his horror, he could see that not only one empty fuel tank had been jettisoned, but two full ones as well. Half of their fuel had been lost at a stroke.

Lindstrand radioed back to the Miyakonojo launch with the bad news. The balloon had only flown about a thousand miles; there were still more than five thousand to go. Lindstrand calculated that they would have to average a speed of 170 m.p.h. to get across on the available fuel – faster than any hot-air balloon had ever flown before. Looking down at the white crests of the waves, visible 30,000 feet below, discouraged any thoughts of ditching in the sea. 'From that moment on,' Branson remembered, 'until we eventually hit the ice in Canada, we both felt the odds were against us ever coming home.'

In the American control room, in San Jose, anxiety began to turn to alarm. No word could be heard from the balloon. In fact, it was passing through an area where the propagation of high-frequency radio waves is poor; radio contact would be lost for six hours. But in the control room, the fear that Branson and Lindstrand might be about to ditch – indeed, might even have done so already – became tangible. By the time radio contact was re-established, San Jose control had already switched to emergency procedure, and were in the throes of mobilising a C130 aircraft and diving crew. (The alarm was contagious. For a short while, news agencies around the world were running the story that the balloon had actually ditched.)

Meanwhile, Branson and Lindstrand were living through the most nerve-racking hours of their lives. With no fuel in reserve, holding the balloon firmly in the jet stream was now absolutely imperative. Night had fallen, but it was impossible to sleep. Every thirty minutes they would monitor the fuel gauge, work out fresh calculations about how much had gone, what was left, how far it might carry them. The angle of the capsule raised fears that the remaining fuel tanks could slip out of their sockets at any moment too, exposing their unprotected inside skin to the temperature of minus 47 degrees centigrade outside. This, in turn, would have cooled the propane to a level where it could not flow up into the burners. Branson and Lindstrand crawled around the capsule as if on eggshells, fearful of even breathing too hard. They took it in turn trying to doze, but sleep brought only nightmares. Far better to stay awake, keep up each other's morale. At one stage, Lindstrand thought he saw a face outside the capsule window. Both had quite forgotten to eat. By the end of the flight all they had consumed was one or two apples, and a handful of chocolate bars. Branson wrote in his notes:

Flown 17 hours and 4 minutes. Feels like a life time. Coming near the dateline. Dropping from 30,000 feet to 29,000 feet because of nasty engine sounds. When we cross the dateline we beat our world hot-air ballooning record. However, right now we are about as far away from help as anyone could ever be, sitting in a tilting capsule with half our fuel gone, terrified that if we move the rest will fall off. Not sure whether war has broken out because we have lost all communication with the outside world . . . Unlikely to reach the coast. But spirits up and the speed we're going is unbelievable.

The log became a way of maintaining wakefulness, concentration. At one point he wrote that their predicament reminded him of a story of a Japanese airliner which had taken off with a faulty tail-plane; unable to land it had simply circled for seven hours until it ran out of fuel and crashed, in which time the passengers and crew composed letters to their loved ones. It was not a particularly cheerful story. 'Things look pretty desperate,' he wrote. 'I'm not certain at this moment that we'll get home . . .'

Two-thirds of the way across the Pacific, Bob Rice came on the radio with a message. If the balloon continued to fly at its present altitude the prevailing wind would carry it in a curve back towards Hawaii. Rice instructed them to drop from 31,000 to 18,000 feet, to pick up a northerly air-flow. Two hundred miles on, Rice instructed them to gain altitude again. It was like a railway train switching points: the balloon was now heading towards Alaska, and Canada's north-west frontier.

They had now been airborne for some forty hours, and flown some 6,500 miles. 'Greatly relieved not to be in mid-Pacific any more,' Branson wrote. 'Just been told by Penni [Pike – his personal assistant] that war has broken out . . .'

Exhausted, their nerves frayed, both men now allowed themselves the thought that they might make it after all. Branson was manning the burner controls, while Lindstrand updated the flight log, when Branson suddenly screamed, 'We're on fire outside!' Lindstrand's immediate thought was 'Impossible!' Nothing burns at 30,000 feet; it was hard enough to get a purpose-built burner working at that altitude. Lindstrand struck his head into the observation dome. To his astonishment he could see that Branson was right. There had been a build-up of propane gas and ice around one of the burners which had ignited in the wind-shear. 'Snowballs' of burning propane were now falling on top of the capsule and the perspex observation dome. If the dome cracked the capsule would instantly depressurise, and Lindstrand and Branson would be sucked up into the envelope above like toothpaste being squeezed out of a tube. 'Take it up,' shouted Lindstrand. Branson fired the burners to make the balloon gain altitude, and at 38,000 feet, starved of oxygen, the fire at last went out. It had been a harrowing ten minutes.

By now, the trip was into its second night. The anxiety about fuel had eased. It had become clear that the balloon would not only make landfall, but have enough to fly inland, affording some degree of choice in a landing site. The jet stream was now carrying the balloon on a course over the Canadian Rockies, towards the north-west frontier. The retrieve team, carried in three Lear jets, were now airborne, and Lindstrand was in radio contact with the local ground services. The worst of the journey was surely now behind them. It was then that Watson Lake Flight Service broke the news that the balloon was flying into an arctic storm, with zero visibility and snow blowing at 35 knots. The three Lear jets peeled away, diverting to an airfield ahead. Branson and Lindstrand's spirits sank. 'Perhaps the famous Branson luck has deserted us this time,' said Lindstrand gravely. They were now some 2,500 miles from where they were originally targeted to land, with no maps, no idea of ground conditions, no helicopters to guide them in. The rigours of the flight, and the see-sawing emotions between fear, relief and fear again, had left both men completely exhausted.

Over the radio, Bob Rice advised them to start descending at 500 feet per minute. It was imperative to land at dawn. Attempting a landing any later in the day would be impossible, because the solar power of the balloon envelope would have kept it aloft, carrying the balloon off to the Arctic. Lindstrand, whose gallows humour was utterly without peer, knew a good story about the Arctic. The bodies of three Swedish adventurers had been found there, dead not through exposure, but through food poisoning from eating a polar bear. He recounted it to Branson, to cheer him up, as the balloon descended at a sickening speed through the howling winds and snow.

At 1,000 feet the balloon suddenly broke out of the storm, into an eerily beautiful world; silent, frozen and white. Branson pulled himself onto the top of the capsule, to look for a place to land. Down below he could see something that looked like earth.

'It's trees!' said Lindstrand.

'No, it's definitely ice,' said Branson.

It was trees, but beyond the tree line Branson could see a frozen lake. Lindstrand initiated a rapid descent, as Branson strapped himself back into his seat. The balloon hit the lake at 800 feet per minute, skidding across a carpet of powdery snow. Lindstrand fired the explosive bolts to release the envelope. They worked! The balloon lurched to a halt as the envelope, liberated from its heavy cargo, bucked and rose a few hundred feet into the air, then floated silently down to vanish behind the screen of trees at the lake's edge.

Branson and Lindstrand were out of the capsule within seconds, scuffling across the snow, half-expecting the capsule to explode into flames behind them. They flung their arms around each other and danced a small jig of delight and disbelief at their good fortune. All around them was perfectly still. On the still, snow-covered surface of the lake was the surreal vision of three giant cans of Pocari Sweat – the empty fuel tanks, which had been torn off as the capsule skidded to a halt. A solitary otter, roused by the noise, waddled into view from the tree line, regarded them curiously, and slowly waddled off again. Within seconds, they were back in the capsule again, wrapping themselves in all the clothes they could find, huddling together for warmth. They had landed in a temperature of minus 30 degrees centigrade.

They set off the emergency beacons, and settled down to wait. Before landing, Branson had been able to say that they were putting down on a lake, by some trees. There are some 200,000 lakes in the north-west frontier; in fact, they had landed some 220 miles from the nearest habitation, 153 miles from the nearest road. It would be almost eight hours, spent shivering in the capsule, before a retrieval helicopter set down on the lake beside them and lifted them to safety.

They had flown a total of 6,761 miles, at an average speed of 127 knots, over a period of 46 hours and 6 minutes. They had flown a longer distance than any hot-air balloon or airship ever.

This had been achieved in an atmosphere which contrasted starkly with the Atlantic crossing of three years before. Then, the balloon landing, and Branson and Lindstrand's close brush with disaster, had been front-page news. But in a time of war, the Pacific flight hardly warranted a mention in the newspapers or on the nightly news. At least that scotched any accusations about publicity stunts.

For Branson, relief at being alive was mixed with a

heady feeling of achievement. 'If you do survive, it's the most wonderful experience to have been through,' he said. 'You feel that surviving such extreme stress is somehow good for you in some way.

'If you're doing something that hasn't been done before it isn't going to be easy – otherwise it would have been done before. Crossing the Atlantic by boat, by balloon, then crossing the Pacific, there has always been that feeling just before starting out of "What's everybody fussing about? It's much easier than people think." But then things don't go according to plan, and you know why they haven't been done before – because they're bloody difficult.'

Having flown the Pacific, he announced, his next challenge would be to fly around the world, with a joint Russian and American balloon team. That too would be bloody difficult. What Branson didn't know was that, this time, persuading his family that he should take part would be more difficult still. Indeed, it would prove bloody impossible.

In early 1992, as the deadline for his participation in the world attempt grew near, his father Ted called a family conference at the house of Richard's youngest sister Vanessa and her husband Robert Devereux. There he gave Branson 'one hell of a lecture' about family responsibilities. 'It was the first time in my life he had ever criticised me,' said Branson. 'Up until then he'd only ever given me support and encouragement. I think he was saving the criticism for a time when it was really important.'

Perhaps, Branson admitted, he was pushing his luck a bit going for a third time. He heeded his father's advice. From now on, Richard Branson was grounded.

Chapter 16

Goodbye To All That

The great business names of the Eighties, the champions of Thatcherism, had begun to fall one by one, undone by greed, calumny, scandal or misfortune. Gerald Ronson, Ralph Halpern, Gerald Ratner, George Walker and – the biggest splash of all – Robert Maxwell.

Even Alan Sugar, whose Amstrad company had seemed impervious to setback, slumped £15m into the red in February of 1992, for the first time since Sugar had founded the company in the Sixties. The recession signalled that the go-go, hot market days of the Eighties had gone.

There had been two notable survivors. There were many differences in style and temperament between Richard Branson and Anita Roddick, but both had come through the slump relatively unscathed for much the same reason: neither Virgin nor Body Shop had succumbed to the temptation of rapid growth outstripping the company's capacity to support itself. Even in its brief period as a public company, Virgin had not taken the customary route of acquisitions, mergers and sell-offs. It had grown by building companies, not buying them, always careful not to over-extend itself too drastically. It was a big company, yet it retained something of the spirit and practices of a small one. At least, that was the principle. In practice, Virgin had long outstripped Richard Branson's capacity to give the whole organisation his full attention.

Nowadays, the airline occupied virtually all of his time and energy. Robert Devereux looked after the Communications arm of the company – publishing, film and video distribution and so on; the retailing arm had never been Branson's great enthusiasm, and required only the occasional grand administrative gesture on his behalf. As for the record company, traditionally Virgin's biggest money-spinner and once the epicentre of Branson's attentions – that was more or less totally under the control of Simon Draper and Ken Berry. Weeks, sometimes months, passed between Branson's visits to the record-company offices, now relocated from the crumbling and overcrowded mansion block on Harrow Road to smarter premises a couple of hundred yards away, beside the Regents Canal.

Branson could still be depended upon to put on a display of enthusiasm and commitment when the situation demanded it. His role to the record company had become that of corporate figurehead, the public face of Virgin, just as Ahmet Ertegun had been at Atlantic, and Chris Blackwell at Island – a star in his own right, with whom other stars could identify. While it was Simon Draper, Ken Berry and, in America, Jordan Harris who set up the deals, and ultimately delivered them, Branson's role – as one friend put it – had become to make the sought-after signings feel 'warm and loved'. When Virgin were wooing the highly successful – and very expensive – American singer Janet Jackson, the deal was finally clinched during a visit to Branson's Oxfordshire home which included a trip in his hot-air balloon.

Like all record labels, Virgin had had its ups and downs over the past few years; its moments of synchronising perfectly with the fickle currents of pop music – and of missing them altogether. But it was still the only remaining independent label of a scale to compete with the major conglomerates.

In America, the Virgin label had gone from strength to strength, taking the increasing dominance of dance-orientated music into its stride. As well as Janet Jackson the label also had Belinda Carlisle and the platinum-selling Paula Abdul. In Britain, fortunes were more mixed. Ten, a Virgin subsidiary, had enjoyed some success with soul and dance music – notably the British band, Soul II Soul, who took the Grammy awards by storm in 1990. But this could not disguise the fact that Virgin's talent for spotting new talent – so well developed in the Eighties with acts like Culture Club and Human League – seemed to have gone temporarily astray. The label now depended heavily on its roster of older, well-established 'AOR' stars like Phil Collins, Genesis, Peter Gabriel, Steve Winwood and Bryan Ferry, whose back catalogues continued to provide steady revenue even in the longueurs between new recordings.

At the beginning of 1992, Branson eventually realised one of his earliest ambitions for Virgin – signing the Rolling Stones. It was almost sixteen years since Branson had first flown halfway round the world and back, attempting to stitch together a deal that would bring the Stones to Virgin. On that occasion he failed; but every time the Rolling Stones' contract had come up for renewal, Branson had contacted the group's financial adviser, Prince Rupert Lowenstein, with the same question: will they join Virgin? Now the answer was yes.

The roster of Virgin acts was bigger now than at any

time in the label's history; from being a lean and hungry operation, it had begun to look increasingly like a top-heavy and somewhat ponderous one. But still, the company was an extremely attractive proposition – and a logical target – for any of the Big Five, fighting it out for supremacy in the market-place. Both Thorn-EMI and the Bertelsmann group discreetly expressed interest. Branson, Draper and Berry began to discuss the idea more seriously among themselves, weighing up the pros and cons. For Branson, the cash would certainly be useful in building up the airline, and for other projects. Against that was the simple argument that the music division remained Virgin's single most valuable asset. Why throw it away? And anyway, there was the relationship with Ken and Simon to consider. The three had been friends and partners in the record company for twenty years. Did anybody want to break that up? What would Berry and Draper do if the company were sold? The questions, and the decision of whether or not to sell, were put on the back-burner.

But for Branson, the question had some bearing on his thoughts about the broader issues of his, and Virgin's, future. He no longer talked of his ambition of turning Virgin into 'the biggest entertainment company in the world' – one of his favourite phrases in the period when Virgin was going to the Stock Market. Perhaps that sort of drum-beating had been largely for the benefit of putative shareholders – shareholders like their chairmen to have vaunting ambition – but it was also true that Branson had changed in the two or three years since then.

The experience of going to the Stock Market, the crash of Black Monday, and the spectacle of other entrepreneurs crashing around him like ninepins, had had a sobering effect. There was little satisfaction, Branson now believed, to be gained from acquisition and growth for its own sake.

In partnership with broadcaster David Frost's company Paradine, Virgin had put in three applications in the race for television franchises in 1991 – for the Thames, Anglia and Southern regions. For the first time, the government had announced that franchises would be awarded on mixed criteria of the highest bidder and the quality of programmes. It was a ludicrous scheme that basically turned independent British broadcasting into a lottery.

Preoccupied with the airline, Branson passed the project over to his old friend Charles Levison to look after. Virgin failed in all three applications. To add insult to injury, they were the only unsuccessful applicant to have made a higher bid than a successful applicant, failing on the 'quality' threshold.

It was an embarrassment for Virgin, but Branson did not seem overly disappointed. In fact, he gave every appearance that he couldn't care less. Trevor Abbott who had by now made the change from group finance director to managing director of the holding company, and who remained Branson's principal 'numbers man', calculated that he and Branson had spent no more than three hours on meetings to do with the TV franchise bid. Branson's reaction on learning that he would not, after all, be running a television channel was almost one of relief.

One evening during the period between Virgin going to the Stock Market and being bought back into private ownership, Branson had sat at dinner, speculating on the possibilities of buying out another record company. This, after all, was what you were supposed to do as a public company when you had money to spare. As the evening and the conversation wore on, and the wine bottle emptied, Branson had idly explored out loud the consequences of such a takeover: the new company is subsumed into the old; certain areas are 'rationalised' – the marketing department, the sales department, the press office and so on; you close down one set of offices, and say goodbye to the elderly commissionaire who has been holding open the door to visitors for the last fifteen years . . . It was no way to carry on . . . By the end of the evening, Branson seemed to have talked himself out of the takeover altogether.

This was not a train of thought one might have heard from Maxwell or Murdoch. But then those closest to Branson recognised that he had always lacked the last 5 per cent of sheer ruthlessness that would put him in a league with a Murdoch or a Maxwell. Branson did not have the brutal singlemindedness to conduct the sort of savage war of attrition which Murdoch had waged on his own workforce in the Wapping dispute of 1985; nor cynically to buy and sell companies (and their workforces) on a whim, and callously dispense with people who displeased him in the manner of Robert Maxwell. People tended to like working for Richard Branson; although executives close to him noted one disadvantage: his reluctance and discomfort at firing people, even those who really *needed* to be fired, meant that this unpleasant task invariably fell to them.

Virgin Atlantic had now lasted twice as long as Laker Airways, a considerable achievement in an increasingly cut-throat and dirty field. It was an achievement that Laker himself gracefully acknowledged at every opportunity. Speaking from his home in the Bahamas on his seventieth birthday, Sir Freddie told newspaper reporters,

'Every morning I give thanks for men like Richard Branson and Michael Bishop [the chairman of British Midland Airways].'

Virgin had confounded everyone's most pessimistic expectations; it had become a profitable airline. But this had only been achieved by a distinct revision of its original form.

From the outset, Virgin Atlantic had marketed itself as an 'economy' airline; the public perception was that it was the heir apparent to Freddie Laker's policy of 'cheap 'n' cheerful' travel for all. Certainly, low fares were crucial to Virgin's marketing ethos. But Branson had quickly realised that Virgin's best chance of survival – of avoiding the fate of Laker – lay in moving away from the perception of Virgin as providing a glorified transatlantic bus service, and instead cultivating the services and image of a sophisticated, business-class airline, concentrating exclusively on long-haul routes.

The Virgin service between Luton and Dublin was shortlived, and the service to Maastricht in Holland was dropped after Branson, travelling on the antiquated Viscount which served the route, overheard a passenger in the seat in front of him saying, 'No wonder they can afford to fly so cheaply to New York when you look at the state of this . . .'

Branson concentrated on upgrading his 'upper class' service as much as possible, offering all sorts of incentives to attract the business traveller. There was a free limo service; sixteen inches more leg room than British Airways offered in its equivalent service; Virgin also claimed a higher ratio of stewardesses to passengers (one for every six passengers, compared with BA's one for every thirteen). This upgrading of service extended into the economy section as well; Virgin aircraft had the most leg room of any flying across the Atlantic, and became the first transatlantic carrier to introduce personalised seat-back videos into its planes. By 1991, nearly half of the airline's income was from business-class travel; and in that same year, Virgin won the *Business Traveller* magazine award for the Best Business Airline, for the fourth year running.

The loyalty of the business traveller was critical in helping Virgin maintain a profitable service in what was becoming an increasingly competitive field. In May 1990, Virgin added Los Angeles to its routes, then Boston. Under new agreements between Britain and America, San Francisco, Washington and Chicago would also be available. Virgin had also acquired licences to fly to Singapore and Australia. And in March of 1992 Branson would fly to Johannesburg to finalise agreements for the regular Virgin service to South Africa.

Branson made no secret of Virgin's ambitions: by 1995 he wanted Virgin's fleet of planes to have expanded to eighteen, and the airline to be flying to the world's top twelve cities. And by then, he announced, he expected Virgin to have 30 per cent of Britain's transatlantic traffic.

For British Airways, Virgin's progress was a source of immense annoyance, and no little concern. In terms of size, Virgin were a mere flea beside British Airways' elephantine operation, yet the flea seemed capable of inflicting a disproportionate amount of discomfort and irritation.

Not only were Virgin encroaching on BA's most profitable routes, but Branson also manifested an infuriating tendency to upstage British Airways at every opportunity. BA's chairman, Lord King, had never forgiven Virgin for apparently stealing British Airways' thunder over the matter of airlifting hostages during the Gulf conflicts; but this was as nothing compared to the more practical threat which Virgin posed. BA had not been pleased when Virgin had first been allowed to take up the Tokyo route, operating three frequencies transferred after the BCal/BA merger, with a fourth frequency added from BA after Virgin had obtained additional aircraft. But BA's displeasure turned to apoplexy in early 1991 when the Civil Aviation Authority forced them to give up four take-off/landing slots at Tokyo's Narita airport in order to accommodate extra Virgin flights.

The background to the CAA decision was both complex and controversial. In May 1990, negotiations between the UK and Japanese authorities had added an extra four frequencies to each side effective from November 1990. However, alongside this agreement on frequencies there was also a capacity limitation at Narita airport, which to all intents and purposes was full. Since 1989, the UK had thirty-eight slots available at Narita, and while an increase in frequencies (number of flights) was agreed, an increase in slots (landing facilities) was not. BA were in the position of being able to re-route flights transiting Narita in two directions to become Narita terminating flights. This effectively meant that BA could increase their Tokyo frequencies while Virgin could not.

In November 1990, Virgin applied to the CAA to vary BA's licence on the Tokyo route in order to limit the number of slots used by BA to 26 (13 flights), and thus enable Virgin to use the other 12 slots (6 flights). In January 1991, the CAA ruled to limit BA to 26 slots (13 flights), thus enabling Virgin to operate two of the additional four frequencies available from the May 1990 bilateral agreement.

Both BA and Virgin appealed against the decision, BA

objecting to the restriction, and Virgin requesting a higher restriction in order to allow Virgin up to eight frequencies a week. The Department of Transport rejected both appeals. BA was thus forced to relinquish four slots at Narita in order to allow Virgin its extra two frequencies. BA were left with fourteen flights a week, and Virgin six. The decision set a critical precedent in CAA thinking, emphasising that in the CAA view, such slots belonged to Britain, not to any one British airline.

Branson greeted the decision with qualified approval: if the CAA were really committed to free competition, he argued, they would have given all four frequencies to Virgin, to help build the alternative competitor to a viable size. Even Branson must have realised that this was about as likely as Lord King taking up sky-diving. But two frequencies, Branson admitted, were better than none.

BA, on the other hand, could barely disguise their fury. Virgin, they claimed, had 'hijacked' their Tokyo operation. BA had been prevented from operating frequencies which were rightfully theirs. For BA, it established a worrying precedent. If this could happen over Tokyo, what would be the situation in other destinations around the world to which Virgin also had plans to fly – Sydney, say, or Johannesburg? Would BA be obliged to share the allocations of these frequencies too?

The Tokyo decision turned up the heat on the rivalry between the two airlines. BA accused Branson of launching 'an onslaught against British Airways and all of its interests'. For his part, Branson warned colleagues that 'we have to be on our mettle day after day'. BA had had no compunction about trying to drive Freddie Laker to the wall; they would do the same to Virgin unless Virgin fought to prevent it happening.

Once upon a time relations between BA and Virgin had

been almost cordial. BA serviced Virgin aircraft. Virgin cabin crew trained on the BA safety chute; the staff of the two airlines mingled amicably. But now a bleak, wintry chill characterised the relationship. It was the question of maintenance that most irritated Branson. Virgin's fleet of aircraft had originally been maintained by BCal, but with the merger of BA and BCal, responsibility passed to BA. Within a year, Virgin had found that its maintenance bill for a reduced service had more than tripled – from BCal's £153 per aircraft hour to BA's £544. Virgin were obliged to strike a new deal with Aer Lingus, which meant Virgin planes being flown to Dublin for servicing. This was typical, Branson believed, of the way in which BA were using their dominant position in the market-place to put an unfair 'squeeze' on Virgin.

Branson's argument was simple. Virgin weren't simply fighting to show an increased profit to shareholders, as BA were; Virgin were fighting for their very survival. And it became increasingly apparent to Branson that survival depended on Virgin being allowed access to Heathrow Airport. Heathrow was not only London's – the world's – most popular airport. It also had longer runways, which reduced fuel costs and enabled aircraft to carry more freight; the average yield per passenger at Heathrow was therefore 15 per cent higher than at Gatwick.

BA's monopoly on Heathrow had long been guaranteed under the CAA Traffic Distribution Rules, known as the 'grandfather rights', which effectively barred any new carrier from using the airport. These had been established in 1977, partly to control the volume of traffic at an increasingly congested Heathrow, partly to encourage the development of scheduled services at Gatwick, and partly to protect the then nationalised British Airways.

Laker had been prevented from flying out of Heathrow. So too had BCal and Air Europe. All had gone under. The CAA had always favoured the development of BCal as a strong second force to British Airways. But BA's assiduous lobbying of government ministers, and Lord King's personal friendship with Margaret Thatcher, had ensured that BCal had received no favours in the period running up to British Airways' privatisation in 1987, and had been ripe for takeover shortly afterwards.

It was Branson's belief that for as long as Virgin were confined to Gatwick, they would always be at a disadvantage in any fare war with BA. BA could slash the prices for their Gatwick routes without losing any revenue on the more popular and lucrative Heathrow routes. The only route out of Heathrow where BA had reduced fares was to Newark, New York – one of Virgin's destinations. It was essentially the same argument that Branson had been making since Virgin's launch: Virgin's low fares were an accurate reflection of their lower overheads, but BA's were simply 'predatory' – loss leaders designed to put Virgin out of business.

As a nationalised concern, Branson argued, BA had perhaps had some claim to be the 'state airline', and therefore eligible for government protection; but since they were now privatised they should be allowed no special privileges. Free competition was in the interest of the consumer – this was the drum Branson banged most consistently. BA called themselves the 'World's Favourite Airline', he argued; but what they in fact wanted was the favouritism of anti-competitive regulations.

In January 1991, Virgin delivered a batch of complaints to the European Commission accusing BA of abusing a dominant market position within the meaning of Article 86 of the Treaty of Rome. This action was likely to take months – if not years – to be ruled on, and would incur hefty legal fees for Virgin in the process; but Branson felt it was necessary, partly to see that justice was done, but also to help dramatise Virgin's petition for permission to fly from Heathrow.

Branson's argument was characteristically blunt: 'All we're asking for is the right to fly against BA from the same airports as BA. Ideally we'd like 50 per cent of the slots, but in practical terms maybe 20 per cent. We're arguing that Virgin, British Midland and Dan Air – the three independent airlines – ought by the year 2000 to have 30 per cent of the routes around the world to BA's 70 per cent.'

BA's argument was equally simple. The future of aviation, they claimed, would be one of big carriers. If Britain were to compete internationally, the country's 'flagship' airline – BA – should be given all the official help and encouragement it could get. Richard Branson, BA alleged, was simply interested in 'creaming off' the best BA routes to make money for himself; Virgin were upstarts and whingers who preached the gospel of free competition, but then complained when the going got tough.

Ever since their inauguration in 1977, the Traffic Distribution Rules governing take-off and landing rights at Heathrow had come under periodic government appraisal. In 1989, the Department of Transport asked the CAA for a review, and the CAA had recommended that the rules should continue. In September 1990, the DoT again asked the CAA for a review, this time in the context of accelerating moves towards liberalisation of airline regulations throughout Europe, and less government intervention.

Airlines were invited to make submissions to the CAA,

which both Virgin and BA did. For the previous two years, Virgin had been lobbying assiduously for the rules to be relaxed. At a meeting with Branson and other Virgin directors in late 1990, the then Secretary of State for Transport, Cecil Parkinson, let it be known that he wanted the rules lifted at the earliest opportunity.

For years, BA had maintained their favoured position at Heathrow with the help of a powerful machine to lobby MPs and government ministers. They gave generously to Conservative Party funds. Lord King was said to be Margaret Thatcher's favourite businessman and a close friend of the Prime Minister's husband Denis. But with Thatcher's departure from the Tory party leadership in November 1990, Lord King's fortunes began to change.

In March 1991, the new Secretary of State for Transport, Malcolm Rifkind, announced that the Traffic Distribution Rules at Heathrow should be changed, virtually deregulating Heathrow, except for some remaining peak-hour limitations on cargo, general and business aviation.

The CAA decision added fresh vitriol to the animosity between BA and Virgin. BA turned on the personal offensive, attacking Branson as a self-publicist whose 'interests are not the customers' interests'. BA, their argument went, was a public company with its shareholders' interests at heart: Richard Branson was simply in it for himself.

Branson and Lord King had met only once, at an aviation awards luncheon. Then, the two men had bantered in an atmosphere of somewhat strained cordiality, Branson suggesting that King should join him on the balloon trip across the Pacific, and King replying jocularly that BA would sponsor it. Now, however, nobody was attempting bonhomie of any sort.

In January 1991, Branson wrote to Lord King complaining about the increasingly personalised nature of BA's accusations: 'I have no idea whether it has been inspired by yourself, but I would like to put on record to you that I resent the level of personal abuse your people at British Airways have resorted to. As the chairman of a small independent airline . . . I have never tried dragging your name into disrepute, and expect your company to behave likewise.'

King's reply was terse: 'Thank you for your letter of 31 January. As I said to the *Sunday Telegraph* ". . . I run my airline, Richard Branson runs his. Best of luck to him." I do not wish and do not intend to say anything more on the subject.'

In July 1991, Virgin began its regular service out of Heathrow. The event was marked by Virgin's characteristic mixture of irreverence, audacity and overkill. On the morning of the inaugural flight, a Virgin 'hit squad' raided the huge model of a British Airways Concorde which stands at the entrance to Heathrow, and covered the BA logos with Virgin insignia. Branson was photographed in front of the plane, dressed in a pirate costume. That evening a huge celebratory party was staged in a marquee within the Heathrow grounds, featuring karaoke, barbecues and a disco which ran into the small hours of the following morning. Lord King did not grace the event with his presence.

King's anger at what appeared to be Virgin's unimpeded encroachment on BA's interests was directed not only at Branson. On 16 July, Lord King announced at the BA shareholders' meeting that the company's traditional donation to Conservative Party funds would be discontinued, as a consequence of the government's aviation policies. Since undergoing privatisation in 1987, BA had paid £180,000 into Tory party coffers; King had never made any secret that it was a way of thanking the Tory government for giving BA management the chance to turn the airline's loss into a profit. But now King's gratitude had worn thin. BA could no longer justify donations, he said, when staff were being asked to make sacrifices and profits were falling.

Branson was taking a short break at La Residencia in Majorca when Lord King's announcement was made. But this was too good a public relations opportunity to be missed: and his response was a small but perfectly formed study in press management. Within an hour of the news breaking, Branson had issued a press release, and was talking personally to British newspaper reporters. The stories which appeared in the newspapers the next day gave much attention to Branson's remarks about King behaving like 'a spoilt child playing at blackmail' and Branson's arguments for 'fair play' in the fare wars.

The following day Branson and Sir Michael Bishop, the chairman of British Midland, issued a joint statement deploring what it described as the 'totally unjustified and unfair criticism' of the government's aviation policy:

Britain is unique in Europe in having the benefit of a genuine multi-airline industry in which free competition is positively encouraged. This is in sharp contrast to most other European countries where inefficient, bureaucratic, state-owned national airlines are protected by their governments against competition. As a result, British business and leisure travellers alike have been able to benefit from greater choice, higher standards of service and lower air fares than their counterparts in other European countries.

The government deserves great credit for this as it is a direct result of its policies. In particular, the success of the current Secretary of State for Transport in opening up Heathrow to new airlines earlier this year was a bold initiative which has encouraged further liberalisation of air travel and which will assist the more rapid development of a truly free market.

Even Malcolm Rifkind must have thought the tribute a touch too effusive. But it was clearly a message designed as much to give him comfort in an hour of need as it was a public relations exercise for Virgin and British Midland.

For Branson, political allegiance had long been a delicate balancing act between idealism and pragmatism. His association with UK 2000 had aligned him too closely with Margaret Thatcher for the comfort of some of his colleagues, not least Ken Berry, who felt that identification with any one political figure or party would be counterproductive for Branson and Virgin as a whole. Berry's reservations over UK 2000 had been well founded – but for the wrong reasons. It was the references to 'Mr Litter' – born of the recurring misunderstanding that the campaign was about 'cleaning up Britain' which would return again and again to haunt Branson, not any taint by association with Tory government policies.

Although Branson had been held up often enough as the epitome of the 'Thatcherite entrepreneur', his relationship with Mrs Thatcher had always been one of polite cordiality rather than friendship. He had dined at Number 10 and Chequers; but he was never one of her favourites, nor among her circle of intimates. Nor did she honour him with the knighthood that the newspapers predicted he was due for whenever the day of the Official

Honours List loomed. Privately, Branson spoke highly of Thatcher's courage and commitment, but lamented her lack of compassion. He welcomed the arrival of her replacement, John Major; the more moderate slant that Major's declarations put on government policy was closer to Branson's own views – which could be roughly defined as a mixture of old-fashioned liberalism on social issues and free-market monetarism in economic matters.

As the dispute with BA ground on, Branson even hinted that he would consider making financial donations to the Tory Party. The idea had never formally been considered by the Virgin board, he told the *Sunday Telegraph*, but 'having said that, if there has ever been a party which we have been impressed by and would feel inclined to support, it is the current Conservative Party'.

However, Lord King's tantrum gave Branson second thoughts. Reflecting on King's decision, and the very fine line which divided patronage from bribery, Branson now decided that businesses making donations to political parties was 'wrong in principle'.

'It's an awkward situation for ministers who are having to make judicial decisions at the same time as their party is receiving cheques from one of the two parties they're making decisions about,' he reflected. 'We definitely wouldn't make any donations for as long as we were directly involved in rulings the government was making.' (The question of Branson's political allegiances would take a further twist in March 1992, in the run-up to the General Election, when Conservative Central Office released a list of 'celebrity' names who had supposedly pledged their vote to the Tory Party, and which included Branson. He immediately contacted Central Office and asked for his name to be withdrawn, on the grounds that he did not support any one political party, 'only policies'.)

The battle between BA and Virgin had now settled into a trench warfare of claim and counter-claim, accusation and innuendo. The battle was being fought in the corridors of the CAA, the government – even the European Commission – and in the columns of the national press. When a *Which?* survey of the world's airlines rated Virgin fourth (after Cathay Pacific, El Al and Swissair) and BA twenty-second, Virgin complained to the Advertising Standards Authority that under the criterion of 'decent, truthful and honest, BA could no longer describe themselves as 'the world's favourite airline'. BA might argue that they were flown by the most people; but on that basis, Virgin argued, the M25 was the world's 'favourite motorway'. The complaint was turned down.

Some months later, a computer company, Psion, ran a press advertisement using Richard Branson's name and the copyline, 'Even the owner of Britain's favourite airline may not have seen our latest personal computer'. This time it was British Airways that complained to the ASA. That complaint too was rejected.

Such incidents were knockabout fun, the sort of mischievous hype which Branson had always delighted in; par for the course. Much more serious, however, was the question of the rumours that had begun to circulate about the state of Virgin's financial health. Was it true, Branson kept being asked, that the airline was losing £3m a week? That it was paying in cash for fuel? That it was in dire danger of going under? None of these things were true, Branson insisted; but the fact that people might think they were true was profoundly alarming. There was no doubt in Branson's mind about where these rumours had emanated from, although it was impossible to prove anything. Branson was convinced that BA were actively running a 'dirty tricks' campaign, deliberately orchestrated to undermine confidence in Virgin among customers and banks at a time when the company was looking for money to fund its expansion plans.

Virgin had received a tip-off from an ex-BA employee. Shortly after the Gulf conflict, it was alleged, a secret 'task force' had been set up within BA with the specific intention of discrediting Virgin and Richard Branson. BA's head of publicity, David Burnside, had recruited an independent 'public relations' man named Brian Basham, whose task was to 'brief' journalists about Virgin Atlantic. Basham was well-known in the City for his work on some of the toughest City takeover bids – work which had earned him the charmless sobriquet of 'the street-fighter'. Branson alleged that Basham had been deliberately spreading false information and rumours about Virgin in the press. Basham's main achievement had been to circulate a report to newspapers emphasising Virgin's 'cash-hungry' nature, drawing attention to Branson's 'Houdini-like' ability in tight corners, and describing him as 'irrational' and 'experimental' in his business approach.

Virgin's list of accusations about 'dirty tricks' grew. BA, it was claimed, had instructed staff at Tokyo not to assist Virgin engineers or receive assistance from them – a breach in longstanding industry tradition on maintenance, which Branson claimed could set 'a highly unprofessional and dangerous precedent'.

Furthermore, Branson alleged, BA had used 'sharp practices' in trying to lure Virgin passengers to BA flights; this included physically 'ambushing' passengers stepping out of the limousines which Virgin provided for 'Upper-Class' passengers and offering them BA tickets at a cheap rate. One passenger, it was alleged, had been offered two free flights to Paris if she cancelled her Virgin flight and went with BA. Others had been offered Concorde flights in return for cashing in Virgin tickets.

BA had not co-operated on ticketing matters, and was refusing to transfer tickets on the phone or to refund Virgin for passengers who had switched from BA. In one month alone, Branson claimed, BA had refused to pay Virgin some £15,000 for tickets transferred in the customary manner. Branson even suspected that he personally was being tailed by a private detective agency trying to drum up some dirt on his personal life.

Eventually, Branson's frustration and anger came to a head. Freddie Laker urged Branson to hit back with all the resources at his disposal – to 'sue, sue, sue . . .' – if Virgin was to avoid the fate that had befallen Laker Airways.

Branson threatened to lodge an official complaint, under EC rules governing fair competition, to the European Commission, the CAA and the DoT. In December 1991, he sent a detailed dossier of his allegations to all BA's non-executive directors, calling on them to launch an urgent internal investigation.

BA's chief executive, Sir Colin Marshall, wrote to Branson denying the allegations, and saying that BA had done nothing in its dealings with Virgin that would depart from normal commercial practice.

In February 1992, Thames Television's *This Week* broadcast a damning investigation into the 'dirty tricks' campaign. This included tapes of Basham briefing a journalist and claiming that Virgin ran a 'dicky business', saying that 'one day, without doubt, an aircraft is going to fall out of the sky', and a former BA employee alleging that a special unit had been set up in BA with the specific intention of discrediting Branson and Virgin. The employee also claimed that an order had gone out to shred any material relating to Virgin when it became clear that Branson was ready to take his grievances to the European Commission. Most damning of all, perhaps, were the scenes of British Airways executives, including their public relations director David Burnside, being ambushed by reporter Richard Lindley as they clambered into their limos, and refusing to comment. BA had refused to take part in the programme. A letter from BA's director of legal affairs, Mervyn Walker, said there was 'no substance' to the allegations of 'dirty tricks', and accused Branson of contriving 'controversy with British Airways to create publicity for himself and his airline'. He added, 'We are not prepared to be provoked into playing Mr Branson's futile game.' Burnside and Basham also announced that they would be taking legal action over the programme.

Branson retorted with a threat that unless BA apologised, gave assurances that the 'dirty' tactics would cease immediately, and removed Brian Basham, then Virgin would sue. There were meetings between lawyers from both sides, but nothing could be resolved. And in March 1992, Virgin appointed lawyers to begin legal proceedings in the American courts under Department of Transportation fair trading laws. In the wake of the *This Week* programme, BA's weekly in-house newspaper *BA News* had published an attack on Virgin under the heading 'Branson Dirty Tricks Claim Unfounded', accusing Branson of fabricating claims in order to garner publicity. Lord King had expressed similar sentiments in a letter to those *This Week* viewers who had written to BA to complain about the allegations. Here was the ammunition for Branson to take the matter to open court in libel proceedings. 'King was effectively calling me a liar,'

Branson said, 'so I sued him.' Three weeks later King counter-sued Branson. The scene was set for what came to be known as 'the mother of all libel battles'. BA's tactics had been deliberately designed, as Branson put it, 'to hit the Achilles' heel' – to undermine the customers' and the banks' confidence in Virgin at a time when the company was in its most vulnerable financial position.

The airline business had changed immeasurably since Virgin's launch in 1984. Increased deregulation in both Britain and America had made it more competitive than ever. The arrival at Heathrow of United and American, the world's biggest airlines, to replace the ailing TWA and PanAm had exacerbated the transatlantic price war. Return tickets for London/New York could now be picked up for under £200 – less than at any time in the previous ten years. (Freddie Laker had been charging £125 each way when he went bust in 1981.)

The Gulf war had increased everyone's problems, pushing up fuel prices, and reducing payloads. Virgin claimed to have suffered less than most; indeed Branson claimed that while British Airways had lost 30 per cent of its load, Virgin had lost only 1 per cent.

But the wider uncertainties of the Gulf conflict, and the deepening recession in Britain, were to have catastrophic consequences in the aviation industry. In one week in May, Virgin felt the shockwaves which dragged down one airline, Air Europe, and almost finished another, Dan Air. Lloyds bank was the principal lending bank for all three airlines. Virgin's overdraft facility with Lloyds had always been flexible; but in the wake of the collapse of Air Europe, and the shakiness of Dan Air, that flexibility suddenly came to an end.

It was a worrying moment for Branson, and a reminder of how fragile any company's fortunes could be.

Branson was reminded of the occasion seven years before, when he had returned from the first ever Virgin flight across the Atlantic to find his bank manager on his doorstep, threatening to freeze the company's funds. Virgin were now a company with a £1.25 billion turnover, but life, it seemed, could still produce its surprises.

For Trevor Abbott, Virgin's policy was to 'go to the supermarket and buy what we need for next week, rather than stocking up for a year'. It had never been company policy, he said, to have 'Hanson PLC-type back-up lines of borrowings, because sure as hell if we had another £100m available, we would spend it'. The idea of heavy borrowings made everyone nervous, particularly when the country was in the midst of the worst recession for ten years, and economic confidence was at rock bottom.

The year 1991 was to be the worst year in the history of civil aviation. The combination of the Gulf war and recession wiped billions off the value of airlines across the world. Virgin Atlantic saw a profit of £8m in 1990 turn into a small loss in 1991, although healthy trading by Virgin's holiday company would allow the Virgin/ Voyager group to show an overall profit of £775,000.

The retail group also showed a loss, of £1m. But in February of 1992, Virgin signed a fifty-fifty partnership with W.H. Smith to run the British Megastores, increasing their value by some £43m. Virgin Communications (computer games, TV post-production, and publishing) showed a profit of £14m, following the sale of the Mastertronic computer games distributor. The most profitable arm of Virgin still remained the Music Group, showing a pre-tax profit of £18m.

Branson took a long, hard look at the books, and began to think again about selling the record company. Virgin did not need the money, he claimed: the net worth of the whole company on paper was some five times its outstanding debt. But his personal priority was to expand the airline – and that would not come cheap. He had already laid plans to sell a share in the airline for £55m, to institutional investors – talks were already well advanced on that – which according to Branson's calculations would be sufficient to fund the expansion of the company. However, some spare cash would not go amiss.

The BA campaign against Virgin had, he admitted, been terribly wearying. 'They tried very hard to damage us and undermine us financially. It was a destructive campaign, particularly in a climate of the worst period in aviation history. I think we had weathered the worst of it. So there was no way we needed to sell the record company, but it was sensible. If the recession had carried on as it was, and the banks had got into more trouble, then we might have been at risk.' It was, he would say, a question of 'prudence, not necessity'.

The principal courtiers were Thorn-EMI and Bertelsmann; but Thorn-EMI eventually took the prize. In March 1992, Virgin Music was sold for £560m.

Branson was given the choice of whether to take the money in cash, or to take shares in Thorn-EMI, which would have made him the single largest shareholder (but not the majority shareholder, of course) in the company. He decided on the cash.

After clearance of Virgin Music debts, Branson himself was left with some £330m. Adding the money which he had personally made from selling the share of the music company to Fujisankei, two years earlier, Branson's personal profit from Virgin records was around £400m. It was agreed that he would stay on as president of the company: a role that satisfied Thorn-EMI's desire to retain Virgin's figurehead, and Branson's desire to maintain some degree of influence over the well-being of the Virgin staff. It would be an unpaid role. 'I've never taken a salary from anyone,' he said, 'and it's a bit late to start now.'

On the day that the sale was announced, Branson addressed the Virgin records staff, thanking them for all their efforts, and reassuring them that they would be well looked after under their new paymasters at EMI. Jon Webster, a company director, and one of the longest-serving members of staff, moved a vote of appreciation and thanks to Branson, Draper and Berry for 'twenty fantastic years'. Branson could feel the tears welling up in his eyes and rolling down his cheeks. Newer members of the Virgin team were moved, and embarrassed, to see him in tears. There were only a handful of staff now who could remember the last time they had seen Branson so upset – eleven years before, when Virgin was fighting for survival, and faced with a staff revolt Branson had pleaded for time and indulgence, with tears in his eyes. The company had struggled out of that crisis – and many more since – to bring them to where they were today. Now Branson was saying goodbye.

Feeling flushed and confused, Branson left the record company and set off at a sprint down Ladbroke Grove, to clear his head. Outside the tube station he caught sight of a news-stand placard – Branson Sells For £560m – and started crying again.

Ken Berry would remain firmly committed to the new Virgin operation. Simon Draper's future was less certain. In recent months, Draper – like Branson – had seemed to be losing interest in the company. He now came in only three days a week. He collected modern art; he was busy restoring his Sussex home, which had once belonged to the patron of surrealism, Edward James; and he was keen on motor-racing. Draper would continue with the new Virgin in his role as chairman, but nobody could be sure for how long.

Another old friend and associate would be saying goodbye. It was more than twenty years since Mike Oldfield had driven up the gravel drive of the Manor studios in a battered Transit van – a shy, awkward and precocious talent – and inadvertently set in motion the train of events that would lead to the launch of the Virgin label. The company had been founded to release Oldfield's *Tubular Bells*; Oldfield had made Virgin's – and Richard Branson's – first fortune. Oldfield had been a Virgin artist ever since, although in later years the relationship had become increasingly tired and habitual. Oldfield felt he was taken for granted, not treated with the respect his contribution to the company deserved; and sales of his records had dwindled, although he remained popular in Europe. Shortly before the sale to Thorn-EMI, Oldfield had offered Virgin first refusal on his new recording, but Virgin were not prepared to meet the asking price, and he had taken it elsewhere. Its title could not have been more poignantly fitting. Richard Branson had founded Virgin to the sound of *Tubular Bells*; he was selling it to the sound of *Tubular Bells 2*.

Chapter 17

'You're Going to Cry Either Way,
Richard. So Just Cry . . .'

The Christmas of 1992 saw Richard Branson enjoying what he would later admit was 'one of the best holidays of my life'.

Relaxing on his Caribbean island of Neckar with a group of friends, Branson swam, snorkelled and sailed. Even in these idyllic surroundings, Branson's family had traditionally found it impossible to insulate him from the intrusions of fax and telephone. But on this occasion, the news from London was only good – newspaper headlines confirming BA's capitulation in the 'dirty tricks' battle.

For nine months, lawyers inside BA had been preparing their case against Branson in a mood of growing frustration and anger. Under the process of legal discovery, whereby both sides in a libel case are obliged to exchange all documentation relevant to the case, BA's lawyers were made aware of the evidence that Virgin had amassed, including the damning testimony from passengers, and BA staff members, about passenger-poaching, the illegal accessing of computer information about Virgin flights and passengers and how BA staff had been instructed by superiors to shred files referring to Virgin for fear of discovery.

The lawyers' trawl through BA's own files offered little in the way of defence. One of the reasons BA had decided to counter-sue Branson was in its belief that Branson was employing undercover agents to undermine BA. But that belief – a distorting mirror of BA's paranoia and the length to which the airline was prepared to go in order to see off Branson's challenge – proved groundless. What emerged instead was chapter and verse on BA's *own* undercover operations against Virgin, conducted in an atmosphere of conspiracy and subterfuge, replete with quasi-espionage style codenames – 'Mission Atlantic', 'Operation Barbara' and 'Covent Garden'.

As the evidence stacked up, it became clear to BA's board of directors that their case had collapsed, and they had no alternative but to offer a settlement.

In December, £485,000 was paid into court on behalf of British Airways in settlement of Branson's claim, and BA indicated it would drop its suit against Branson and foot the legal costs of both sides.

Branson agonised over whether to accept the settlement, or press on with his libel action. His lawyers advised him to settle. A court case would be a protracted, and costly, exercise; and there was no guarantee a jury would award damages comparable to the sum BA were offering.

So it was that on 11 January, a sun-tanned, relaxed and extremely happy Richard Branson presented himself in the High Court for the concluding act of 'the mother of all libel battles'. In a statement which had been fought and gnawed over by respective teams of lawyers, BA and Lord King apologised 'unreservedly for the injury caused to the reputation and feelings of Richard Branson and Virgin Atlantic' by the articles in *BA News* and Lord King's letters. The statement went on to admit that Brian

Basham had attempted to place 'hostile and discreditable stories' in the press, and that aspects of BA's conduct gave Branson 'serious concern about the activities of a number of British Airways employees and of Mr Basham, and their potential effect on the business interests and reputation of Virgin Atlantic and Richard Branson'.

Brian Basham's name had been included in the apology at the insistence of Virgin's lawyers. Basham, wise to the fact that the loyalty of his employers BA had stopped some distance short of the High Court, had prepared his own statement; that at no time had he acted 'without the knowledge or approval of the British Airways Board', and that he had tried to 'discourage BA from disseminating disparaging and unsubstantiated rumours' about Richard Branson. Basham's statement went on to say that he did not accept the references to him in BA's apology as 'an accurate summary of his actions on behalf of BA'.

The amount of BA's final settlement was £610,000: £500,000 to Branson himself, £110,000 to Virgin Atlantic. Branson shared the £500,000 among his entire airline staff as a vote of thanks. BA also paid costs estimated at £4.5m.

Within BA, the libel settlement exploded like a neutron bomb.

In their High Court statement, BA's lawyers had insisted that 'the directors of British Airways were not party to any concerted campaign against Richard Branson and Virgin Atlantic'. Under pressure from the airline's institutional investors, Lord King and chief executive Colin Marshall were obliged to sign pledges affirming that they had not 'implemented or authorised' any of the 'disreputable business practices' for which the airline had apologised in court, or 'any press campaign or other improper action against Virgin Atlantic Airways or Mr Branson'. The chairman of BA's non-executive directors, Sir Michael Angus, added emphasis to the executives' defence, stating that Sir Colin Marshall 'did not know' about any of these 'disreputable activities'.

The disingenuousness was breathtaking. A book on the affair, *Dirty Tricks* written by Martyn Gregory, the producer of the *This Week* programme which had initially brought BA's activities against Virgin into the public domain, subsequently demonstrated how the responsibility for the campaign went to the very top of the BA hierarchy. It was King and Marshall who had initially authorised Brian Basham's press campaign against Branson. Lord King himself had encouraged Basham to circulate a story – never substantiated – about council workmen refusing to move refuse bags from outside Heaven, the gay nightclub owned by Branson, for fear of AIDS-infected syringes. Marshall had authorised the briefing document, circulated by Basham, designed to undermine press and City confidence in Virgin's business, and signed the cheque for £46,000 paying Basham for it. It was Robert Ayling, as BA's director of marketing and operations, who had been in charge of the department from which BA employees had been working to lure passengers from Virgin to BA flights in both Britain and America.

Human sacrifices were nonetheless demanded, and duly delivered. David Burnside, BA's head of corporate affairs, was sacked. Brian Basham, 'the streetfighter' who had been left bleeding on the courtroom floor by his own employers, was now peremptorily dumped on the pavement. Basham was to exact his revenge, by being a crucial witness against King and Marshall in a *World In Action* programme on the affair, made by Martyn Gregory, and in Gregory's book *Dirty Tricks*.

Nor was Basham ready to make friends with Branson. In March 1994, at a party at the Ivy to launch *Dirty Tricks*, Basham twice refused to shake hands with Branson, offering the supreme insult – 'I would rather kiss Jeremy Beadle'.

For Lord King, the case was to prove a crushing personal blow. Margaret Thatcher's favourite business-man, a principal flagbearer of the Thatcher ethic of freebooting and rapacious capitalistic enterprise, had made the fatal mistake of underestimating his younger, less orthodox opponent. Within BA, Branson had been known disparagingly as the 'grinning pullover' – a nick-name in which both frivolity and contempt jostled for the upper hand. 'If Richard Branson had worn a pair of steel-rimmed glasses, a double-breasted suit and shaved off his beard, I would have taken him seriously,' King later admitted. 'As it was, I couldn't.' In this he had made the grievous error of judgement which others had made in the years before him, when negotiating record licensing and distribution deals, of being lulled into a false and fatal sense of security by Branson's casual appearance, toothy grin and air of blithe insouciance.

At the end of January, King was obliged to grit his teeth once more as Virgin walked off with the third successive Airline of the Year award, and six other prizes. His handshake with Richard Branson at the awards dinner at the Grosvenor House Hotel was a small victory of politesse over rancour.

King's fate had already been sealed. He had been plan-ning to step down formally as chairman of BA in July 1993, after bidding goodbye at the summer's Annual General Meeting. But the thought of facing a tempestuous and embittered meeting of shareholders was not appealing. In February, a BA board meeting named Colin Marshall as the new chairman of BA, with Robert Ayling as managing-director. After 12 years as chairman, it was announced, King would assume the post of honorary president.

A scrummage of reporters greeted him outside the BA offices. 'Lord King, have you resigned because of the dirty tricks?', asked Joan Thirkettle, the ITN reporter. 'No,' King barked back, 'Madam.' 'Why not?' chorused the hacks. Turning on his heel, King breathed to his minders, 'Fuck 'em all . . .'

In the offices of Virgin Atlantic, BA's capitulation was celebrated in a mood of delirium. While the British media joined in a ritualistic savaging of BA and its hierarchy, congratulatory messages poured in; Labour's Shadow Transport Secretary John Prescott was among a number of MPs who telephoned to apologise for not having believed Branson's accusations.

Dignified in triumph, Branson was careful not to gloat over his victory, but quick to capitalise on it, suggesting that passengers might wish to express their disapproval of unethical behaviour by selecting seats on independent airlines. 'I would not say black BA, but if passengers feel that having read what BA did, they are shocked by it, as they should, the best way to ensure a strong independent airline industry in the future and make sure British Airways don't get their way is to make sure they fly Virgin or another independent carrier.'

Within three months of the settlement, Virgin was claiming that loads had increased by 20 per cent.

For Branson, the victory constituted not only a wel-come respite from the anxiety and uncertainty which had dogged the airline over the past two years, but 'a coming of age' for Virgin. Not only had BA's capitulation provided Branson with the most stunning publicity coup in British commercial history; not only had he been personally vindicated, but the credibility of Virgin as a world airline had been restored.

Mendacious as the stories had been about Virgin paying for fuel and running 'a dicky business', they had nonetheless had the effect of undermining confidence in Virgin not only among some passengers, but in the airline industry as a whole. But within weeks of the libel ruling, Branson was in negotiation with both Boeing and Airbus Industrie for the purchase of two new Boeing 747–400s, and four of the new Airbus A340s, with options for two more of each aircraft.

The 'list-price' of a Boeing 747–400 is $180m; of an Airbus A340, $110m. But Branson was able to take advantage of a slack market to negotiate a favourable price, on the basis of lease-purchase agreements by which Virgin had acquired all their aircraft.

Branson would tell friends, only half jokingly, that, actually, the impetus for upgrading his fleet was due to the desire to upgrade the in-flight video equipment in economy class on Virgin planes from six to fourteen channels. 'We wanted to borrow $20m to put new equipment into the planes, but we were turned down. So we got on to Boeing and said if we buy some new 747–400s, will you throw in a fourteen-channel video? They said, yes. It was the same with the Airbus. The bizarre thing in life is when you can't borrow $20m for new video systems, but you *can* borrow $2bn for new planes.'

The first new Airbus arrived in December 1993, in a manner which, once again, demonstrated that the gods of publicity smiled on Richard Branson. One of the first congratulatory telegrams Branson received following BA's capitulation in court was from the Princess of

Wales – a simple message with the single exclamation – 'Hurrah!'

Branson wrote back, asking whether she would inaugurate Virgin's new aircraft. 'Because our Airbus is so beautiful, so sleek and largely British built I can't think of a more appropriate person to name it.' To which Diana replied. 'I am flattered that you think Airbus and I have such similarities. I am also told it is of mixed European heritage and has a very wide body. Despite this I will be delighted to name your aircraft. I will leave our guests to decide which of us had the more accurate description.'

Since the announcement in December 1992 that the Prince and Princess of Wales were separating, interest in the Princess's movements had reached a level of unparalleled frenzy. Shortly before the unveiling, the Princess announced that she would be withdrawing from public life; christening Virgin's new Airbus would be her last public engagement, a piece of serendipitous timing which ensured that every newspaper and paparazzo was present at the ceremony . . .

Branson rose to the occasion with his customary egalitarian informality, throwing an arm around the Princess and planting a kiss on her cheek. 'If you look on the right, you'll see Granny's castle,' he joked as they flew over Windsor. The press, in a fit of self-righteousness – and uncharacteristic protocol – described his behaviour as 'cringeworthy'.

The mood of optimism inculcated by the victory over BA was consolidated by two more developments. In October 1993 Branson drew on £45m of the money he had received from the sale of the record company to buy back the 10 per cent share which Seibu Saison, the Japanese hotel and supermarkets group, had bought in the airline three years previously.

Seven months later the British government ratified what Branson would describe as 'the single most important deal Virgin has ever done', with Delta, America's third-largest airline. Delta already had flights from four American cities into Gatwick, but none into Heathrow, the prime British airport. The new agreement combined the two airlines' frequent-flyer programmes – a powerful incentive for regular transatlantic passengers – and provided a computer code share, by which Delta passengers would be directly routed through to Heathrow, on Virgin planes, and Virgin passengers would have access to some 200 American cities through Delta's internal flights. As part of the agreement, Delta contracted to pay Virgin $150m a year to block-book seating on Virgin aircraft, as well as sharing terminal facilities.

Buoyed by the success of the 'dirty tricks' action, Virgin pressed ahead with an expansion of routes. It launched a daily service to Athens and one to Dublin – from the London City airport – both operated by franchisees flying under Virgin colours. In February 1994 Virgin launched its Hong Kong route, to be followed in May by a regular service to San Francisco.

For Branson the growth of the airline provided new challenges to his abiding belief that for companies to be beautiful they had to be small. Virgin's expansion would bring 700 new employees into the company in 1994. Branson began to toy with ideas to break the airline down into more manageable parts, including a scheme to divide the 3,000 cabin crew into thirty groups, each with its own 'team-leader', which would allow each team to fly the airline's most glamorous routes and foster a sense of team comradeship and loyalty.

Through all of this, the situation with BA had come no

nearer to final resolution. The court case in January 1993 had dealt with libel damages to Branson. It had not dealt with the matter of compensation to Virgin for damage inflicted by BA's 'dirty tricks' activities, which Branson estimated at one stage resulted in as many as six out of ten upper-class passengers being switched from Virgin flights by BA agents.

In the aftermath of the libel action, Sir Colin Marshall and Robert Ayling arrived at Branson's home for 'peace talks', and to hammer out an agreement between Virgin and BA which would obviate the protracted and expensive business of both sides going back to court.

The talks dragged on interminably in an atmosphere of mutual suspicion and distrust. Virgin were seeking a figure which, in Branson's mind, would reflect the seriousness of BA's 'dirty tricks' campaign, and the costs it had exacted on Virgin's business. In real terms, Branson estimated this should have been in the order of tens of millions of pounds. In the event, he indicated he would be prepared to accept £13m to call the matter closed.

BA offered £9m. Branson was inclined to accept the figure, but balked at the two conditions BA wanted to impose: that he should return all the documents that had been given to his lawyers during the process of discovery in the libel case; and that he agree to sign a clause prohibiting him from ever speaking about the 'dirty tricks' campaign again. Ayling claimed that all BA were seeking was a simple agreement 'not to rake over the events of the past'. Branson argued that such a gag would restrict Virgin's ability to refer to the case in any further actions or to provide information to any other airline involved in a similar dispute. On a more prosaic level, he added, the agreement would prohibit him even from so much as mentioning the case were he ever to write his autobiography in the years to come.

In June 1993, Christopher Chataway, the chairman of the CAA, attempted to broker a settlement which would have dropped the gagging clause. BA refused. Branson's determination to pursue BA through the courts for redress was now applied with a vengeance.

In May 1993 he launched another court action against BA, for breach of copyright, arising from the computer information which BA had been illegally accessing for nearly three years.

That was followed by a complaint to the European Commission, alleging continued anti-competitive activity. And in October 1993, he filed an anti-trust action in New York, claiming damages of $325m (£220m) for BA's 'illegal, anti-competitive and monopolistic activities'.

'In an ideal world,' Branson remarked, 'after losing the libel case, BA would have eaten humble pie, paid us the damages and we could have both got on with it. But they decided to drag it out. Perhaps they felt we'd get bored with it; the public would get bored with it; that it would wear us down going through the courts for years in the States. For whatever reason, they took this approach.'

For Branson, obtaining satisfaction in the American courts was a matter of economic redress and principle, as well as a means of establishing a bench mark on such fundamental competition issues as travel-agent discounts and corporate discounts.

The battle against BA had been a steep learning curve for Branson. Building Virgin over twenty years, he had become accustomed to making quick decisions and reaping quick results. But the defence of Virgin's name in the face of BA's campaign had been a protracted and wearing battle against a powerful and cunning enemy. It had taught Branson patience and perseverance.

The indifference and, in some cases, hostility of the business press to his original claims about BA's 'dirty tricks' had sown the seeds of distrust in Branson, and taught him that 'financial journalism' often depends as much on mutual back-scratching and 'disinformation' carefully planted by corporate P.R.s as it does on the facts. The resilience of BA's hierarchy, their apparent imperviousness either to shame or retribution, remained an abiding puzzle.

'The fascinating thing in life,' he remarked, 'is how individuals who can be almost crooked in their approach to things, can still remain in positions of power and be completely and utterly accepted as respectable business-men within a month or two.'

Among the public at large, the BA verdict had the effect of elevating Branson almost to the status of national hero; the David, as any number of newspaper stories belaboured, who had slain Lord King's Goliath. A survey commissioned by the TSB, and published in May 1993, revealed that Branson was now the role model most young people in Britain would like to emulate, number one in a field which included such improbable choices as the comedian Lenny Henry, Anita Roddick and John Major. Dr David Lewis, a consultant youth psychologist who analysed the findings, said, 'There's an F Factor to Branson: he's got fame, fortune and fun.'

Most parents surveyed also approved the choice of Branson – the first time since the 1950s that the two had matched, according to Lewis.

Fatuous as such polls may be (could *any* young person seriously see John Major as a role model?), it nonetheless provided an interesting weather-vane both of Branson's indelible public profile, and the values of Britain's young. Branson had found his constituency. Forged in the era of social idealism, flourishing in the age of the entrepreneur, Branson appeared to combine both elements in one; the grinning nonconformist who had taken on 'the suits' and beaten them at their own game.

He was the businessman whose success had effected his entry into the most gilded social circles, yet who still showed a dangerous propensity for puncturing formality with some outlandish prank. At a *Business Traveller* dinner where Virgin won the award for 'World's Best Business Class' for the fourth year running, Branson celebrated by grabbing the presenter of the award, Ivana Trump, and turning her upside down, to the inevitable fusillade of flashbulbs. Invited to the Mexican retreat of millionaire businessman James Goldsmith for an environmental conference, Branson succeeded in being asked to leave after one day, for committing the heinous crime of pushing Goldsmith into the swimming-pool.

The potency of such a figure was not lost on the *Economist* magazine, which in May 1994 ran a story entitled 'Richard Branson, PM' speculating that in a time when party politics had degenerated into a pattern of recrimination and mud-slinging, and when the electorate's cynicism towards politicians was at an all-time low, Branson was the one figure in British public life who might usefully enter politics on his own ticket. 'It is not hard to imagine a platform with voter-appeal,' wrote the *Economist*. 'It would be pro-enterprise, pro-consumer and patriotic. But it would also be kind to the weak, keen on education and health, and in favour of fun.' As a thumbnail analysis of Branson's beliefs and priorities, it was not inaccurate. But as prophecy it was wildly improbable. Branson would be about as likely to invite Lord King, Colin Marshall and Brian Basham on a week's skiing holiday as he would be to run for political office.

By the beginning of 1994, Richard Branson stood at the apex of a pyramid of companies with a combined revenue estimated at £1,500m. There was Virgin Travel, the business dearest to Branson's heart, which included the airline and holiday business; Virgin Retail, which had grown from the first record shop, above the shoeshop in Oxford Street, to include Megastores throughout Britain and Europe, Japan, North America and Australia. There was Virgin Communications, run by Branson's brother-in-law Robert Devereux, operating a host of media and entertainment related businesses, including a publishing arm; the radio station 1215AM; video games and interactive CD-ROM software; and studios in London, Los Angeles and Mexico City offering post-production services for video, broadcast and advertising companies; there was the Virgin Hotels Group, operating clubs and hotels in Britain and Spain, and responsible for the management of Neckar Island. And there was Virgin Investments, which included a hot-air balloon and airship company and the Storm model agency.

Branson had long yearned for an opportunity to break into national radio – more particularly, to provide a commercial rival for the BBC's national pop station, Radio One. It finally came in 1992, when Virgin bid £1.9m to the Radio Authority for the annual licence to run a commercial rock station on the 1215AM frequency, previously held by Radio Three. Virgin had conceived a station which would follow the model of the American 'classic rock' stations, with programming geared to the 'thirty-something' audience, who bought albums rather than singles and who, it was presumed, were jaded with the incessant diet of dance music provided by Radio One and the chart-oriented pop of local commercial radio. The proposal had one fundamental flaw. The AM frequency meant it would be impossible to broadcast in stereo, a severe handicap to a station broadcasting 'quality' rock to an audience whose tuners and car stereos were habitually locked to FM. But Branson reasoned it would at least give Virgin a degree of purchase on the airwaves, and put Virgin in 'pole position' if and when an FM frequency became available – a strategy he likened to the airline initially winning permission to fly out of Gatwick, and then campaigning to fly out of Heathrow.

Even before the station was launched, on 30 April, in the customary champagne foam of publicity, it was struck by problems. Parts of the transmission equipment Virgin had inherited from the BBC dated back to 1957. Tests revealed that the transmission quality in London was far below expectations, necessitating a hasty investment in new equipment. Notwithstanding the improvements, the AM signal was to prove a major detriment to the prospective 'CD-generation' listenership, accustomed to listening to music on state-of-the-art home tuners and FM car radios.

On its launch, Branson said he firmly expected the station to be in profit within three years. But the optimism quickly evaporated. In October it was revealed that Virgin 1215 had an audience of fewer than 3m people, 200,000 less than Radio 3 – a loss of half a million since the station's launch in April, and 430,000 short of the 3.3m target figure promised to advertisers.

The AM frequency was not the only factor. It had quickly become apparent that Virgin's musical policy was not finding favour with listeners. A decision was made to leaven the reliance on tried-and-tested favourites such as Led Zeppelin and the Stones, with a larger proportion of new music. Initial research had also suggested that Virgin's target audience wanted more music, less talk from deejays. Before the launch, Branson had spelt out that Virgin would 'let the music do the talking' and specifically avoid disc-jockeys who 'like hearing the sound of their own voices too much'. But it quickly became apparent that the early research was wrong, and that listeners craved companionship as well as music. Within twelve months, Virgin had a breakfast-show as chatty as any in music radio, and had supplemented its cast of diffident musos with Nick Abbott – Britain's first 'shock-jock', on the model of American radio's garrulous and opinionated Howard Stern.

From the outset, Branson realised that the long-term future of the station rested on whether or not he could secure an FM frequency. No sooner was Virgin 1215 on the air than Branson was in meetings with the BBC's director-general John Birt and head of radio Liz Forgan, arguing that, as a predominantly speech-oriented station, Radio Four should swap its FM frequency for Virgin's AM one.

In June 1993, Lord Chalfont, chairman of the Radio Authority, warned that he would block any such proposal. The Radio Authority, Chalfont argued, had advertised – and Virgin had accepted – an AM frequency, and higher bids might have come forward had there been any indication of an FM frequency becoming available.

Branson persisted. A month later he announced that Virgin engineers had found that an extra national FM station could be created from local BBC frequencies, and offered to hand back his AM frequency to the BBC for talk radio if he was allowed the FM frequency. A Virgin FM station, he argued, could attract up to 10m listeners and generate up to £20m for the Radio Authority. The BBC poured cold water on Branson's proposal as 'a mighty complicated web of frequency allocation'.

A further opportunity presented itself early in 1994, when the Radio Authority announced that 105 to 108FM, a frequency used by the emergency services, would be allocated for radio from January 1996, and asked for comments from the industry on how it should be utilised. Branson's was among 450 submissions, arguing that he should be allowed to swap his 1215AM frequency for the FM one. To support his proposal, Branson launched a campaign on air encouraging listeners to sign a petition for the switch to FM. There was some consternation within Virgin that the plan would backfire by simply drawing listeners' attention to the inadequacies of the AM frequency. But the campaign gathered more than 600,000 signatures, and by the time of the Radio Authority's decision, in May 1994, the official RAJAR audience figures were showing that Virgin 1215 had begun to turn the corner, with the station showing a 'weekly reach' of 3.3m people – a 27 per cent increase on the previous quarter.

The campaign was not enough to persuade Lord Chalfont, however. The Radio Authority ruled that the available frequencies would be allocated on a local basis to community and hospital radio services.

In a letter to Lord Chalfont, Branson warned that without an FM licence there could be no guarantee that Virgin would still be on air in five years' time. Virgin 1215, he believed, could sustain profitability on its AM frequency with an audience of 4m, but the campaign for an FM frequency would continue.

The rejection by the Radio Authority was a bitter blow for Branson. It came in a week in which he was awaiting three major government decisions. The verdict of the Radio Authority was one. And one strike against. A ruling from the Monopolies and Mergers Commission on the merger between Virgin and W.H. Smith, which would give the new combine 30 per cent of the record-retailing outlets in Britain, was another. That was passed. One strike for. Branson would learn of the third, and most important, ruling of the day after the Radio Authority had passed its verdict. The news, when it came, would constitute what Branson would describe as the 'biggest set-back of my life'.

The combination of Branson's growing wealth and position, and the injunction which had shadowed him since his childhood to 'do something useful, Richard' had expressed itself in various ways over the years. The Mates campaign and establishing the Virgin Healthcare Foundation had given him experience in the way in which the resources of a large commercial organisation could be deployed to charitable ends. The evacuation of Britons from Baghdad following Iraq's invasion of Kuwait (which had so enraged Lord King and been a significant catalyst for the whole 'dirty tricks' campaign) and the airlift of supplies to refugees in Jordan, had been another crucial factor in Branson's life, coming as it did in a period when Branson was most racked with self doubt and the existential questions which traditionally plague those in middle life. Branson would later describe the airlifts as the most satisfying accomplishment of his life – but one that was to be eclipsed by yet another project.

Branson's thoughts first began to turn to the idea of a national lottery in 1987, when, on holiday with friends in Ireland, he was introduced to a man named John Fitzpatrick, who ran the Irish lottery, which raised millions of pounds for government-nominated projects. Branson wrote to Margaret Thatcher, suggesting the idea of a similar lottery in Britain, to raise money, supplementary to NHS budgets, for preventive health schemes. There the matter rested until 1993, when the government passed the National Lottery Act, and announced it would be accepting submissions from interested parties to run the lottery on a licence basis.

An Office of the National Lottery, Oflot, was established, with an accountant, Peter Davis, as its director-general, to regulate and administer the awarding of the licence.

What was being proposed was, in effect, the creation at a stroke of Britain's largest consumer industry. The government estimated that a National Lottery should receive up to £4bn a year, of which half would be spent on prizes and around 12 per cent go to the Treasury as tax. A quarter would go to a National Lottery Distribution Fund, established to channel money into 'five good causes' nominated by Peter Brooke, the National Heritage Secretary: the arts, sports, heritage, charities and the Millennium Fund, set up by John Major to plan celebrations for the year 2000. The remainder of the income would be divided between retailers, advertisers and running costs. That would leave around 1 per cent in profit – as much as £40m to £50m for the operator.

Branson had no doubt that he wanted to be involved in a bid for the lottery, but his immediate thought was, why should it be run at a profit? A charitable foundation could run the lottery at cost, generating a huge amount of money for charities not covered by the NLDF. And the 'feel good' factor among the public of playing in a lottery for charity would increase the income of the lottery overall, bringing more money into the NLDF.

A team began to assemble. John Jackson, the director of the Virgin Healthcare Foundation at the time of the Mates launch, who had gone on to work with Anita

Roddick at Bodyshop, and Anne Leache, the present head of the Healthcare Foundation, drew up a scheme for a charitable foundation to dispense the lottery profits; John Fitzpatrick from the Irish lottery was made chief executive designate of the new UK Lottery Foundation. Lord Young, the former Trade Minister and now executive chairman of Cable and Wireless, was named as its chairman. Other members of the consortium included the computer-company IBM, who would provide the *materiel* and expertise for installing terminals in outlets selling lottery tickets, Mars Confectionery and the advertising agency J. Walter Thompson.

The UK Lottery Foundation bid was formally announced in December. By then, seven other major contenders had already thrown their hats into the ring. Foremost among them were the Camelot Group (a consortium of Cadbury Schweppes, De La Rue, Racal Electronics, ICL and GTECH, a company with considerable experience of running state lotteries in America); the Great British Lottery Company (Granada, Vodafone, Associated Newspapers, Carlton and Hambros Bank); and a consortium headed by N.M. Rothschild, the merchant bank, in association with the Australian lottery enterprise Tattersall's.

Branson's was the only bid made on a strictly non-profit basis. In its proposals, the UK Lottery Foundation predicted a turnover of £37bn over the six-and-a-half-year period of the licence, generating a contribution of £10.5bn to the NLDF, but with as much as £600m a year extra going to other charities – a figure that would potentially make the UK Lottery Foundation the largest charitable foundation in the country.

Branson approached the lottery bid with an enthusiasm which he had not shown for any project since the launch of the airline ten years before. He lobbied his friends and contacts in business and politics for support. Friends found themselves being solicited for ideas about the best way of distributing the lottery profits. What were the priorities? Homelessness? Job creation for the young? Preventive medicine?

An NOP Poll, conducted on behalf of the UK Lottery Foundation, suggested that the idea had caught the public imagination too. Seventy-two per cent of respondents said they wanted any profits from a national lottery to be donated to good causes. And 64 per cent said they would be 'more likely' to play in a lottery that raised money for good causes than in a lottery run for private profit.

On the morning that the Oflot decision was going to be announced, a huge banner was hung across the front of Branson's office in Holland Park. '£11bn going to good causes. One new millionaire a day every day. Our profits are your profits. The UK Lottery Foundation.'

Two doors away, in the living-room of Branson's home, a small group gathered around the fax machine: Branson, Lord Young, John Jackson, Anne Leache, John Fitzpatrick, Branson's lawyer Colin Howes, and Branson's old friend, Simon Draper. Draper had severed his connections with Virgin records altogether, and launched a new business, producing state-of-the-art limited edition books on two of his enthusiasms – pheasants and motorcars – setting up office just around the corner from Branson's home. Branson was beside himself with anticipation. 'If we get it, Simon, I'm going to cry,' Branson confided to Draper. 'What shall I do?'

'Richard,' said Draper, 'you'll cry if you're successful, you'll cry if you fail – just cry.'

Oflot had announced that the decision would be made public on the Stock Exchange screens at 10.00 a.m. At

9.57, the fax machine started chattering. Branson tore the sheet out of the machine and took in the news.

'I can't believe it,' he muttered. 'I can't believe it.' The franchise, he announced to his colleagues, had been awarded to the Camelot Group.

Fifty of the staff who had worked on the lottery bid had gathered in the garden at the back of the office, drinking coffee and awaiting the result. Branson made his way over to break the bad news, then turned to face the press corps assembled on the pavement outside. Sensing the anger, as well as the disappointment, that Branson was feeling, Will Whitehorn, his young public relations and right-hand man, had quietly urged Branson to put on a brave face: congratulate the winners; point out that even if the UK Lottery Foundation had lost the bid, simply by taking part it had forced its rivals to modify their bids in a way that would increase the amount that would be going to good causes.

But Branson found it impossible to be equivocal. Raising a game smile, but struggling to keep the anger out of his voice, he told the assembled reporters that he had learned of the decision in a 'nasty little fax', which had given no reason why the Lottery Foundation bid had failed.

The lottery bid, he said, was 'the most important thing I could have done in my lifetime. There will be nothing else in my lifetime which could equal this.

'Generally speaking,' he added, 'I agree with the government that organisations need profits and a fair return for shareholders who take risks. With this particular business there is no risk, it's a licence to print money . . . For a few shareholders to cream off hundreds of millions of pounds from this I think is absolutely wrong.' In an interview with Radio Four he would amplify the attack.

'It is completely and utterly wrong for the government to award the lottery and profits to a handful of companies when they are not taking any risks,' he said. 'Of all the decisions I have ever seen any government make over many, many years I reckon this is perhaps the most crass.'

Outside his office, a new banner was unfurled over the old, its use as a backdrop for celebratory photographs no longer required. 'Best of luck to all involved in the lottery. You win some, you lose some,' read the new message. The predominant images that would appear in the next morning's newspapers would be of a dejected Branson, lost in thought.

Sitting on a sofa in the living-room of the Holland Park house, where he had plotted so many triumphs, Branson now fielded a stream of telephone calls offering sympathy and commiseration. Surrounded by advisers, he explored the possibilities of seeking a judicial review of the decision (the idea was dropped). He telephoned John Prescott and Tony Blair, the two front-runners in the forthcoming election to the Labour Party leadership, suggesting that if a Labour government got into power the lottery should be nationalised. If they did that, Branson said, he would happily accept the abandonment of plans to privatise the railways, notwithstanding Virgin's interests.

In explaining his decision to choose Camelot, Peter Davis, the director-general of Oflot, said that he had been guided strictly by his duty to choose the bid which would maximise the net revenues available for good causes.

Camelot had predicted a turnover of £32bn over six and a half years, generating £9bn for the NLDF, but pledged that if they were to reach the £37bn turnover predicted by the UK Lottery Foundation they could top the £10.5bn figure that the Lottery Foundation pledged to the NLDF.

The Camelot infrastructure, Davis believed, made it the best equipped of all bidders to get terminals into shops and maximise ticket sales. Most crucially, Davis was not persuaded by Branson's argument that a lottery run for charity would attract more players than one run for profit. On the contrary, Davis argued that a lottery run for profit would be more efficient. *The Times* newspaper was among those who found this argument dispiriting. 'In many businesses that might be a reasonable assumption,' it stated in an editorial on the day after the decision, 'but in a virtually risk-free government-sponsored monopoly the need for shareholder profits . . . is not at all clear. Profit is not the only possible motivator of all human endeavour; if the Government seems to believe this, it could yet turn the excellent idea of a National Lottery into a rod for its own back.'

Branson believed that Davis had 'measured the mood of the country completely wrongly'. Davis's arguments about business efficiency made no dent in Branson's belief in the strength, and the moral probity, of the UK Lottery Foundation bid.

Privately, he wondered to friends whether other factors had not come into play. Perhaps his high profile as a public figure had weighed against him, and that a successful bid would have cemented in the public's mind the idea that the lottery was a 'Richard Branson enterprise', rather than a government one. Perhaps, too, his reluctance to 'play the establishment game' had been a factor. Branson felt sure that his continued refusal to support the Conservative party publicly or privately, or to donate to Tory party funds, constituted 'a black mark' against him.

Working on the lottery, he said, he had 'found a direction', which embraced everything he most enjoyed doing, everything he thought most worthwhile. 'It entailed launching a new project, which I enjoy and which I'm quite good at; we had a wonderful group of people. And then there was that lovely feeling that we would be able to achieve wonders.' He had sunk £1m of his own money into the bid. 'From a personal point of view, spending £1m for a return of possibly £3bn in good causes seems like a good return . . . Obviously, that makes one feel good. If you're in a position in life to do something that important then you should do it. And there is nothing ever in my life, in the past or ahead of me, that could equal that degree of importance.

'I don't want to waste this position I find myself in, which is a fairly unique position. I'm held in reasonable esteem by the public, and being in a position to achieve quite a lot . . . from one's own selfish point of view it just seems stupid to waste it. So it's important after the lottery that the next direction I go in is not just doing things for doing things' sake, but it does have a reasonable clear path.'

On the day after the lottery announcement, Richard Branson drove up from London to attend a further special party in the grounds of the Manor recording studios – the twenty-first birthday of Virgin Records. For those who had been associated with the company, or followed its fortunes, over the previous twenty-one years, it was a night of mixed emotions. The shoestring operation, run by the 'Earl's Court Hippies' of the early seventies now nestled within the corporate bosom of Thorn-EMI. Where once the atmosphere would have been of *laissez faire* informality, it was now of corporate efficiency. Guests traipsing through the mud were greeted at the entrance by a sign, warning them that they were waiving all rights in the event of their appearing in a television film that was being made of the event.

Richard Branson, founder, until 1992 chairman, of Virgin Records, and still the company's life president, found himself in the improbable position of being refused entry to one of the hospitality tents because he lacked the appropriate laminated pass.

Familiar faces loomed from the past: Branson's original partner and oldest friend, Nik Powell; Ken Berry, for so long Branson's first lieutenant in the record company, who had stayed on with Virgin after the sale and who, the previous day, had learned of his promotion to managing-director of the new parent company, Thorn-EMI; Tom Newman, with whom Branson had first discovered the Manor all those years ago, and who had gone on to produce *Tubular Bells*; Stephen Navin, for many years Virgin's lawyer, now working with Simon Draper. Others were conspicuous by their absence: Draper himself. Mike Oldfield, on whom the fortunes of the company had originally been founded. John Varnom, who had joined Branson in the days of *Student* magazine and stayed with Virgin up to the time of the Sex Pistols. And, not surprisingly perhaps, Malcolm McLaren.

A stage had been erected in the grounds, where a representation of the new and old of Virgin performed: Soul II Soul; BBM – a new 'supergroup' (in a distinctly seventies meaning of the term) made up of Jack Bruce, Ginger Baker and the guitarist Gary Moore; and Boy George, who pointedly dedicated 'Do You Really Want to Hurt Me' to 'all the people who were fired' following Thorn-EMI's takeover. More than 100 had lost their jobs.

As the evening progressed, Branson, overwhelmed by

the deluge of faces from the past, and the disappointments of the immediate present, seemed unsure whether to laugh or cry.

Within a month, the following would happen. Richard Branson would open negotiations with Air France to lease Concordes to fly out of Heathrow under Virgin colours, in direct competition to British Airways.

He would announce his intention to bid for a local FM licence in London – where Virgin's AM transmissions were particularly poor – as part of a new strategy to build Virgin radio on a network of city stations on the FM frequency.

He would have discussions with the ambassador of the new South Africa, to establish a lottery, along the lines of the UK Lottery Foundation proposals, to raise funds for that country's regeneration.

And driving his family along the M40 from London to his Oxford home in the early hours of the morning, he would swerve to avoid another motorist, causing his Range Rover to turn upside down and skid 100 yards along the motorway on its roof. The car was a total wreck. Miraculously, Branson and his family were pulled out of the wreckage with only minor cuts and bruises, leaving him to reflect that, when all was said and done, he really *was* the luckiest man alive.

Chapter 18

Brand Wars

With the sale of Virgin Records to Thorn-EMI in 1992, Richard Branson experienced a sensation he had not felt for the last twenty years: freedom from financial anxiety. The days of nervously juggling figures and begging for loans, of bank managers presenting themselves on his doorstep to demand the repayment of overdrafts, were over – at least for the foreseeable future. For the first time in Virgin's history there was money to spare.

The business that Branson was left with spanned the globe. With the airline at its core, Virgin had a foot in retailing, video, film distribution, holidays. From its earliest days the growth of Virgin had been built around a careful diversification from its core business into related activities. Mail-order records led to recording studios, to the record label, music publishing, video and film. The airline had been a leap into the unknown, but that in turn had spawned the holiday business, hotels. Virgin, it seemed, had cornered the market in the 'feel good' industry. There had been failures along the way, but the public perception was that whatever Virgin's name was attached to appeared to turn to gold.

Virgin had become a by-word for value-for-money,

reliability, youthful cachet, a certain anti-establishment élan. It had attained that Holy Grail in the world of marketing – a 24-carat brand name. In 1993 an article appeared in *PR Week* – the bible of the public relations industry – analysing the strength of Virgin as a brand name. The article suggested that the Virgin brand had a 99 per cent recognition factor in Britain, and that Branson himself had a 98 per cent recognition factor. A third of the British population would be more likely to buy a Virgin product because of their high opinion of Branson.

Branson had always demonstrated a supreme indifference to the conventions of business – he wore the fact that he had never read a business book almost as a badge of pride, and had always run Virgin by instinct rather than theory. He was similarly immune to the use of business jargon. But now he began to talk about 'branding' at every opportunity.

The *PR Week* research, he admitted, had 'freed up any inhibitions I had about branching out', and given him ammunition to fight those within Virgin more cautious about expanding into new fields. The Virgin brand, he argued, not only inspired confidence in customers. It was a powerful inducement to potential partners, who could see that their investment was at least partly guaranteed by the enormous saleability of the Virgin name. It opened up a myriad of possibilities for joint ventures incorporating the Virgin name and other people's money.

Two products built on precisely that basis had already met with mixed fortunes. Virgin Vodka came out of a joint venture with William Grant, the producers of Glenfiddich Whisky. Vodka, Branson reasoned, was a 'young' drink that would appeal to Virgin's natural constituency. But the Virgin brand never provided a serious challenge to the market leaders Smirnoff.

Virgin Computers grew out of the purchase of a small computer company called Euro Magnetics which licensed the Virgin brand name to ICL. Virgin had no control over the marketing of the product; they simply received a royalty. But the product had nothing new to offer in a rapidly expanding market, and when ICL was taken over by the Japanese company Fujitsi, the line quietly folded.

Branson had learned a salutary lesson: that licensing Virgin's name had potential pitfalls. Whatever Virgin attached its name to in the future, the company should retain at least a 50 per cent interest; and the product, and its marketing, should be innovative and exciting.

At first appraisal, the proposal put to Branson by Cott Corporation to produce and market a cola drink under the Virgin name did not seem either particularly innovative or exciting – cola, is cola, is cola. But Branson was confident he could market Virgin Cola as a fun alternative to Coke and Pepsi. More than that, what appealed to him were the logistics of the challenge. Cola is one of the biggest businesses in the world. The combined sales of Coca-Cola and Pepsico total some $48bn. Both are long-established brands, market-place Goliaths just begging for a David to appear with an impudent sling-shot to knock them off their pedestal. 'Coca-Cola,' Branson reasoned, 'is the biggest brand name in the world, the most profitable company in the world, and it has the least competition of any company in the world. I felt that just challenging it, in itself, was synonymous with what Virgin stood for.'

The Cott Corporation had licensed a formula for cola from an American company, Royal Crown Cola, which had tried, and failed, to launch its own competitor to

Coke and Pepsi. Cott had fallen back on manufacturing cola for supermarkets to sell under their own brand name. The successful launch of Sainsbury's Classic Cola, manufactured by Cott, in April 1994 provided another incentive for Branson.

Virgin and Cott signed a 50–50 deal to manufacture and market Virgin Cola. The Cola business had obvious value in terms of synergy to Virgin. Branson could cut back on costs by serving Virgin Cola on his airline, in his nightclubs and hotels. But these were mere drops in the cola ocean. Branson needed to get his cola into supermarkets, corner stores and filling-stations if he was to challenge the market dominance of Coke and Pepsi.

In June 1994, in order to establish a foothold in supermarkets, Branson approached Sir Ian McLaurin, the chairman of Tesco, and persuaded him that rather than following Sainsbury's lead and branding their own cola, Tesco should take exclusive rights on Virgin for a year. Virgin Cola was launched in a fizz of publicity in October 1994, pitched as a young, brash and fun alternative to the market-leader – 'the unreal thing' as the tongue-in-cheek slogan had it. It quickly established a toe-hold in Tesco, outselling Pepsi and hard on the heels of Coke.

Within a couple of months of the launch, the press were reporting that Branson was claiming that he was already making £1m a week profit from Virgin Cola, and that the business would be worth at least £500m 'within a year or two'. Branson was obliged to point out that he had actually said turnover, not profit.

Virgin Cola was followed by a line of soft drinks, marketed by Branson with his typical mixture of panache and bare-faced cheek. He agreed to a cameo appearance, water ski-ing in the television series 'Baywatch', on the proviso that he was towed into camera-shot by an airship bearing the Virgin Cola logo. Working on 'Baywatch' with Pamela Anderson led to her promoting the Virgin Energy drink – marketed with a message on the can stating that, 'Despite what you may have heard, there is absolutely no scientific evidence that Virgin Energy is an aphrodisiac' – and to Virgin styling a cola bottle modelled on her distinctive shape, 'the Pammy'.

Lacking the huge advertising budgets of Coke or Pepsi, Branson fell back on his tried-and-tested methods of scene-stealing. In 1996, in a bid to maintain their foothold in the cola wars, Pepsi made the strategic move to change the colour of their cans from red to blue. The launch in Britain was planned, in conditions of utmost secrecy, for 2 April. But not quite secret enough. On 1 April, a series of newspaper advertisements appeared showing a blue can of Virgin Cola with the slogan 'Blue Can Warning', and a message informing consumers that thanks to new developments in packaging technology in the event of cola turning flat the can would turn blue. 'Virgin strongly advises its customers to avoid all blue cans,' the message went on. 'They are clearly out of date.'

But April Fool jokes and Pamela Anderson were not enough to disguise the fact that while the drink itself was not going flat, the business plan was. Coca-Cola had responded to Virgin's challenge with a full-frontal sales and marketing attack, stymying Virgin's inroads into newsagents and filling-stations. (Coke's annual marketing and advertising spend was around £34m, compared to Virgin's £4m.)

After two years, Virgin Cola was showing a £2.3m loss, and rather than achieving its target of 10 per cent of the take-home cola market, Virgin had attained only 5.3 per cent.

In 1996, Virgin renegotiated the contract with Cott, maintaining the 50–50 share in the British business, but giving Virgin a 90 per cent shareholding in overseas development.

By the end of 1997, Branson was claiming that the tide had begun to turn. Virgin had signed distribution deals with four more supermarket chains – Asda, William Morrison, Safeway and Somerfield – along with Shell and Texaco for distribution in their filling-stations. Virgin's own market research was showing that the drink had attained a 7 per cent share in the cola market and projecting a rise to 10 per cent within twelve months. (Research by A.C. Neilsen, however, suggested the brand had attained just 4 per cent of the market by October 1997, a rise from 3.3 per cent in October 1996.) Furthermore, Virgin claimed, in places where both products were stocked Virgin was out-selling Pepsi. More tellingly, Branson was looking forward to launching Virgin Cola in America in 1998, at a cost of some $20m, and predicting with a smile that, 'we're either going to be a huge success or fall flat on our faces'.

The launch of Virgin Cola had one peculiar knock-on effect which typified Branson's approach to business. In 1995, Virgin were approached by Luke Johnson, who had set up the Pizza Express chain, asking whether they would be interested in joining him in bidding for the 129 MGM cinemas which were being sold by Credit Lyonnaise.

Branson's first instinct was to say no. But no sooner had he put the phone down than a thought occurred to him. He made another call: how much cola is sold in MGM cinemas? The equivalent of 30 million cans, he was told. Thirty million people sampling Virgin Cola . . .

perhaps, Branson reasoned, Virgin should be going into the cinema business after all.

The more Branson thought about cinemas, the more it appealed to him. Given the Virgin treatment, he reasoned, cinemas could be transformed into palaces of fun: airline-style Pullman seats, the chance to buy CDs and books, to play laser games. 'We want to create a proper entertainment experience,' he announced, 'instead of just getting people to go to films.'

Virgin and Pizza Express joined forces to enter the bidding for MGM. When the price reached £150m, Pizza Express dropped out. Virgin quickly found a new partner, the Craig Corporation, an American cinema operator. When the bidding passed £165m, Craig too dropped out. In a frantic scramble to put together a bid before the deadline ran out, Trevor Abbott contacted an American venture capital company, the Texas Pacific Group, whose track record included rescuing Branson's airline rival Continental from Chapter 11 bankruptcy.

In June 1995, with TPG as partners, Virgin paid £195m to take control of MGM Cinemas. His first move was to sell off the ninety single-screen cinemas that came with the package to a team who had been managing the MGM chain before Virgin's acquisition. Branson retained the plum cinemas, suitable for renovation and refurbishment. To this he planned to add a dozen purpose-built multiplexes, including multi-screen cinemas, restaurants, games areas and shops.

Emblazoned on aircraft, megastore and cinema fronts and cola cans, the Virgin brand was now so ubiquitous that John Murphy, the chairman of the brand consultancy Interbrand, was moved to remark that, 'Unless they poison someone or start applying the brand to inappropriate products such as pension funds or photocopiers, I doubt whether the Virgin brand will be diluted'. Branson had no plans to manufacture photocopiers. But pension funds . . . Now there was an idea.

Rowan Gormley had joined Virgin from Electra Venture Capital in 1991, helping Branson to put together a bid for the Gatwick Express at the time when the Conservative government were first bruiting the idea of privatising the railways. Gormley stayed on in the company, working to a loose brief of sifting through the dozens of business proposals which landed on Branson's desk each morning and generating new ideas. When Gormley approached Branson with the suggestion that Virgin should take a close look at the pensions and life-insurance business, even Branson had his doubts. At the age of forty-six, Branson had never given much thought to pensions. Such was his personal wealth that it was hardly necessary. But the way Branson lived his life was antithetical to all that pensions implied; Branson lived almost day-by-day, too galvanised by the excitement of the moment to give much consideration to the future. Furthermore, pensions were neither glamorous nor sexy.

But Gormley made a persuasive case. A huge share of the payments people make for life insurance and pensions, Gormley argued, goes towards administration and overheads. Then there were the enormous commissions that fund managers and investment companies took for handling people's money. Now think of the telephone, said Gormley. First Direct, the telephone bank, had gained more than 500,000 customers since being set up by the Midland in 1989. Direct Line, the phone-based insurance company, had gained 10 per cent of the car insurance market since its launch in 1985. Virgin could offer a low-cost insurance policy using the same techniques. And with the infrastructure in place, the service could be extended to offer pensions, PEPs and personal banking.

Entering into a 50–50 partnership with Norwich Union, Branson launched Virgin Direct. After some consideration it was decided that the best product to put on to the market first was an index tracking Personal Equity Plan, or PEP. For all Margaret Thatcher's vision of Britain as a share-owning democracy in the 1980s, relatively few people had actually bought into it. Around ten million people in Britain own shares, but few actively follow the stock market. With an index tracking PEP, linked to the performance of the best companies on the stock market, investors can play the stock market without the trouble, and high commissions, of brokers or fund managers. And rather than monitoring a portfolio of disparate shares, PEP holders could simply watch the index to see how their investment was faring.

Index linking funds had been a well-kept secret in investment circles, partly because time and again it was proved that they performed better than investment fund managers. After analysing the performance of both the FTSE-100 (the top 100 stock market shares) and the FTSE-800, Virgin Direct decided to link their PEP scheme to the FTSE-800.

'I can't walk past a fat and complacent business sector without wanting to shake it up a bit,' said Branson on the launch of Virgin Direct. He was banking on the Virgin name, he said, to allay the distrust which people traditionally had for the City and investment schemes. 'The Virgin name is trusted, especially by younger people. The consumer has been taken for a ride for too long by an industry which has been able to hide its charges.'

Virgin Direct set up an office in Norwich, staffed by 100 people recruited from Norwich Union, and opened the telephone lines. Sir John Harvey-Jones was photographed being the first person to sign up for the plan. The Virgin PEP quickly became the fastest-selling product in the financial market. By the end of its first year, Virgin Direct had sold £400m of PEPs to 75,000 investors. By the end of 1997, Branson was claiming that 200,000 people had invested in the scheme, and more than £1bn was under Virgin Direct management. By then, Virgin had bought out Norwich Union's share in the business, after the Norwich had balked at extending the business into life insurance, and taken on a new partner, Australian Mutual Provident. By the end of 1997, Virgin were offering mortgages and banking facilities. After spending twenty years fighting with banks, Richard Branson had ended up owning one.

Virgin Atlantic remained the jewel in Branson's crown, and the most profitable arm of the Virgin empire. In the year 1995–96, Virgin Travel – the holding group which encompassed the airline and holiday business – showed a profit of £84m, and Virgin were claiming that, measured in terms of profit against turnover, it was one of the most profitable airlines in the world. It remained Branson's abiding hands-on interest. Two or three days a week he would drive to the airline's headquarters at Gatwick for meetings. The upper-class visitors-book and letters of complaint from passengers remained among his principal reading matter.

Branson's target of a few years earlier of twelve destinations had been reached with the recent addition of flights to Hong Kong, Washington and Johannesburg. Virgin now had flights on nine of the twelve most popular long-haul routes out of London.

But, inevitably, he now had no intention of stopping

there. There were proposals to fly to Las Vegas, Toronto, Moscow, Cape Town and Shanghai. And in June 1996 Virgin paid £40m for a 90 per cent share in a small Brussels-based airline, Euro Belg, which was rechristened Virgin Express, offering a low-cost, no frills service between various European capitals.

The preparations for the anti-trust case against BA in America were proving increasingly onerous. As the case entered the 'discovery' phase, in which the parties involved exchange documents, Virgin had been obliged to install a new computer system, at a cost of $2m, in order to cope with processing the estimated one million documents from BA; a sum that Branson hoped would be adequately compensated for if the ruling were to go in his favour. If the American court were to decide that BA needed to be taught a lesson, the $325m that Virgin Atlantic were claiming could, theoretically, be tripled to $1bn.

But now Virgin Atlantic was facing another threat from BA.

In June 1996, BA announced their intention to form an alliance with the giant American Airlines that would co-ordinate passenger and cargo flights, code sharing and frequent flyer programmes. The alliance, they claimed, could come into effect from April 1997, pending regulatory approval.

Flights between Britain and America are governed by an agreement between the two countries known as Bermuda 11, which determines who can fly where and how often between the two countries. Approval for the BA–AA alliance came to hinge on a liberalisation of Bermuda 11, the so-called 'open skies' question.

The American government made it clear that they wanted more American carriers to be given access to

Heathrow, the top international choice of high-paying business travellers, and an important staging post for flights into Europe. Britain allowed just two American airlines, American and United, to fly into Heathrow. US officials were insisting that Heathrow be opened to other American carriers before the BA–AA alliance could be approved. But talks had proceeded in an increasing mood of resentment among British negotiators over what they regarded as American intransigence, demanding the freedom for more US airlines to use Heathrow while at the same time attempting to impose tight restrictions on the freedom of British carriers to operate within the US.

Branson was all in favour of the liberalisation of Bermuda 11, and open skies. The airline business, he argued, should be no different from any other. Just as Virgin could open a Megastore in New York or Los Angeles, and Tower Records could open a store in Piccadilly, so Virgin should be allowed to operate internal flights in America giving, say, SouthWest Airlines a run for their money; and SouthWest should be able to operate in Europe.

What Branson objected to was the way in which the open skies question had been linked to the granting of anti-trust immunity to the BA–AA alliance. Rather than encouraging competition, he argued, the alliance would quash it. The proposed deal, he said, would be 'a de facto merger in everything except the legal sense'. Together, BA and AA would account for 62 per cent of the UK–US market, and on many routes they would have a total monopoly. It would give BA–AA 80 per cent of peak take-off and landing slots across the Atlantic, which, in turn, would give the two carriers tremendous leverage in setting prices.

Branson was not the only person to find fault with the

proposal. Both the Office of Fair Trading in Britain and the European Commission concluded that the alliance would severely reduce competition. The OFT proposed a limited confiscation of slots at Heathrow in order to maintain a degree of fair competition. The EC went further; its competition commissioner Karel Van Miert made it clear that BA would have to give up 350 Heathrow Airport slots to get the alliance cleared. Branson believed that the alliance was so anti-competitive that it should not be agreed at any price. Virgin passengers were left in no doubts about his feelings; the fuselage of Virgin planes started flying the slogan, 'BA–AA – No Way'.

In August 1997, Branson presented evidence to a special sitting of the House of Representatives Committee on Transport and Infrastructure at the American Embassy in London. If the alliance were to go ahead, he argued, it could be, 'one of the most outrageous developments in the history of air transportation'. The alliance, he pointed out, was opposed by 'every single consumer body' in the US and UK, including the Consumer Federation of America, the Consumers Union and the Consumers Association of Great Britain. 'Add to this impressive list the fact that the GAO [the General Accounting Office, the investigative arm of the US legislature], the European Commission, the UK Office of Fair Trading and numerous Members of Congress and Members of Parliament have found this alliance to be unequivocally anti-competitive and wholly unacceptable in its present form. Such an overwhelming weight of opinion cannot be ignored.'

British Airways argued that the alliance would promote competition and cut fares. 'Virgin wants to maintain its cosy position at Heathrow with access denied to airlines such as Continental, US Airways, Delta, TWA and Northwest,' said BA's chief executive Bob Ayling. 'It appears that Virgin is afraid of competition.'

Nothing, Branson retorted, could be further from the truth, 'nor designed to make me more angry. Virgin,' he said, 'welcome competition, provided it is fair competition, always has and always will. It would be a great tragedy if Robert Ayling and [American Airlines' chairman] Bob Crandall were allowed to swoop in like a pair of international jewel thieves in the dead of the night to snatch away the precious gem of competition.'

By the end of 1997, the proposed alliance had still not met with regulatory approval, and BA and AA were said to be discussing ways in which a less ambitious partnership might be formed if the original proposals were delayed or killed outright. Branson was vowing to fight on.

Airlines, hotels, a travel company, radio, a model agency, publishing, cinemas, soft drinks, personal finance – Branson's appetite for expansion seemed limitless. He announced plans for a Virgin clothing company, trading under the name Victory, in a 50–50 partnership with Rory McCarthy, a businessman who had made his fortune out of laser game arcades, and who shared Branson's enthusiasm for life-risking exploits: McCarthy held the world sky-diving altitude record.

There was a line of Virgin cosmetics in the offing – named Vie – and a business serving weddings, Virgin Bride. He had even announced his intention to go back into the record business. The Virgin name, as a music company, was now the property of Thorn-EMI. The new label would be called V2.

In 1996, the *Sunday Times* published an analysis of the Virgin empire. It showed a grouping of more than twenty separate 'umbrella' companies (controlling almost 200 private companies) with combined sales of £1.8bn and annual profits of £114m, when associates were included. Were Virgin to be quoted on the Stock Market, the *Sunday Times* concluded, it would be challenging for a position in the FTSE-100 index.

Instead of the traditional hierarchal model of a handful of businesses, all reporting to a holding company, Virgin was made up of a myriad apparently unconnected operations, many of them joint ventures with outside investors. Only Branson and a handful of key executives had an overall view. The empire Branson had created was what the Japanese call a *keiretsu* – a family of companies that use a brand name across a range of unconnected business areas. The Mitsubishi name, for example, is attached to cars, electrical appliances, textiles and a bank; Yamaha manufacture tennis rackets as well as motorcycles.

Branson preferred to describe his new, expansionist mood as 'inquisitive' rather than 'acquisitive', 'inquisitive meaning I love getting out and finding out about things I know little about, which results in us being fairly acquisitive. Anything we take on I treat like a university education. I completely immerse myself in the new business. I try to find out why other people are doing it badly and how we can get in there and do it better. I love the challenge of trying to turn big companies upside down, of seeing if we can do things differently, of delivering good value for money and, hopefully, paying the bills at the end of the day.'

The question was whether Branson wasn't diversifying too far, too fast. As Branson himself had acknowledged time and again, the most important asset any company has is its reputation: put your name on a product that doesn't come up to scratch and the whole company is brought into disrepute. The reputation which Virgin had built up over the years was based on value for money, quality, reliability, innovation, an indefinable, but none-theless palpable, sense of fun. Successes were trumpeted to the skies. Failures tended to be quietly buried. But with every new venture which Virgin took on the imperative to maintain standards, and the risk of them being under-mined, grew greater. And what would expansion mean to Virgin's image of the maverick, 'the underdog', in tune with the tastes and sensibilities of the man in the street, pitching itself against the might of faceless corporations? Part of Branson's skill had been in personalising every battle he fought. The dirty tricks war was not simply a backyard dust-up between a big airline and a small one. It was big, bad British Airways vs Richard Branson, the people's champion. How much longer could Branson purport to be 'David' when Virgin itself was daily grow-ing to Goliath-like proportions?

Throughout the history of Virgin, Branson's head-strong enthusiasm for what he called 'new challenges' had been tempered, and in some cases actively resisted, by more cautious voices, a resistance which had only served to inspire Branson's enthusiasm to even greater heights.

In 1984, Simon Draper and Ken Berry had cautioned him that going into the airline business could mean the end of Virgin. And the rapid expansion in the 90s caused similar alarm among some of the company's inner cadre. James Kydd, the new head of Virgin's trading arm, was openly sceptical about whether Virgin should be in the life insurance business. Virgin, he reasoned, was a com-pany synonymous with fun. 'Life insurance is effectively about death.' Trevor Abbott was sceptical about both life insurance – what is an entertainment company doing in the financial services sector? – and the cola venture. So too was Robert Devereux, Branson's brother-in-law. Coca-Cola had established a virtually unassailable position as number one in the market, Devereux argued; Virgin could never compete with its advertising and promotion budget. He had another, telling, point to make. The Virgin name, he argued, was synonymous with quality and endurance. 'Do we really want to see the name Virgin on a crumpled cola can lying in a gutter?'

Devereux had joined Virgin in 1982 to oversee the company's move into publishing, and gone on to develop Virgin's interests in film and video. He had become a millionaire in his own right, but now his enthusiasm for the business was waning, and he was expressing a wish to do something 'more creative' on his own account. At the end of 1996 he quietly withdrew from Virgin to become chairman of the Film Consortium, a project set up in conjunction with Branson and his old friend and former partner Nik Powell, to develop films using money from the National Lottery.

With Devereux gone, the inner-core of individuals who had surrounded Branson through the 80s had now all but disappeared.

Trevor Abbott, who had joined Virgin in 1984 as group finance director, prior to the ill-fated stock market launch, and gone on to become Branson's principal 'numbers man', was also taking an increasingly low profile in the company. Abbott had recruited Stephen Murphy in 1992, from the Burton group, as his own replacement as group finance director, and gone on to found his own venture capital company, Passport. But he maintained an interest in Virgin's retail operation and remained a director of the Virgin travel group.

Brad Rosser, a tough-talking Australian, had been

recruited from the management consultants, McKinsey, to oversee corporate development. Simon Burke, who had joined Virgin in 1987 as an accountant, and gone on to become managing director of Virgin retail, now occupied the post of chief executive of Virgin Entertainment, which included the new cinemas, and the international retail division.

From his earliest days in business, Branson had required a foil – someone to bounce ideas off, a lightning-rod for his enthusiasms, a confidant for his worries. It was a role that, at various times in his life, had been filled by Jonathan Gems, Nik Powell, Simon Draper, Ken Berry and Robert Devereux. Increasingly, this was a role now filled by Will Whitehorn. Whitehorn had joined Virgin in 1987, at the age of twenty-seven, as director of press and public relations. But in an organisation that placed such enormous value on presentation and image, his role had always gone beyond the customary press relations duties of cultivating stories favourable to Virgin and fire-fighting critical ones. Over the years, Whitehorn had become Branson's *de facto* right hand man, 'a sort of Minister without Portfolio', as Branson himself would put it. Loyal, enthusiastic and tireless – his boyish appearance and casual dress an echo of Branson's own – Whitehorn had become a constant presence at Branson's side, a valued adviser in the development of airline strategy and the dirty tricks war against British Airways, and in Branson's bid for the National Lottery. And it was Whitehorn who, in 1991, had taken the telephone call which would inadvertently lead Virgin into their most ambitious, and potentially most hazardous, area of diversification – railways.

With the proposed government nationalisation of the railways on the news agenda, a *Sunday Telegraph* reporter named Toby Helm took a 'flyer' on a slow Friday night and phoned Branson's office to ask whether, in the event of privatisation, Virgin would be applying for a rail franchise. By a curious serendipity Branson had just returned from Japan, where he had taken the bullet train from Tokyo to Kyoto. The range of on-board entertainments and services had prompted Branson to muse on why trains in Britain couldn't provide the same diversions for passengers as aeroplanes. But until Helm's telephone call it had never seriously occurred to Branson that Virgin should be in the railways business. 'Phone him back,' Branson told Whitehorn in a moment of impulse, 'and say we're considering it . . .'

The morning after the *Sunday Telegraph* story appeared, the Virgin office was inundated with telephone calls from sundry people offering their expertise and advice for Virgin's new venture. Among them was a transport economist named Jim Steer, who was to become Virgin's rail consultant. Within a week, Virgin had registered three possible rail trading names: Virgin Rail, Virgin Express and Virgin Flyer. Branson was in the rail business.

'I was once considering, if ever I wrote a book, calling it, "Talking Ahead of Myself",' Branson recalled. 'That's something I'm apt to do sometimes, through boredom in interviews and having said the same thing over and over again. This definitely was a case of that.'

Branson's rail ambitions lay in two separate spheres – national and continental. In May 1994, Virgin announced that it was joining a consortium, London and Continental Railways – which included Warburgs, the American construction company Bechtel, National Express coaches and Blue Circle cement – to build and run the all-passenger high-speed trains through the new

Channel Tunnel from London to Paris and Brussels. In the absence of air routes to Europe, Branson saw the proposal as a way to compete directly with BA and Air France for business traffic to the Continent.

In 1996, Virgin entered into partnership with a group of financial institutions, including Bankers Trust New York Corp, Texas Pacific Group, J.P. Morgan and Electra Fleming, to pay £60m for two national rail franchises. And in January 1997, Virgin Trains were secured a fifteen-year franchise to run the InterCity West Coast Main Line, between London and Scotland, along with the franchise for smaller Cross Country routes radiating from Birmingham. Like other franchisees, Virgin Rail would benefit from a government subsidy given to buyers of the loss-making parts of British Rail. But Virgin and its partners pledged to cover £1bn of subsidies from operating profits over the fifteen years of the franchise.

Buying what Branson took to describing as 'a train set' flatly contradicted the established Virgin ethos of 'growing businesses'. Rather than quietly nurturing a company away from the glare of the public spotlight, Branson had bought a huge, labyrinthine organisation replete with problems. With the West Coast Main Line, Branson had inherited one of the busiest in Britain, linking London with Birmingham, Manchester, Liverpool and Glasgow. It was also probably the worst. The line and its rolling stock had suffered from a chronic lack of government investment over the previous thirty years. The Office of Passenger Rail Franchise published figures showing that the two routes Virgin had acquired had the worst punctuality and service records of the entire network. Rather than recruiting its own staff, Virgin had inherited a work-force of some 3,000 with firmly entrenched practices.

The expectations on Branson to transform a dilapidated and demoralised operation and perform a miracle were enormous, and so were the risks. Virgin had worked for thirteen years to develop a bedrock of goodwill among its airline passengers. It could be argued that this goodwill would transfer to passengers riding trains bearing the Virgin livery. But in simple numbers terms, the requirement to maintain standards of customer care and efficiency on railways was even higher than on airlines. Around 5.3m people a year fly with Virgin. Some 25m people would be riding Virgin trains. The possibility of enhancing the Virgin name was enormous; but so was the possibility of damaging it.

Branson announced plans for an immediate refurbishment of the entire fleet of 100 trains, at a cost of £150m. He set about streamlining the operation, cutting the administrative bureaucracy that existed to run the two networks, and replacing it with a slimmed-down head office in Birmingham. Service staff and drivers were introduced to 'charm-school training'. It quickly became apparent however that the Virgin name in itself was not enough to work miracles. Within a matter of months, Branson had run into a chorus of complaints about train timetables and the inefficiency of telephone enquiries and bookings. Virgin, he pointed out, had set itself the challenge of 'undoing thirty years of neglect, demoralisation and structural decline'. Things would not change overnight.

But commentators eagerly seized on the problems to attack Branson personally. Writing in the *Guardian*, Mark Lawson acidly noted that as Branson 'has rapidly expanded from airlines to fizzy drinks to financial investment to cinemas to clothes and now railways, many have felt that this level of promiscuity should be recognised by

505

formally changing the company's trade name from Virgin to Whore'.

In the *New Statesman*, the former government minister David Mellor complained about the loos, the sandwiches and the timetables. 'Marvellous,' he wrote, 'to discover that beneath all the bullshit this part of Branson's empire is as badly run as if a mere mortal were in charge.'

Stung by the criticism, and acutely conscious, as ever, of the perils of bad press, Branson took out a series of newspaper advertisements explaining the difficulties which Virgin had inherited with the lines and outlining the plans to rectify them. At a press conference in November, Virgin unveiled their plans to introduce 55 revolutionary tilting trains on the West Coast Main Line by 2001, which would cut the journey time from London to Manchester to 1 hour 45 minutes, and a new fleet of 75 diesel trains for the Cross Country Line. The total cost of replacing the fleet would be £750m. The improvements package included a £2.1bn investment by Railtrack, in return for a share of Virgin's revenue, to replace track and signalling, increasing line speeds first to 125 m.p.h. and ultimately to 140 m.p.h. The improvements, Virgin predicted, would double the number of passengers travelling on Virgin trains from around 25 million in 1997 to an estimated 50 million by 2005.

By the end of 1997, Virgin were making plans to float Virgin Rail on the stock market – Branson's first flirtation with the market since taking the Virgin Group back into private ownership in 1988 – with analysts valuing the company in the event of flotation at more than £250m. 'This is the biggest challenge Virgin has ever taken on,' Branson said, knowing only too well that Virgin's reputation, and its fortunes, rested on the outcome. 'But I think, by the year 2002, people who remember how things were under British Rail will cite Virgin Rail as an example of the radical transformation for the better which has taken place.'

If they didn't, he acknowledged, it would be a disaster.

Ever since his emergence into the public eye in the eighties, Richard Branson had always been careful not to pledge allegiance to any one political party.

In the seventies, his admiration for Roy Jenkins had led Branson to become a supporter of the SDP (while declining their invitation to contribute to the party's funds). His attitude to Margaret Thatcher was more ambivalent. While Virgin had profited from some of the Thatcher governments' economic policies throughout the eighties, Branson had never been able to bring himself to support her social policies. Nor were the two ever personally close. Branson never forgot that Thatcher had been largely responsible for the misunderstanding that had arisen over his involvement with UK 2000, its transformation in the public eye from a job-creation scheme to an 'anti-litter campaign' and the ridicule that had followed. When she joined Branson at the helm of *Challenger II* on its triumphal journey up the Thames of 1986, it was a photo-opportunity of convenience rather than love; a chance for her to align herself with a popular hero, for him to fly the flag and receive official benediction for his accomplishments. Branson was a successful businessman – a phenomenon – and in many ways an exemplar of the Tory belief in entrepreneurial vigour, but he was never a member of 'the club', that loose alliance of industrialists, power-brokers and politicians, united by a combination of old school, monetary and party allegiance. His relationship with John Major was never one of anything but cordial pragmatism on both sides.

The new leader of the Labour party, Tony Blair, was a different proposition, however. In the spring of 1996, Branson visited Blair at his Islington home. Branson had two issues he particularly wanted to discuss. Tobacco advertising, and the lottery. Branson felt strongly that a Labour government should be enforcing a ban on cigarette advertising, and on the sponsorship of sporting events by tobacco companies. And he wanted to press home personally his point that when Camelot's licence to run the lottery expired, it should be run as a non-profit-making exercise, with profits going to health and education. During the meeting the Labour leader, in relaxed mood, had slipped off his shoes. Afterwards, he walked Branson down the street to find a taxi, still in his stockinged feet. A kindred spirit, thought Branson.

The two met several times after that. Blair introduced Branson to Gordon Brown, who asked him if he would join a committee to investigate how best to spend the windfall tax that a Labour government proposed to impose on the utility companies, but Branson declined. Labour were keen for Branson's endorsement, but Branson stuck to his principle of non-alignment. If you are in business, he reasoned, there will be occasions, such as the proposed merger between BA and American Airlines, when the government will be acting as judge, and strict independence was the best course. But as John Major's government struggled from crisis to chaos to the depths of sleaze, Branson found himself increasingly tempted to support Labour publicly.

In March 1996, in a letter to *The Times*, Branson waded into the 'cash for questions' scandal engulfing the Conservative government, suggesting that Tory MPs embroiled in the scandal should be de-selected by their constituencies. Shortly afterwards, Branson was approached through an intermediary to see if he would consider standing as an independent candidate in the Tatton constituency against Neil Hamilton, the Tory MP. Branson declined. Privately, he promised Tony Blair that if the opinion polls showed a fall below a 5 per cent Labour lead he would come out publicly and endorse Blair for Prime Minister. In the event, it was unnecessary. Labour romped home with the biggest parliamentary majority in post-war history.

In April 1996, Branson was in New York for the opening of a Virgin Megastore on Times Square. The opening involved Branson, dressed in a space suit, being lowered in a silver ball several storeys down the side of the new store. His exuberant mood was only slightly tempered by the presentation, on the same day, of a law suit.

Elizabeth Hlinko, a former public relations manager with Virgin Atlantic in America, filed a suit in a Manhattan district court alleging that Branson had made unwanted advances to her at a cricket afternoon at his Oxford home in May 1994. The suit alleged that 'in the presence of other employees and guests . . . Branson made unwelcome advances to [Hlinko] by fondling and grabbing her breasts'. Hlinko also accused Branson, and David Tait, executive vice-president of Virgin Atlantic in charge of American operations, of discrimination, suggesting that after the incident she had been frozen out of the company and forced to resign.

Branson was shocked at the allegations. He had always prided himself on amiable and informal relations with his employees, close, but not *that* close. Responding publicly to the allegation, he said that he had no recollection of the incident whatsoever. His wife, family and friends and a number of journalists had also been at the party. It was hardly likely . . .

Sexual harassment suits had become a growth industry in American legal circles; a justifiable riposte to the unwanted advances of bosses on their subordinates in some instances; in others, a way for disgruntled or opportunistic employees to make a killing. Privately, Branson told friends that Elizabeth Hlinko was 'trying it on'. Three months before the case was filed, he claimed, he had been contacted by Hlinko's lawyers offering an out of court settlement. Branson declined, saying he would fight the case.

Shortly afterwards, another former Virgin employee Lorna Brissett-Romans announced that she too would be filing suit, claiming that Branson had 'fondled her buttocks' at a party for Virgin executives in Florida. A third woman also announced her intention to file suit.

In the first step of what promised to be a protracted case, Branson made an application to 'strike out' the Hlinko suit. That application was scheduled to be heard in January 1998. The date was significant in more ways than one. January was when Branson expected to be fighting a libel case against Guy Snowden, the chairman of the lottery equipment company GTECH. It was also the time when, in an ideal world, he was hoping to be 30,000 feet in the air, traversing the world in a hot-air balloon.

Richard Branson had tried hard to honour the promise made to his family in 1990, after his successful crossing of the Pacific by hot-air balloon, that he would stay grounded. He had abandoned a plan to fly around the world with a joint Russian and American balloon team – a project that had eventually fizzled out without Branson's commitment. And, in public at least, he stuck stoically to the line about abiding by his family's wishes and remaining firmly anchored behind his desk.

His wife Joan knew better. She had long since resigned herself to the impossibility of persuading her husband to curb his sense of adventure. Branson seemed to need the adrenaline rush of putting his life and his fortunes on the edge. Just as the growth of his business empire could be seen as one long, sustained dice with risk, so there seemed to be some need in Branson to challenge himself by putting his life in danger.

Per Lindstrand's reminders that a circumnavigation of the globe by hot-air balloon remained one of the world's last, great untried challenges were guaranteed to wear away whatever resistance Branson might have felt to taking to the skies once more. Reluctantly, his family and friends began to give way . . .

The announcement, in 1995, that Branson and Lindstrand would be attempting to fly around the world in a new balloon, *Global Challenger*, raised familiar alarms among his business associates. Those with long memories could recall the damage which had arisen from the Atlantic crossing in 1987, when Virgin was a publicly quoted company on the Stock Exchange. A television film showing Branson practising sky-diving – and failing to pull the right ripcord – wiped 15p off the share-price – some £15m off the value of the company, overnight.

Branson was no longer accountable to shareholders or non-executive directors, but there was a palpable tremor of anxiety among his partners in joint holdings about the damage that would be done to Virgin-related businesses in the event of mishap during the round-the-world attempt. One city analyst opined that without Branson at the helm, the Virgin group could lose at least a third of its value. Another, more heartlessly, suggested that any fatality would be seen as 'a heroic gesture' that would promote the Virgin brand.

Branson and Lindstrand had acquired a third member of the team for their round-the-world attempt: Rory McCarthy, Branson's new partner in developing a line of Virgin clothing, and a man who seemed equally determined to risk his life at every opportunity. McCarthy piloted his own jet-plane, and was the holder of the world's sky-diving and hang-gliding altitude records.

As with the Atlantic and Pacific crossings, the balloon team would be hitching a lift in the jet-stream at an altitude of 30,000 feet. If all went according to plan, the 174ft-high *Global Challenger* would fly some 24,000 miles over some seventy countries in roughly eighteen days. Branson jocularly talked about landing in his garden in Oxfordshire. On previous attempts, the balloons had been emblazoned with the logo of Virgin Atlantic. This time it would be branded with Virgin Cola.

Meteorological conditions determined a three-month 'window' of possibility when the jet-stream would be at its most amenable: between November and January. The original plan was to launch from Greenwich. But at length it was decided that Morocco was more appropriate.

In January 1996, the team arrived at the putative launch site, a military airbase outside Marrakech. The day Branson and Lindstrand arrived it began to rain. And it didn't stop. For a week, the balloon team, and an accompanying circus of press and media, kicked their heels under the lowering sky. There were excursions to the *souk*, dinners, belly-dancing evenings. There were instant friendships, furtive affairs, stomach upsets, souvenirs bought and regretted. But there was no launch. Disconsolate, the team packed the enormous balloon and capsule back into their containers and returned to England.

Twelve months later, the team reassembled once again in Marrakech. The weather could not have been kinder. A warm sun shone in a cloudless blue sky, and the barest breeze rippled across the launch site. The presence of mountains had proved a fortuitous omen on the previous balloon attempts. The successful Atlantic crossing had begun in the shadow of Sugarloaf mountain; the flight across the Pacific in the shadow of Mount Tajachiko; now, from the airbase in Marrakech one could look across to the snow-peaked Atlas mountains, magisterial on the horizon.

This time there was to be no waiting. Lindstrand had arrived in Marrakech with his engineering and launch team. Branson arrived with twenty-four hours to go to the launch. Family and friends had flown to join him; his parents, Joan and the children, his two sisters Lindi and Vanessa. On the evening before the launch, Branson packed the last of his personal belongings into the capsule, including his reading matter for the journey: a copy of Julian Barnes' short stories; an *SAS Survival Guide* and a *Fodor's World Guide* – presumably to choose a good restaurant in the event of a forced landing in India or Japan. Returning to the hotel, he declined dinner, instead popping a nutritional pill and a mild sleeping tablet to enable him to calm his nerves and snatch a few hours' sleep before dawn.

He was awoken with bad news. Rory McCarthy had been suffering a heavy cold which had turned into acute bronchitis. After examining McCarthy, the team doctor, Tim Evans, had decided that the risk of his developing pneumonia in the pressurised air of the capsule was simply too great. McCarthy was grounded.

Branson came downstairs to the empty hotel lounge, where he was joined by McCarthy, barely able to restrain his tears. Branson wrapped his friend in a consoling bear-hug. Branson and Lindstrand could not fly the balloon alone, but there was someone in reserve.

Alex Ritchie, fifty-two, was a senior engineer on the project, who had designed the pressurisation system for the capsule. He had no experience of flying at the kind of altitudes the balloon would reach, and he had never sky-dived – a requirement in the event of a high-altitude catastrophe – but he knew every nut, bolt and wire in the capsule. He would prove to be a fortuitous replacement.

At the launch site, the flyers were greeted by the spectacular sight of the inflated envelope, glistening like a huge pearl earring against the cloudless blue sky. Beneath the envelope, the capsule looked ludicrously fragile, girdled with propane gas tanks painted to resemble giant Virgin Cola and Virgin Energy cans.

The Moroccan authorities had contrived a touchingly impressive departure. Arrayed around a perimeter fence was an honour guard of uniformed airmen and traditional Berber dancers and musicians. A phalanx of horsemen galloped into view, brandishing antique muskets, occasioning a mild frisson of anxiety that a ceremonial volley of gunfire might inadvertently sabotage the project altogether.

For two hours, Branson, Lindstrand and Ritchie waited, as the crew made last minute adjustments to the craft, including vacuuming the last speck of dust out of the capsule, lest it damage the delicate pressurisation system. Lindstrand had estimated that if the balloon had not taken off by midday, the wind would have risen to the point that a launch would be impossible. A few minutes after 11 a.m., the three flyers walked across the tarmac for a last word with the media. 'We're about to embark on a great adventure,' said Branson, 'and we're very sorry to have kept you waiting.' Then Branson sprinted across to where his family were waiting to give a final hug to Joan, Holly and Sam.

At the foot of the balloon, the three flyers posed for a final team photograph before climbing inside. At 11.19 a.m. the explosive bolts to release the capsule were detonated and, to the accompaniment of a clatter of drums, and the deafening roar of military helicopters circling above, the balloon soared smoothly into the sky.

Almost immediately, the problems began. Instead of a steady climb to 30,000 feet as planned, the balloon shot up at a rate of 2,000 feet a minute, forcing the crew to dump helium in an attempt to slow it down. But this only had the effect of slowing the ascent too much, obliging them to jettison the ballast of lead-shot and water.

Eventually, stabilised at 30,000 feet, the balloon sailed effortlessly along for three hours. But as darkness began to fall, and the helium in the balloon began to cool, another set of problems set in. Theoretically, the hot-air system should have kept the balloon aloft. Instead, it began to descend at the rate of 2,000 feet a minute. In mounting desperation, the crew began to throw out almost everything inside the capsule that wasn't screwed down: food, papers, cushions, supplies (only later did they discover they had also jettisoned a package containing $2,000 emergency cash).

Still the balloon continued to fall. There was one piece of surplus weight that could make all the difference. The canisters around the capsule each contained a tonne of propane. 'We've got to jettison one of the containers,' said Lindstrand. The three men shot each other nervous glances. Someone would have to climb on to the roof of the bucking capsule in pitch darkness and unscrew the bolts.

'I know the system better than anybody,' said Ritchie. 'I'll do it.' Attaching a safety line, he gingerly edged his way through the hatch and on to the roof and began loosening the bolts. One by one, they came free, and the canister spun free. The fall had been arrested at 5,000 feet.

Gradually the balloon began to climb again, to 12,000 feet, then to fall, then to rise. At 25,000 feet, it began its final descent, drifting down to 7,000 feet in less than five hours. By then, Lindstrand had acknowledged that it was hopeless to continue. 'We're putting it down,' he said.

Eighteen hours after taking off from Marrakech, the balloon put down in the desert of north-west Algeria, close to the Echarbechar military base. Branson, Lindstrand and Ritchie climbed out of the capsule to find themselves staring down the gun-barrels of a group of Algerian soldiers. Branson grappled for the Arabic *mot juste*. 'Allah . . . ?' he said, hopefully.

For Branson, there was no doubt who had been the hero of the hour. 'Alex had designed and built much of the system that he eventually had to release in order to save himself and us. I don't think anyone else could have done what he did. He showed unbelievable bravery by climbing on to the roof, held on only by tank straps. I truly believe he saved our lives.'

It had cost £3m for the *Global Challenger* to travel just 400 miles. But on the day afterwards nobody in the marketing industry was doubting that it was money well spent. A leading British PR man, Eugene Beer, pointed out that simply by taking off and landing, Branson had 'outdone Pepsi fourfold – and they spent £300m on their "turning blue campaign", including repainting Concorde blue'. Calculating the advertising value of the abortive attempt in terms of column inches in newspapers and minutes on worldwide news, one American advertising executive expressed the view that 'there aren't enough zeros to do the maths'.

To Branson that was hardly the point. The challenge had failed, ergo, they would try again. In his call to the project centre after landing Branson confessed that his one thought as the balloon plummeted earthwards was, 'What the fuck am I doing up here ... I remember thinking that if I ever get through this I am definitely not doing it again.'

Safely on the ground, however, there was no doubt in his mind that there would be another attempt. 'It really is terrifying,' he mused, 'that within four hours you could want to do it all over again.'

In December 1997, the *Global Challenger* team embarked once again for Marrakech, to await a suitable weather pattern for a launch. For Branson, it was to be a race against time in more ways than one. If the balloon did not launch before the end of December, the attempt would have to be abandoned in order for Branson to attend the GTECH court hearing in America. Either way, Richard Branson was preparing, once again, to put himself on the line.

Index

Note: The abbreviation RB is used in the index for Richard Branson. *il.* indicates there is an illustration of the subject referred to.